FRASER
GOLD 1858!

FRASER

THE FOUNDING OF BRITISH COLUMBIA

GOLD 1858!

NETTA STERNE

WSU PRESS

Washington State University Press
Pullman, Washington

Washington State University Press
PO Box 645910
Pullman, WA 99164-5910
Phone 800-354-7360; FAX 509-335-8568
© 1998 by the Board of Regents of Washington State University
All rights reserved
First printing 1998

Printed and bound in the United States of America on pH neutral, acid-free paper. Reproduction or transmission of material contained in this publication in excess of that permitted by copyright law is prohibited without permission in writing from the publisher.

Library of Congress Cataloging-in-Publication Data
Sterne, Netta, 1923-
    Fraser gold 1858! the founding of British Columbia / by Netta Sterne.
      p.   cm.
    Includes bibliographical references (p.   ) and index.
    ISBN 0-87422-164-1 (pbk. : alk. paper). — ISBN 0-87422-165-X (hdb. : alk. paper)
    1. British Columbia—History.   2. British Columbia—History—Sources.   3. British Colum-
bia—Gold discoveries.   I. Title.
    F1088.S85 1998
    971.1—dc21   98-14831
                                                               CIP

Cover: "H.B. Co. Fort Langley, Left Bank of Fraser River," by artist James Madison Alden of the U.S. Boundary Commission, 1858.

DEDICATION

To Ron
Chris and Susan

CONTENTS

Illustrations

ACKNOWLEDGMENTS

IN SHARING THIS STUDY of one uniquely interesting year in our past, I should explain that I am not a historian—just another interested reader of Pacific Northwest history. The genesis of my book was simple curiosity: In the spring of 1858 a new gold rush brought a great wave of miners across the northern border of the United States into British territory (later that year to be named British Columbia). The old territorial dispute between Great Britain and the United States, of course, had long been settled—the Oregon Treaty of 1846 having established the boundary line at the 49th parallel. Now, however, the United States population south of that boundary line had burgeoned, while the British territory remained undeveloped and with virtually no white population. How then, in the face of the gold rush "invasion," was British law to be established in the gold fields?

This question, which led to others, has been a pleasant preoccupation over recent years, and I gratefully acknowledge the sources of many answers. These include the several authors/historians whose works are here listed in the Select Bibliography.

Also deserving of appreciation, for their excellent research facilities and the helpfulness of staff members, are the Provincial Archives of British Columbia in Victoria, and the University of British Columbia in Vancouver. Thanks are due also to the staff of the Vancouver Public Library's Special Collections Division, and especially to the Division's head, Marjorie Kevlahan, now retiring; she will be greatly missed.

To John Gonzales, Reference Librarian at the California State Library in Sacramento, I am grateful for his kind guidance to newspaper citations and microfiche copy. Kathleen M. O'Connor, archivist at the National Archives-Pacific Sierra Region, San Bruno, was very helpful in providing a list of Selected Archival Repositories in California, and also the *Guide to Records in the National Archives Pacific Sierra Region*.

During visits to Britain I was able to find, in newspaper archives, contemporary accounts of the relationships in 1858 between the British government, the new colony of British Columbia, and the Hudson's Bay Company. I gratefully acknowledge the helpfulness of the staff at the British Library in London, and the Scottish National Library in Edinburgh. Also in London, the National Maritime Museum at Greenwich was a friendly source of information concerning the Brunel ship, the *Leviathan*.

In particular, I must extend my appreciation to the staff of the Washington State University Press for their talented work in designing and producing this book; and my personal thanks to Glen Lindeman, Editor, for providing excellent advice, invaluable contributions, and constant encouragement. I am grateful also to Dr. John H. Monnett, Professor of History at Metropolitan State College of Denver, in Denver, Colorado, for his review of the manuscript and his helpful suggestions.

Let me also express my respect and admiration for all writers of histories more extensive than this one.

Netta Sterne
Vancouver, British Columbia
May 1998

PREFACE

T HE CALIFORNIA GOLD RUSH of 1849 was the precursor, and an indirect cause, of the 1858 gold rush which brought miners from the American West, including many veteran "Forty-niners," northward into a wilderness called New Caledonia (now British Columbia). At that time, Vancouver Island was a separate colony, whose population and government did not extend to the enormous mainland territory of New Caledonia. Thus, it was mainly these adventurers from the State of California and the territories of Oregon and Washington who became the first large white population, and some of the earliest settlers, in British Columbia.

By a fateful coincidence, it was in February of that same year that Britain's long-standing Palmerston Government was defeated—to be replaced, temporarily, by a new Government determined to create a new British colony west of the Rocky Mountains. Consequently, it was in that same year, coincident with the arrival of the first sizeable white population, that the Colony of British Columbia was born.

The purpose of this book is to chronicle the events of that uniquely important and interesting year in our Pacific Northwest history, letting much of the story unfold through the words of some who were there at the time—miners and prospectors, merchants and entrepreneurs, officers and statesmen, and "the media" of the day, those American and British newspaper reporters who were privileged to cover one of the great stories of the century.

"H.B. Co. Fort Langley, Left Bank of Fraser River," by James Madison Alden of the U.S. Boundary Commission, 1858. A large Indian village of traditional cedar-plank houses stands on the north shore. The inhabitants have hauled their numerous canoes up the bank beyond reach of the Fraser's current. *Record Group 76, National Archives, Washington, D.C.*

1
THE GOLD RUSH BEGINS

THEY WERE AMONG the first arrivals, vanguard of the motley army of adventurers now advancing by sea and land toward the new gold country. Their long trek had brought them beyond Washington Territory's northern border to where the Fraser River flows into the Gulf of Georgia. Behind them lay Fort Langley and the Hudson's Bay Company store, which had provided their small group with some additional supplies. Now, heading upriver, they had only their own resources to rely upon and only such provisions as their small craft could carry. In this wild country they would find none of the amenities of civilization—only a few, far-separated fur-trading posts. Before them lay an infinity of snow-frosted mountains, rushing waters, densely forested foothills—an inconstant scene of changing light and fugitive colour; sunshine vying with rain clouds; mists that drifted in the valleys and haunted the forests.

To the native Indians this land was home. Nature was their provider, and to gather her seasonal bounty they might travel freely in sturdy canoes upon familiar highways of water, or on foot along well trodden trails, often precipitously daunting to any white man. But, for the newly arrived strangers, the country was formidable, to travel through it incredibly arduous. Fifty years earlier, Simon Fraser[1] had found it so when, as the first white man to explore "the great river" that was to bear his name, he had (against the advice of the Indians) led his expedition on a terrifying canoe journey downstream over rapids boiling through rocky canyons, and by portages along Indian trails which, practicable enough for the accustomed and sure-footed natives, were to the white men mere flimsy structures of vines and tree branches, swaying perilously hundreds of feet over the wild river.

Now, in this spring of 1858, began the great new adventure already bringing hordes of men from Washington, Oregon, and California northward into New Caledonia. Some earlier prospectors had explored this wilderness, and a few had returned to Washington in the fall of 1857 with news of gold they had found in the "Couteau" region[2] of the Fraser and Thompson rivers.

On March 21, 1858, the schooner *Wild Pigeon* had arrived at Steilacoom bringing the startling news that several pounds of gold from the Fraser River country had been traded to the Hudson's Bay Company by Indians; that some 300 men had left Vancouver Island in search of Fraser River gold; and that many logging camps and mills, and also the Bellingham Bay Company's coal mines, were near closing down for want of labour—most employees having taken off to join the new gold rush.[3]

From Portland to San Francisco it had become known, by April, that a shipment of Fraser River gold had been received, for assay, from the Hudson's Bay Company. Throughout the West, the existence of northern gold, long rumoured and now confirmed, became the talk of the people and the preoccupation of the press. Nothing now could hold back the masses impatient to pack their gear and head north to the new eldorado.

Since the great gold rush of 1849 had opened up the American West, the youthful and turbulent State of California had prospered, its population grown in less than a decade from fewer than 100,000 to nearly 400,000. But by the mid-1850s, the surface wealth which had yielded to the pans and rockers of the Forty-niners was depleted, and California gold mining had become the business of large companies better equipped to reach the deeper lode. Now the dream of new-found gold was renewed, and many a veteran Forty-niner was joining in the general exodus.

From the first blush of spring until summer's end the great exodus would continue, leaving mines, farms, and industries abandoned, and employers bereft of their work force. In San Francisco, the *Daily Alta California* of April 23, 1858, lamented:

> There is no telling when this system of depopulation is to stop. At the present time, the boats from the interior come down every night, loaded with miners and others, all bound for Fraser's River. The hotels of this city are fairly crammed with people waiting for an opportunity to leave: while reports also reach us from various points in the interior, that parties are setting out overland for the same locality. Throughout the length and breadth of the State, the "Fraser River Fever" seems to have seized hold of the people, and threatens to break up, or at least seriously disarrange for the time being the entire mining business of the State—and for all classes of labour, mining and otherwise, a marked rise must be looked for. To fill the void that will be created by the departure of the hundreds and thousands who are now leaving, or who will leave hereafter, we require a new immigration from other States and other countries.[4]

A further consideration, however, of this "all absorbing topic of the time," predicted beneficial results:

> What effect the discovery of gold in the British possessions will have on California it is impossible at this time to speculate. There can, however, be no doubt that for some time after the facilities for reaching the far distant mines have been increased there will be an immense migration from this State. This will, as a matter of course, be of great benefit to our mercantile and agricultural interests. For a long period the supplies will have to be drawn from here. Oregon and Washington Territory being so near the new gold mines, their citizens will flock to them as the surest and speediest way of accumulating wealth. So soon as the news reaches the Eastern States and Europe, we may expect an immense immigration, which will, in transit, be compelled to remain for a time with us. In all probability a large number will be induced by the superior facilities and comforts afforded in California either to occupy the places vacated by the restless portion of our population or still further develop the hidden resources of this State, which, in our opinion, will still prove as rich as any territory further north.

The same account, though, acknowledged the inconvenience of the sudden flight from the state of needed workers:

> The desire to emigrate is fast increasing in California. Several hundreds have left in the last fortnight, and many thousands more are preparing to leave. This hegira is already causing inconvenience to employers of labour. At Grass Valley 600 miners are waiting a favourable report from 20 of their fellows, who have been sent to explore, to depart in a body. These are all, or nearly all, Cornishmen, who came to this country from England or Australia. Indeed, all British subjects who are not well off or bound down by engagements will leave. They are delighted at the opportunity of getting once more under the protection of "the old flag." Several of the quartz mills at Grass Valley have had to stop for want of hands, and others are only able to continue working by an increase of wages to the miners.

But no inducement could stem the tide. By mid-April the first massive wave of gold seekers was headed inexorably towards New Caledonia.

——

1. Margaret A. Ormsby, *British Columbia: A History* (Toronto: MacMillans in Canada, 1958), 37.
2. "Couteau" was a name of Indian and French-Canadian derivation applied to the locality and its native inhabitants.
3. Ezra Meeker, *Pioneer Reminiscences of Puget Sound* (Seattle, 1905); see chapter 21, "The Fraser River Stampede," 162-70.
4. *Daily Alta California* (San Francisco), April 23, 1858.

2
DOUGLAS OF VANCOUVER ISLAND

F AR DISTANT AS IT WAS from the mother country, New Caledonia had
remained largely unknown and had received little attention from the
British government. Only for its strategic importance had neighbouring
Vancouver Island, with its splendid natural harbours, been named a British Crown Colony in 1849. The entire island was leased, for a token payment, to the Hudson's Bay Company (HBC) on the company's promise
(largely unfulfilled) to increase the white population by encouraging immigration from Britain. The company's regional chief, James Douglas, had
been appointed governor of the island, which had become home to a few
hundred colonists. Fort Victoria, with its seaport, was the colony's center
of population and seat of government. As the port of call nearest to New
Caledonia, Victoria was destined to be a focal point of the gold rush for all
who arrived by sea.

The Hudson's Bay Company, foreseeing the loss by treaty of its Oregon holdings to the United States, had chosen southern Vancouver Island
for the building of an alternative headquarters. It was Douglas who, in
1843, had chosen the site for Fort Victoria, which in 1849 had become the
HBC's Pacific Coast base. Douglas and his officers brought the same civilized, well supplied, disciplined way of life to Fort Victoria that previously
had been theirs at Fort Vancouver on the Columbia River under Chief
Factor Dr. John McLoughlin (who is sometimes remembered as "the father of Oregon" because of his compassionate helpfulness to the early
American settlers—which incurred for him the disapproval of high-ranking HBC officials).

Douglas was not Vancouver Island's first governor, but Richard
Blanshard, the young English barrister who had the misfortune to precede
him in that appointment, had returned to England within a year of his
arrival in Victoria, greatly disappointed by his reception in the colony and
in his prospects there; and Douglas' authority had remained supreme.

Douglas was, in effect, "our man in Victoria" both for the British government and for the mighty, London-based Hudson's Bay Company, virtually an empire in its own right. That this empire was built upon the slaughter of animals, to near extinction of species, was of no consequence in an age when killing or capturing wild creatures was both profitable commerce and prestigious sport. And the Indians—sophisticated intertribal traders and quite astute in their dealings with white men—were not averse to plundering nature for those animal skins which, since the beginning of the fur trade, had so greatly increased their wealth and resources that the fur trade era has been called "the 'golden age' of Indian art."[1]

Disapproved by the white fur traders, but still in practice, was an intertribal trade in slaves—captives from raids or wars.[2] As symbols of wealth and power for the owners, slaves were included among the valuable "gifts" dispensed at important potlatches. In terms of "fair trade," a Hudson's Bay blanket to the Indians might perhaps be likened in value to a fine fur coat in the European market. Goods which were "commonplace" to the white men had greater value in the Indian villages because of their rarity. Even so, the natives could well discern between good and poor quality trade goods. Staple items of trade were blankets, muskets, powder, shot, cloth, molasses, rice, bread, and biscuits. Secondary barter items, also often given as "presents" in trading encounters, included tobacco, beads, buttons, brass wire, chisels, needles, thread, knives, scissors, stockings, and apples.[3]

Monitoring of these and other imports, and the planning for exporting furs and other produce of the country, were among the most important aspects of James Douglas' administrative duties for the HBC. Douglas, a man of impressive stature, great dignity, and legendary courage, had served in the North American fur trade, with its continent-wide network of trading posts, since coming from Scotland as a boy of sixteen. Born in Lanarkshire, Scotland, in 1803, he was the son of John Douglas, who owned sugar estates in Demerara, British Guiana. Young James attended school in Lanark and later in England, at Chester, where he acquired, from an excellent French tutor, his lifelong ability to speak a very polished French.[4]

A talented administrator and lifelong scholar, Douglas was now, at fifty-four, the HBC's Chief Factor for the Pacific Coast. Formal in manner, strong-willed, and certainly a formidable opponent, Douglas was yet a kindly man, a devoted husband and father, and he loved his beautiful wild country. Of his happy memories, he wrote: "The retrospect is full of charms; images of the morning breezes, the bright sky, the glowing sunrise, the rushing waters, the roaring cataract—the dark forest, the flowery plains, the impressive mountains in their pure white covering of snow, rise before me, at this moment, as vividly as ever and old as I am, my heart bounds at the bare recollection of scenes I loved so well."[5]

Earlier in his career, when Douglas served the company in Oregon under the British flag, he had seen that disputed territory ceded to the United States by the Oregon Treaty of 1846 after large numbers of Americans had settled there. Now, under ominously similar circumstances, he was concerned not only with the threat to British sovereignty, but also with the likelihood that the great influx of Americans could lead to conflicts with the Indians. The year before (in July 1857), he had mentioned in a despatch to London: "A new element of difficulty in exploring the gold country has been interposed through the opposition of the native Indian tribes of Thompson's River, who have lately taken the high-handed, though probably not unwise course, of expelling all the parties of gold-diggers, composed chiefly of persons from the American territories, who had forced an entrance into their country."[6]

In fact, as early as 1856 the HBC, having accepted for trade small amounts of gold at its fur posts, knew full well that wealth, though of uncertain quantities, lay in New Caledonia's streams. Douglas feared it was a secret that would not be contained, and the Couteau Indians, who increasingly were involved in the mining of gold, also were concerned of its import. (In 1854-55, for example, 400 to 500 Oregon and Washington wealth seekers had swept eastward through the Cascade Range into the Fort Colvile area, where the Pacific Northwest region's first significant gold strike had occurred along the Canada-U.S. border. This rush of men helped precipitate the outbreak of a major Indian war in the summer of 1855, which squelched much of the mining activity in northern Washington Territory for a time. Consequently, some of these men, including some southern Plateau Indian prospectors, eventually straggled northward to the rich gravels of the Couteau region.)

Aware of the Indians' desire "to monopolize the precious metal for their own benefit" and their fear that mining would drive off the salmon, their staple food, Douglas had given strict orders to his own people that there should be no mining without the Indians' consent. But he could not prevent the intrusions by American prospectors, nor prevent their spreading the news of their gold discoveries. Nor did he know, until the gold rush provided proof, how extensive and valuable the region's gold deposits really were. A similar "rush" to the Queen Charlotte Islands in 1852 had proved unfruitful and short-lived (though it had caused the British government to extend Douglas' authority to those islands).

Knowing that any significant gold discovery would bring a great influx of Americans into the country, Douglas had for two years past been warning the Colonial Office in London that such an invasion was likely, and he had urged that military aid be sent out from England to safeguard British sovereignty. However, the Palmerston government, and specifically its Colonial Secretary Henry Labouchere, declined to commit resources for the protection of this remote, unsettled region from which little revenue could be expected. Consequently, Douglas faced the present emergency, and the enormous new responsibilities that were to follow, with totally inadequate resources. He was to find his uncommon abilities tested as never before.

"You can imagine," an on-the-scene news reporter wrote in June 1858,

> the severe tax which the sudden influx of such a multitude, composed of such materials, must have imposed upon the representative of the Hudson's Bay Company. The full weight of it fell upon the Governor, for he is not only Governor of the Colony, administering the Government as the representative of the Crown, but he is also chief factor for the Hudson's Bay Company, intrusted with the direction of its affairs. His is in no enviable position I can assure you—no sinecure. Plenty of work, of annoyance, of worry, of unjust and unreasonable blame, of great responsibility and anxiety. I was curious to see how he bore himself under it all—whether he was flurried or calm. He cultivates the latter virtue. My next query was, does he do his work well? A short enumeration of his measures must answer this question. I soon saw through his system—that is, I saw what enables him to work his way easily and quietly through such mazes of difficulties as were continually recurring. He has long been accustomed to power, to the direction of affairs, to command, to assume responsibility, and to direct others. His present duties, suddenly multiplied as they are day by day, and distracting as they would be to many less trained officers, come easy to him. He is an old hand at this sort of thing, in short, and he is a man of unquestionable talent—"mighty clever," as a [navy midshipman] remarked.[7]

Yet another contemporary view of Douglas was expressed, in November 1858, by Vancouver Island resident Alfred Waddington:

> Every thing depends then on the Governor . . . he has been habituated almost from childhood to the mean, petty, despotic dealings of the Hudson's Bay Company. On that account alone I signed a petition against his renomination . . . So far, his acts though tardy have been

judicious and liberal, considering circumstances and the many difficulties he has had to contend with. He knows the country thoroughly,
was the founder and originator of Victoria, and his best interests and
affections belong here. But attached as he has been and still is to the
Hudson's Bay Company, he has a hard game to play as Colonial Governor; whose province it now is, to assist the country in emerging
from the swaddling clothes of that same monopoly, and finally freeing
itself from Colonial restrictions obtain self-government with popular
institutions. If his efforts tend that way, and he succeeds, it will re-
dound to his honor.[8]

1. Wilson Duff, *The Indian History of British Columbia, Volume 1: The Impact of the
   White Man* (Victoria: Provincial Museum of British Columbia, 1969), 59.
2. For an extensive account of Indian slavery, see Robert H. Ruby and John A. Brown,
   Indian Slavery in the Pacific Northwest (Spokane: Arthur H. Clark, 1993).
3. Duff, *The Indian History of British Columbia,* 57; reference is made to Joyce A. Wike,
   "*The Effect of the Maritime Fur Trade on Northwest Coast Indian Society,*" Ph.D. disser-
   tation, Columbia University, 1951.
4. For a biography of James Douglas, see Walter N. Sage, *Sir James Douglas and British
   Columbia* (Toronto: University of Toronto Press, 1930).
5. Parliamentary Papers Relating to British Columbia. Governor Douglas, Correspondence Outward, Miscellaneous Letters, November 30, 1859, to December 8, 1863;
   March 19, 1859, pp. 130-31.
6. Ibid. Despatch, July 15, 1857, from Governor Douglas to the Right Hon. Henry
   Labouchere, M.P. Also quoted in *British Columbia and Vancouver's Island: A Complete
   Hand-Book, Replete with the Latest Information Concerning the Newly-Discovered Gold
   Fields* (London: W. Penny, 1858), 24.
7. *The Times* (London), August 27, 1858; quoted account is from a San Francisco corre-
   spondent dated June 24, 1858. The visiting correspondent's firsthand report on
   Vancouver Island and the New Caledonia gold fields also appeared in Robert M.
   Ballantyne, ed., *Handbook to the New Gold Fields: A Full Account of the Richness and
   Extent of the Fraser and Thompson River Gold Mines* (Edinburgh: A. Strahan; and Lon-
   don: Hamilton, Adams, 1858), 57-66.
8. Alfred Waddington, *The Fraser Mines Vindicated, or, The History of Four Months*
   (Victoria, 1858), 35-36. Waddington's 54-page book was printed in circa late-
   November 1858, by P. DeGarro, of Wharf Street, Victoria, and sold for fifty cents.
   This promotional assessment of Victoria and the Fraser mines was one of the first
   books to be published in the Vancouver Island colony.

Long-time experience as an HBC official and governor of Vancouver Island prepared James Douglas for the monumental task of overseeing thousands of gold seekers rushing into the New Caledonia wilderness in a few months' time. *Provincial Archives of British Columbia, Victoria.*

3
ARRIVAL BY SEA

ON APRIL 25, 1858, the arrival of the first gold-rush ship from California to reach Victoria shattered the tranquillity of that remote outpost. It was a Sunday, and from the hillside overlooking the harbour church-going Victoria citizens witnessed a happening perhaps as astonishing to them as a landing from Mars. There in the harbour, the San Francisco steamer *Commodore*, newly docked, was disembarking a seemingly endless stream of ruggedly attired men, all heavily laden with gear and firearms. Four hundred and fifty by actual count, they exceeded in number the entire population of Victoria! The men were of many nationalities, mostly American, British, French, and German, and they included a small group of Blacks—a few of the many who came north in those pre-Civil War days seeking a treasure more precious than gold.

To Governor Douglas, the arrival of the miners came as no surprise. Four months earlier, in an official despatch to London he had written: "The reputed wealth of the Couteau Mines is causing much excitement among the population of the United States' territories of Washington and Oregon, and I have no doubt that a great number of people from those territories will be attracted thither with the return of the fine weather in the spring."[1] At about the same time, Douglas had alerted his men at the Hudson's Bay posts on the mainland to be prepared for the arrival of gold seekers and had warned his company officers in Victoria of the great changes that lay ahead.

As the *Commodore*'s passengers disembarked and assembled, they were greeted officially by Governor Douglas, the sole representative of British authority. Douglas was pleasantly surprised to find the newcomers well behaved, and generally well supplied with equipment and capital. Fifty who chose to remain in Victoria were made welcome. (Among these were merchants and entrepreneurs who soon would be responsible for the dramatically swift commercial development in Victoria.) For the others, the mainland's gold fields beckoned, but few craft were available to cross Georgia Strait, a distance of some eighty miles from Victoria to Fort Langley on the banks of the Fraser River.

Some men hired Indian paddlers and canoes; others built crude boats or rafts, many of which were reduced to flotsam as their passengers perished tragically in rough waters. The two-day voyage from Victoria required an overnight stop at one of the many intervening islands; on the second day, with luck, the men reached Fort Langley, thirty miles up the Fraser. But the rampaging river, swollen by melting mountain snows, also would claim its victims. Douglas reported in a May 19 despatch to Lord Stanley, the Colonial Secretary in London: "Many accidents have happened in the dangerous rapids of that river, a great number of canoes having been dashed to pieces and their cargoes swept away by the impetuous stream, while of the ill-fated adventurers who accompanied them, many have been swept into eternity."[2]

In this despatch, Douglas made reference to "boats and other small craft from the American shore" continually entering Fraser River. He also remarked:

> The American steamer Commodore returned to this port from San Francisco two days ago with four hundred passengers for the Gold Mines, who are preparing to leave in boats and canoes for Fraser's River. The excitement about the Couteau Gold Mines is on the increase and people are pushing from all quarters in that direction.
>
> On all sides the Americans are striving to force a passage into the Gold District through their own territories, attempts being made at once to open roads from Bellingham, from Nisqually, and by way of the Columbia River.
>
> I am now convinced that it is utterly impossible through any means within our power, to close the Gold District against the entrance of foreigners, as long as gold is found in abundance, in which case the country will soon be overrun and occupied by a large white population, whether it be agreeable to our wishes or not; while, on the contrary, it is no less certain that the excitement on the subject will soon altogether cease, if the diggings prove unremunerative, and the crowds now gathering on the banks of Fraser's River will in that case soon abandon the country and return to their homes. The evil will then work its own cure without interposition on our part.

Clearly, then, Douglas in those early days considered the gold rush to be an "evil," the failure of which he would welcome. When, however, the "evil" was confirmed by success, Douglas was to prove his adaptability, winning admiration and respect for his enlightened helpfulness to the miners and for his firm management of the gold country's affairs under the most difficult of circumstances.

A report in the *New York Times* stated that fifty canoes had reached Fort Langley between May 27 and June 5, with an average of six passengers in each. The article continued:

> The Governor of the Hudson's Bay Company, with four directors, and Captain Prevost of the British steamer Satellite, had proceeded to Fort Yale, where they appointed Custom-house officers. They were cordially received by the miners on the various bars along the river, and appointed magistrates from among them. The Hudson's Bay Company is pursuing a conciliatory course and keeping favour successfully.[3]

Being governor only of Vancouver Island, Douglas had no status in New Caledonia except as Chief Factor of the Hudson's Bay Company. Nevertheless, he boldly assumed governmental authority over the gold region. He issued official proclamations and regulations. Repeating a strategy he had used successfully during the earlier gold-rush invasion of the Queen Charlotte Islands, he required every miner to purchase a mining licence in the name of the Queen, thus affirming British sovereignty, besides procuring needed revenues.

At the same time, Douglas took steps to protect the interests of the Hudson's Bay Company. Besides imposing restrictions on shipping and trade, he exacted "head money" from foreigners entering the country and required "compensation" for infringement of the company's trading rights. These measures, like the HBC monopoly itself, soon would succumb to legal and political circumstances, as well as to government edict, but they answered Douglas' immediate need to take control.

Surely Douglas could not have enforced such regulations in the face of a virtual foreign occupation had he not been able to control the various points of access to the Fraser River. This he was able to do, initially, with the aid of two Royal Navy survey vessels, H.M.S. *Satellite* and H.M.S. *Plumper*, already stationed at Vancouver Island. A merchant vessel, the *Recovery*, chartered by Douglas and manned by officers and men of the H.M.S. *Satellite* and carrying civilian revenue officers, also was stationed on the Fraser River to prevent smuggling and licence evasion.

Although the captains commanding the *Satellite* and *Plumper* were very willing to aid Governor Douglas in maintaining order and security, it soon became evident that their resources were insufficient to meet the need.

By summer, miners' guidebooks and maps were hastily prepared by printers in San Francisco, London, and Edinburgh as word of the great gold strike circled the globe. This map is from John Domer, *New British Gold Fields* . . . (London, 1858).

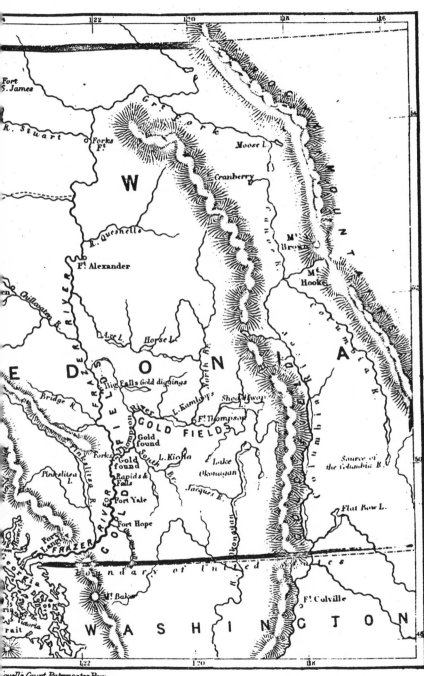

Hoping that additional naval support might be obtained with some speed, Douglas wrote in early May to Rear Admiral Baynes, the newly appointed Commander in Chief of Her Majesty's Forces in the Pacific:

> I have very lately addressed a communication to the Right Honourable Secretary for the Colonies, directing his attention to the prodigious emigration of United States citizens, and other foreigners, from California and Oregon, in consequence of the discovery of gold on Fraser's River within the British Possessions on this coast.
>
> To prevent the entrance of those people into the British territory is, perhaps, altogether impossible with any force that could be collected within a reasonable time, but what may be easily accomplished is, to maintain the authority of the Government, to preserve the peace, to punish offences, and to enforce obedience to the laws, until Her Majesty's Government are in a position to take more decided steps for administering the Government of the country.
>
> I therefore take the liberty of making application to you for a sufficient force to aid and assist in maintaining the Queen's authority, until further instructions are received from England.
>
> The Satellite and Plumper are both at present employed on this part of the coast, but being on special service I do not feel at liberty to tax them too severely for assistance, though I am convinced that both Captains Prevost and Richards will afford me every assistance. I therefore think it highly necessary that the naval force in this quarter should be largely reinforced, especially as there is no limit to the possible amount of immigration into the Gold Region should the country prove productive; and I shall not be at all surprised if, in that case, there be an influx, in course of a few months, of twenty or thirty thousand people. I, as a matter of course, feel deeply anxious about the results which may arise in the altered circumstances of the country, and desirous of seeing such measures taken as may have the effect of protecting the interests of the British Crown.[4]

But it would be several weeks before Douglas received a response, and that a negative one, from Admiral Baynes.

The male colonists of Vancouver Island likewise not being immune to the gold fever, their absence soon was felt in the colony. A citizen of Victoria wrote in a private letter dated April 18:

> There is no news here now; everything is very dull since the people left for the mines. The latter are very rich but are nearly all overflowed from the snow melting on the mountains. They will not be workable again before the end of July; then will be the grand rush. The company are getting all the cream. We expect all the Victoria people back soon to wait until the water falls.[5]

Shipload after shipload, the miners continued to come—many of the ships' crews then deserting to join their passengers in the great treasure hunt. A correspondent for the London *Times*, writing from San Francisco, reported:

> Trade has revived considerably of late, owing in a measure to the business done for Puget Sound . . . Ships suffer great inconvenience from the scarcity of sailors, who are all taking themselves off to the new mines. Wages hence to Puget Sound for able bodied seamen have risen to $35 a month, and will soon advance beyond this rate.

And, Captain Prevost of H.M.S. *Satellite*, writing to advise the Admiralty that gold miners were coming in great numbers from Washington, Oregon, and California, added:

> By the last account steamers, and even sailing ships are being chartered to convey passengers to Puget Sound, or to Vancouver Island, whence they have to find their way to the diggings by canoe. I have heard that all the crews of the ships to Puget Sound have deserted, and have gone to the diggings. I am happy to say that as yet I have not lost a single man from the Satellite since the information was received, and I have every reason to hope that I may not be unfortunate in this respect, although, doubtless, soon the temptation to desert will be of no ordinary character.

Before long, however, a bonus of one dollar a day had to be paid to the sailors of the *Satellite* as an inducement not to desert[6] (a dollar a day, in 1858, was quite persuasive).

The battered old *Commodore*, which had brought the first shipload of miners, continued her runs between San Francisco and Victoria. Tragedy struck on June 21: "A dreadful disaster occurred at Victoria, by which some thirteen persons were drowned. A small boat, called the Alcatraz, while conveying an overload of passengers from the steamer Commodore to the shore, was capsized, and precipitated some thirty-four into the water, of whom thirteen were drowned."[7]

But the *Commodore*, and other old, unseaworthy vessels, all chronically and dangerously overloaded, continued to gather great profits for their owners.

Notable among the earliest arrivals in Victoria was a Nova Scotian, the former William Alexander Smith, who legally had changed his name to Amor De Cosmos (perhaps an intentional language mix conveying his "love of the world"). De Cosmos, a real estate speculator, arrived from

California by sea in May, and in December started a newspaper, the *British Colonist*. Editorially, he immediately made it plain that his "love of the world" did not extend to the Hudson's Bay Company and Governor Douglas, whom he considered undemocratic and nonprogressive. De Cosmos was to be successful in politics—promoting union with Canada and becoming premier of the province in 1872: "He was a demagogue, and was to write a large part of the country's history in the next thirty-five years."[8]

1. Parliamentary Papers Relating to British Columbia. Despatch, No. 6 (35), Governor Douglas to Right Hon. Henry Labouchere, M.P., December 29, 1857. Also quoted in *British Columbia and Vancouver's Island: A Complete Hand-Book, Replete with the Latest Information Concerning the Newly-Discovered Gold Fields* (London: W. Penny, 1858), 26.
2. Ibid. Despatch, Governor Douglas to Lord Stanley, Part I, p. 11, May 19, 1858.
3. *New York Times*, June 21, 1858. Letter from San Francisco correspondent; reprinted in *The Times* (London), July 30, 1858.
4. Parliamentary Papers Relating to British Columbia. Despatch, No. 7, p. 27, Governor Douglas to Rear-Admiral Baynes, May 12, 1858.
5. Letter from Victoria dated April 18, 1858, in *Daily Alta California* (San Francisco), May 3, 1858.
6. Parliamentary Papers Relating to British Columbia. Despatch, Governor Douglas to Lord Stanley, July 26, 1858, pp. 24-25.
7. From the *San Francisco Bulletin*, June 28, 1858; reprinted in the *Daily Scotsman* (Edinburgh), August 10, 1858.
8. B.A. McKelvie, *Pageant of B.C.* (Toronto: Thomas Nelson and Sons, 1955), 184-85.

4
GETTING THERE

For every one of the thousands of men preparing to trek northward to the new gold country the question was the same: How do we get there? Here was an immediate market for maps and guidebooks, and several were quickly prepared and published in California and England. Of these, probably the best and most popular was Alexander Caulfield Anderson's *Hand-Book and Map to the Gold Region of Frazer's and Thompson's Rivers, with Table of Distances,* published in San Francisco (price $1.50).

Anderson, an explorer, geographer, naturalist, and retired HBC Chief Trader, was a grandson of the distinguished Scottish botanist Dr. James Anderson. He later would be acknowledged as, "one of the most scholarly intellectuals of the pioneers in the province."[1] Anderson's knowledge of the Fraser River country was extensive. As early as 1846 he had discovered a route through the Harrison, Seton, and Anderson lakes areas—a route eventually utilized by miners to reach the "Forks," later called Lytton, where the Thompson River flows into the Fraser. When, with the establishment of the international boundary in the 1846 Oregon Treaty, the HBC was forced to abandon its Columbia Basin trails, it was Anderson who led the three grueling expeditions north of the 49th parallel to search out (at cost of great hardship to men and animals, and some loss of life to both) an alternative transportation system for the company.

In his *Hand-Book*, Anderson described "two distinct lines of approach to these mines: one by the direct route through Frazer's River; the other by way of the Columbia River, by Portland and the Dalles, and thence with pack animals through the trails [in the Columbia Basin, Washington Territory] used until recently by the Hudson's Bay Company, for their communications and for transport of supplies for the interior."[2] On the Columbia River between Portland and The Dalles, Anderson explained, "every facility of Steam Navigation exists," and this voyage would take, "part of two days, the intervening night being passed at the Cascades, where travellers are well accommodated." (According to a contemporary April 1858 news report, "saddles, accoutrements, clothing, supplies and a complete outfit" could be purchased at Portland, Vancouver, or The Dalles; the steamboat fare from Portland to The Dalles was $11; and, at The Dalles "the best Indian horses" could be had for from $20 to $40.[3] And, according to the pioneer historian Ezra Meeker, "more than a thousand men were congregated at The Dalles at one time preparing to make the trip northward."[4])

For the next stage of the journey from The Dalles with horses, Anderson offered two alternatives—one across the "Yackama" (Yakima) Valley, requiring five days' march with packs; the other more easterly by way of the HBC's old Fort Walla Walla, requiring eight days' march with packs. The trails converged northward at Priest's Rapids on the central Columbia, and there was "good grass by both routes." Anderson explained that the first route by the "Yackama Valley," though the shorter of the two by cutting off the great bend of the Columbia River, was the least practicable—the double crossing of the Columbia being a serious obstacle, and the "Yackama River" when high being, "a troublesome impediment. For this reason, I should prefer the longer route by Walla-Walla; and the more so, as it is passable at all seasons, which the other is not, owing to snow in the mountains."

Proceeding, then, from the junction of the Walla Walla and Columbia rivers, Anderson outlined a nineteen-day march by way of the east bank of the Columbia, Grand Coulee, Fort Okanogan, Rat Lake, Upper Bonaparte River, Similkameen Forks, Red Earth Forks, Nicola River, to "Nic-o-meen . . . the commencement of the mining region, as so far declared"; thence (on the nineteenth day from Walla Walla) to the Forks of Thompson's River, making in all a journey of twenty-seven days from The Dalles.

Anderson's 31-page *Hand-Book* was well worth the purchase, for it offered a wealth of information regarding the country and climate. It mentioned encampment sites; every significant stream, lake, and river; fording places and ferrying points ("horses here being swum"); and every difficulty or obstacle to be encountered. Anderson even advised that near the Similkameen Forks:

> There is usually a pretty large concourse of Indians at this point during the salmon season. It is good policy to supply the chief with a little tobacco to smoke with his followers. Good will is thus cheaply secured.[5]

(Well travelled in 1858, the Columbia River trails were to see another burgeoning of traffic in the early 1860s with the great rush to the Cariboo mines of central British Columbia.[6])

The second of Anderson's proposed lines of approach was the direct route by sea to the Fraser River. In the first season of the gold rush, this approach was the one favoured by most miners, since overland travel in the interior was slow and arduous, and hostile Columbia Basin tribes made it even more hazardous than usual due to the Yakima war (1855-58). For most travellers, the approach by sea required them first to take passage from San Francisco or Washington and Oregon harbours to Victoria on Vancouver Island, the nearest port to New Caledonia. A *Times* correspondent described the journey from San Francisco:

> The voyage from San Francisco to Vancouver Island, which, in a steamer, is made all the way within sight of the coast, is one of the most agreeable when the voyager is favoured with fine weather. I know of no other more picturesque out of the Mediterranean. The navigation is so simple that a schoolboy could sail a steamer, for a series of eighteen headlands which jut out into the ocean all along the coasts of California, Oregon and Washington Territory serve as landmarks to direct the mariner in his course. All he has to do is to steer from one to another; from Point Reyes outside the Golden Gate to Point Arena, the next in succession, and so on until he comes to Cape Flattery, upon rounding which he enters the Straits of Fuca towards the end of his voyage.[7]

The writer further described the beauty of the coastal scenery and praised the "pre-eminent" harbour of Esquimalt, located three miles west of Victoria and its smaller port. Here the voyage ended. Esquimalt, as this and other reporters observed, was a harbour of such great capacity that it could even accommodate Britain's newly constructed, giant ship *Leviathan*, which was very much in the international news at the time. According to the reporter at Esquimalt: "Captain Richards pointed out to me the position in which the *Leviathan* should lie if she comes out" to the West Coast.

Another reporter had noted:

> That harbour is . . . easy of access at all seasons and with a depth of water sufficient to admit the Leviathan, or any other monster . . . Her seagoing capacity once fairly tested, what is to prevent her making a venture in this direction with half a colony at once within her gigantic ribs? The pleasure of seeing the world's wonder in the waters of the Pacific may yet be ours.[8]

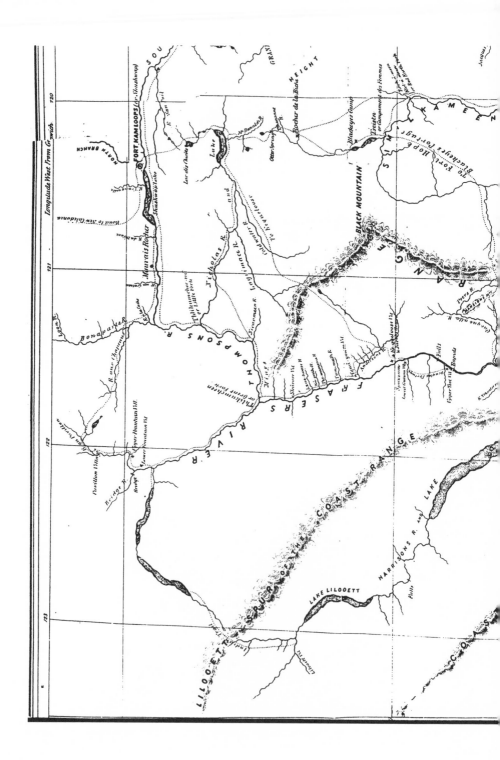

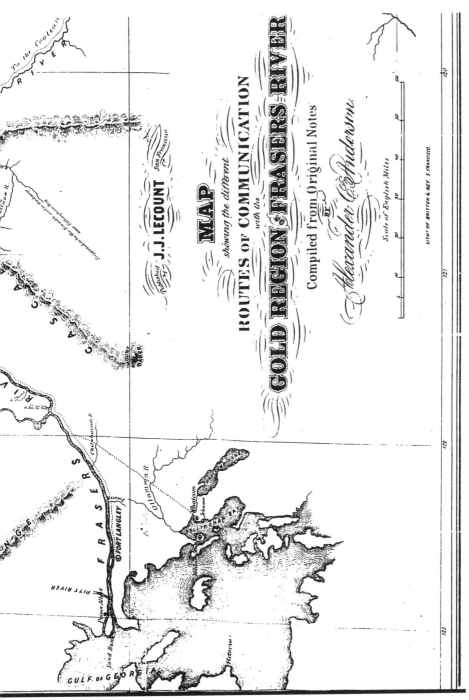

A section of Alexander C. Anderson's map, from *Hand-Book and Map to the Gold Region of Frazer's and Thompson's River . . .* (San Francisco, 1858).

(But this was not to be. The *Leviathan*—vastly larger than any ship then afloat—was designed by the genius Isambard Kingdom Brunel (1806-59) and launched January 31, 1858. In 1859 her name was changed to *Great Eastern*. After three years as a passenger ship between Southampton and New York, she was placed in service for the laying of the transatlantic telegraph cable, which she completed in July 1866. "Ahead of her time by 50 years," the *Leviathan,* as she was known in 1858, never saw service in the Pacific. As the *Great Eastern*, however, she retains an important place in history, as do the many other inspired works of her creator, Brunel.[9])

From Esquimalt, most of the passengers walked the short distance to Victoria where they made arrangements for passage across the Strait of Georgia to New Caledonia and the Fraser River. In describing the distances and difficulties to be encountered in journeying upriver on the Fraser, Anderson indicated that Fort Langley was about twenty-five miles above the river's mouth; to the next post, Fort Hope, was about sixty-nine miles; from thence past Fort Yale "to the foot of the 'Falls,'" twelve miles farther. "Let me here remark," Anderson noted, "that there is no practicable way of reaching this point from Fort Langley except by water."

He further noted that above Fort Yale:

> The series of rapids called "the Falls" is about three miles in length. There is no such abrupt descent as the name implies. At low water these rapids may be ascended with light craft, by making portages; but at the higher stages of the water they present a difficulty almost insurmountable. During the summer season, the rocky shores of the "Falls" are thronged by Indians from the lower country, who resort thither for the salmon fishery. A ceaseless feud, I may here mention, prevails between the Couteau and the lower Indians, who differ from each other widely in many respects.

This "standing feud," he later added, "is kept alive by a treacherous murder every now and then, as occasion presents."

Anderson advised the miners not to proceed by boat on the Fraser farther than the Falls:

> Assuming the miner to have reached the foot of the Falls by batteau or other conveyance . . . the more formidable impediments to his progress are still in advance . . . The alternative is to proceed on foot; but . . . the trail is a rough one, full of painful inequalities. It would, therefore, be impracticable to convey in this way more than a very limited amount of provisions, to say nothing of tools and other necessaries for mining operations.

Anderson warned that "serious consideration" should be given to "the difficulties which embarrass this route" to the upper Fraser and the Forks, "until some better system be organized than at present exists."[10]

Later that year, in fact, Anderson was destined to direct the first road building expedition here. Fortunately, during this first season most of the miners found gold without proceeding into the dangerous, less accessible regions beyond Yale and the Falls. Near Fort Hope, a sandbar had been found to be rich in gold, and within weeks, from this point up as far as Yale, miners were frantically at work at every bend along the lower river—and at least thirty of these locations yielded riches.[11]

1. E.O.S. Scholefield and R.E. Gosnell, *A History of British Columbia: Volume 2, Biography* (Vancouver: British Columbia Historical Association, 1913), [8].
2. Alexander C. Anderson, *Hand-Book and Map to the Gold Region of Frazer's and Thompson's Rivers, with Table of Distances* (San Francisco: J.J. LeCount, 1858), 4. On the title page, Anderson is described as "Late Chief Trader Hudson Bay Co's Service." Anderson dated the Preface to his *Hand-Book* as "May 3, 1858" at "Cathlamet" on the lower Columbia River in Washington Territory.
3. "From the Northern Coast," *Daily Alta California* (San Francisco), April 23, 1858; includes a *Portland Standard* report concerning the route via Portland, Oregon.
4. Ezra Meeker, *Pioneer Reminiscences of Puget Sound* (Seattle: Lowman and Hanford, 1905), 169.
5. Anderson, *Hand-Book and Map to the Gold Region of Frazer's and Thompson's Rivers*, 11-18.
6. For a detailed account of the late 1850s-early 1860s miners' trails to Canada via eastern Washington's Columbia Basin country, see Ron Anglin, *Forgotten Trails: Historical Sources of the Columbia's Big Bend Country*, edited with contributions by Glen W. Lindeman (Pullman: Washington State University Press, 1995), especially chapter VII, "Gold Rush Travelers."
7. Report from San Francisco dated June 24, in *The Times* (London), August 27, 1858.
8. Report from Victoria correspondent dated June 17, in *The Times* (London), August 10, 1858.
9. See J. Adams and P. Elkin, *Isambard Kingdom Brunel*, or A. Kludas, "The Great Eastern," in *Great Passenger Ships of the World*, Volume 1.
10. Anderson, *Hand-Book and Map to the Gold Region of Frazer's and Thompson's Rivers*, 4-6, 8-9, 20.
11. The names given to the gold-bearing bars by the miners in the Fraser River country indicated "the predominance of Americans and especially of Californians: 'Fifty-four Forty,' 'Union,' 'Santa Clara,' 'American,' 'Puget Sound,' 'Yankee Doodle,' 'Eagle,' 'Texas,' 'Ohio,' 'New York,' 'Washington,' 'Madison,' 'Tehama,' 'Boston,' 'Mormon,' 'Yankee Flat,' 'Angel's Flat,' and . . . 'Stranglers,'—the slang name applied in California to the members of the Vigilance Committee"; Frederic W. Howay, W.N. Sage, and H.F. Angus. *British Columbia and the United States: The North Pacific Slope from Fur Trade to Aviation*, ed. by H.F. Angus (New York: Russell and Russell, 1942 [1970]), 154-55.

An 1857 view of San Francisco's Lombard, North Point, and Greenwich street docks. A year later, many thousands of excited California miners, including veteran "Forty-niners," embarked through the Golden Gate for the Fraser River country. *San Francisco Maritime National Historical Park.*

5
THE FIRST NEWS REPORTS

Now we have seen the GOLD, and seen the men who dig it,
and are satisfied.

THUS BEGAN, IN LATE APRIL 1858, one of the first of an excited flurry of
on-the-scene accounts (soon to be circulated world-wide) from West
Coast correspondents and other travelers to the newly opening goldfields.
The report continued: "There is no doubt in the minds of any of us as to
the existence of gold and the richness of the deposits. The field, too, is very
extensive, and I do not believe its limits are one half known yet." But he
warned:

> The river is high and rapid, and is absolutely impassable to boats of
> any kind. The trail is through dense forest, and is impassable to any-
> thing except an Indian or a hunter . . . The people of Whatcom are
> now cutting a road from Whatcom, to strike the Hudson's Bay
> Company's road along the river; this once through, and the mines can
> easily be got at.

(The reporter could not know that this ambitious Whatcom road project
through mountainous country was doomed to failure.)

> Provisions are enormously high just now on Fraser's River, reaching
> the fabulous prices of the winter of '49 in California, but as soon as
> the river falls and the trail is open, they will descend to a reasonable
> rate . . . There is no doubt of the richness of the diggings, men being
> able to make from five to twelve dollars a day easily, and that, too,
> with the rudest implements . . . mere rough rockers, dug out from the
> solid wood. If so, why you can figure for yourself what could be done
> with "Long toms" and "sluices". . . A miner at McCaw's Rapids, be-
> yond Fort Yale, wrote on the last day of April, "We have prospected on
> several bars, and on one of them we got from six cents to twenty-five
> cents to the pan, and took only top dirt. On another we got from five
> cents to ten cents to the pan. We could not stop at the former place, as
> the Indians would not allow us . . . The Indians were all at work them-
> selves . . . At the latter place we cannot work to advantage without a

quicksilver machine. An old California miner says that this place very closely resembles the north fork of the American River in California, and that he believes richer mines will be discovered here than have ever been discovered in California . . . A few miles below this there is a party of whites, who were to have a sluice in operation either today or tomorrow. An Indian has just arrived in a canoe, and he tells me the sluice is in operation, and that they are taking out "hi-yu" (or plenty) gold.[1]

At about the same time, the *Puget Sound Herald* of Steilacoom, Washington Territory, stated:

The steamer Sea Bird brings still later and more definite news from the gold diggings on Thompson's and Fraser's Rivers. Miners are at work, and in many well known cases, taking out almost fabulous amounts. An Indian belonging to the Spokane country comes as a passenger on the Sea Bird. He is direct from Frazer's River, where he has been mining during the past winter; he reports that for six days in succession, he dug one hundred dollars worth of gold dust each day— many days thirty or forty dollars—and at no time did he make less than four dollars per day. Mr. Peabody, of Whatcom, is also a passenger by the Sea Bird; he has lately returned from the mining country, and very nearly corroborates all former reports. He picked up gold in many places, and found miners doing well, although the season is not the most favourable . . . the question is settled beyond a doubt that gold can be found in Frazer's and Thompson's Rivers in as large quantities as ever found in California. Mr. Peabody was on a visit to the mining country on business connected with the Boundary Commission, and not for the purpose of mining or discovering mines.[2]

On April 23, an Olympia newspaper, the *Pioneer and Democrat,* reported:

We delayed going to press this morning until a late hour, in expectation of the arrival of the steamer Sea Bird, from Bellingham Bay and intermediate ports, with further intelligence from the Frazer River gold mines . . . Adventurers, gold-ward bound, continue to concentrate here in considerable numbers . . .

The Sea Bird has arrived. The news from the gold region north is most encouraging. Gold is represented to exist at intervals from Fort Hope as far northward as has yet been prospected. Frazer's River is represented as still navigable for good substantial canoes.

However, the same report gave this warning:

From recent intelligence received from Frazer's River, we are assured that it would be quite unsafe for parties at this time, to attempt to ascend it in canoes or small boats. The river is rising rapidly, and the current and rapids are becoming furious. Two parties, recently, lost nearly all their outfits from the upsetting of their canoes in the rapids. The pack trail from Bellingham Bay to Fort Hope is now, perhaps, very nearly completed, but adventurers to the mines should remember that as yet they cannot obtain transportation thither from Bellingham Bay, and should provide themselves with animals before quitting the southern settlements. There will be no trouble in getting transportation for themselves and animals at that point.[3]

In early May, a correspondent for *The Times* reported from Whatcom on Bellingham Bay:

From the mines the news is quite as favourable as any yet received. Mr. Giddings estimates that upwards of twenty thousand dollars had been received at Whatcom by merchants within the week preceding his departure, in payment for goods. Miners were arriving and departing every day; those arriving invariably making their stay as short as possible. A party had returned to Whatcom a few days previous to Mr. Gidding's departure, who had proceeded as far as Fort Hope, where they met a large company just from the mines, to whom they disposed of provisions at about four hundred per cent above cost. The miners instantly retraced their steps, while the others returned to Whatcom.

In San Francisco on May 19, *The Times* correspondent wrote:

Two vessels have arrived here from the British possessions in the northwest since the despatch of my last letter on the 8th inst. The last steamer from Vancouver's Island arrived the day before yesterday. The richness of the new gold mines is fully confirmed.

The Times' reporter continued with an account from a special correspondent of a San Francisco newspaper, writing from Fort Langley:

A returned miner, whose name is given, and who was two months in the diggings, earned from fifteen dollars to twenty dollars per day in his claim. He brought down with him two thousand, five hundred dollars worth of gold dust, which he sold at Fort Langley. There are numbers of men here with gold. They all intend to return to the mines with provisions, which they came down for.

From Victoria, a gentleman writes on the 9th inst.: Yesterday the Hudson's Bay Company's steampropeller Otter, arrived here from Fort Langley, one of their trading posts on the Fraser River, and brought gold dust valued at thirty-five thousand dollars—judging from the fact that its weight was as much as one man could conveniently carry. Heavy gold is found ten miles from the mouth of Thompson's River, at a place called Necowman. The heaviest nugget yet found was eight dollars and twenty-five cents. Bank and river mining is going on between the forks and big falls of Fraser River, into which Thompson River runs. The number of miners now working is estimated by one of their number, from whom I received the above, at one thousand men—all of whom, he assured me, were doing well. To quote his figures, they were making from ten to forty dollars per day . . . We learn that miners located near the forks of Thompson River, about two hundred miles distant from the mouth of the Fraser River, are successfully at work. The higher up the richer the diggings, it would appear . . . Some fifty or more men are at work a few miles above Fort Yale. Mr. McCaw ascended the river some twenty miles above Fort Yale, and assures us that the diggings are rich along the whole of that distance. The gold is found on and within six inches of the surface.[4]

But, the *San Francisco Bulletin* of May 18 cautioned the miners against, "too speedy a departure for the Fraser River":

In the first place, the journey is long and laborious, the transportation rude and uncertain, while provisions are scarce and dear. They will also be compelled to live under laws entirely different from ours, but which, to our shame be it said, afford more protection to life and property. The Governor of the Hudson's Bay Company, Mr. Douglas, is a humane, intelligent gentleman, possessed of a remarkable degree of firmness of character and administrative talent. He is determined to preserve order and maintain British law, and he has the military strength to enforce his rule. The miners will be governed by the same laws as now prevail in Australia. The license which is exacted from the miners will be devoted to defraying the expense of the Government and military force for their protection.[5]

Quite apart from the gold-rush excitement, these were colourful times in the West. On June 4, a *Times* correspondent reported:

We have had four fires in San Francisco in the last fortnight. Among the property destroyed was the French theatre. The country did not escape so easily; several fires of a serious and disastrous character have occurred within the same brief period. There has also been a good sprinkling of lynching throughout the country, some of it for horse-stealing and some for murder.

Still, the gold rush continued to dominate the news:

Labour of all kinds continues, and carpenters find additional employment in making wooden houses for transportation to the gold mines . . . As a result of all this emigration, business in the interior is becoming much deranged. The operations of the country merchants are checked; rents and the value of property in the interior towns are diminishing. Some of the merchants are "liquidating," and some have already moved their business to San Francisco, to take advantage of the business which has sprung up between that port and the northwest . . . The increase in business will bring an increase of immigration to the city, for there is every reason to believe, judging from past experience, that a considerable proportion of the emigration from Europe, the Atlantic States, and Australia will rest here; that the city will increase rapidly, and that an advance in the value of property must ensue in consequence.[6]

The *San Francisco Bulletin* likewise commented on the "lively business" which the gold rush had engendered in San Francisco: "Scarcely one of the emigrants leaves San Francisco without disbursing more or less money, and it will not be too high an estimate to assert that before the lapse of another week $1,000.00 will be added to our daily circulation since the epidemic commenced raging." But what San Francisco might expect to gain, Sacramento feared to lose. "To show the extent of the dread of the interior newspapers caused by the recent exodus of population," stated the *New York Times:*

> Sacramento journals telegraphed two days since to their reporters in the city that they should send up only the worst features of the news then expected from the North. But the accounts came overwhelmingly confirmative of all and more than all that had before been received; they could not hold back, and have already coursed over the wires, adding fuel to the flames, and causing the fever to rage with ten times its former violence.

A report noted that of the thousands of passengers leaving on steamers and sailing ships for the mines, at least one fourth were not being enumerated in the custom-house clearances. According to the *New York Times* correspondent in San Francisco:

> Fully 12,000 persons have departed for the land of promise in the last two months, and probably the actual total is not less than 15,000 . . . and it is safe to assume, from all present appearances, that the entire exodus from California during the first six months of the Frazer River fever will reach the enormous figure of 40,000. The rapidity and extent of this emigration have never been paralleled . . . The gold is found everywhere, and even during the extreme height of the river parties are averaging from ten dollars to twenty dollars per day, digging in the banks or on the upper edge of the bars, nearly all of which are overflowed. Big strikes of from fifty dollars to two hundred and fifty dollars are frequently reported. Nearly all the work at present is carried on between Forts Langley and Yale, and for some twenty or thirty miles

above the latter, an entire distance along the river of about one hundred miles. Some few are digging on Harrison River and other tributaries, where the gold is found in larger particles. Those who were engaged in mining on the forks of Thompson River show still richer yields, but have been compelled to leave on account of the high stage of the water, the want of provisions, and the opposition of the Indians . . . At Hill's Bar those at work had averaged fifty dollars per day the whole time they had been there . . . All the letters received . . . from the various ports on the Sound and from the diggings furnish corroborative testimony as to the extent and richness of the new placers . . . The impression of all who have gone is unanimous and conclusive as to the great fact of new gold fields now being explored, equal to any ever yet developed in California or elsewhere. No steamer has yet returned with more than twelve or fifteen passengers, and nearly every one of them had come down to obtain supplies for himself or his party left behind at the diggings. They all say they are going back in a few weeks, and that nothing is lost by not getting there in a month or so, as the river will remain very high for that length of time. And yet with this convincing proof of the common declaration of all who are on the ground, that there is no use of being in a hurry about starting, the people of California refuse to hold back one single day, and rush off with resistless speed, making almost every sacrifice, and apparently regarding nothing valuable in comparison with a passage paid to Frazer River, and a bare sufficiency to set foot on the new diggings in the north.[7]

Tragically, that "bare sufficiency" often proved quite inadequate to miners who, depending upon immediate access to gold dust to purchase supplies, found rising flood waters preventing them from reaching it. Some were forced to return home, while others, lacking return fare, had good reason to regret leaving California.

———

1. Report dated April 27 from Olympia, Washington Territory, in the *Daily Alta California* (San Francisco), May 3, 1858.
2. April report from the *Puget Sound Herald*, Steilacoom, Washington Territory, reprinted in the *Daily Alta California* (San Francisco), May 3, 1858.
3. Account from the *Pioneer and Democrat*, Olympia, Washington Territory, April 23, 1858, reprinted in the *Daily Alta California* (San Francisco), May 3, 1858.
4. Reports of correspondents, *The Times* (London), May 1858, *passim*.
5. *San Francisco Bulletin*, May 18, 1858.
6. Report of San Francisco correspondent, June 4, 1858, in *The Times* (London).
7. "The Gold Diggings on Fraser River," from San Francisco correspondent, June 21, 1858, in the *New York Times* and reprinted in *The Times* (London). Also quoted in John Domer, *New British Gold Fields* (London: W.H. Angel [1858]), 44, 46-47.

Alexander Caulfield Anderson—former HBC trader, diligent trailblazer, and author of one of the best guidebooks to the British Columbia gold fields. *Provincial Archives of British Columbia, Victoria.*

6
ROADS TO RICHES

BY LAND AND SEA, the gold rush continued into early summer, as communities across the West vied with each other to cash in on the new commerce. A San Francisco correspondent writing in early June described how the exodus continued to affect the Golden State, and he made recommendations for traveling north overland from California:

> From California the exodus of miners continues. Some thousands have left by sea, and great numbers are going overland, starting from Shasta and from Yreka, in the northern portion of this state, and travelling through Oregon to the new El Dorado. This is a perfectly practicable route, and the journey can be accomplished in about eighteen days.
>
> The excitement in the interior is universal. I was up the country this week, and returned only last night, so that I had an opportunity of judging for myself. From every point of the compass squads of miners were to be seen making for San Francisco to ship themselves off: and I heard of arrangements having been completed for driving stock overland, to meet the demands of the new population congregating in the Puget Sound country. One man had purchased a drove of mules, and another had speculated in 200 Californian horses, to supply the demand for "packing." These two "ventures" were to proceed overland in two days hence. The speculator in horses had been at Fraser River, and returned convinced of the judiciousness of his "spec." He spoke of the overland trip with enthusiasm—plenty of game and of grass, a fine climate, and no molestation from Indians.
>
> In fact, I found the interior quite in a ferment, the whole floating population either "on the move" or preparing to start; while traders, cattle-dealers, contractors, and all the enterprising persons in business who could manage to leave, were maturing arrangements to join the general exodus. Persons travelling in the mining region reckon that in three months 50,000 souls will have left California.[1]

As gold fever spread to other states, a St. Paul, Minnesota, news column rather over optimistically recommended a northerly route to the mines via the upper Midwest. Under the headline, "How to Get to the Fraser River," it advised:

> We believe the most feasible route to be through St. Paul for that region of country, as another season will make evident. That part of British America lying north of this, and extending to the Pacific, has, until within a late date, been a *terra incognito* to most intelligent people, owing to the care which the Hudson's Bay Company has exercised in suppressing all information of the richness, fertility, and exuberance of the soil, and salubrity of the climate of a large territory over which their chartered rights have extended.

Having gained information at "several meetings held in St. Paul," the reporter continued:

> From these reports we learn that the distance from St Paul to the gold mines on Fraser River is as follows:—St Paul to Pembina, 450 miles: Pembina to Carlton House, 600 miles; Carlton House to Edmonton, 400 miles; Edmonton to Fraser River (a branch of Fraser), 200 miles— total, 1650 miles. It is estimated that in view of the facilities afforded by the face of the country, and the continuous line of Hudson's Bay Company's posts, that this journey can be accomplished in seventy days, at an expense to a company of ten persons of 180 dols. each.
>
> There are many reasons why the above-mentioned route is the best from the valley of the Mississippi to the Pacific. One is, it has more water, timber, and game than those which start from the Missouri. Another is, there is no danger of molestation from Indians on this northern route. Another and very important one is, that the ridge of the Rocky Mountains, which, west of Missouri, hunches up like a camel's back, gradually flattens out; so the transit on the northern route is comparatively easy.
>
> It would not be at all surprising should the Fraser River gold tract, which Governor Stephens *[sic]* [former Washington Territorial Governor Isaac I. Stevens, currently the territorial delegate to Congress] states extends in our possessions as far down as Southern Oregon, be found the richest on the Continent. The discoveries and yield thus far warrant such a belief.[2]

On the West Coast, the burgeoning maritime traffic caused keen competition between Washington's coastal communities, with each claiming to offer the most advantageous access to the Fraser River. Bellingham Bay being in early favour, a *Puget Sound Herald* item of June 25, 1858, stated: "The Cortez arrived at Steilacoom on the 22nd bringing mails, freight and 1,083 passengers; 137 got off at Victoria and the remainder go on to Bellingham Bay bound for Fraser River."[3]

A citizen of Port Townsend, taking exception to published claims that Bellingham Bay offered superior advantages, wrote in early July:

> Now, sirs, how is it that we, old timers on Puget Sound, have been so deceived as to these great advantages lately brought into notice? Until we ascertained the fact through the columns of the papers, Bellingham Bay was looked upon as the most dangerous point for a vessel to approach, to be found from Cape Flattery to Olympia, and in support of this assertion I will give you the names of steamers known to have been ashore on reefs, islands, and flats, in their attempt to reach the Bay.

Port Townsend, he claimed, "with the finest trail above us [Snoqualmie Pass, across Puget Sound in the Cascade Range], and the river travel below . . . controls all the routes now in use, and those contemplated." He also stated that a party of "Puget Sound boys, from Olympia, Steilacoom, Seattle, and other points on the Sound" had left Port Townsend two weeks earlier for Skagit River, to find gold or, failing in that, to follow the river through the Cascade Range, and from there reach the Thompson River. Meanwhile, another party, 100 strong, had left Seattle for the Thompson River through Snoqualmie Pass: "The route by the Snoqualmie Pass is a fixed fact, and no better proof is wanted than to know those composing the company, many of them volunteers during the late Indian war, and connected with the Northern Battalion which was stationed near this pass."[4]

Of the many proposed "roads to riches," not all fulfilled their promise. In Whatcom on Bellingham Bay, the merchants—already reaping profits from trade with Fraser River miners—hoped to make their small town an important center of gold-rush traffic by constructing a trail some 150 miles eastward through the Cascades directly to the junction of the Thompson and Fraser rivers. According to pioneer historian Ezra Meeker: "If a trail could be constructed through the mountains from Whatcom, then the town would at once bloom into a city, and the fortunes of townsite proprietors would be made, and all might go to the mines whose spirit moved them."[5]

This would be a significant improvement over taking Whatcom's indirect and unsatisfactory lowland trail system to the "lower" Fraser that then was being used. After raising funds by subscription, a well-known engineer, Captain W. W. DeLacy, was recruited to lead a party to search out a pass through the mountains. Another group of men followed behind to cut the trail. After them came hundreds of hopeful prospectors, who marched along for many miles before discovering that the trail suddenly ended, with the worst of the mountains still ahead. DeLacy, apparently despairing of finding a pass, had disappeared. As Meeker recalled: "Meanwhile, the trail out from Whatcom for forty or fifty miles became well worn by men and animals going and returning, I saw sixty men with heavy packs on their backs start out in one company, every one of whom had to come back after floundering in the mountains for weeks."

Another party set out from Whatcom to proceed through Snoqualmie Pass, but they failed to reach the open country east of the mountains. In yet another venture described by Meeker: "W.H. Pearson, the intrepid scout . . . conducted a party of eighty-two persons, sixty-seven of whom packed their bedding and food on their backs, through the Snoqualmie Pass to the Wenatchee, where they were met by the Indians in such numbers and threatening mood that nearly all beat a hasty retreat."[6] (East of the Cascades, hostilities had flared up again between elements of several tribes and the Americans—mainly miners and U.S. troops. After a short period of truce, gold seekers intruding on Indian lands, as well as large brigades of Fraser-bound miners passing through the Columbia Basin, had been a major cause of a resumption of the Yakima war in the summer of 1858.)

Alfred Waddington, a proponent for Victoria, observed and summed up the competition between American communities, as well as the subsequent rise of Victoria as a key focal point for the mining excitement. Writing in November 1858, he noted that Port Townsend initially had the advantage in the spring of 1858,

> probably on account of its Custom house, and as being the port of entry of the Sound; and forthwith streets were laid out, houses went up, lots too went up, and were sold and resold, and every body flocked to Port Townsend.
>
> There were other speculators, however, who . . . pointed out the faults of Port Townsend; her open roadstead, her uncertain anchorage in the stream, and above all her distance from Fraser river. Watcom [sic] was certainly much nearer, but what was to give the greatest attraction to Watcom was the Bellingham Bay trail, which had just been started . . . [O]f all the extraordinary ideas that have been broached, that of cutting a perilous, and finally impracticable, trail 120 miles long, over high mountains and perpetual snows, in order **not** to make use of a navigable river [the Fraser] close by, is about the most extraordinary . . . It was the greatest humbug of the season, and the first of a long series of disappointments to the California miner.
>
> In the meantime numbers of adventurers began to assemble in both these places, and merchants hesitated whether they should ship

their goods to Watcom or to Port Townsend. Watcom, however, got the upper hand . . . [and] proved somehow or other that its very inconveniences were advantages; that the three-quarters of a mile of a mud flat in front of it was useful, and the exposure of the bay to the south winds more convenient than otherwise. The steamers, however, soon found out that the mud flat was not so very convenient; and in order to avoid it, a new city was proposed and started about a mile off, at Sehome. This town though intended to be the third big city, attained no great importance, nor ever rose above the rank of an annex to Watcom.

Hundreds of miners from all parts of the Sound and from California, to whom we may add a good stock of gamblers, pickpockets, swindlers, and men of broken down fortunes, were now congregated at Watcom, anxiously awaiting for the opening of the trail. And as the trail did not open, nor was very likely to open, people got tired . . .

In the mean time a few modest traders, who were acquainted with the Sound, and the advantages of Victoria as a good harbour . . . had made up their minds to go there and try their fortunes . . .

At length, the first steamer succeeded in getting up the [Fraser] river and reaching Fort Hope, thus proving the river to be navigable. This was a thunderbolt for the new cities, and from this moment the influx of population to Victoria became overwhelming . . . This immigration was so sudden, that people had to spend their nights in the streets or bushes, according to choice, for there were no hotels sufficient to receive them. Victoria had at last been discovered, everybody was bound for Victoria, nobody could stop anywhere else, for there, and there alone, were fortunes, and large fortunes, to be made . . .

Never perhaps was there so large an immigration in so short a space of time into so small a place . . .

Shops, stores, and wooden shanties of every description, and in every direction, were now seen going up, and nothing was to be heard but the stroke of the chisel or hammer. In six weeks 225 buildings, of which nearly 200 were stores, and of these 59 belonging to jobbers or importers, had been added to a village of 800 inhabitants; and . . . the whole country around the town was covered with tents, resembling the encampment of an army.[7]

---

1. Report from correspondent in San Francisco, June 4, 1858, in *The Times* (London), July 14, 1858. Also quoted in John Domer, *New British Gold Fields: A Guide to British Columbia and Vancouver Island, with Coloured Map, Showing the Gold and Coal Fields, Constructed from Authentic Sources* (London: W.H. Angel [1858]), 31-32. *The Times* account likewise appeared in Robert M. Ballantyne, ed., *Handbook to the New Gold Fields: A Full Account of the Richness and Extent of the Fraser and Thompson River Gold Mines* (Edinburgh: A. Strahan; and London: Hamilton, Adams, 1858), 47.

2. From a St. Paul, Minnesota, news column, dated July 14, 1858, reprinted in the *Daily Scotsman* (Edinburgh), August 16, 1858.

3. *Puget Sound Herald* (Steilacoom, Washington Territory), June 25, 1858.

4. "From our Puget Sound correspondent," July 8, 1858, in the *Daily Alta California* (San Francisco), July 16, 1858. Seattle, Olympia, and Steilacoom likewise vied for the mining trade, but their locations on Puget Sound were too far south to allow them to compete effectively with Port Townsend, Whatcom, and Victoria.

5. Ezra Meeker, *Pioneer Reminiscences of Puget Sound* (Seattle: Lowman and Hanford, 1905), 167.

6. Ibid., 168.

7. Alfred Waddington, *The Fraser Mines Vindicated, or, The History of Four Months* (Victoria: P. DeGarro, 1858), 8-10, 16, 18.

7

DOUGLAS REPORTS;
BRITAIN RESPONDS

B Y MID MAY, so great a volume of traffic had landed at Victoria and departed for New Caledonia that Governor Douglas decided to inspect the mining operations and see for himself how the miners were faring along the Fraser River.[1] On May 19, Douglas wrote to Lord Stanley: "I propose in a few days hence to make an excursion to the Falls of Fraser's River for the purpose of inquiring into the state of the country, on which I will report to you on my return."

Douglas and his party crossed the Strait of Georgia by company boat to the mouth of the Fraser, and subsequently, in a June 10 despatch addressed to Lord Stanley, Douglas described this expedition and the conditions then prevailing along the Fraser:

> In consequence of the requisition for assistance made on Captain Prevost, Her Majesty's ship Satellite was anchored off the mouth of Fraser's River, where I joined her on the following day, with the Hudson's Bay Company's propeller Otter, in which we proceeded up Fraser's River, with the Satellite's launch and gig in tow, to Fort Langley, distant about thirty miles from the mouth of the river.
>
> From Fort Langley we pursued our upward journey, in canoes manned chiefly by native Indians, and accompanied by Captain Prevost in his gig, manned by six of the Satellite's seamen.
>
> After journeying four days, we reached Fort Hope, the next establishment of the Hudson's Bay Company on Fraser's River, and about eighty miles distant from Fort Langley.
>
> The actual gold diggings commence on a bar of Fraser's River about one mile below the point on which Fort Hope is situated, and from that point upwards to the commencement of the Falls, a distance of twenty miles, we found several parties of miners successfully engaged in digging for gold on as many partially uncovered river bars; the number of whites on these bars being about one hundred and ninety men, and there was probably double that number of native

Indians, promiscuously engaged with the whites in the same exciting pursuit.

The digging became sensibly richer as we ascended the stream as far as Hill's Bar, four miles below the Falls, which is the richest point workable in the present high state of the river. The gold on these bars is taken entirely from the surface, there being no excavations on any of them deeper than two feet, as the flow of water from the river prevents their sinking to a greater depth.

Mr. Hill, the party after whom the bar is named, produced for inspection the product of his morning's (six hours') work, the result being very nearly six ounces of clean float gold, worth one hundred dollars in money, giving a return of fifty dollars a day for each man employed.

The greatest instance of mining success which I heard of in the course of our journey fell to the lot of a party of three men, who made one hundred and ninety ounces of gold dust in seven working days on Sailor's Bar, a place about ten miles above the Falls, giving a return of nearly nine ounces a day for each man employed.

Thirty miners arrived from the upper country during our stay at the Falls, with very favourable reports as to its productiveness in gold. They told me that they had prospected the banks of Fraser's River as far as the Great Falls, forty miles beyond the confluence of Thompson's River, and also many of its tributary streams, in all of which they found gold, frequently in pieces ranging from twenty-four grains to half an ounce in weight, and they also observed that the gold was larger in size and coarser the further they ascended the river. Thus, for example, the gold found below the Falls is in thin bright scales or minute particles, while that found at the Great Falls is in pieces ranging, as before said, from twenty-four grains to half an ounce in weight; a circumstance which the miner believes to be indicative of a richer country beyond . . . Those miners were prevented going further into the country for want of food, which compelled their return to the settlements for supplies. They were very successful about the Great Falls, and made from ten to thirty dollars to the man a day.

William C. Johnson, an old California miner, told me that he had prospected Harrison's River, and had travelled from thence to the Great Falls of Fraser's River, and that he had observed in the course of his journey much gold-bearing quartz, and the most promising indications of placer gold. Another old miner assured me that he had found large quantities of gold-bearing quartz in the mountains near Fort Hope, which he thinks will pay better than the California quartz rock; a report which was confirmed by other miners. The miners generally assert that the Fraser's River is richer than any "three rivers" in California.

Thompson's River and its tributary streams are known to be auriferous, and I have just heard from Mr. McLean, one of the Hudson's

Bay Company officers, that gold has also been lately discovered on the banks of the Great Lake.

Mr. Richard Hicks, a respectable miner at Fort Yale, assured me that he had found "flour gold," that is, gold in powder, floating on the waters of Fraser's River during the freshet, and he is of opinion that by means of quicksilver, gold will be found in every part of Fraser's River, even to its discharge into the Gulf of Georgia.

In summary, Douglas stated:

Evidence is thus obtained of the existence of gold over a vast extent of country situated both north and south of Fraser's River, and the conviction is gradually forcing itself upon my mind, that not only Fraser's River and its tributary streams, but also the whole country situated to the eastward of the Gulf of Georgia, as far north as Johnstone's Straits, is one continued bed of gold of incalculable value and extent . . . Your Lordship will not be surprised to learn that, under these circumstances, the gold excitement throughout the Colony, California and Oregon, continues unabated. Crowds of people are coming in from all quarters. The American steamer Commodore arrived on the 13th instant from San Francisco with four hundred and fifty passengers, and the steamer Panama came in yesterday from the same port with seven hundred and fifty passengers, and other vessels are reported to be on the way.

Douglas concluded with an urgent appeal to the Colonial Secretary:

In consequence of the unceasing demands upon my time by the crowds of people who are flocking to this place, and the want of assistance, my secretary, Mr. Golledge, being greatly overworked, I have been compelled to prepare this report in the midst of numberless interruptions, and I beg that its inaccuracies may be overlooked and that I may receive your instructions by return post, as the case is urgent, and calls for rapid and decisive measures in the outset, for in the course of a few months there may be one hundred thousand people in the country.[2]

Later that month, Rear Admiral Baynes aboard his flagship *Ganges* at Callao, Peru, sent a note to Douglas tersely acknowledging receipt of Douglas' early May letter requesting naval support. Baynes stated that a copy had been forwarded to the Lords Commissioners of the Admiralty. With the note sent to Douglas, Baynes included a copy of his letter to the Admiralty, stating that he was unable to send additional ships to Vancouver Island "without distressing other parts" of his station.[3]

Disappointed, the beleaguered Douglas notified the Colonial Secretary:

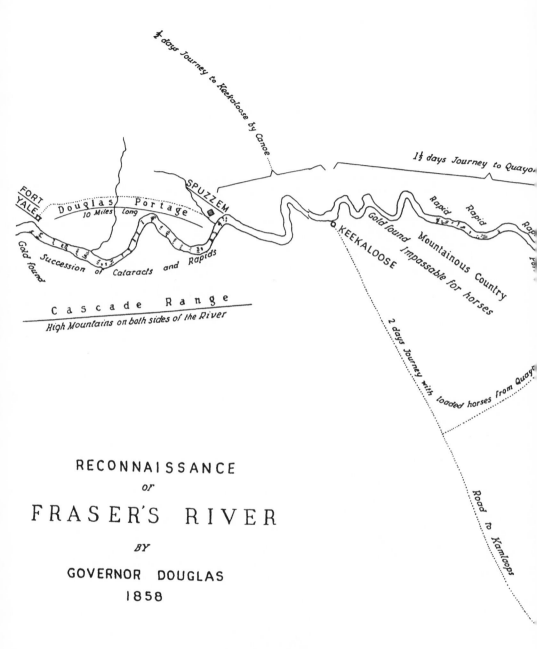

RECONNAISSANCE
of
FRASER'S RIVER
BY
GOVERNOR DOUGLAS
1858

From Angus M. Gunn, *British Columbia: Landforms and Settlement* (1968).

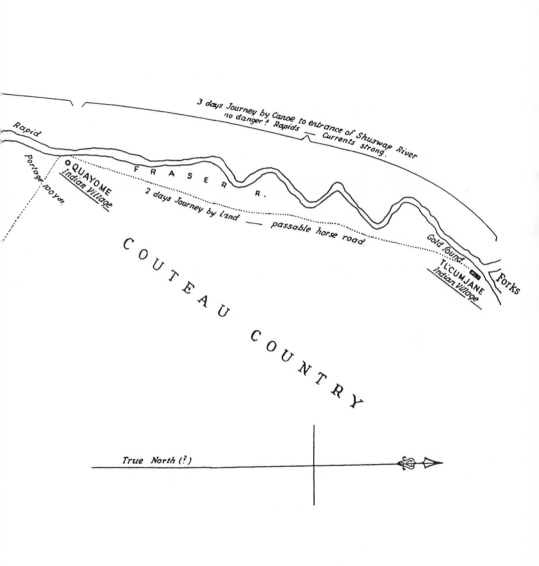

Rapid

Portage 100 yds.

○ QUAYOME
Indian Village

F R A S E R   R.

3 days Journey by Canoe to entrance of Shuswap River
no danger. Rapids ⌒ Currents strong.

2 days Journey by Land — passable horse road.

Gold found.

TL'CUMJANE
Indian Village

Forks

C O U T E A U   C O U N T R Y

True North (?)

I infer from Admiral Baynes' letter that he cannot furnish any additional force; neither does it appear from his letter that he entertains any hopes of being able to aid or assist in protecting the country; so that I am left to depend upon the casual aid received from the Satellite and Plumper, whose excellent Commanders, Captains Prevost and Richards, have merited my warmest thanks for their cordial and zealous cooperation in all the protective measures adopted by this Government.

The settlements on the seaboard require no other protection than those ships can afford; but a force is wanted for the service of the interior, which can be spared neither from the Satellite nor Plumper, both being here on special service, the latter on the coast survey, and the former for the objects of the Boundary Commission.

There are now about ten thousand foreign miners in Fraser's River, and upwards of three thousand of that number are profitably engaged in gold mining.

I have appointed Sub-Commissioners to mark out the mining claims, and to receive the duty of 21s. a month payable on each claim. Those officers require support, and the miners demand protection, while I have not a single man to detach to either of their assistance. The affairs of government might be carried on smoothly with even a single company of infantry; but at present I must under Providence, depend in great measure on personal influence and management; a position inconsistent with the dignity of the Queen's Government. I therefore trust that you will take our case into consideration, and direct such reinforcements to be sent to this country as Her Majesty's Government may deem necessary.[4]

Unknown to Douglas, the British government already was deeply concerned about the situation on the Pacific Coast and was responding with all possible speed. The process of sending civil and military reinforcements was underway, and naval assistance was the subject of an extensive correspondence between the Colonial Office and the Admiralty. But communication between distant London and Victoria was not swift. Each official despatch, typically containing letters in numbered sequence on a variety of matters, had to be painstakingly hand-written. It could take two months or more by sea for a despatch from Douglas to reach London, and each subject covered might then merit consideration, consultation, and decision-making by various officials, requiring multiple copies to be penned and circulated. The issues raised by the gold rush, being of special interest and importance, required discussion and planning by various authorities before the return despatch, containing responses and further directives, could be prepared. Sent then by a ship of the Royal Mail Steam Packet

Company, leaving Southampton on a regular schedule, the despatch might take two months or more for delivery via Panama to Victoria. Douglas might therefore expect to receive a response to his appeals some six months after sending them.

In the meantime, for six months after the start of the gold rush, he had to deal with the situation on his own initiative, for not until near year's end did the additional resources he so urgently needed begin to arrive.

1. Douglas made three trips to the mainland gold fields in 1858—the first occurred in the early summer of 1858, described here, then in late August-September, and again in November. See Margaret A. Ormsby, *British Columbia: A History* (Toronto: MacMillans in Canada, 1958), 157-63.
2. Parliamentary Papers Relating to British Columbia. Despatch, No. 2 (24), pp. 13-14, Governor Douglas to Lord Stanley, June 10, 1858.
3. Ibid. Despatch, No. 8 (34), p. 28, August 10, 1858; Rear-Admiral Baynes, Callao, to Governor Douglas, June 28, 1858.
4. Ibid. Governor Douglas to Lord Stanley, August 10, 1858.

"View of Victoria, Vancouver's Island," from the *Illustrated News of the World*, 1858. Victoria's rapid building expansion and the great surge of shipping activity during the gold rush are evident in this scene. *Provincial Archives of British Columbia, Victoria.*

8
THE COMPANY IN QUESTION

ADDING TO THE DIFFICULTIES of the miners in their early gold prospecting operations were the official restrictions imposed on them to protect the interests of the Hudson's Bay Company. The London *Times,* whose editorial columns were supportive of the HBC, published an editorial decrying the gold rush "invasion," and stated:

> The authorities of the Hudson's Bay Company are evidently alarmed at the prospect of such an invasion. They have issued a proclamation warning persons from entering Fraser's River for the purpose of trade, such acts being contrary to law and infringements upon the exclusive rights of the Hudson's Bay Company; and that all persons, boats, and ships, found fourteen days after the date of the proclamation in Fraser's River, or in any of the bays, rivers, or creeks of the British possessions on the north-west coast of America, without a licence from the Hudson's Bay Company, shall be liable to forfeiture, and will be seized and condemned according to law.[1]

A letter written from Sailor's Diggings on May 12, 1858, reported good earnings, but the writer complained:

> All the trading with the Indians is prohibited, and no merchandise of any description, beyond a miner's supply for six months, is allowed to pass up. Mr. Samuel McCaw, of Steilacoom, had some two thousand dollars' worth of merchandise seized and confiscated at Fort Langley by the officers of the Hudson's Bay Company. The goods of Messrs. Tilton and Gibson, as well as their vessel the Black Duck, shared a similar fate.[2]

Douglas had proposed to the U.S. Pacific Mail Steam Ship Company, in California, a one-year agreement whereby the Americans could place their steamers and staff of experienced officers on the navigable routes between Victoria and the falls of the Fraser River for the transport of goods and passengers. However, they would be allowed to carry *only* Hudson's Bay Company goods and no passengers, "except such as have taken out and paid for a gold-mining licence and permit from the Government of Vancouver Island." The steamship company also would be required to pay compensation to the Hudson's Bay Company at the rate of $2 head money for each passenger carried on the Fraser River. This proposal, mentioned in Douglas' May 19 despatch to Lord Stanley,[3] was rejected not only by the Pacific Mail Steam Ship Company, but also by the British government.

Concern in this regard also was expressed by *The Times'* San Francisco reporter. While allowing that, "the Company is eulogized for the leniency with which it has hitherto taken into consideration the destitute condition of some of the miners on their first arrival," and also that, "the Company does not charge exorbitant rates for its goods," he declared:

> But it is seriously objected that they have established a close monopoly in their own favour, under colour of the provisions of their charter. No vessel is allowed to enter the Fraser River without first obtaining a permit at Victoria. The sufferance costs $12 for a decked vessel, and $6 for open boats. All vessels of every nationality must take out this permit and pay their fees. No exceptions of any kind are made in favour of British vessels; and the British man-of-war Satellite is stationed off the entrance of the river to enforce the conditions of the sufferance, to stop all vessels or boats of any description from entering without a permit . . . Her British Majesty's steam-ship Satellite, Captain Prevost, has received orders to maintain a close blockade of Fraser's River, with a view to prevent the further ascent of trading vessels . . . I give no opinion upon the measures of the Hudson's Bay Company. From all I have learned they have behaved with liberality and in an accommodating manner to the emigrants hitherto. This permit business is the first ground of complaint, and they may be in the right for aught I know at present. But matters cannot long rest in peace and quietness as they are now. The British Government will act wisely in taking prompt measures to meet the emergency which has so suddenly arisen.[4]

As a veteran servant of the HBC, indoctrinated since his youth in the company's ways, Douglas, even as the colonial governor of Vancouver Island, always had followed HBC policy—despite complaints from colonists forced to purchase necessities at the company's high rates and from outsiders whose attempts to settle or to trade in the country were thwarted by the company monopoly. Complaints (some of which reached the Home Government) increased in number with the start of the gold rush, as Douglas sought to preserve the *status quo* against an overwhelming tide of free enterprise. In June, when Douglas had gone so far as to prohibit free passage on the Fraser of American steamships sorely needed for the transport of miners and supplies, a resolution signed by six Vancouver Island colonists was addressed to him as governor, begging him to adopt more liberal measures, and further stating:

> We cannot therefore, consider without serious apprehension the state of confusion and distress which must ensue when the vast numbers now swelling the tide of immigration shall have settled on these shores, should the present restrictions imposed upon trade by the Hudson's Bay Company continue in force.
>
> We beg to draw your Excellency's attention to the great inconvenience that is suffered by all classes, and by the mining community in particular, for the want of a reliable steam communication between this port and the mining districts; a want which has already caused the loss of many valuable lives. Such a state of things is deplorable in this age, and the more to be regretted when we consider that the means of supplying this want are at hand, and freely offered, but are rejected by the exclusive policy of the Hudson's Bay Company.
>
> It was with great satisfaction that the public heard that on the 5th instant your Excellency had given permission to the American steamers, Surprise and Sea Bird to carry passengers from this port up Fraser's River, but it heard with deep regret that this permission was given for one trip only.
>
> We would especially point out for your Excellency's most serious consideration how highly injurious is this state of things to the interests and progress of this important Colony. Many British subjects have recently come here, anxious to make this their home, and have invested in property to a considerable amount, and numbers of their friends are only waiting their advice to follow; but they find their ardour damped and their operations checked by the monopolizing policy of the Hudson's Bay Company. In the meantime, thousands of our countrymen from California are daily passing this beautiful island to settle upon American soil, because they see no fair field offered for their enterprise under the British flag.
>
> We feel assured that your Excellency will at once perceive that in bringing the objects of this memorial so prominently before you we are actuated by an earnest desire to advance the interests of this Colony, by providing for the welfare of settlers, and holding out inducements to early immigration, convinced that this is only to be obtained by the speedy adoption of the liberal measures embodied in the Resolution we have submitted.[5]

Since settlement of its vast territories always had been opposed by the Hudson's Bay Company, as being contrary to HBC interests, Douglas probably received this appeal without much enthusiasm. However, he was to have little choice in the matter. His restrictions on American shipping and trade were soon to be withdrawn, as illegal, on instructions from the Home Government.

Also inevitably affected on Vancouver Island was the company's selective immigration policy, which heretofore had barred free access for settlers, and had ensured a limited population based upon the class structure and social conventions of Victorian Britain. Included in a small, exclusive social circle headed by the governor were the land owners, prominent citizens and officials, visiting naval officers, and the company's clerks and officers (called "gentlemen," as distinct from labourers and workers). Lower on the social scale were the immigrants who, fleeing poverty in their homeland, had been shipped out from Britain by the company or the land owners. After six-months' passage round the Horn, they served as coal miners, farmhands, and servants. The labour force also included native Indians, and Sandwich Islanders (Hawaiians), called "Tanakas."

Within a few weeks of the arrival of the first shipload of miners, hundreds of new buildings were erected in Victoria. On surrounding sites, miners encamped in a crowded "tent city." Victoria was declared a free port, and massive shipments of merchandise arrived from San Francisco. Wells Fargo and other express companies opened offices. American merchants and businessmen advertised their wares and services in the *Victoria Gazette* (founded by an American company in June 1858) which with its circulation and revenues rapidly expanding, soon moved into larger quarters. And—symbolic of the changing social order—two newly arrived merchants opened the first of many new stores, ending the monopoly of the Hudson's Bay Company.

Yet, the HBC, through its very presence—in its trading posts and brigade trails, efficient organization and talented officers, and established peaceable relations with the Indians—was to be, however unwillingly, an important and beneficial influence during the initial occupation and settlement of the gold-rush territory. And, undoubtedly, the successful progress of the young colony owed much to the early presence of James Douglas of the Hudson's Bay Company.

————

1. *Daily Scotsman* (Edinburgh), July 13, 1858; extract from letter of New York correspondent for *The Times*, June 29, 1858. "An extract" of the "Sailor's Diggings, May 12th 1858" letter also is included in John Domer, *New British Gold Fields: A Guide to British Columbia and Vancouver Island, with Coloured Map, Showing the Gold and Coal Fields, Constructed from Authentic Sources* (London: W.H. Angel [1858]), 51.

2. *The Times* (London), July 30, 1858; reprinted from the *New York Times*, June 21, 1858.
3. Parliamentary Papers Relating to British Columbia. Despatch, Part I, p. 12, item 10, Governor Douglas to Lord Stanley, May 19, 1858.
4. Report of San Francisco correspondent, June 4, 1858, in *The Times* (London), July 14, 1858.
5. Parliamentary Papers Relating to British Columbia. Despatch, No. 25, pp. 15-16, Resolution, signed "James Yates [and five other persons]," June 9, 1858.

FORT LANGLEY, FRAZER'S RIVER.

From *Harper's Weekly,* October 9, 1858.

9

A NEWLY FAMOUS LAND

IN THE BRITISH PRESS meanwhile, New Caledonia, its name heretofore virtually unheard of and its location on earth unknown, was now receiving pride of place among news columns dealing with the important topics of the day—*mutiny in India . . . anti-slave trade measures . . . conditions in lunatic asylums . . . a bill to abolish the East India Company . . . triumphal reception at Cherbourg for Emperor Napoleon III and the Empress Eugenie . . . agonies of surgery eliminated by medical miracle chloroform.*

Reports from the West Coast normally appeared in New York and London newspapers a month or two after their date of origin. One especially exuberant report from a correspondent in Victoria, dated June 10, 1858, appeared in the London *Times* on August 14:

> I presume ere this the gold discoveries of which I have written before, have caused some little excitement at home; if not, they ought to have done, and Vancouver Island should no longer be a place of geographical doubt. The gold exists from the mouth of the Fraser River for at least two hundred miles up, and most likely much further, but it has not been explored; hitherto anyone working on its banks has been able to obtain gold in abundance and without extraordinary labour; the gold at present obtained has been within a foot of the surface, and is supposed to have averaged about ten dollars per diem to each man engaged in mining. Of course, some obtain more, some less, but all get gold. Thompson River is quite as rich in gold as Fraser River; in fact the whole country about Fraser and Thompson Rivers are mere beds of gold, so abundant as to make it quite disgusting. I have seen pounds and pounds of it, and hope ere long to feast my eyes upon tons of the precious metal; but not a bit of it, unfortunately, is my own.
>
> Before three months are over our heads we expect to see at least fifty thousand miners at work. At present steamers are running up from California bringing five hundred to one thousand passengers at a time; sometimes they call here, at other times go to American ports near the boundary line, of which Bellingham Bay is the most

frequented, but which in a very short time must give up the ghost to more favoured spots. In fact, Victoria and Esquimalt harbour in Vancouver's Island, where we reside, will be the spot to which nearly all vessels and steamers will go and depart from. There is no harbour like Esquimalt on the American coast; it is certainly a magnificent harbour; all the land about it has been bought up, and eighty pounds an acre is not considered a high price where good water frontage can be had. Those who held land there have made something by it, for it was sold by the Colonial Government at one pound per acre. I suppose Fraser River is not more than sixty or seventy miles from here, with beautiful navigation for steamboats.

Correspondents from several places on the Sound, both in the English and American territories, men of various nationalities, write that the country on the Fraser River is rich in gold . . . This is the burden of every song from Victoria, Vancouver's Island, Port Townsend, Bellingham Bay, Olympia, Whatcom, Sehome, Portland, and other places. Wherever a letter can be posted, or a steamer boarded in the north-western countries of Oregon, Washington, and the British territory the same news is wafted to San Francisco . . . When I add to this statement of facts from the Fraser River already given, that we have received many more accounts of mining having been carried on in April and May in several other places besides those mentioned in my statement, and with the like good results; that sundry persons have reported having seen returned miners on the coast of Puget Sound and elsewhere in the British and American territories with considerable quantities of gold; and when I add, further, what two of the principal San Francisco papers have told us, that two miners had $6,000 between them, one of whom said his last day's work amounted to $144, both statements given as ascertained facts; that one man had a shot bag filled with gold, and another fifty ounces, the two latter statements given on hearsay—when I add all this to my statement, I shall have given a pretty fair summary of all that is known here as yet concerning the new gold country.

"My own conclusion," *The Times* correspondent finally stated, "is that the Fraser and its tributary, the Thompson, are rivers rich in gold, and that I have no reliable evidence of the existence of gold fields beyond those rivers . . . Yet the stories of what was seen, and heard, and could be earned, have sufficed to unhinge the masses, and to produce an excitement which results in an unparalleled exodus." The same reporter, however, having first presented the "sunny side of the picture," went on to point out:

But the sun does not always shine upon the miner in New Caledonia. Overlooking the disagreeables and risks of the voyage from San Francisco, made, at high rates of fare, in crazy old vessels, not one of which

is really seaworthy, where men and women were crowded "like her-
rings in a barrel," . . . as a misery of short duration—only five or six
days—we come to where the miner finds himself dropped on the beach
at Victoria, Bellingham, or elsewhere.

Now his real difficulties and hardships commence, and his help-
lessness becomes painfully apparent. He is from one hundred to two
hundred and fifty miles from the mines, without food and without
shelter, in a variable climate. Several of his fellows tell the tale of his
troubles in a few short but significant items:

"Canoes very scarce; the price has risen from $50 and $80 to
$100 each. Many parties have built light boats for themselves, but
they did not answer."

: "We have got up, but we had a hard time coming."

: "Jordan is a hard road to travel; lost all our outfit, except flour.
Our canoe was capsized in the Falls, and was broken to pieces. Six
other canoes capsized and smashed the same day near the same place.
Four whites and two Indians belonging to these six canoes drowned."

: "Provisions high up the river are exorbitant, of course, as they
can only be brought up in canoes requiring long portages. Here's the
tariff at Sailor's Bar and other bars: Flour, $100 a barrel, worth in San
Francisco $11 to $12; Molasses, $6 a gallon; Pork, $1 per lb.; Ham,
$1.25 per lb.; Beans, $1 per lb.; Picks, $6, and Shovels, $2 each."

: "There were no fresh provisions; I should have been greatly
surprised to hear that there had been."

: "At Fort Hope there was nothing to be had but dried salmon."

: "At Fort Langley plenty of black flour at $9 a hundred, and salt
salmon at four for $1."[1]

What lively visions of scurvy these reports conjure up!

A June 14 report from San Francisco, later appearing in Edinburgh's
Daily Scotsman on August 5, stated:

The fever all over the State is intense, and few have escaped its conta-
gion. From Yreka to the north, bordering on Oregon, to San Diego in
the extreme south, the masses are in commotion; and from Shasta,
one of the northern, to Mariposa, one of the southern mining countries, miners and others are flocking to San Francisco in thousands on
their way to New Caledonia.

Naturally, the business derangements and the social inconveniences of this general and sudden exodus will be considerable. An old
country would be prostrated by them for a time. Here we are more
self-reliant from habit. The first bad effects will be felt by the commercial community. Then again, capital will come to a standstill. The
quartz mills are stopping for lack of hands, and all new enterprises of
every kind must be suspended from the same cause. The ordinary relations of life are being reversed. We are becoming primitive. "When

Adam delved and Eve span, where was then the gentleman?" If our Eves would spin we would not complain so much, but our domestic Eves are going to Vancouver Island to become ladies. It is a great reproach upon our gallantry, but we can't keep the women.

The same June 14 report quoted the narrative of a man who had left his "claim" in charge of two partners, and travelled to San Francisco with some of the "dust" he had dug above Sailor's Bar. The man, "connected with a business firm in" San Francisco, returned to the Fraser River with supplies and provisions. He described the country as,

> very rich and beautiful, but high and mountainous. You are surrounded by mountains entirely. There is plenty of timber and everything a miner can wish for, except game and provisions . . . "There are plenty of salmon in the river, and brown bears in the woods. They (the bears) are very good eating." They are much more accommodating than their 'grizzly' brethren of California, whose flesh is as tough as shoe-leather. "Wherever we 'prospected' (above Fort Yale) we found gold—at some places more, at others less; but we found gold EVERYWHERE . . . At the Rapids or Falls, twenty odd miles above Fort Yale, where the water fell fifteen feet over the rocks and prevented our ascending higher (by canoe) we prospected and found gold very plenty. Near the Falls and from Sailor's Bar up, many miners were at work, all with rockers.

"Another authority," the same reporter continued,

> a California miner, known in San Francisco, also lately returned from the Fraser and Thompson rivers, testifies to the existence of gold in great quantity. "This statement," he says, "is true; gold does exist, in this new country, and there is no doubt in my mind that the upper mines are much like the upper mines of California. The first diggings are not far from Puget Sound; but there, as in California, the richest mines will be found far up in the mountains."[2]

On the bars of the Fraser River, late into June, good fortune and high spirits continued to reign. A correspondent for the *San Francisco Bulletin* noted:

> The steamer Surprise reached Fort Langley, on Frazer River, June 5th, and proceeded to Fort Hope, arriving there next day. The steamer is the first that has ascended the river above Fort Langley, and could have gone to Fort Yale had her supply of coal not been limited. The navigation of the river for 150 miles from its mouth is thus established.[3]

Also in June, a Puget Sound newspaper reporter interviewed Joseph T. Bush, who had come down from the Fraser to replenish his supplies.

The account appeared in the London *Times* not many weeks later. Bush claimed that some parties on the river were making $100 a day with rockers, and that all of the miners were doing well. Between Fort Hope and Sailor's Diggings there were, when he left, about 350 miners. Only 35 or 40 men were at work on the Thompson River. The observation also was made that:

> Two miners of Steilacoom returned last evening from Frazer River in a canoe, after an absence of six weeks. They state that during a low stage of the river they made fifteen dollars per day each. Four rockers near them were making from four to nine and a half ounces per day.

Two trains with provisions had arrived through the interior from The Dalles, said Bush, and at Fort Langley provisions were abundant and cheap. He also noted: "The river is represented as in good navigable condition for canoes as high up as Fort Yale, beyond which point they cannot go with safety. The Hudson's Bay Company are actively engaged in repairing the Fort."[4]

A June 21 report in the *San Francisco Globe*, which like so many of these accounts later appeared in the London *Times*, stated:

> On Sunday we received a visit from Messrs. Edward Campbell and Joseph Blanch, both boatmen, well known in this city, who have just returned from the mines on Frazer River . . . Six of them . . . all of them boatmen in San Francisco . . . left this city on the steamer Commodore and took a whaleboat with them, in which they performed the remainder of the trip from Victoria to Hill's Bar, one hundred and fifty miles above the mouth of Frazer River, and two miles below Fort Yale. They mined for ten days in the Bar until compelled to desist from the rise in the river, in which time they took out one thousand three hundred and forty dollars. They used but one rocker, and have no doubt they could have done much better with proper appliances. There were from sixty to seventy white men at work on Hill's Bar, and from four hundred to five hundred Indians, men, women, and children.

The *Globe* also noted that, "the narrative of these gentlemen exactly agrees with that of Mr. Henry Ettling, published in the *[San Francisco] Herald* of yesterday."[5] Henry Ettling's report, also later appearing in the *New York Times* and London *Times*, stated that he and his partner bought a canoe at Port Townsend for $50. They then navigated to the mouth of the Fraser in three days and thence upriver to Hill's Bar in seven more days. At Hill's Bar they found seventy American miners at work:

Mr. Ettling and his partner had never mined before, and were, consequently, green at the business. Nevertheless they realised together six ounces in the five days. Being unsupplied with a rocker they cut down a tree, made a rough substitute for a rocker, and perforated the holes with an iron spoon. The miners on the river appear to be well satisfied with their operations.

The impression of all who have gone is unanimous and conclusive as to the great fact of the new gold fields now being explored being equal to any ever yet developed in California or elsewhere. No steamer had yet returned with more than 12 or 15 passengers, and nearly every one of these has come down to obtain supplies for himself or his party left behind at the diggings . . .

Fortunately, so far no serious disturbances have occurred, save one near Fort Hope, in which an Indian chief and a white man were killed. The Indians were greatly aroused, but Mr. Allard, an agent of the Hudson's Bay Company, succeeded in pacifying them.

Nearly all the work at present is carried on between Fort Langley and Yale, and for some 20 or 30 miles above the latter, an entire distance along the river of about 100 miles. Some few are digging on Harrison River and other tributaries, where the gold is found in larger particles. Those who were engaged in mining on the forks of Thompson's River show still richer yields, but have been compelled to leave on account of the high stage of the water, the want of provisions, and the opposition of the Indians.

The *Sacramento Union* estimates the emigration from this State to New Caledonia to have already exceeded, 12,000. It states that from the 1st of May to the 15th of June, 9,000 passengers left Sacramento for San Francisco, against 5,800 during a previous period of six weeks. The arrivals by up-river steamers in San Francisco during the last week have averaged 500 nightly of the Frazer River bound, and it is safe to say that the departures from this city for the north will have reached the same daily average.[6]

The San Francisco correspondent for the *New York Times*, on June 21, listed fifteen vessels that had sailed in a fortnight for Victoria and the Puget Sound ports, and he added:

The departures for Fraser River from San Francisco have not been less than 6000 in the period of two weeks . . . At least twenty sailing vessels—clipper-ships, barks, brigs, and schooners—are now advertised to sail with quick despatch, some of the smaller class to take passengers through to Fort Langley, stopping at Victoria to obtain permits to pass up Frazer River, at the mouth of which the British steamer Satellite is stationed to guard against unlicensed ingress [which was aided by a launch, manned by 20 men, stationed at Fort Langley, to search boats going up]. The price of first-class cabin passage by steamer to

Victoria is sixty-five dollars; thirty-five dollars in the steerage. The sailing craft charge from sixty dollars down to twenty-five dollars.

Reporting extensively on the "wondrous news" of the gold rush and the "vast commotion" created in California, the *New York Times* correspondent had concluded:

> It is no longer doubted or disputed that a new gold country awaits development in the north, as rich in its resources as California or Australia . . . Already it is found by the record that 9,216 registered passengers have left this port in steamers and sailing vessels for the new mines. It is well known that at least one-fourth of those departing are not enumerated in the clearances at the Custom-house. The steamship Cortes, which sailed on the 17th inst., really carried about 1,400 passengers, but only 900 were reported. So, too, the Panama sailed, June 14th, with about 900 passengers, when her clearance was for 570. Fully 12,000 persons have departed for the land of promise in the last two months, and probably the actual total is not less than 15,000. That the next two months will carry off an equal number there is no question; and it is safe to assume, from all present appearances, that the entire exodus from California during the first six months of the Frazer River fever will reach the enormous figure of 40,000. The rapidity and extent of this emigration has never been paralleled.[7]

On June 28, a correspondent for the London *Times* reported from New York:

> The Moses Taylor arrived from Aspinwall on Sunday with $1,799,502 in gold. The reports of the gold discoveries on Frazer's River are fully confirmed. All doubt in regard to the richness of the mines is dispelled.

In July, President James Buchanan appointed John Nugent, editor of the *San Francisco Herald*, as special agent "to make proper representation" to the United States citizens in the new gold country, "with the view of preventing collisions or outbreaks in that quarter." The *New York Times* commented: "It is pleasant to reflect that we have fairly earned the courtesy which Britain extends to our miners by our own liberality in California, and it is earnestly to be hoped that peace and good will may characterize their intercourse with British subjects and with the British authorities."[8]

———

1. Report from Victoria correspondent, "The New Gold Diggings," in *The Times* (London), August 14, 1858.
2. Extract of letter from *The Times* San Francisco correspondent, dated June 14, 1858, in the *Daily Scotsman* (Edinburgh), August 5, 1858. A portion of this account later

was quoted in *Guide Book for British Columbia, &c., by a Successful Digger, Containing Practical Information for the Emigrant, and other Useful Matter* (London: n.p., 1862), 12.

3. San Francisco correspondent's report for the *New York Times*, June 21, 1858; item from special correspondent of the *Bulletin*, reprinted in *The Times* (London), July 30, 1858. Also quoted in John Domer, *New British Gold Fields: A Guide to British Columbia and Vancouver Island, with Coloured Map, Showing the Gold and Coal Fields, Constructed from Authentic Sources* (London: W.H. Angel [1858]), 45.

4. From "a Puget Sound newspaper," in *The Times* (London), July 30, 1858. Also quoted in Domer, *New British Gold Fields*, 51.

5. *San Francisco Globe*, June 21, 1858, reprinted in *The Times* (London), July 30, 1858. Also quoted in Domer, *New British Gold Fields*, 48-49, and Robert M. Ballantyne, ed., *Handbook to the New Gold Fields: A Full Account of the Richness and Extent of the Fraser and Thompson River Gold Mines* (Edinburgh: A. Strahan; and London: Hamilton, Adams, 1858), 18.

6. *San Francisco Herald*, June 20, 1858, reprinted in the *New York Times*, July 21, 1858, and *The Times* (London), July 30, 1858. Ettling's account also was quoted in Domer, *New British Gold Fields*, 48, 50.

7. Extract of letter from New York correspondent, dated June 29, 1858; "Gold Discoveries on the Fraser River," later reprinted in the *Daily Scotsman* (Edinburgh). Also quoted in Domer, *New British Gold Fields*, 47, 50.

8. *New York Times*, July 28, 1858, reprinted in *The Times* (London), August 12, 1858. John Nugent, however, proved unsuited and ineffectual as a U.S. agent and his tenure fortunately proved short lived—September 20 to November 13, 1858; Frederic W. Howay, W.N. Sage, and H.F. Angus. *British Columbia and the United States: The North Pacific Slope from Fur Trade to Aviation,* ed. by H.F. Angus (New York: Russell and Russell, 1942 [1970]), 158.

10
Douglas as Peacekeeper

THE INDIANS, AS PARTICIPANTS in the fur trade, had become accustomed to generally peaceful, even amicable, relations with the British, and particularly the Hudson's Bay Company. Governor Douglas' own wife, Amelia (later Lady Douglas), had both a Scottish and a Cree heritage; mixed marriages such as that of her parents were common in fur-trade society.

In the western United States, however, relations between white settlers and Indians frequently were hostile. Douglas feared that importing this hostility into British territory could provoke bloody warfare. He therefore again appealed to the Colonial Office to send troops to occupy the territory, explaining in a June 15 despatch: "The recent defeat of Colonel Steptoe's detachments of United States troops, consisting of dragoons and infantry, by the Indians of Oregon territory [actually, Washington Territory], has greatly increased the natural audacity of the savage, and the difficulty of managing them. It will require, I fear, the nicest tact to avoid a disastrous Indian war."[1]

He enclosed, as added persuasion, an extract from the May 28 issue of the *Pioneer and Democrat*, a Washington Territory newspaper. Under the headline, "Another Indian War—Startling Intelligence," it described,

> the defeat, on the 16th instant, at the first crossing of Snake River, about 30 miles above its junction with the Columbia, of the command of Colonel Steptoe. The command consisted of five companies of 400 men. The Indians are reported as having been 1,500 strong, and composed of the Snake, Palouse, and other tribes. The action resulted in three officers and fifty men killed . . . The Indians took two howitzers which belonged to the command, and all but sixty pack animals. In fact, so complete is said to have been the rout, that the officer in command was compelled to fall back with the utmost precipitation. The battle took place while the regulars were in the act of crossing the river.

Colonel Steptoe had proceeded into the Snake country peaceably to treat with them, or proceed to hostilities, if necessary.[2] The object of his visit was probably of a similar character with that of Major Haller, some three years since, and which resulted in a like unfortunate manner. Major Haller, our readers will remember, proceeded thence with a force of 104 men, and in a peaceable manner demanded the murderers of the emigrants of 1854. The result was, that instead of bringing to justice these depredators and murderers, he brought home the bodies of 22 of his command, killed or wounded, on litters.[3]

This tragic account may have reminded London that the Pacific Coast colonists always had been massively outnumbered by tribal peoples, and of the dangers inherent in that imbalance. However, although Douglas was asked to continue sending, "newspapers which contain matters worthy of attention," his request for military aid was in vain. Instead, the confidence of Her Majesty's Government in Douglas' peacekeeping abilities was expressed in a letter from the new Colonial Secretary, Sir Edward Bulwer Lytton (the famous writer was also an able colonial administrator):

At this distance, and with the imperfect means of knowledge which I possess, I am reluctant to offer, as yet, any suggestion as to the prevention of affrays between the Indians and immigrants. This question is of so local a character that it must be solved by your knowledge and experience, and I commit it to you, in the full persuasion that you will pay every regard to the interests of the Natives which an enlightened humanity can suggest.[4]

In subsequent despatches, Lytton frequently instructed Douglas that the Indians must, under every circumstance, receive fair and considerate treatment—a sentiment also expressed by other cabinet members during Parliamentary discussions regarding New Caledonia.[5] The government's confidence in Douglas' peacekeeping abilities was tested during his June visit to the Falls of Fraser River. When he and his men arrived at Hill's Bar, Douglas found,

the white miners were in a state of great alarm on account of a serious affray which had just occurred with the native Indians, who mustered under arms in a tumultuous manner, and threatened to make a clean sweep of the whole body of miners assembled there.

The quarrel arose out of a series of provocations on both sides, and from the jealousy of the savages, who naturally feel annoyed at the large quantities of gold taken from this country by the white miners. I lectured them soundly about their conduct on that occasion, and took the leader in the affray, an Indian highly connected in their way, and of great influence, resolution, and energy of character, into the Government service, and found him exceedingly useful in settling other Indian difficulties.

I also spoke with great plainness of speech to the white miners, who were nearly all foreigners, representing nearly every nation in Europe. I refused to grant them any rights of occupation to the soil, and told them distinctly that Her Majesty's Government ignored their very existence in that part of the country, which was not open for the purposes of settlement, and they were permitted to remain there merely on sufferance; that no abuses would be tolerated; and that the laws would protect the rights of the Indian, no less than those of the white man.

Douglas appointed a Justice of the Peace at Hill's Bar, and instructed the Indians to take any grievances to him. Douglas also appointed Indian magistrates and instructed them to, "bring forward, when required, any man of their several tribes who may be charged with offences against the laws of the country." Thus did Douglas set some ground rules for the peaceful coexistence of miners and natives, while at the same time possibly preventing a massacre. But he predicted: "without the exercise of unceasing vigilance on the part of Government, Indian troubles will sooner or later occur." [6]

1. Parliamentary Papers Relating to British Columbia. Despatch, No. 4 (26), p.17, item 9, Governor Douglas to Lord Stanley, June 15, 1858.
2. *Pioneer and Democrat* (Olympia, Washington Territory), May 28, 1858. This newspaper account of Steptoe's defeat was based mostly on hearsay. Though correct in some details, it is quite inaccurate in others, particularly in misrepresenting the locations of events and exaggerating the size of the armed camps and the number of casualties. Regardless, the battle was a large one by Indian war standards and hard-fought. Here is a brief, but accurate portrayal from a modern source: "On May 6 [1858] . . . [Lt. Col. E.J.] Steptoe and a command of over 150 mounted soldiers, packers, and Nez Perce Indian guides left the U.S. Army's Fort Walla Walla . . . to search for Indian cattle thieves, to parley with the Spokanes, and to investigate reports of increasing Indian hostility toward American miners around Fort Colvile . . . [The] command traveled northward through the heart of the Palouse country. Near modern-day Rosalia, perhaps 600 mounted warriors—Spokanes, Palouses, Coeur d'Alenes, Yakimas, and elements from other tribes—met the troops and warned Steptoe not to continue north. Steptoe obliged, but, regardless, a bloody running fight developed the next day, May 17. After an all-day battle, the command, having suffered considerable losses, was surrounded at nightfall on a hilltop with only three bullets left per man. Under the cover of darkness, the troops quietly abandoned their position to attempt a desperate dash for the Snake River. After a 70-mile flight, alternately riding and dismounting to walk the horses, they reached the Snake a few miles below the mouth of the Clearwater

where friendly Nez Perce canoed the exhausted soldiers across to safety and guarded the tired horses. In a few days, the dispirited command arrived back at Fort Walla Walla." Ron Anglin, *Forgotten Trails: Historical Sources of the Columbia's Big Bend Country*, ed. with contributions by Glen W. Lindeman (Pullman: Washington State University Press, 1995), 128-30.

Consequently, the U.S. Army abandoned its heretofore peace policy of 1856, 1857, and early 1858, in which the military had been excluding white settlers from eastern Washington and eastern Oregon to prevent friction with the tribes. However, resumption of military action in 1858 was due not only to Steptoe's defeat, but also because tribesmen clashed with large brigades of Fraser-bound miners intruding northward across native homelands in the Yakima, Wenatchee, Grand Coulee, and Okanogan areas. With overwhelming reinforcements, the army completed the conquest of the Inland Northwest in two campaigns in the late summer of 1858, ending the Yakima war of 1855-58 (Ibid., 150).

3. Major Granville Haller's fight had been the first major engagement of the Yakima war. Haller's regulars, seeking the murderers of Indian agent Andrew J. Bolan and some miners, were defeated by Yakima and Klickitat warriors in the Simcoe Mountains of south-central Washington in October 1855 (Ibid., 128).

4. Parliamentary Papers Relating to British Columbia. Despatch, No. 6 (6), pp. 45-46, item 3, Sir E.B. Lytton to Governor Douglas, July 31, 1858.

5. Despite such well intentioned paternalism, the aboriginal people were to suffer in future years from often misguided government policies and costly but inappropriate bureaucracies.

6. Parliamentary Papers Relating to British Columbia. Despatch, No. 4 (26), p.16, items 3-9, Governor Douglas to Lord Stanley.

11
GOLD MINERS ALL

Among the thousands of miners who came to the Fraser River in 1858, there was a high degree of literacy and of good conduct, for these men represented every walk of life, many nationalities, and many diverse careers—the latter abandoned, if only temporarily, for the grand adventure. What they necessarily had in common was the courage and resourcefulness to venture through hundreds of miles of wilderness to seek fortune by their own hard work.

There were exceptions, of course—the outlaws, gamblers, opportunists, and liquor merchants who infested the gold camps; the drifters and the improvident, caught up in the gold rush, but ill-prepared for its hardships. The latter were mentioned by a reporter writing from San Francisco: "I was informed by a gentleman from the interior [of California], who observed the exodus now taking place with much interest, that the greater part of it was composed of idlers and vagabonds who had been hanging about the different mining towns and camps 'out of luck,' doing nothing, and ready for anything that might 'turn up,' but now industrious foreigners, French and German, are departing in great numbers."[1]

Among the most stalwart and law-abiding of the miners were the Chinese, about whom the *San Francisco Bulletin* of May 18 reported:

> The new gold region is destined to be a rich harvest for the Chinese. Being prevented from coming to California by the stringent law recently passed by our legislators, and in the British possessions being afforded the same protection and facilities as the whites, the Fraser River mines will soon be crowded with hordes of these people from their own overgrown population in China. Already the heads of the different Chinese companies in this State are making arrangements to ship their countrymen at present among us. We have ample news of what is doing in China by a merchant vessel which came in this morning, making the passage in fifty days from Hongkong. She brings a crowd of Chinamen, who will no doubt find their way to the north,

now that a late law of this State prohibits their importation into California.

In spite of being afforded by law "the same protection and facilities as the whites," the Chinese who remained in Canada after the gold rush, and those who came later, were to experience in varying degrees at different periods, that prejudice and discrimination that seemingly are inevitable in any country towards people of a foreign race and different colour. (In the xenophobic Orient, white foreigners have been, historically, the unwelcome "barbarians.") But the Chinese, by their hard work, intelligence, and good citizenship, earned success and respect in their adopted country, contributing considerably to its culture, character, and prosperity.

The early gold-rush population also included many British and European expatriates, some of whom had been variously employed in the United States, but also others who came direct from Europe on hearing the early reports of New Caledonia gold. One such was the British author and adventurer Kinahan Cornwallis, who previously had visited and written about the gold fields in Australia and California. In April 1858, he again departed England, this time for Vancouver Island and New Caledonia. He was destined to quickly write and publish (in London, late 1858) one of the most entertaining, readable, and informative accounts of the Fraser River gold rush, titled *The New El Dorado; or British Columbia.*[2]

After a thirty-five day voyage from Liverpool via New York and the Isthmus of Panama, Cornwallis landed at San Francisco on May 29, and joined in with hundreds of his fellow passengers:

> On shore we go, leaping like so many frogs from the whole side-length of the steamer . . . We go with the crowd to 'book' for the next steamer to Victoria—we have to wait our turn—there are at least five hundred before us, and just as many coming up behind . . .
>
> Once more I stand on the shores of California, and the bay of San Francisco.

Cornwallis next rhapsodized at length about the natural beauty of this part of California, and continued:

> San Francisco itself is all life and animation, full of revelry and delight; the very streets and wharfs seem to groan beneath the weight, and the hotels and saloons swarm with the daring adventurers destined for the El Dorado . . . Down the Sacramento pours night after night a torrent of future British Columbians. It is useless to attempt to stem the tide: in the rush, the words of advice and the voice of reason are equally

unheeded . . . Even newspaper men, the last and least credulous in the world, are making off,—all seem determined upon exploring for themselves . . . although those who are now there, from whom letters have been received, advise intending emigrants not to start for a month til the river falls, yet every steamer, clipper ship, or barque, which sets sail for the north, is filled with passengers, and hundreds have to be left behind for want of accommodation-room for them.

To Cornwallis, San Francisco appeared much as it had when he had been there in 1855 during the California gold rush. Red-, blue-, and gray-shirted miners laden with picks, shovels, pans, blankets, and rockers again thronged the streets and over-ran the stores. Thousands of dollars were being exchanged for "revolvers, rifles, shot, guns, and knives; pickaxes, shovels, and hoes, rocker iron drills and rifle boxes, flannel shirts, thick coats and pants, waterproofs, oilcloths, and water-boots" by miners eager to complete their kits before embarking for New Caledonia. At the same time in Stockton and Sacramento, thousands of men lined up for conveyance to San Francisco. Between one man and another, the question was no longer—are you going? but when?

On a "bright and beaming" early June morning, the steamer *Cortes*, with Cornwallis among its nearly 1,500 passengers, left San Francisco for the six-day voyage to Vancouver Island. "I blended up my voice with the farewell of that mighty crowd in a hearty, hopeful cheer to those collected on shore."

"As the paddle-wheels flew round," and finally after "the cheers of those on shore died faintly away in the distance" and "the waving of hats ceased," Cornwallis turned his attention to his fellow passengers. He noted several travelling groups of from three to six men, all seemingly well supplied with mining tools and provisions. Some had packed whaleboats—small watercraft—in which to complete their journey to the mines. The "swarthy, restless" passengers "walked backwards and forwards, and guessed and calculated, either on deck or in the cabins, from early morning till midnight." Their shipboard meals included "pork and beans, pickles and molasses . . . thrown together on the one plate, and hurried into obscurity with all the impetuosity of an ardent gusto and excitement peculiar to themselves."

"On the morning of the sixth day from San Francisco, the bold shore of the destined island was presented to our longing view, and in two hours" the *Cortes* dropped anchor in Esquimalt harbour. Men went ashore as fast as boats could be sent to take them off. They set out immediately on foot for Victoria, a distance eastward of three miles.

Those few who had earlier passed this way in more tranquil days now found dramatic change. Where formerly a few travelers "had floundered in the mud without meeting a single soul, there was now to be seen a crowd of foot travellers who were making their way from the port to the town. Carts, vans, and express wagons also covered the thoroughfare which presented the busiest scene imaginable. The new El Dorado was drawing men in thousands from California, and the majority of them some time or other passed over the muddy road from Esquimalt to Victoria."[3]

To continue in Cornwallis' words: "[In Victoria] we lost no time in repairing to the government gold licence office, where we tendered our five dollars each, in exchange for a monthly voucher, privileging us to dig, which also was our necessary passport to travel up river, for without it we could not have proceeded along the mainland. This tax was frankly paid, but heartily denounced."

Cornwallis observed that Victoria, "wore a highly flourishing and pleasing appearance, the most notable feature in the shop and trading line being the scarcity of anything like hotels; there were five places, however, where liquor was sold, the proprietor of each having to pay the Hudson's Bay Company a licence fee of no less than [120 pounds] per annum for the privilege." Cornwallis spent some time strolling "a little way inland along green Jamaican-looking lanes, running like channels through a continent of cultivation." He admired the beauty of the island and the fertility of its well cultivated soil, until, "at five o'clock . . . I embarked on board the American steamer Surprize [sic],— which had just returned from Fort Hope with Governor Douglas and suite. He is a fine old, jolly looking Scotchman, very gentlemanly and agreeable."[4]

This early June voyage of the *Surprise* to Fort Hope was mentioned in a despatch by Douglas, who wrote: "Two steamers, the Surprize and Seabird, both owned by American citizens, ply with passengers between this port and Fraser's River, the former having made her way up that stream as far as Fort Hope, one hundred miles from the sea. The miners by that means reach their destination with safety and despatch."[5]

The fare from Victoria to Fort Hope was, Cornwallis stated,

twenty dollars without distinction, whereas the San Francisco steamers' fares varied from thirty to sixty-five dollars. We passed and saluted the steamer Satellite, as we entered the mouth of the river, after crossing, or rather rounding, the Strait of Juan de Fuca, which separates the island from the mainland, and after that, threaded our way amongst the canoes past Fort Langley and the mouth of the Harrison River, towards Fort Hope, which we reached early on the morning of the second day afterwards; having sailed a hundred and sixty miles in all from Victoria.[6]

1. *The Times* (London), June 14, 1858; extract in the *Daily Scotsman* (Edinburgh), August 5, 1858.
2. Kinahan Cornwallis, *The New El Dorado; or British Columbia* (London: T.C. Newby, 1858).
3. Walter N. Sage, *Sir James Douglas and British Columbia* (Toronto: University of Toronto Press, 1930), 21.
4. Cornwallis, *The New El Dorado*, 150, 179-87.
5. Parliamentary Papers Relating to British Columbia. Despatch, No. 28 (6), Governor Douglas to Lord Stanley, June 15, 1858.
6. Cornwallis, *The New El Dorado*, 187-88. Carter Museum, 1975.

"Noon on the Frazer, Our Bivouc beyond the 'Forks,'" depicts Kinahan Cornwallis' party unloading a canoe and settling in around a cooking fire. This unknown English artist's fanciful view of British Columbia gold miners served as the frontispiece to Cornwallis' *The New El Dorado; or British Columbia* (London, 1858, 2nd ed.).

12
CORNWALLIS AND COMPANY

It was KINAHAN CORNWALLIS' good fortune to fall in with a company of hardy and experienced Californians who were determined to reach richer gold deposits that lay beyond the lower river. Here was his opportunity, as a writer, to record the day-to-day experiences of men who ventured farther than most along the Fraser in 1858.

The *Surprise* having landed them at Fort Hope, the companions found the early June weather delightful. The riverbanks were thronged with miners—all merry and excited—rocking and digging away with great success. Cornwallis, equipped only with a geological shovel he had purchased in San Francisco, worked for only three hours—his day's gains proving considerably less than those of his more industrious and better equipped companions. (Possibly, Cornwallis initially was more of a writer and observer than a serious digger; as time went on, however, he clearly from his own account became infected with the same "fever" that inspired the Californians.)

At Fort Hope the companions spent the night in a large, octagonal tent, for which privilege each paid three dollars, "being half a dollar in excess of the charge at the hotel-palaces of New York." The German proprietor had himself only just arrived by the previous steamer from San Francisco. Having set up his canvas "hotel," he had furnished it with skins on which Cornwallis, the proprietor, and thirteen others, after having dined on tea and muttonchops, reclined, "talking and medicinal-brandy drinking till about ten o'clock . . . All slept with their revolvers and gold under their variously improvised pillows." The next morning:

> The river was a little lower than on the previous day, and miners were busy, either singly or in twos, rocking the washing stuff; it requires two to work a rocker well, one to dig and the other to wash and collect the "bits." Some who had not brought rockers with them, were engaged in making them out of green timber; the bottom, however, a thin metal plate punctured with holes, had to be purchased, and at an

exorbitant price—one of my fellow boarders have given forty dollars for one; a thing that in England would cost about eighteen pence, and in San Francisco two dollars and a half. But the necessity for a rocker in wet diggings is all but absolute. For my own part, I gave four dollars for a pan, and worked that in lieu of a rocker, making about four bits each washing.

On the next morning—their third day on the river—Cornwallis with five others, having purchased a canoe for eighty dollars, left Fort Hope at seven o'clock and set off for Fort Yale. "Two or three miles below" Fort Yale, they came to Hill's Bar ("a sandy flat about five hundred yards in length"). They found this place crowded with some 500 Indians ("men, squaws, and children"), while about eighty white miners also were at work here:

> These were averaging from fifteen to twenty-five dollars a day each man. Provisions were exceedingly dear and scarce, flour selling at eighty dollars the barrel, bacon at seventy-five cents per pound, and butter at a dollar per pound. A party of twenty miners had set out on the previous day to prospect for dry diggings in the interior, under guidance of a batch of Indians, who said there was plenty (hihew) of gold to be found, but no tidings of their success had yet been heard of. The population were subsisting chiefly upon deer's flesh and salmon, both of which were abundant. My companions went "in for a dig" . . . at this place, but being anxious to explore new spots, did not remain beyond noon on the day following.

"Under the pilotage of an Indian, whom we had engaged at eight dollars a day wages," the party portaged the rapids just above Fort Yale and eventually made their way far upstream to a point beyond the "Forks"— the junction of the Thompson and Fraser rivers—"making about a hundred and seventy miles in all from the river's mouth." At this location they worked for only six hours, making good yields of forty-eight to eighty dollars for each man, but then decided to continue on upriver.

The Indians here were fewer in number, "but were as well stocked with gold as the white men. They carried it about with them in skin pouches and bags containing from one hundred to five hundred dollars' worth." (As with the white men who "struck it rich," it would be interesting to know how the wealth gathered by the Indian miners affected their future.) The Indians were very friendly, "and manifested the most kindly feelings towards us, frolicking about in the highest glee imaginable."

As the company proceeded, they had, of course, left the larger population of miners behind them, until only a few were to be seen along the river. Cornwallis wrote:

As for provisions and habitations, at this stage, they were both equally scarce. We had to run down river three miles, towards Sailors' Bar, before we arrived at a newly constructed store of green timber, where flour was selling at a hundred dollars the barrel; molasses, seven dollars a gallon; pork, a dollar per pound; tea four dollars per pound; sugar, two dollars per pound; beans, one dollar per pound; picks at six dollars each, and shovels three dollars each; and where we were taken in for the night at three dollars a head.

That night the men slept in the one-room store—Cornwallis on "a wooden bench covered over with a bear skin," while "about twenty others . . . were variously located about the store."

Up and about on yet another beautiful morning, the party decided to press higher up the river:

We set out with a newly-engaged Indian, with the view of passing the upper falls, either by land portage or skilful steersmanship; the latter, however, we were warned against trusting to, as two miners and an Indian had been drowned in the attempt to pass through, their canoe being also smashed to pieces, five days previously . . .

On reaching the falls we disembarked, each man carrying his own "kit," and our Indian pilot the canoe. Had it not been for the unusually high state of the river at this particular time and season, we could have easily avoided making the portage, but as the river ran, it was the wisest thing we could do to abstain from trying it . . . after proceeding nearly a mile, the canoes were again laid on the water, and our oars plashed away . . . At dusk, feeling hot and tired, we drew up in a small natural cove on the right bank of the river, partly overhung by a species of water-willow . . . [and] stepped ashore . . . I dwelt with something like rhapsody on the picturesque region of mountain and forest which delighted my admiring, not to say astonished gaze . . . and I thought it the loveliest clime it had ever been my changeful lot to wander in.

Not an Indian was to be seen, the woodland was deserted. We began, of course, with our usual avidity, to explore and prospect, from the instant of our mooring the canoe, while our native pilot collected faggots for a fire . . . and very soon the crackling of the pile of leaves and branches which our Indian pilot had collected, was heard.

The fire was not really needed for warmth, but was used to cook some dried salmon and make tea. Here, Cornwallis remarked upon the rather sudden change in the climate and character of the country, for they were approaching the drier region that lies inland from the coastal rain forest. Beyond a belt of trees flanking the river, "deeply-grassed" prairie land now stretched for miles, bounded by mountains to the north and forests to the west, but, southward, open as far as the eye could see. As the men gathered by the fire for the night, Cornwallis brought out his treasured opossum rug to sleep on, which he had acquired during similar excursions in Australia. Around him the others laid their blankets on the ground and settled down for the night, as "the howling of a wolf and the cries of other animals of the wilderness were heard from time to time coming faintly from the distance."

Soon after daybreak on the following morning, the men were again hard at work, finding gold "everywhere." Cornwallis noted, "my only surprise was, that a region so palpably auriferous should have remained so long unproclaimed and hidden from the gaze of civilization."

The Cornwallis party appeared to be the first miners to have prospected at this particular location. They had heard that another party of six had gone farther upriver and were thought to have diverged southwest into the interior. (Small parties of miners, of course, already had penetrated into this country in 1858 and a couple of years preceding.) Cornwallis and his companions, hoping to find still better diggings upstream, soon abandoned their rich, "Willow Bank" deposits. They rowed swiftly along on rapid and shoaly waters, "the navigation of which was both intricate and dangerous, towards—the mountains now transformed into—visionary gold."

Farther upriver they found the banks lined with low shrubs, weeds, and grasses. There were many skittish waterfowl, one of which, a duck, Cornwallis shot for provisions. "As of the latter," Cornwallis wrote:

> Our stock was becoming very attenuated, owing to the absence of natives; we, however, expected to meet with them every hour, when we should be able to negociate [sic] for the purchase of bears' flesh, wild vegetables, and fresh salmon . . . We had to make another portage at about four o'clock in the afternoon, in order to keep clear of the rapids, and proceeded in the same order as on the last similar occasion, carrying our own "kit," while the Indian walked along with the canoe on his back; he was a fine intelligent fellow, about six feet in height, and as kind-hearted a guide as I ever had the pleasure of being associated with in any enterprize. We only gave him four dollars a-day for his services, as he had the advantage of making a "pile" on the journey, if luck threw it in his way—a pile being, in digger parlance, a small fortune in "dust" or "nuggets." We had scarcely got the canoe into water again on the other side of the rapids, when I caught sight of an ordinary-sized brown bear, standing with one paw bent forward on a shelving part of the river's bank, about twenty yards a-head.

The bear having been dispatched with a single shot through the head, the Indian soon had prepared steaks for cooking. To the party's surprise, still no natives were to be seen, but the Indian guide assured them that they soon would "meet with plenty of them . . . that their encampments lay at some miles' distant from the shores of the river, generally near a creek or lagoon." At day's end, having consumed their dinner together with tea and "a quantum of brandy," the party was camping beneath trees near the river when, shortly after dusk, came rain, thunder, and lightning lasting about two hours. After that, "flies and other insects seemed to spring into life."

In the morning a little after breakfast, the men were startled by the sudden appearance of about 100 Indians, apparently fierce and warlike, followed by about 20 others on horseback—galloping furiously and prancing about, "in the most humorously despotic style, yelling and brandishing arms in savage glee." Like their friendly guide, Jack, these were Carrier Indians, and it was not long before Jack had communicated the white men's goodwill. Friendship was established by Cornwallis making a gift to the chief of a pocket knife. After this, the Indians agreed to trade provisions to the miners. A group of Indians set off to their village to fetch provisions, while others examined, with the greatest curiosity and delight, all of the belongings of the white men, ransacking everything and, "eating up the remains of Bruin's carcase *[sic]* with evident satisfaction, and making temporary use of everything not actually in hand or on our backs, and all this in the most perfect good humour and friendship."

"The detachment returned with provisions"; the miners' possessions were restored; the natives sat down and fed; and the miners filled their pockets with gold—for, as Cornwallis stated, "the banks of the river were literally strewed with gold; the natives rooted it up with sticks, and the heart of the El Dorado seemed already reached." As the men dug away, one of the party made twenty-two ounces of gold, and others panned like amounts. Cornwallis himself "turned up sixteen small nuggets" worth about $250, "and this with an amount of labour which could only be called amusement."

That evening, more canoes arrived from the lower river, each landing six or so miners, all of whom were heartily welcomed. That night, while the natives retired to their own camp, the miners engaged in revelry encouraged by "some excellent brandy." Cornwallis calculated, "we were now . . . about two hundred and eighty miles from the river's mouth, and one hundred and forty from the mountains."

Next morning came another fleet of canoes. These came downriver, however, bringing some 200 Carrier Indians, all armed warriors and wildly whooping, but, like the others, peaceful and friendly. They, too, were most inquisitive; Cornwallis' opossum rug of Australian origin again was passed around hand-to-hand with much delight, and with fascination for its great size "and the stitching which held the skins together." Cornwallis had to resort to the greatest tact in resisting their invitations to part with it.

It was, Cornwallis recalled, "a sun-burnt, motley group" that camped by the riverside. All were merry, for the day's yield had greatly exceeded that of any previous day. One man, "a stringy, dried-up looking Kentuckian," had made nearly $500 using a rocker. There were also "four long, slo[o]p-built, semi-civilized-looking" Missouri men "with heavy rifles nearly as long as themselves," who had travelled overland to the California gold mines, and had lately travelled through Oregon to the Fraser, being "clever enough to 'shirk the license' on the way." These four each had an axe; they proposed to build logs cabins on the following day. There also was an Englishman from Bristol, who had run away to sea and, eventually reaching California, deserted his ship for the Sierra gold fields. In California, he did well in the diggings, but after each of his "good strikes" invariably spent all his profits on "a jolly spree." Like most of the others, he had come north by steamer from California. The company also included three Frenchmen, who were partners; two Germans; and four more Americans—"a surgeon, a lawyer, a conjurer, and a photographic artist." Not forgetting, of course, the presence of an aristocratic English author, it clearly was a "motley group" that spent that night in comfort around the camp fire, "in the happy confidence of safety. And this was . . . adjoining a camp of reported warlike Indians . . . I would thus as readily trust myself to their power as I would to humanity of the white skin." [1]

————

1. Kinahan Cornwallis, *The New El Dorado; or British Columbia* (London: T.C. Newby, 1858), 188-91, 193-96, 199-201, 203, 205-07, 209-12, 214-31, 234-41.

13
THE JOURNEY HOME

I
N THE MORNING, the Missouri men set to work chopping down pine
trees, while another man cut up some bear meat bought from the Indians, and cooked it for breakfast, "gridiron fashion across a burning fag-
got." Cornwallis, meanwhile, "enjoyed a refreshing bath in the river." Then
he partook of breakfast, "the best part of which was the tea: a beverage
which I felt almost as necessary to my existence." By this time, "the Indians were flocking down to us like so many geese to their pond."

"After breakfast the work of trimming the logs and washing the gold
proceeded briskly," until it was time for a midday meal. Consistent with
Cornwallis' continuing good fortune, one of the Frenchmen in the company happened to be an excellent cook. He had been a restaurant keeper in
California, and would rather cook than dig for gold. The miners soon
hired him to do so at $10 a day. The meal he served, Cornwallis recounted,
"consisted of a savoury dish of stewed squirrels, a 'pan' half full of
transmogrified deer's and bear's flesh, converted into a harricot [sic] with
the assistance of wild vegetables, and some yam-like cereal called potatoes
[probably the Native American wild staple, camas roots], grown and supplied by the Indians." Later offerings included a variety of other bear-meat
recipes, with "grasshopper sauce . . . prairie greens and yam potatoes . . .
also a pudding stuffed with wild raspberries, and half-a-dozen other wild
things which we did not at all expect, but which turned out very well."
Cornwallis speculated that if the camp were "dead broke" out of provisions, this "cook would have dished us up a very palatable pottage of landscape herbage, and made soup out of the few knife handles we were possessed
of, or, better still, out of my persecuted opossum-skin rug." However, he
added, "We had plenty of salmon, and a few small fish, so that we were not
compelled to confine ourselves to squirrels and bear's-flesh." After dinner,
the four Missouri men returned to the work of house-building, using "the

newly cut timber of the forest, and a few nails which they had brought overland."

On this and following days, the yield of gold continued to be extremely rich, but this was no longer a "novelty." The men hardly even mentioned it. For Cornwallis, too, the excitement was fading. The river no longer was navigable, being full of rocks around which the waters whirled wildly. Though the natives indicated that a further portage would lead to deep, smooth water, "we should have had to travel hundreds of miles further up, following the river's course, before reaching its source in the Rocky Mountains." Perhaps the other members of the company also felt they had gone far enough, for, though Cornwallis did not state it, the building of cabins and the routine of cooking may have signalled that the company was settling into its final "diggings."

But Cornwallis was ready, now, to go home. "I had seen enough of the upper country to satisfy me as to its richness, and now felt a longing to observe life elsewhere." (His readers might have wished they could have learned what the future held for his companions, and in what diverse directions their new-found wealth would take them; but, that "motley group" we must leave forever gathering gold on the upper Fraser.)

Cornwallis sold his share in the canoe, and set out accompanied by "two painted Indians, in a canoe belonging to their tribe." Now he was anxious to reach Victoria and to "invest" several thousand dollars of his gold dust: "which, indeed, I felt it agreeably oppressive to carry . . . We shot down the river like an arrow, passing by . . . the respective bars of Canoe, La Fontaine, and Foster, and bivouacing *[sic]* for the night on the right bank of the river, where we made a portage, [and] reached the 'Forks,' distant about one hundred and sixty miles from the river's mouth, and six miles below Mormon Bar, an hour before noon on the second day out."

Here the Indians, not wishing to descend further, departed with their canoe. Cornwallis purchased another canoe for $120, "from a party of Frenchmen at the Thompson River junction, in which I proceeded with another Indian down the river as far as Fort Yale (which was then undergoing repairs) making a portage along the Cascade Mountains on the way."

At Fort Yale, Cornwallis spent the night "in a square tent-store kept by an Illinois man." Here, "tents were numerous, and wooden houses and stores were going up every day. The 'dry diggings' being worked on a creek parallel with Hunter's Bar, a few miles further down . . . were turning out very rich."

On the next morning, Cornwallis proceeded downriver, "passing hundreds of boats and canoes on the way." On reaching Fort Hope, he sold the canoe which had carried him down from the Forks, and, paying $20 for steamer passage, left on the same day for Vancouver Island. There were very few passengers on board. Twelve miles below Fort Hope, they "passed the steamer *Sea-bird* grounded on a bar," yet manned by her captain who looked "extremely disgusted." At Fort Langley, only two or three more passengers boarded the steamer. The next day at noon, the steamer "came to an anchor in the placid and baylike harbour of Esquimalt."

At Esquimalt, the harbour was alive with ships "and boats of all sizes and shapes," including Indian canoes, some guided by native girls, that plied between the shore and the shipping. A large, newly constructed store and wharf were the center of activity for a throng of Americans and Europeans, as well as Chinese, Blacks, and Sandwich Islanders, and Italian fishermen/boatmen from San Francisco. Cornwallis and his fellow passengers "took boat together" from Esquimalt to Victoria. Here again fortune favoured him, for on that same day, "a Company's land sale was going on at the office of Victoria Fort . . . the scramble for lots was of course tremendous." The price per lot was $100 (an increase from $50 two months before), and almost all of the lots purchased were destined to change hands quickly at greatly increased prices. One man "in a liquor store" told Cornwallis that he had purchased a $50 lot two months previously and had just sold it for $7,000.[1]

The land sales also were mentioned by Alfred Waddington who wrote: "The opening of the land office was announced several days before hand, and also the hour for 9 o'clock; but before four in the morning the door was already besieged, and at nine the crowd was such that it was useless for those who had come rather late to think of getting a place or lot."[2]

Cornwallis could not penetrate the scramble for lots on that day: "I had never been in such a crowd since the year of 'fifty-five, when I waited my turn for letters in front of the San Francisco post-office after the arrival of the United States Mail." But, during the next day, and on the day following, by dint of early rising and perseverance, he managed to buy the permitted limit of six lots, each 60 by 120 feet, at the standard price of $100.

> I thought myself very lucky in having been able to enter thus cheaply into a landed proprietorship, which promised to be about the best paying thing even in a gold country . . . I really felt it quite worth the

passage-money from New York, to see the rampant excitement, and to watch the eager speculation going on amongst the disordered community assembled together at Victoria. There were individuals who but two weeks previously had been plodding their way in San Francisco, tolerably well satisfied with the profits of a small and legitimate business, who now looked upon themselves, and were looked upon by others, as *millionaires*. They would tell you that they owned a thousand or twelve hundred lots in the town of Esquimalt—or Squimalt as it was pronounced— which cost them but five dollars an acre but a few days since— and which they now sold at as many thousands per acre.

Shortly, on June 27, the San Francisco steamer *Republic* arrived bringing 1,300 Californians, all burdened with the usual baggage and weapons. After they embarked, Cornwallis noted:

> Most of them walked across from Esquimalt [to Victoria] in preference to waiting for boats to bring them round. I had a sight of them on the road, and a curious and exciting sight it was. The entire length of the road was lined with them. They were all "packed," that is, they all carried more or less baggage across their shoulders, and were all equipped with the universal revolver, many of them carrying a brace of such, as well as a bowie-knife . . . I also recognized the arrival of some notorious San Francisco "sharps," whose coming was by no means grateful to the well-disposed . . . Moreover, the steamer Surprize had also just arrived from Fort Hope, bringing reports of the most dazzling description. The river was rapidly falling, and the yield was, as a natural consequence, increasing, and was expected to be prodigious; the present average in some places being forty dollars to the man per day, and in others double that amount. There was a Vancouver Indian, a passenger by her, who had brought twenty-seven pounds' weight of 'dust' and nuggets, slung round his body in bags and belts . . . and there were several Americans and Frenchmen also by her with even larger amounts . . . The Surprize was to leave again for Fort Hope on the day following—people lived as much in a day here as they do in a month elsewhere—and would take about four hundred passengers, the balance of the number by the Republic having either to wait for the steamer following, or to take boats and canoes, that is, as many as could get them . . . The Republic was unexpectedly announced to leave next morning for Bellingham Bay . . . from thence to proceed to San Francisco.

Cornwallis, being now "as impatient to get to Europe as the majority of the people were to get to the diggings," sold three of his lots within three hours, making a profit of more than $20,000. The other three he retained, "till after my return from Europe, *en route* to which I now intended proceeding by the Republic." On the following morning, Cornwallis boarded ship, carrying a single valise, his opossum rug, and a precious burden of gold. Ten minutes later, the *Republic* was off, "with half-a-dozen cabin passengers only, and these composed of San Francisco merchants and miners returning for supplies." During a two-hour stop at Sehome on Bellingham Bay, Cornwallis rode a wagon as far as the town of Whatcom, which was noted (for a time) as the home of numerous California "sharps" and other rough characters. The town consisted "of about a hundred houses, chiefly wooden, and mostly occupied as stores, restaurants, and gambling houses." He also noted that the purported trail from Bellingham to the gold fields was "bogus news." The steamer meanwhile had picked up eight more passengers, now making fourteen in all.

On July 3, at seven o'clock in the evening, the *Republic* arrived at San Francisco. Cornwallis observed: "The city of people were of course half-mad for news . . . Extras were at once issued from the newspaper offices, and the whole place was in even greater ferment than when I had left it, more than a month before . . . even greater and more than that which characterized Victoria." The next day being the Fourth of July, "there was much talking, feasting, and rejoicing" in San Francisco. "But still all these things were subordinate to, and swallowed up by, the gold excitement."

"On the next day," Cornwallis "embarked on board the steamer, Golden Gate, for Panama," where he crossed "the isthmus by railway, and took steamer from Colon, or Aspinwall, as the Americans" called it, "to the island of St. Thomas." Then again he was bound for Southampton, arriving "in the month of August."

So it was that Cornwallis, having absented himself from England for four months, was now in a position to settle his accounts with certain creditors who perhaps had helped motivate his departure. (Of his decision to leave England he had written, in the early spring: "Unanimously resolved that we go to the diggings, and take our petty cash with us instead of into the Queen's Bench.")

Cornwallis wasted little or no time in supplying his publisher with the account of his adventures, for that same year saw the release of his book, *The New El Dorado; or British Columbia*, which he dedicated to the Colonial Secretary, Sir Edward Bulwer Lytton:

> . . . for his brilliant genius, and as a slight but reflected evidence of the universal popularity of his able political administration, more especially in the founding and constitution of British Columbia.

In his conclusion, Cornwallis praised British Columbia's "salubrious climate" and its agricultural potential, as well as its mineral wealth—"five hundred thousand square miles of the richest and most splendid country in the world." And, Kinahan Cornwallis, who by his own courageous enterprise had regained fortune's favour, advised his fellow Britons: "Men who have been groping in the hazy squalor of poverty for years in this country, and might remain so forever, may at once make a plunge into the arena of wealth and all its attending glory, by embarking for the golden shores of our El Dorado."[3]

1. Kinahan Cornwallis, *The New El Dorado; or British Columbia* (London: T.C. Newby, 1858), 244-60.
2. Alfred Waddington, *The Fraser Mines Vindicated, or, The History of Four Months* (Victoria: P. DeGarro, 1858), 19.
3. Cornwallis, *The New El Dorado,* iii, 260-61, 269-70, 281-82, 293-94, 296, 298-301, 304-05, 308-09.

14
THE JULY FLOODING

IF ANYTHING COULD HAVE discouraged the faint of heart from migrating northward, it might have been a photographer's advertisement that appeared in California's *Grass Valley Telegraph* of June 11:

> Persons about going to Frazer's River, will do well to call upon Mr. Wood at his Rooms on Hill Street, and leave a resemblance of themselves with their friends. Should they ever live to return it will be quite a matter of curiosity, to notice the ravages which time and hardship will have made upon them; and should they never return from the frozen regions of the north, such a memento will be cherished by their friends here as a priceless gift.

Nevertheless, the exodus continued, and in late June a San Francisco correspondent wrote: "Those who have lately travelled through the mountains [of California's mining region] say that the principal roads in the interior present an appearance similar to the retreat of a routed army. Stages, express wagons, and vehicles of every character are called into requisition for the immediate emergency, and all are crammed, while whole battalions are pressing forward on horse or muleback and on foot."[1]

Also in late June, the *San Francisco Bulletin* reported:

> As during the fortnight previous, the last fifteen days have been occupied almost exclusively with Fraser River matters. The new gold mines at the north have been in everybody's mind and in everybody's mouth. The press of the entire State has been almost monopolized by accounts and letters from there; and every line on the subject has been seized and read with the utmost avidity. The exodus from California of emigrants from that region has continued unabated; steamers and sailing vessels, some of the former of the largest class, have been called into requisition to accommodate the travel . . . As yet, there seems to be no falling off of the number who are travelling. The interior towns are being deserted, and operations in parts of our mining country will for a time cease. Property in various parts of California has necessarily

depreciated. In many places the depreciation is unreasonably great; and perhaps a better time for investing money profitably in property in California never existed than at present. Mining claims, paying splendidly, and real estate, have been sold by individuals afflicted with the "Fraser River fever" at less than half of their real value. Our latest news from Victoria (Vancouver's Island) reach to the 28th June and from the new mines to the 26th June.

But the account continued on an ominous note: "At that time there were an immense number of miners on the banks of Frazer River, waiting for the stream to fall, to enable them to go to work on the bars, which are said to be fabulously rich."[2]

The phrase, "waiting for the stream to fall," was a reference to seasonal flooding as the Fraser River swelled increasingly from the melting of mountain snows, preventing the miners from digging. The most fortunate miners were those who had reached the diggings before the spring inundation of the riverbanks became most severe. Still, the northward migration to the Fraser continued, despite advice from Governor Douglas and from newspaper correspondents that it would be wiser, now, to wait until the floodwaters receded. All such warnings went unheeded, with the result that many men—especially those who came without sufficient resources to wait out the flooding—had their hopes replaced by disappointment, frustration, and even hunger. During July, many miners returned home, thwarted by the conditions then prevailing on the lower river. All subsequent reports of their hardships received more than full coverage in San Francisco newspapers—not only to provide due warning to would-be miners, but also, some suggested, in the vain hope of discouraging workers from leaving the state. Most earlier news reports about the gold rush had been positive, but during the time of the worst flooding some expressed an extremely gloomy view of the miners' circumstances and prospects. In a report to *The Times* of London, a correspondent in San Francisco stated: "The misstatements of the American newspapers on all matters touching the Fraser River gold mines are quite monstrous. They give most perverted statements upon every subject, all of which get into the papers here and make much of what they publish unreliable."[3]

On July 7, a *Daily Alta California* report drew upon, "the statements of several returned miners, who have been up the river and prospected it for a distance of twenty miles: Their accounts are gloomy in the extreme, and are but a commencement of what may be expected." And the same report continued under extended headlines—"Desperate situation of the miners . . .

Scarcity of provisions . . . Hard times now and starvation ahead . . . Destitution among Californians"—expounding upon the question of how soon the floodwaters might be expected to recede: "That will certainly not be until the latter part of August. This is as certain as that the sun rises and sets. Let nothing to the contrary deceive you, readers, in this respect."

But, in fact, the floodwaters were receding, and miners were again successfully digging by early August. A further paragraph, under the heading "Returned disappointed miners," referred to complaints of "nothing to eat, no gold, starvation, cold weather, savage Indians, monopolizing Hudson's Bay Company, etc., etc. These results are exactly what has been predicted by far-seeing men."

But again, in fact, "cold weather" in midsummer would be surprising; and the Hudson's Bay Company, though indeed a monopoly, had earned the respect and admiration of the miners, and in fact had done its best to mitigate hardship and hunger; and as for "savage Indians," this was not the view of some who expressed admiration and respect for the Fraser River Indians, finding them strong and intelligent and—to those who gave them due consideration and respect—friendly and helpful. The report urged readers against leaving for the gold fields until the floods receded, but then went on:

> Mr. Pike, who returned some weeks since to San Francisco, with $3,500 in gold dust, from Sailor's Bar, arrived here last week, and started back to his claim with two partners, in the last trip of the Surprise. He has another partner holding the claim until the water falls again so as to allow them to work. Mr. D. Duyer, coal dealer, of your city, and Mr. Hathaway went up in the same boat; both are acquaintances of Mr. Pike, and go with him. Perhaps this is an instance where the suggestions I have thrown out above might be departed from, as Mr. Pike has a claim, and knows precisely where to go and what to do. The party went well supplied with provisions.[4]

It was true that among those who put their faith in the early glowing reports from the mines, there were some who would return not with fortunes in gold, but with tales of hardship and disappointment. Among those was one Morris Anderson, of Sacramento, who told an *Alta California* reporter,

> he had waited, hungry, together with three or four hundred others, for the steamer Cortez, advertised to leave for San Francisco on a Saturday but delayed until Monday. "The officers of the steamship were very attentive, particularly about the time we were going on board,

insisting that every man should pay thirty dollars. One poor fellow had only twenty dollars, and upon making this fact known was ordered back by the kind hearted purser, and told to keep off."

(This was, of course, the same steamer *Cortes*, which, at the beginning of June, had brought from San Francisco hundreds of more fortunate miners, including Kinahan Cornwallis.) Anderson concluded:

> Finally, I am back in San Francisco, light in pocket, but thank fortune that matters are no worse, and that I have escaped from the grand humbug with life and health. I have suffered untold hardships, and am out at least three hundred dollars. Still, I am truly thankful to Providence for my deliverance. Fraser River I pronounce emphatically the worst and most shameful deception ever practiced upon an intelligent people.[5]

But, interestingly, another report in the same newspaper, on July 14, mentioned that miners without means to support themselves "might get employment in a thousand ways, for labourers are in great demand at Victoria just now."[6]

A long letter was published in the *San Francisco Daily Times*, pleading that something be done "for humanity's sake" for the "destitute and starving" Fraser River miners; castigating the steamship companies for having, for profit, brought them to misery; and suggesting, "they fear to allow those unfortunates to return, else their tales of suffering and hardships may put a stop to the exodus." In response, under the heading "Pitiful if True," the *Victoria Gazette* of July 28, 1858, quipped:

> There is an antiquated (perhaps an antediluvian story) about a man who employed a lawyer to prosecute one who had injured him, and who was affected to tears by the touching appeal of his counsel. In the depth of his self-sympathy he exclaimed, 'Never till now did I know how I have suffered' . . . Now as far as Victoria is concerned, anyone resident here must consider the 'starvation and destitution' story absurd.[7]

On July 26, Douglas wrote to London: "Notwithstanding the great number of people assembled at Fraser's River, it does not appear that there has been a large production of gold, as most of the river bars are still inundated; nevertheless the miners have unwavering faith in the richness of the country, and are in great spirits in anticipation of any early fall in the river."[8]

But of course, not all the miners shared the "unwavering faith" and "great spirits" which Douglas had observed. Towards the end of July, as the flooding of the bars continued, more and more disgruntled men were giving up and returning to California. On the night of July 31, a large body of returning miners, having crossed from the mainland, descended on Victoria as an angry, rioting mob, forcing Douglas to call up the man-of-war H.M.S. *Plumper*, which hastened to Victoria, but arrived after the riot had ended. The miners, after "letting off steam," and having forcibly retrieved one of their number who had been arrested, had dispersed peacefully.

When at last the floodwaters receded, those miners who had waited at the diggings, and those newly arrived, were rewarded by the deposits of fine gold which were again found in abundance. As a British news report, dated to August 5, stated:

> The water in the numerous streams was at last beginning to fall for the season, and the snow in the mountains, which heretofore has fed them, is pretty nearly exhausted. A good many miners are already working on the bars in the river, and some of them are doing well. All were quite sanguine that as soon as the streams fell they would take out large quantities of gold. A new route has been discovered to the Upper Fraser River region, by the way of Harrison and Lillooet rivers and lakes, and some easy trails. This was considered of great value as one of the principal difficulties heretofore to be contended against was the difficulty of transporting provisions to the upper waters of Fraser River, where the principal diggings are said to be located.

(As more miners became enabled, by new trails and an improved supply situation, to work the richer gold bars beyond the lower river, Victoria gradually was to become a somewhat less essential destination. In time, Victoria's fortunes would temporarily decline as the fabulous Cariboo discoveries of the early 1860s made the new mining towns of Richfield and Barkerville, on William's Creek deep in central British Columbia, the magnets for gold miners.)

The August 5 account continued: "The Hudson's Bay Company now permit all persons to take up an unrestricted quantity of provisions to the mining region, and there seemed to be little or no suffering there now for the want of food. The Hudson's Bay Company and its officers have acted with the utmost fairness and liberality in all their dealings with the miners and others, and are very popular and universally respected."[9]

By early August, then, fortune was again favouring the Fraser River gold miners. A report from Fort Yale and Victoria, dated August 11 to 14 and published in the "Foreign Intelligence" columns of the *Daily Scotsman*, stated:

Up to one week of the latest dates from the mining region the river remained too high for operation on the bars. This had caused great despondency among the people on the banks of the stream, who were waiting for the water to subside. About the 5th of August the river began to fall, and on the 11th—our latest date—many miners had been working on the bars for several days. The yield of gold was very rich. The lowest accounts put it down at $7 and $8 to the man per day; the highest at $50 to $75. Provisions were plentiful in the mines, and comparatively cheap. No rich "dry diggings" had yet been discovered to any extent. The miners were pushing up towards the head of the stream, and now that the waters are subsiding they will experience less difficulty on the way.[10]

On August 21, despite some lingering flooding, the news continued promising. *The Times* report of that date stated:

Wherever mining has been carried on, the bed of the river has yielded gold in abundance, and nearly all the miners who have worked on it concur in the opinion that gold exists in remunerating quantities.

About a week ago some $12,000 worth of gold dust came down to Victoria, all from Fraser River, and the day before yesterday the Hudson's Bay Company steamer, the Otter, brought down an amount estimated at about the value of $30,000, belonging to different miners. It is impossible to ascertain the quantity with accuracy, but I should think the above not an over-estimate, from the fact that upwards of $25,000 of the gold dust was offered to the Company on sale.

The following is a summary (condensed) of the news brought by the passengers and correspondence of the Otter from Fraser River:— About $25,000 a week could be purchased from the miners on the river, although they are reluctant to sell more than suffices to supply their immediate wants in provisions, etc.

The Otter brought down about 600 ounces from the Texas Bar, the greatest portion of which was obtained by "sluicing." The earnings of this place ranged from $15 to $40 per man per day. On Puget Sound Bar, 40 rockers, three men to each, were at work doing well. On Sacramento Bar, 15 rockers at work; Emery's Bar, 36 rockers, the miners earning $6 to $8 each. Another account reports five companies at work on the bar, making from $8 to $25 per day to the hand. At Hill's Bar 100 rockers and 400 men at work, averaging an ounce a day to the hand, and some lucky "strikes" were made which yielded as high as $30 per day to the hand. At Fort Yale not much doing. At Fort Yale Bar several companies making $15 to $20 per day per man. At Pike's Bar 80 ounces had been got out in three days.[11]

From all accounts, then, some of the men who rushed to New Caledonia during that first summer had gone ill-prepared and despite the many warnings that the Fraser River country, especially in the flood season, was no California. Nevertheless, fortunes were won by many who came well-prepared, and with luck on their side; and a great abundance of gold still awaited those who came later and prospected farther. As that first season ended, Alfred Waddington wrote:

> The greater part of those who have left on account of the winter, have done well here, and have quietly taken home their earnings, with the intention of returning in the spring. It is well known that this class of miners, who never talk much about their gold dust, unless to particular friends, and never trust it out of their own pockets, or the lining of their clothes, have taken away large quantities with them; much more so than the sums officially set down.
>
> Thus . . . whilst those who are gone away . . . assert loudly that there is little or no gold; those who have remained and have given the country a fair trial, who are working still and making money are convinced of the contrary . . . Indeed every thing we see and hear corroborates the fact that there is gold in plenty; and the steady increase in the amount of dust, which has been coming down by every steamer, begins to convince even the most incredulous.[12]

1. From San Francisco correspondent, *New York Times*, June 21, 1858; reprinted in *The Times* (London), July 30, 1858. Also quoted in John Domer, *New British Gold Fields: A Guide to British Columbia and Vancouver Island, with Coloured Map, Showing the Gold and Coal Fields, Constructed from Authentic Sources* (London: W.H. Angel [1858]), 47.
2. *San Francisco Bulletin*, June 28, 1858; reprinted in the *Daily Scotsman* (Edinburgh), August 10, 1858.
3. Report dated July 15 from San Francisco correspondent, *The Times* (London), August 27, 1858.
4. News from Victoria to July 7, 1858, *Daily Alta California* (San Francisco), July 12, 1858.
5. "Arrival of the Cortez," *Daily Alta California* (San Francisco), July 16, 1858.
6. *Daily Alta California* (San Francisco), July 14, 1858.
7. *Victoria Gazette*, July 24, 1858.
8. Parliamentary Papers Relating to British Columbia. Despatch, July 26, 1858, item 13, p. 23, Governor Douglas to Lord Stanley.
9. "Foreign Intelligence," an account from San Francisco dated to August 5, 1858, in the *Daily Scotsman* (Edinburgh), September 28, 1858.
10. From Fort Yale to July 11, and advice from Victoria to July 14, in the *Daily Scotsman* (Edinburgh), September 28, 1858.
11. "British Columbia—From Our Own Correspondent," dated August 21, 1858, *The Times* (London).
12. Alfred Waddington, *The Fraser Mines Vindicated, or, The History of Four Months* (Victoria: P. DeGarro, 1858), 40-41.

FORT YALE AND THE GOLD HUNTERS' CAMP, FRAZER'S RIVER.

From *Harper's Weekly*, October 9, 1858.

15
MIDSUMMER ON THE FRASER

IGNORANT OF THE EXTENSIVE planning and decision-making going on in London to send naval support and military and civil personnel to his aid, Douglas worked on ceaselessly through the summer, with scant assistance, to control an ever-increasing population. Also unaware that Sir Edward Bulwer Lytton was now Colonial Secretary and that forthcoming directives from London would bear Lytton's signature, Douglas continued to address his despatches to Lord Stanley, who had resigned from that position. On July 1, Douglas wrote to Lord Stanley:

> I have lately received a communication from Mr. Travaillot, a gentleman who has resided for some months past in the Couteau Gold Diggings. He represents the country as exceedingly rich, and abounding in gold, fully to as great an extent as California in its better days.
>
> Every succeeding report tends to confirm my belief as to the great value and extent of the auriferous deposits in this country.[1]

In his communication to Douglas, Captain Travaillot had included estimates of the generous gold yields obtained at Mormon Bar, six miles above the Fraser River's junction with the Thompson River, and also at the "dry diggings" on tableland sixty-four miles above the junction. Also in his July 1 communication, Douglas reported;

> The excitement on the subject of the Fraser's River Gold Mines has been more than ever exhibited in the rush of people from all parts of the coast to this Colony. The Custom-house books of this place show a return of: 19 steam ships, 9 sailing ditto, 14 decked boats, which have entered the port of Victoria since the 19th of May last, having 6,133 passengers on board, all either bound directly for Fraser's River, or proposing to settle at this place, with the view of entering into business connections with parties at the mines.
>
> The ascertained number of persons who had actually sailed from the port of San Francisco, with the intention of going into Fraser's River mines was 10,573, and there was no abatement in the demand

for passages, every vessel being taken up as soon as advertised to sail for Vancouver's Island.

Those statements give a proximate idea of the number of persons at and on the way to Fraser's River from California and other more distant countries, but do not represent the increase of population derived from the United States territories of Washington and Oregon, through parties of adventurers who have entered the British Possessions by land. We are, therefore, led to the inference that this country and Fraser's River have gained an increase of 10,000 inhabitants within the last six weeks, and the tide of immigration continues to roll onward without any prospect of abatement.[2]

At this time, the *Surprise* remained as the only steamer plying between Victoria and Fort Hope, and this service was insufficient for the hordes of miners, many of whom, of necessity, still ventured crossing the Strait of Georgia in small craft. A San Francisco correspondent described the departure from Victoria, on July 6, of a fleet of such small boats bound for the Fraser River:

> A novel scene was presented yesterday noon. About forty skiffs, canoes and boats, containing from sixteen to four men each, numbering in all some four hundred, started from Boatman's Cove, in front of the Fort, and put out across the Sound to Fraser River. These canoes and skiffs have been bought of the Indians or built here during the last fortnight, and hundreds of others are being made. The Lilliputian fleet left amid repeated cheers, and steered boldly out on their dangerous voyage. They kept together as much as possible, in case of accident. It is feared that some disaster will happen to some of them in crossing the rough waters of the Sound. Why are not other steamboats sent up here? Two more, beside the *Surprise*, might do a good business in freight and passengers.[3]

Despite his restrictions on shipping, however, Governor Douglas was quickly earning the respect and confidence of the miners for himself and the Hudson's Bay Company; this was apparent in a July 7 report in the San Francisco press:

> In reviewing the course of the Company, it must be admitted that they have been actuated by a general desire to act fairly throughout this excitement. The price of (Vancouver Island) lots they have kept uniformly to $100—though those to whom they sold have made fortunes by them; and flour, which our speculators would have rushed up to starvation prices, has been kept at $20 to $25 per bbl., and even now quantities are bought by outsiders at these prices, and sold at advances. This, however, it is difficult to do, as they will not allow one person to take more than 800 lbs.

They also keep a crowd of bakers at work who are allowed to sell loaves at such a price as will admit of a poor man's getting something to eat. The miners appreciate all this, and while they deprecate the monthly license, and the exclusive trade arrangements, they give the Company full credit for their liberality.

The same reporter wrote also:

Governor Douglas delivered an address to a large assemblage of miners, day before yesterday, in the fort grounds. He assured them that the Hudson's Bay Company had made every exertion to procure provisions to meet this unexpected immigration, and that they would only charge a reasonable commercial profit. It would be his aim to keep down the price of flour by having a good stock constantly on hand at the Company's warehouses—that in a few weeks more, they expected to have light draft steamers on the river, by which ample supplies of provisions could be sent up to the stations, and that thenceforth miners would not have to return to Victoria for supplies. He replied to several general inquiries as to his own belief in the gold stories, that he had faith in them, having known of them long ago; he advised the people not to hurry up there for the present.[4]

But again this advice—warning of the increasing flooding of the riverbanks—went unheeded; the optimism of the gold miner could be cured only by bitter experience.

On July 8, the steamer *Surprise* arrived at Victoria from Fort Hope, carrying men returning from the mines. Among those waiting at Victoria to take the steamer's four a.m. return trip to Fort Hope on the following morning was the "Fraser River Special Travelling Correspondent" for the *Daily Alta California*. He reported that the discouraging news brought by those returning from the mines,

dampened the ardor of many persons. During the day, several miners' outfits were posted about town for sale. But there are too many persons here eager to get into the mountains, who have invested their all in their determination to dig for gold on Fraser River, to be turned back by any circumstance, save their own dear-bought experience . . . [The *Surprise's* passenger list] numbered 240 passengers, some of whom, I know, will not have one dollar in hand when we land at Fort Hope, and they take the chances up the river rather than remain below, where they might get employment in a thousand ways, for laborers are in great demand at Victoria just now. These 240 men are taking along 200 lbs of freight each, that being the limit per man on the steamer. The price of passage is increased this trip $5, and the expense of getting to Fort Hope from Victoria is, today, from $40 to $50 per man. Thus: passage, $25; license, $5; freight, $4 to $7; meals, $1 each; berths,

$1 each night. The trip requires two days. As you leave at daylight, you must be on board the night before.

As the voyage commenced, the reporter was enchanted by the island scenery off Victoria, and dwelt at length upon the beauty of snow-topped mountains and the pleasures of sailing among the numerous islands, until,

> some 25 miles out, we came up with the fleet of boats which left yesterday for the mines. They are flat boats, and Indian canoes, capable of carrying from two to eight men, with their tents and 200 lbs of freight. They were to row all night, with the expectation of being able to reach the Gulf of Georgia and cross it before the wind rises. Forty of these boats were to start today in company. Will they all reach their destination? How many anxious hearts are waiting the return of those who shall be heard of no more? The coasters which come in report that almost every day boats are picked up, sometimes abandoned at sea, sometimes smashed upon the shore.

Continuing on, "we were six hours running to the 49th Parallel, into the clear waters of the Georgia Gulf." Proceeding on into the mouth of the Fraser River, the *Surprise* passed Fort Langley, which the reporter observed was "a fine farm," with horses, dogs, acres of cleared land, and a high stockade of upright logs enclosing the HBC's warehouses and offices, "all old and black with exposure to many storms." The fields were fenced, and the general appearance was "one of neatness and thrift." From its elevated position, the fort commanded a view of the coast for many miles around.

Many miners were camped above and below the fort and along the riverbanks. A boat from upriver, coming alongside, reported that the river above Yale had risen three feet in two days, driving all the miners off the bars, and that many people there were hungry and "would gladly return, but have no money to pay their passage and cannot work until the waters fall." But reports also were received of abundant coarse gold having been discovered on Harrison River, "which empties into the Fraser, 25 miles above."

On the way to Fort Hope, the *Surprise* passed many men rowing boats both upriver and down, those going down shouting greetings as they glided by, "while the upward bound, still tugging at the oar, look with weary eyes . . . This hunt for gold in these tortuous regions is terrible."

"On the second day of the voyage, July 10th, daylight broke at 3 o'clock, and the Surprise steamed onward, passing many Indian camps on the shore, and many miners and their boats at every point along the river;

also the steamer Sea Bird, listed and stuck on a sand-bar in mid-stream." (Kinahan Cornwallis, on his return downstream, also had noted the *Sea Bird*'s misfortune.)

Soon, "we had entered the mountains." From that moment until the *Surprise* reached Fort Hope at one o'clock, the reporter was lost in the scenic splendour that surrounded him: "Who shall describe it? Language fails . . . Words are beggarly and unmeaning." In his multitude of superlatives, one sentence, still true, perhaps said it all:

"There is no more enchanting scenery in the world than is here."[5]

---

1. Parliamentary Papers Relating to British Columbia. Despatch, No. 6 (29), p. 19, item 7, Governor Douglas to Lord Stanley, July 1, 1858.
2. Ibid., items 1-3.
3. "Departure of Canoe Fleet," *Daily Alta California* (San Francisco), July 12, 1858.
4. Ibid., "The Hudson's Bay Company."
5. "From Our Fraser River Special Travelling Correspondent," from Fort Hope, July 10, 1858, *Daily Alta California* (San Francisco), July 16, 1858.

Of Scottish and Cree Indian ancestry, Amelia Douglas typified the cultured wife of a high-ranking official in the HBC's rigid social order. *Provincial Archives of British Columbia, Victoria.*

16
DOUGLAS CARRIES ON

"THE AGENTS OF THE Hudson's Bay Company," Douglas wrote in a despatch on July 26, "have laid in large quantities of mining tools and provisions for the use of the miners, which they supply at merely remunerative prices, greatly to the advantage and satisfaction of the mining population . . . To supply the mining population with food, we have licensed two American steam vessels to ply the waters of Fraser's River, and one of these vessels has succeeded in reaching the Falls, or Fort Yale, about one hundred and thirty miles from the discharge of the Fraser into the Gulf of Georgia."

This epic run was made on July 21 by the sternwheeler *Umatilla*, which fought its way upstream from Fort Hope to Fort Yale, urged on by the miners on board with much shouting and gunfire. After a five-hour struggle, she reached Yale, and met with a joyful reception—whereupon the captain invited the leading citizens of Yale to a banquet. A few days later on July 25, the *Umatilla*, carrying eighty passengers and a special correspondent from the *Victoria Gazette*, made a trial run from Fort Langley to Harrison River and Harrison Lake, establishing the navigability of this waterway.

Douglas' July 26 despatch continued:

> I have accounts of 5,000 ounces of gold dust which have been actually exported from Fraser's River since the month of May last, and we have estimated that as much as half that quantity has been carried away in small quantities by return miners, comprising, as I believe, the whole export of gold dust for that period.
>
> We are therefore led to believe that the miners are hoarding up their gold dust, either from not being in immediate want of supplies, or more probably from not knowing how to remit or where to place it in security, and for that reason, among others, I am considering the ways and means of having their savings conveyed to the sea coast under Government escort, and placing them in charge of a public treasurer,

until they are called for by the depositors, the conveyance and other expenses to be defrayed by a charge on the deposits. The advantages expected from that measure are manifold. We hope, for instance, to draw the gold by that means to this Colony, from whence, instead of being exported to other countries, it will find its way to England in return for our own manufactures.[1]

Burdened as he was at that time with administrative responsibilities, Douglas had little opportunity to leave his desk in Victoria. His prediction to Lord Stanley on June 10, that "in the course of a few months there may be one hundred thousand people in the country," seemed to be proving true, for in addition to the hordes of men in California coming overland to San Francisco to take ship's passage to Vancouver Island, there were by then thousands of steamer passengers arriving in San Francisco from Sacramento, for the same purpose. According to a *Sacramento Union* report, arrivals by upriver steamer in San Francisco during one week had averaged 500 nightly.[2]

On July 19, the officers and men of the British Boundary Commission, who had sailed from England on April 2, were ceremoniously welcomed to Victoria by Governor Douglas. The commission, comprising four Royal Engineer officers, a surgeon, and a veterinarian, and accompanied by fifty-six non-commissioned officers and highly skilled men of the Royal Engineers, had been appointed to determine (in conjunction with the United States Boundary Commission) the exact dividing line between American and British territories along the 49th parallel. Among those observing the ceremonies was a large gathering of gold miners, some of whom took advantage of an opportunity to question Douglas concerning their prospects in the country. "With that courtesy that has been an invariable accompaniment of his conduct toward all new-comers," wrote a reporter for the *Victoria Gazette* of July 24, "His Excellency complied, and made the following remarks:"

> My Friends:—You wish me to speak to you about Fraser's River, and to get my advice about going there, and my opinion of the country. Now I will tell you all plainly, that I will not take the responsibility of giving any advice on the subject. You have all heard what has been said of Fraser's River, and I know nothing more about the gold than has already been told you by others.
>
> Had you sent to ask my opinion about Fraser's River before you left California, I would have told you, one and all, not to leave your quiet homes; not to give up the substance for a shadow, and to wait

patiently until something more definite was known about the country. Now, suppose I *were* to tell you so. Suppose I were to advise you, one and all, to return immediately to your homes, without going further, what would the answer be? Why, you would all refuse to do so; you would all say that course will never suit. After the trouble and expense we have had in coming here, we must go to the end—we must see the elephant. And perhaps you might think that I had some object to gain in keeping you from going to Fraser's River.

Now I know, men, what you wish me to tell you. You wish me to say there are lots of gold in Fraser's River, but that I will not say, because I am not certain of the fact myself. But this I will tell you as my own settled opinion, that I think the country is full of gold, and that east and north and south of Fraser's River, there is a gold field of incalculable value and extent. I have told our glorious Queen so; and I now tell you so, and if I mistake not, you are the very men who can prove by your courage and enterprise, whether my opinion be right or wrong.

Remember, I do not give you that statement as an established fact, but simply as an opinion, founded on what I have actually seen myself, and heard from others who know the country.

Now what more can I say to you, but go on and prospect, and in a few short weeks you will be able to tell me what Fraser's River is. Take mining tools and food in abundance; you will then be independent of others, and may go to whatever part of the country you choose. I would not advise you to go beyond Fort Yale with your canoes, as the river is dangerous above that point; neither would I advise you to take the Fort Hope road, as you cannot carry enough of provisions to last you over the journey.

The route by Harrison's River is I think the best, and we are now preparing to get a road opened that way; in fact I expect to see teams and wagons on the twenty mile portage that divides that river from Anderson's Lake, before many months are over. That is a safe and accessible route at all seasons to Upper Fraser's River.

Let me say one word about the Indians. They are all friendly, and all thievish; therefore have an eye to your things, and do not leave them exposed, for in that case the Indians will steal them.[3]

(The Indians—who considered the miners themselves to be "thievish" for taking the gold—might well have coveted the tools brought by the miners. In a December 1857 despatch, Douglas had mentioned that small quantities of gold were being traded to the company by the Indians, but that "they are, however, at present almost destitute of tools for moving the soil, and of washing implements for separating the gold from the earthy matrix, and have therefore to pick it out with knives, or to use their fingers for that purpose."[4])

Douglas continued in his address to the crowd of miners and Royal Engineers in Victoria:

> Get on with them [Indians] as quietly as you can, and Government will protect you. Be careful of your revolvers, and be not too ready to use them in your own cause.
>
> The law of the land will do its work without fear and without favour. Therefore appeal to it in all cases; let it do justice between man and man; let it defend your rights and avenge your wrongs.
>
> Now my friends go and prosper; there is hard work before you, and I hope you will be repaid with rich strikes and big nuggets.
>
> One word about the views of Government. The miner who acts in submission to the laws and pays the Queen's dues like an honest man, shall be protected in person and property, and as soon as good and trusty men are found, measures will be taken for the conveyance and escort of gold from the mines to this place. Every miner will give in his own sack, and his own weight, and have it addressed and sealed in his own presence, and get a receipt for a sack said to contain so much gold dust. It will be deposited in the Public Treasury at Victoria, and delivered to the owner on production of the deposit receipt. There will be a charge made for the expense of conveyance, but that will be a small matter compared to the security of your property. I now wish you all well, and shall not detain you by any further remarks.[5]

---

1. Parliamentary Papers Relating to British Columbia. Despatch, July 26, 1858, p. 23, Governor Douglas to Lord Stanley.
2. *Sacramento Union* report reprinted in the *New York Times*, June 21, 1858, and *The Times* (London), July 30, 1858. See also, John Domer, *New British Gold Fields: A Guide to British Columbia and Vancouver Island, with Coloured Map, Showing the Gold and Coal Fields, Constructed from Authentic Sources* (London: W.H. Angel [1858]), 47.
3. "Address of Gov. Douglas to the Miners in Victoria," *Victoria Gazette*, July 24, 1858.
4. Parliamentary Papers Relating to British Columbia. Extract of Despatch No. 6 (35), Governor Douglas to Right Hon. Henry Labouchere, M.P., December 29, 1857. Also quoted in *British Columbia and Vancouver's Island: A Complete Hand-Book, Replete with the Latest Information Concerning the Newly-Discovered Gold Fields* (London: W. Penny, 1858), 26.
5. *Victoria Gazette*, July 24, 1858.

17
THE MINERS BUILD A ROAD

THE CALIFORNIA PROSPECTORS knew from experience that the presence of fine gold in the lower Fraser indicated the existence of heavier, richer deposits farther upriver, and this was confirmed by the findings of those prospectors who had reached the upper country. The lack of roads and transportation from the lower river was, however, a major impediment to the progress of mining operations beyond Fort Yale. True to the assurance he had given to the miners in his July 19 speech—that a route was to be opened by Harrison River—Douglas lost no time in addressing this need. As he explained in his despatch to Lord Stanley on July 26:

> Another important object I have in view is the improvement of the internal communications of the country, which at present are, for all practical purposes, nearly inaccessible beyond Fort Yale, in consequence of a range of mountains running north and south, which there interpose an almost insurmountable barrier to the progress of trade.
>
> To the eastward of that range of mountains the country is open, and comparatively level, and the construction of good roads would be a matter of easy accomplishment; in fact, it is even at present almost everywhere accessible for pack horses.
>
> It is therefore evident that the construction of a good road through that mountain barrier, though passable in the first instance only for pack horses, would be of prodigious advantage to the country; and such a road might, I think, be carried through the valley of Harrison's River, at a moderate expense, to a point near the Great Falls of Fraser's River to the eastward of the mountains in question, from whence the country is easy of access; and should no Instructions militating with that design be in the meantime received from Her Majesty's Government, I will probably make the attempt in course of the present summer.[1]

In a further despatch on August 19, Douglas reported, with obvious pride and pleasure, a remarkable project undertaken through the cooperation of a large body of miners:

We have commenced the work of improving the internal communications of the country, as referred to in the 17th paragraph of my Despatch No. 31 of the 26th of July last, a party of 500 men being now engaged in opening a road into Upper Fraser's River by the valley of Harrison's River.

A stern wheel steam vessel is now running to the upper extremity of Harrison's Lake, from whence we have commenced cutting a road through the forest on the left bank of Harrison's River and Lillooet Lake to connect Anderson's with Harrison's Lake, the total distance between these two points being about 80 miles of land carriage over a generally level country.

The men employed in that important enterprise are gold miners, composed of many nations, British subjects, Americans, French, Germans, Danes, Africans, and Chinese, who volunteered their services immediately on our wish to open a practicable route into the interior of the Fraser's River District being made known to the public. They, moreover, proffered their services on terms so peculiar in themselves, and so advantageous for the country, that it would have been unwise of me to decline them. Each man, for example, on being enrolled into the corps, paid into our hands the sum of 25 dollars, as security for good conduct. They receive no remuneration in the form of pay; the Government having merely to supply them with food while employed on the road, and to transport them free of expense to the commencement of the road on Harrison's Lake, where the money deposit of 25 dollars is to be repaid to them in provisions, at Victoria prices, when the road is finished. The cost of the work will therefore not be heavy, nor exceed our means of repayment out of the revenues of the Gold District.

The organization of the corps is simple, yet effective, it being divided into 20 companies of 25 men, and each company under the command of a Captain, who carries all orders into effect, reports to the Commander of the corps, and draws upon the Commissary for the weekly supplies of food.

An engineer, with guides and Indians acquainted with the country, blazes the trees, and marks out the road, in advance of the main body.

I have lately received the most cheering accounts of the progress of the party who were working assiduously, and had then cut through about 15 miles from the commencement of the road on Harrison's Lake, and will, I trust, carry it through with the same degree of spirit as they now exhibit.[2]

This newsworthy project was duly reported by the press:

This route will be by Harrison's River, a tributary of the Fraser, emptying into the latter about midway between Langley and Fort Hope.

The Harrison River is fed by a chain of lakes found to be navigable by small steamers already plying on them. A portage of 50 miles from the highest of these lakes will strike the mineral country on Fraser's River, about 40 miles above the junction of the Thompson. This route is progressing rapidly, and will soon be open, and will save the dangerous navigation and laborious portages of the Fraser River at and above Fort Yale.[3]

The first company of miners, led by Alexander Caulfield Anderson, left Victoria on August 5 for Fort Langley; thence to Harrison Lake, proceeding by steamboat to the north end of the lake; and there, at the southern terminal of the proposed road, trail cutting commenced on August 9. The miners proposed that the terminal be named for Anderson; however, Anderson chose the name Port Douglas, to honour the governor. (Later that year, Anderson was to become British Columbia's first Postmaster-General—on November 30, 1858, he notified the public that mails would be forwarded "by every favourable opportunity" to Langley, Hope, and Yale, the price of postage to be five cents.)

By early September, the last company of miners was working toward the road's completion. The calibre of the men undertaking that expedition, and the conditions then prevailing, were evident in a report published in the *Victoria Gazette*, under the headline:

FROM THE LILLOOET-HARRISON ROAD-CUTTING EXPEDITION:

Terminus of Trail on Big Lillooet Lake, Sept. 5th, 1858: The work on the Trail has lately been a little impeded by rainy weather, and much more by the non-arrival of the mules, which necessitates so much extra packing (on our backs) and in some cases has caused a total cessation of work, rather than entail this labour in an additional degree by removal to a greater distance from the depot. The advanced companies, however, have been somewhat relieved, by purchases of some essential articles, made from the sufferers by boat-wreck on the river— thus verifying the old adage.

It was with increased pity and admiration that we now looked on the boats that were forcing their way up-stream, inch by inch, as it were, now rowing and paddling, sometimes with poles, then their navigators wading in and against the swift current, and towing the heavily laden crafts.—Surely, we thought, these men, at all events, will dearly earn even a large "pile," and they have our hearty good wishes.

We have passed the two largest streams that intersect our path, which respectively required bridges of about thirty and forty yards long, and our party are pressing vigorously forward . . .

At length, passing over dates and details—we reached the rapids at the foot of the little lake, and a boiling cauldron it is. Here we found a small assemblage of Indians, young and old, male and female, and quite a collection of boats and canoes of the hardy white adventurers who had so far surmounted the difficulties of this perilous and highly laborious navigation.

We here noticed several fishing stations and rancheries, also an aboriginal burying place . . . There, also, we found a large patch of grass, almost the only one as yet met with on this rocky route, although there is no lack of heavy timber—chiefly spruce, pine, cedar and hemlock, and in at least one bottom, a regular growth of cypress.

It was with great pleasure that we greeted the placid waters of the little lake, and we pushed our way along the thickly clad slopes of the huge granite hills that hem in the water-course, with renewed vigour until we had attained a point within about a couple of miles of the terminus of the trail on the big lake.

On August 26, evidence of a tragedy was discovered by members of the expedition:

This day we performed the melancholy office of burying the body of a man found in the river—name unknown—supposed to have been in the water ten days. Deceased seemed to have been about five feet six or seven inches in height, of middle age, and had red whiskers. Had on a dark, frock coat, two woolen shirts, brown ribbed cassimere pants, and cotton socks (one of them being blue and the other white). All of the pockets were wrong side out, although the coat was buttoned across the breast, and no doubt was entertained by those present that the body had been searched and robbed.

The men of the expedition buried the body and marked the grave with wooden slabs. Three days later, on August 29, they encountered the party of which the dead man had been a member, and which identified him as having been Antonio Forlano, an Italian, who had on his person "a considerable sum in gold and silver," and a watch (all, of course, now missing). Forlano was said to have been lost by drowning, on August 8, about five miles from the mouth of the river.

This party also informed us that they had about 15 or 16 cwt. of provision on the river, which they would be willing to dispose of to the H.B.Co's agents, in case of need, to be delivered on the Big Lillooet Lake, if required—which, in the present scarcity, we were very glad to hear was the case, and our captain at once forwarded the intelligence to headquarters.[4]

The 108-mile road, with its many bridges and portages, was finally completed by mid-October, and by November mule trains were passing through to Lillooet. The route was, as Douglas had predicted, "of prodigious advantage to the country."

Lytton wrote to Douglas, sincerely praising the miners for their road-building accomplishment, and expressing the hope that under Douglas' continued "able and cheerful influence" they might equally "unite in the formation of a Police, in the establishment of law . . . in short, in all which may make individual life secure and the community prosperous." Lytton concluded: "I trust you will assure the hardy and spirited men who have assisted in this preliminary undertaking how much their conduct is appreciated by Her Majesty's Government."[5]

Though better roads were later constructed by the elite Royal Engineers who were soon to arrive from Britain, it is worth remembering that this very first road through the mountain barrier was constructed voluntarily in this, the colony's first year, by the gold miners themselves—those "British subjects, Americans, French, Germans, Danes, Africans, and Chinese," about which Douglas had written with pride, and Lytton with praise.

---

1. Parliamentary Papers Relating to British Columbia. Despatch, No. 31, p. 23, Governor Douglas to Lord Stanley, July 26, 1858.
2. Ibid., No. 8 (34), pp. 27-28, Governor Douglas to Lord Stanley, August 19, 1858.
3. Report from Victoria correspondent, August 21, 1858, in *The Times* (London), October 12, 1858.
4. *Victoria Gazette*, August and September 1858, *passim*.
5. Parliamentary Papers Relating to British Columbia. Despatch No. 30 (30), p. 71, item 10, Sir E.B. Lytton to Governor Douglas, October 16, 1858.

As the new Colonial Secretary, Sir Edward Bulwer Lytton (1803-73) envisioned a crown colony west of the Rockies as a geopolitical counterbalance to the thriving territories and states of the American West. This painting by H.W. Pickersgill depicts the 1st Baron as a young man (1831). *National Portrait Gallery, London.*

18
A New Parliament vs. the Hudson's Bay Company

Douglas could not know, until the news reached him in September, that a bill had been introduced in Parliament by the new Colonial Secretary, Sir Edward Bulwer Lytton, to create a Crown Colony in New Caledonia. It was a most fateful coincidence that this year, in which the gold rush brought the first sizeable white population to the territory, was also the year when there came to power in Great Britain a new Government dedicated to the colonization and settlement of Britain's undeveloped North American possessions, including New Caledonia. To that end, the new Government was determined to challenge the time-honoured privileges of the Hudson's Bay Company, whose monopolistic policies in British North America, from the Atlantic to the Pacific, had discouraged settlement, leaving the territories undeveloped and vulnerable to United States expansionism.

Lord Palmerston's long-standing Government had been defeated, temporarily, in February 1858, and under the short-lived administration of the Earl of Derby, the post of Secretary of State for the Colonies had been filled briefly by Lord Stanley, and then by Lytton. The brief change of Government, and Lytton's appointment as Colonial Secretary, had great significance with respect to policies relating to the North American territories, especially since Henry Labouchere, as Colonial Secretary in the former Government, held opposite views to those of Lytton regarding the necessity for settlement and colonization as opposed to the continuance of the Hudson's Bay Company's privileges.

In a speech to the House of Commons, Mr. John Roebuck, M.P. (who had been raised in Canada and who was a leader of the colonization plan) expressed his support of Lytton's policies. Roebuck's statements, as paraphrased by a reporter in the July 21 issue of *The Times,* were that:

The English possessed a portion of the American continent stretching from the Atlantic to the Pacific, north of the great lakes. Prince Edward's Island, Nova Scotia, New Brunswick, Lower and Upper Canada, were colonies when the English became possessed of the country, and since that time they had not added to the territory one acre of land in the way of colonization. In the meantime the Americans had increased from 13 to 36 independent States, and from 3,000,000 population to very nearly 30,000,000, while the English had remained idle; and though they had seen the Americans become one of the greatest nations, they, notwithstanding that they had the means, had effected nothing as a counterpoise to the Americans. He wished to see this state of things ended; but he was met by a curious observation. Canada . . . was a strip of land along the shores of the St. Lawrence, and in the reign of Charles II. certain persons asked and obtained from the Crown certain portions of territory which they called the Hudson's Bay territory. At that time Canada belonged to France, and France was supposed to have dominion to the North Pole; but, with that curious habit which then belonged to all the nations of the earth with respect to wild lands, Charles II. dealt with these wild lands as if they belonged to nobody, and gave the Hudson's Bay Company power with respect to that territory and those wild lands. (The hon. gentleman here recited the terms of the charter granting to the Hudson's Bay Company the sole right to trade and commerce) . . .

The Times account included Roebuck's brief outline of the history of the fur trade, and continued with:

He meant to bring no charge against the Hudson's Bay Company. They had done what by their nature, as a company, they were called on to do; but he asked the House to consider the circumstances under which the company acted. It was a fur company, and a fur company by its very nature was opposed to colonization. Where wild animals congregated, there man could not live; and the introduction of man as a colonist drove away the fur-bearing animals, and put an end to all fur companies. The Hudson's Bay Company, following up their own interest, had maintained the territory in its wildest state, and had kept out colonization. In this state of things he appealed to the House of Commons, and said that they had the means in their hands to advance civilization over an uncultivated territory, and to carry there all the arts and happiness and all the improvement in manners, laws, and religion which attended civilization, making the territory, what it was intended to be, a happy home for millions of people. (Hear, hear.) . . .[1]

It was Lytton who had proposed creating a new colony west of the Rocky Mountains. Regarding his bill, intoduced to the House of Commons on July 1, Lytton had declared on July 8 that the Thompson River district was "one of the finest countries in the British dominions, possessing a climate far superior to that of countries in the same latitude on the other side of the mountains." Mentioning its wealth of fisheries, timber, and coal, he went on: "From Thompson River and Colville districts to the Rocky Mountains, and from the 49th Parallel some 350 miles north, a more beautiful region does not exist. Therefore, apart from the gold fields, this country affords the highest promise of becoming a flourishing and important colony." (And regarding the Vancouver Island harbour of Esquimalt, Lytton declared it to be "the best harbour north of San Francisco as far north as Sitka, the Russian settlement.")

Lytton's bill to create this new Colony was mentioned again in the House of Commons on July 20, 1858, during discussion of the findings of the Select Committee which had, since 1857, investigated the activities of the Hudson's Bay Company. The proceedings (reported shortly in the "Parliamentary Intelligence" section of *The Times*[2]), dealt with three resolutions. The House had no difficulty in reaching majority agreement on the first resolution, that renewal of the Company's privileges, granted under license for twenty one-year terms (and due for renewal on May 30, 1859), was no longer necessarily appropriate; and on the third resolution, that colonization, long delayed by the Company, must proceed. Most contentious was the second resolution, that the validity of the Company's charter "ought at once to be determined by process of law." As Roebuck had alluded to in his speech to the House, the venerable charter dated from 1670, in which year Prince Rupert and seventeen other noblemen and gentlemen had received from King Charles II a charter granting them a monopoly of trade "in all lands watered by streams flowing into Hudson's Bay."

Prince Rupert had first requested the charter in 1668, influenced by the French explorers Radisson and Groseilliers who, having discovered the rich potential of fur resources in the Hudson Bay region, had urged Prince Rupert and others to mount an expedition to trade with the Indians. Another object avowed by the Company, but not pursued, was to seek out a Northwest Passage to the Orient. King Charles also granted the Company (then incorporated as The Governor and Company of Adventurers of England Trading into Hudson's Bay) "the complete lordship and entire legislative, judicial, and executive power" over these lands (thus giving away virtually half a continent).

From the beginning the charter was questionable, since the Crown could not legally grant what it did not possess and the land in question belonged at that time to France (and was not ceded to Britain until the Treaty of Utrecht in 1713). Over the course of many years, the question of the charter's legitimacy occasionally had been raised, but as there never was a pressing incentive to try the matter in a court of law, and there always were influential voices (including those of Company shareholders) to speak out against such action, the charter had become hallowed by time. Now, however, the question had assumed a new urgency, since the fur-trading Company, being by its very nature opposed to colonization and to competitive trade, had discouraged any growth of population in the British territories.

In addition to the territory granted by Charles II, the Hudson's Bay Company had held under licence, since 1821 (when it amalgamated with the rival North West Company of Montreal), the monopoly of trade in the vast lands west and northwest of the original charter territory; also, in 1849, when Vancouver Island was made a Crown Colony, the HBC had been granted a lease of the island for a nominal annual rent of seven shillings, on the condition that the Company encourage immigration from Great Britain and the Dominions. The western territories not covered by the charter might be reclaimed at will by the government for purposes of colonization. However, the question of whether or not the Company would be entitled to claim compensation if lands granted by the charter were removed from its jurisdiction remained to be settled in law.

After introducing the resolutions, John Roebuck concluded that the Company had no such rights as claimed under the charter, and that if it had, Parliament should purchase the Company out; and he hoped that Lytton, as the new Secretary for the Colonies, would take immediate steps to ascertain the Company's legal rights.

Lytton announced that he intended to place the matter of the charter's validity before the Government's legal officers. As for the licence renewal, he said that the Government

> will certainly not renew the licence over any part of the Indian territory which promises early settlement; but they will renew it for a limited period over the more remote and northern regions. The Government would retain the right to withdraw the licence, and would retain the Imperial rights to fisheries and mines, 'and whatever may call forth human industry and enterprise in pursuits more congenial to our age than the gloomy trade in the skins of animals.'

Lytton reminded the House that in 1837, when applying for a renewal of licence in the Red River region, the Company had stated it intended to settle that region with immigrants from Britain, and to establish a valuable export trade in agricultural produce. He pointed out that these were "sanguine hopes; not realized since 1837 under the auspices of the Company, but which may be more rapidly fulfilled when the Company withdraws from the place the shadow of its chilling protection."

Granting "the expedience of substituting, and in one connecting frontier line, the colonies of Great Britain for the hunting grounds of a trading company," Lytton stated, "Already, by the Pacific, Vancouver's Island has been added to the social communities of mankind. Already, in the large territory west of the Rocky Mountains, from the American frontier up to the Russian domains, we are laying the foundations of what may become hereafter a magnificent abode for the human race."[3]

Lord Bury, a member of the Select Committee, pointed out to the House that the late Government had been opposed to investigating the validity of the rights claimed by the Company and had stated that it was only up to "persons in Canada . . . to contest" those rights. But Lord Bury thought "when a question was certain to arise as to whether a large amount of compensation for these supposed rights was to be given to the company, it was a matter which very much concerned both the House and the Government. (Hear, hear.)." The former Government had suggested that Canada might acquire from the HBC "such portions of the territory as were required by Canada for the purpose of settlement," but Lord Bury contended it was a matter of such importance that it concerned not just the Company and Canada, but the whole British empire—"The real point at issue was whether the company should continue their monopoly, should keep closed doors, should put up a 'no thoroughfare' board at every inlet into this country, or whether it should be thrown open to the enterprise of all Her Majesty's subjects. (Hear, hear.)."

Lord Bury also stated that he personally (as a member of the Select Committee) had investigated how far the Company's claim was "founded on truth and justice." Outside of the House, he pointed out,

> he seldom heard that territory mentioned without being more or less associated with the terms "barren," "sterile," "ice-bound," "unfit for colonization and the support of human beings." But that was an entirely erroneous supposition. (Hear, hear). It might be true that comparatively only a small portion of this vast territory was fitted for colonization, but it was no less true that that comparatively small portion consisted of something like 500,000 square miles, and would afford occupation and means of subsistence to, he believed, every person

of full age in Her Majesty's dominions, both in the colonies and at home. (Hear, hear.) . . .

Lord Bury went on to describe the variety and magnificence of the lands in question, and he pointed out that every year "the teeming population of the United States advanced northwards, and very soon would overstep the boundary which marked the commencement of British territory."

Among those Members who defended the Company was, of course, Labouchere, who, as the former Secretary for the Colonies, considered "it was his duty to say for this Company that in dealing with them he had not found them unwilling to listen to him when he impressed on them the necessity of attending to the general interests of the country, and he had no doubt that the right hon. baronet opposite [Lytton] had also heard the Company express the same desire to meet the wishes of the Government and the interests of the country as far as they could do consistently with a fair regard to the interests of the members of the Company."

Having thus confirmed the Company's priorities, Labouchere went on to suggest that the Crown already had power to establish colonies in the territory that was under licence to the Company. Again, according to *The Times* reporter:

> He agreed with those who said it would be a matter of great convenience if the rights of the Company under their charter were ascertained . . . This was no new question, for more than 100 years ago the Government of the day were also anxious to have information on the same point, and referred to their law officers . . . who gave it as their opinion that, considering how long the Company had enjoyed and acted under the charter, it would not be advisable for the Crown to make any express or implied declaration against it, until there was some judgment of a court of law on the matter . . .

Regarding the current debate, Labouchere continued:

> Let the Government take such portion of the territory as they might for colonization, but let them not throw open the whole of those vast lands without having first secured the means for preserving peace and order. (Hear, hear.) With respect to the resolutions which had been moved, he could not advise the House to concur in them. It was premature to attempt to cut those knots, which required careful untying by such resolutions . . .

But a majority of speakers in the House of Commons at this time expressed views such as those of Mr. Gilpin, M.P., which were summarized as follows: "That the Company had the keys of a vast outlet for the industry and enterprise of Englishmen; that this outlet had been closed against civilized man, and as their claims conflicted with colonial and Imperial interests, and were also at variance with legal rights, he trusted these would be speedily extinguished."

Lord Gladstone—a future Prime Minister (1868), and former Colonial Secretary—had long been keenly interested in colonial affairs. Gladstone reminded the House that Sir George Simpson, the former governor of the Hudson's Bay Company, had been among those (twenty-four witnesses in all) questioned by the Select Committee. After he retired from the Company, Simpson had written a book, *Journal of a Journey from the Red River Settlement across the Rocky Mountains* (1847), in part of which he described the North American territories which he knew so well, as being ideally suited for colonization. When questioned before the Committee, however, he had told a very different story. In Gladstone's words:

> Here is a large portion of the surface of the earth with regard to the character of which we have been systematically kept in darkness (hear, hear): for those who had information to give, have also had an interest directly opposed to their imparting it. I am at liberty to say so, because I refer only to public documents; and as an illustration of the truth of what I have said, I need only direct attention to the interesting and important work of Governor Simpson, who gives a glowing description of the capabilities and fitness for colonization of a considerable portion of the territories of the Hudson's Bay Company. (Hear, hear.) Last year my right honourable friend the then Secretary of State for the Colonies moved for, and the House granted, a committee to inquire into the affairs of the Hudson's Bay Company. Before that committee questions were raised seriously involving all their rights. Governor Simpson was examined before it, and the honourable and learned member for Sheffield [Roebuck], and other gentlemen, questioned him upon the agricultural and colonizing capabilities of the territories of the Company. An entire change had come over the spirit of his dream. (Hear, hear.) He represented that these territories were bound by frost and banked by fog, and that woe betide any unfortunate individuals who might by a reckless spirit of adventure be so far diverted from the path of prudence as to endeavour to settle in those parts. (Hear, hear.) And when some member of the committee, with inconvenient curiosity, ferreted out the book of Governor Simpson, and made quotations from it, the governor, with all his ingenuity, which is not small, was greatly puzzled, and indeed entirely failed to reconcile the account of the country which he had given as an author, and that which he gave as Governor of the Hudson's Bay Company, when the object was to prove to the committee that it was useless to pluck

and feather the Company because they had got nothing which was worth having.

Gladstone also reminded the House that in 1849 he had moved on an address, which was unanimously adopted by the House, "praying that the Crown would be pleased to take legal steps for the purpose of testing and ascertaining the validity of the rights of the Company." The Colonial Secretary at the time, Earl Grey, had avoided the intended judicial decision and had instead obtained from the Company an *ex parte* statement of their claim, and upon this obtained from the law officers of the Crown their opinion that "they saw no reason to question the charter upon the case stated to them." At the same time, Earl Grey had persuaded a humble university student, "a most meritorious man but in humble circumstances who was struggling to pay for his own education," that it was open to him as a private individual to try the question on behalf of the public, at his own cost and expense. Lord Gladstone continued:

> The truth is, that a great part of this country is highly valuable for colonizing purposes, and it is impossible to state in too strong language the proposition, that the Hudson's Bay Company is, by its very existence and its character the enemy of colonization. (Hear, hear.) All its traditions, all its habits, all its establishments, the fruit of generations, all its purposes and arrangements, are not only not directed to colonization, but are directed to purposes the attainment of which requires that colonization should be absolutely excluded. (Hear, hear.) . . .

Roebuck, in his closing remarks, also drew attention to Governor Simpson's inconsistency. Referring to claims of the Company's supporters that "the territory was not worth being colonized," Roebuck pointed out that "upon that point he might refer to the authority of Governor Simpson before he became Sir. G. Simpson, and had no interest in not telling the truth."

This was a sad outcome for George Simpson, the clever Scottish boy who, making the fur trade his life's career, had achieved the high rank of HBC governor after the Hudson's Bay and North West companies united in 1821. Then twenty-nine years of age, he afterwards had travelled over the continent, at record speeds and with boundless energy, imposing astute and forceful control over the Company's affairs in the wilderness outposts. Venerated as His Excellency, Governor in Chief of all the Hudson's Bay Company territories in North America, and as the all-powerful source of career advancement or of ignominy, he had been received by Company personnel everywhere with pomp and ceremony befitting royalty. ("A man so aware of his own importance that he chose to arrive on horseback with plenty of fanfare—the pipes playing and the cavalry preceded by flag bearers."[4]) Now sixty-six years old, he was comfortably retired, honoured, and knighted, and but for this upstart government—which was to last only a year—no discredit would have marred these last two years of his life.

During this session, Roebuck introduced another subject dear to his heart—a railway to be built across the continent, creating a direct communication between England, Halifax, and Vancouver Island, and uniting with China. If Lytton were to carry out "this magnificent scheme," Roebuck suggested, "he would have achieved greater things than even he had done for literature, and would be remembered as a great colonial administrator." (As seemingly impossible as this visionary scheme appeared at the time, Roebuck lived to see the Canadian Pacific Railway's transcontinental line under construction a quarter of a century later.)

With the return to power of Lord Palmerston's Government in June of the following year (1859), Lord Derby's administration was ended, and Lytton was replaced as Colonial Secretary by the Duke of Newcastle. It did not happen that the legality of the HBC's charter was ever settled, and the Company continued operating under the privileges it had been granted until, some ten years later, the lands covered by the charter were bought out by the Government of Canada on terms beneficial to the Company (which continued to prosper, rich in property and with innumerable corporate interests). During Lytton's brief tenure, however, the HBC's monopoly west of the Rocky Mountains was brought to an end, and Lytton's new colony, British Columbia, was established.

Writing to Douglas on August 14, Lytton made clear his awareness that Douglas himself had not been forthcoming regarding the richness of the territory's resources, suggesting:

> As . . . our Department has been left singularly in ignorance of much that should enter into considerations of general policy, and on which non-official opinions are constantly volunteered . . . you might find someone capable of assisting, under your superintendence, in furnishing me, as early as possible . . . information as may guide the British Government to the best and readiest means of developing the various and the differing resources both of the island and the mainland; resources which have so strangely been concealed for ages, which are now so suddenly brought to light, and which may be destined to effect, at no very distant period, a marked and permanent change in the commerce and navigation of the known world.[5]

1. *The Times* (London), July 21, 1858.
2. Ibid., July 22, 1858.
3. Ibid. See also, *British Columbia and Vancouver's Island: A Complete Hand-Book, Replete with the Latest Information Concerning the Newly-Discovered Gold Fields* (London: W. Penny, 1858), 61-62.
4. Jan Gould, *Women of British Columbia* (Saanichton, BC: Hancock House, 1975), 48.
5. Parliamentary Papers Relating to British Columbia. Despatch, No. 8 (8), pp. 48-49, item 16, Sir E.B. Lytton to Governor Douglas, August 14, 1858. A portion of Gladstone's speech before Parliament also was quoted in *British Columbia and Vancouver's Island*, 9-10.

19
THE CRIMINAL ELEMENT

CONTRARY TO POPULAR BELIEF, the majesty of British law did not prevail, entirely, immediately, and magically, in British Columbia—not in that first year, nor for some little time after, for, despite the very high calibre of those few officials first appointed to the colonial service from Great Britain, they did not arrive until year's end. It was to be some time after that before sufficient support personnel were available to fully enforce the laws with respect to murder, theft, smuggling, claim jumping, liquor sales, tax evasion, and general mischief.

Of the general population of the gold fields, Douglas observed, in July: "About two thirds of the emigrants from California are supposed to be English and French; the other third are Germans, and native citizens of the United States. There is no congeniality of feeling among the emigrants, and provided there be no generally felt grievance to unite them in one common cause there will, in my opinion, always be a great majority of the population ready to support the measures of Government."[1]

This was true. Most miners wanted only to dig for gold, and were supportive of any rule of law that enabled them to work in peace. In the absence of reliable official personnel, however, an element of lawlessness soon became evident—for among those who had joined the gold rush a minority were criminals, including fugitives from California's vigilance committees, and each of the mining communities seemed to have its share of these miscreants.

At Fort Langley it was common practice to sell liquor without a licence, to both whites and Indians. Boats and canoes were stolen on the river, brought to Fort Langley, and sold. There were beatings, robberies, and thefts, and, as William H. Bevis, the Revenue Officer at Fort Langley reported, "the constant firing of pistols and guns is getting dangerous, particularly during the night-time. The practice of gambling is becoming very

glaring, and to endeavour to prevent the same would, I fear, be useless."
Bevis told how,

> a man by the name of Joseph Miller went into the house of Mr. W.B.
> Bolton, for the purpose of taking a drink as he says, and that he had
> no sooner entered the house when he was knocked down, and kicked
> in the face and severely cut about the head; his trouser pocket contain-
> ing $340 in gold dust was cut out, his watch cut from the guard, and,
> in fact, the man was very much abused, and, as far as I can learn, by a
> party of men who appear to have very little means of obtaining a
> livelihood.

Bevis also noted that the same criminals had stated their intention of
shooting Hudson's Bay Company cattle, but he concluded: "Any attempt
to arrest the criminals on my part would, I fear, be attended with some
trouble, as our force here is so small, and where *[sic]* I to call on all good
citizens to aid me, from present appearances there would, I fear, be very
little response; and in the many little cases of petty thieving which almost
nightly occur, I am afraid the people will take the law into their own hands
and punish the offenders."[2]

And a report from Sailor's Diggings stated:

> We learn that a man named Charles Adams, well known hereabouts,
> was killed by Charles McDonald, of this place, near the mouth of
> Frazer River. It seems that they were in partnership in their operations
> in the mines, and that Adams was making off with all the funds of the
> concern, when he was overtaken and shot dead. McDonald is said to
> be at Whatcom awaiting requisition and trial.[3]

The criminal element at Hill's Bar gained particular notoriety under
the leadership of one Ned McGowan, long known to the police of San
Francisco. A man of many talents—not the least of which was his uncommon ability to cheat justice—McGowan was as charming and persuasive
as he was unscrupulous. He had been, variously, a lawyer, politician, and
police captain, but throughout his varied career he had consistently dealt
in corruption and consorted with criminals, to such extent that the Vigilance Committee called him "the chief of the vultures."

Charged in San Francisco as an accessory to murder, McGowan had
escaped to Mexico, returning to San Francisco the following year when the
Vigilantes disbanded. He began a new career, publishing a newspaper so
scurrilous that in February 1858 it was seized by the San Francisco police.
Joining the gold rush to Fraser River, he acquired ownership of a gold
claim at Hill's Bar and became a leader among his fellow criminal expatriates.

From Yale, in August, Governor Douglas received the shocking news that many white men had been murdered by Indians; and although a further report (from Richard Hicks, the Assistant Commissioner of Crown Lands at Yale) stated that the first report had been greatly exaggerated and only two deaths had occurred, Douglas, informing Lord Stanley, wrote: "I am nevertheless preparing for an excursion to Fraser's River, with a small military force of 35 men, composed of 14 sappers and miners [Royal Engineers of the Boundary Commission] furnished by Major Hawkins; and Lieutenant Jones with 20 Marines, kindly furnished by Captain Prevost of Her Majesty's Ship Satellite."[4] This would be Douglas' second trip to the gold fields since the mining excitement had begun in March and April.

When Douglas and his men arrived at Yale, the hostilities had ended—but Douglas, observing the white men involved, believed he "had never seen a crowd of more ruffianly looking men," and, in addressing them, he found them surly in acknowledging the authority of the Crown. To assert the rule of law, Douglas sent for the Crown Solicitor of Vancouver Island to preside at a murder trial in Hope. Since there was no gaol, the accused, being found guilty, was sentenced to banishment from the region. Douglas also appointed special constables from among the miners, and set up temporary courts of law at Yale and Hope. Even so, the peaceable majority of the miners asked him to appoint additional magistrates.

At this time, while awaiting the arrival of official personnel from England, Douglas was forced to make some immediate appointments of his own. Few suitable candidates were to be found—most men, of course, being interested only in digging for gold—and not all those appointed proved satisfactory. Douglas must have welcomed the timely arrival from Australia of so promising and personable a candidate as Captain P.D. Whannell, whom he promptly appointed as Justice of the Peace at Yale, the most populous mining community. But when (in the following spring, 1859) news of Whannell's appointment reached Australia, the Chief of Police in Melbourne was to receive an interesting letter from Whannell's former commanding officer:

> Sir,—Referring to my recent verbal communication, I have now the honor of acquainting you that a person of the name of Whannell, who for some time held a situation in the Customs Department here, absconded from this Colony in the month of November, 1856, accompanied by the wife of a resident in Melbourne whose name I have not learned, leaving his own wife and family behind totally unprovided for.
>   Whannell was a private trooper in the Victoria Volunteer Yeomanry Corps under my command, and at the time of his enrolment

[sic] represented himself as having been formerly in a light cavalry regiment in India, as to which I had some reason afterward for expressing my doubts in consequence of his ignorance of ordinary Cavalry exercise and field movements. Nothing whatever was heard of Whannell after his departure until very lately, when the following paragraph appeared in one of the Melbourne newspapers:—

"*British Columbia.*—His Excellency Governor Douglas has been pleased to appoint as Justice of the Peace at Fort Yale, *Captain* B. Whannell, of the Victoria Yeomanry Cavalry in Australia, late of Nigaria Cavalry in the East Indies."

If Whannell represented himself to His Excellency Governor Douglas as having been a Captain or even a commissioned officer in the Victoria Yeomanry Cavalry he told a deliberate falsehood. The uniform of that Corps is a very expensive one, that of the ranks being mounted with gold lace precisely the same as a commissioned officer, and I have no doubt that this has assisted Whannell in some measure, if he appeared in that uniform, in imposing upon the Governor with the tale of being a commissioned officer.

I deem it my duty, as commanding officer of the Royal Victoria Yeomanry Corps . . . [to take] some steps for the purpose of making known to Governor Douglas that Whannell is an absconder, and that if he has represented himself to His Excellency Governor Douglas as having held a Commission in the Victoria Yeomanry Corps (now called "Royal" by Her Majesty's permission) he (Whannell) has been guilty of falsehood and wilful imposition. Under these circumstances it has occurred to me that the most direct course would be to communicate the facts to His Excellency Governor Douglas thro the office of the Secretary of State for the Colonies, but of course I defer to your better judgment in such matters.

Herewith I beg leave to forward for your further information a letter addressed to me from the Customs Department of date 27 ult., mentioning the precise date of Whannell's departure and of his subsequent dismissal from the service by the Governor in Council.

Whannell's name was erased from the roll of members of the Royal Victoria Yeomanry Corps, he having been reported as an absconder and absent without leave.

I have the honor, etc.
(signed) Jas. H. Ross
Lt. Col. Commanding R.V.Y.C.[5]

At Yale in November 1858, meanwhile, the Assistant Commissioner of Crown Lands, Richard Hicks, wrote to Douglas: "I beg to thank Your Excellency for the appointment of Captain Whannell as a Justice of the Peace for Fort Yale. He will certainly relieve me of much labour"—and later:

Captain Whannell and Lady arrived this evening about five o'Clock. Mrs. W.[hannell] I very much like. She appears like a fine young English Lady. The Captain is busy making his house arrangements. I have afforded him every assistance.

Is it Your Excellency's desire that a Cottage residence should be built for their use? if so, I should feel obliged for your assent.[6]

"Captain" Whannell's true identity apparently remained undiscovered for some time. Further communications from Yale, however, reflected no such friendly feelings as those at first expressed by Richard Hicks, for between Whannell and Hicks (both quite unsuited for office) it was not long before the pot was calling the kettle black—each accusing the other of unbecoming conduct, such as public drunkenness and of using official authority for personal gain. They were not alone in these accusations, for the miners under their jurisdiction complained bitterly of their corrupt and inefficient administration. Official inquiry eventually was to reveal that Hicks had been criminally negligent in the performance of official duties, while ensuring that his official power to grant leases, licenses, and permits brought him a substantial, illicit share of all profits. (Hicks, the charges against him of bribery and corruption being well proven, was soon dismissed from office.) Yet Hicks spitefully wrote several letters to Douglas admonishing Whannell for this same kind of behaviour:

The fees in Fort Yale alone must amount to many thousand dollars per annum. Mr. Whannell's office must be more lucrative than the Governor of the Colony. He little remembers his own condition when he kept a low liquor-shop at Shaw's Flat, California, or he would pity poor miners instead of exacting from their industry to keep him in luxury.[7]

From this, and from Hicks' reference to "Mr." Whannell, it might be guessed that some miners from California had recognized "Captain" Whannell from earlier encounters at "Shaw's Flat."

Before such revelations appeared in 1859, however, Whannell, by the end of 1858, had sent a dramatic and somewhat hysterical report to Governor Douglas:

Sir,—I have the honor to inform your Excellency that on the 24th inst. one William Foster, a notorious character and gambler, shot one Bernard Rice, a miner, in open daylight and has absconded. I have used every precaution and exerted every possible means in my power to capture the criminal, but to no purpose as yet. He has been hidden by his associates here as well as on Hill's Bar, among whom is that notorious villain, Edward McGowan.

I have closed up all the Gambling Saloons, appointed three men on the Police Forse [*sic*], and taken on several special constables on pay, as I could not arrange otherwise, and a large force is absolutely necessary here at the present crisis.

I have also to inform your Excellency that Edward McGowan came up this day to this town at the head of a lawless band of ruffians; broke open the Jail and liberated a Prisoner, in the person of Hickson, Constable at Hill's Bar, whom I committed this day for contempt of Court and insubordination.

Mr. Perrier, Justice of the peace at Hill's Bar, issued a Warrant for my arrest for the above act and dispatched a band of Sworn in special constables composed of the most notorious characters in that locality, and of which number was McGowan.

I pronounce Mr. Perrier totally unfit to serve in any capacity under Her Majesty's Government.

This town and district are in a state bordering on anarchy; my own and the lives of the citizens are in imminent peril. I beg your Excellency will afford us prompt aid. I have applied to Captain Grant for assistance already, as troops can easily be billeted in this town.

An effective blow must at once be struck on the operations of these outlaws, else I tremble for the welfare of this Colony.

In conclusion, I beg to report to your Excellency that at the present time, owing to Mr. Perrier's act this day, my authority is set at defiance and I am, as it were, a mere cipher.

With due deference to your Excellency, I must state that should an armed force not be convenient to be sent up here at once, I shall be under the necessity of tendering my resignation.

To Mr. G. Tennent, the bearer of this, I beg to refer your Excellency, as he is aware of all that occurred here from the date of the murder of Bernard Rice. Before concluding I must state that the *whole* of these disturbances at Fort Yale have originated in the acts of Mr. Richard Hicks, whom I do not hesitate to denounce as an unprincipled and corrupt Public Officer and a disgrace to the Government under which he has served.

I have dismissed Hickson, the Constable at Hill's Bar, but the Justice there has put him on again; that man is also in league with McGowan's party.

> I have the honour to be, Sir, Your Excellency's most Obedient Servant, (Signed) P.B. Whannell
> Justice of the Peace, District of Fort Yale.[8]

Given the dramatic circumstances described by Whannel, and considering the supposed involvement of the notorious and dangerous

McGowan faction, Douglas had no choice but to take immediate action and despatch an expedition to Fort Yale, at excessive cost and despite the severe hardships and difficulties of winter travel. At Yale (which only part of the expedition was, initially, able to reach—the river being ice-bound) all was found now to be calm. An investigation revealed that McGowan, far from inciting insurrection, was for once blameless; his actions and those of his followers had been ordered by George Perrier, the Justice of the Peace at Hill's Bar, who had sworn in McGowan and others as special constables. That a man had been murdered and the killer had escaped was true, but almost irrelevant. Primarily, the conflict between Yale and Hill's Bar had been caused by their respective Justices, rivalling each other in foolish self-importance, and each taking absurdly inappropriate actions to assert authority.

One Bernard Rice having been shot by a man named Foster, Whannell "in his anxiety to prevent the ends of justice from being defeated, had imprisoned Foster's partner [Adams] and a servant named Allmeyer, whom he intended to call as witnesses, requiring enormous bail for their appearance . . . which amounted, the killer, Foster, having by this time absconded, to a sentence of perpetual imprisonment upon an innocent witness."[9]

Also "oppressively treated" by Whannell was a coloured man, Dixon, who had complained to Whannell of having been assaulted by two men, Burns and Farrell. Whannell issued warrants for the arrest of Burns and Farrell, and put Dixon (the injured party) in gaol to ensure his presence at prosecution. Burns and Farrell, being arrested, were taken before Perrier, the aforementioned Justice of the Peace at Hill's Bar, one and a half miles distant. Perrier sent his constable to fetch Dixon, but Whannell, demanding that Burns and Farrell be brought before him, refused to release Dixon, and put Perrier's constable in gaol for refusing his order.

By now, regarding these two investigations, Whannell had imprisoned an injured party, witnesses, and constable—everybody but the guilty. It was then that McGowan and his fellow special constables—sworn in by Perrier and all fully armed—descended upon Yale and seized Whannell and his gaoler. Whannell was then brought before Perrier at Hill's Bar and "fined twenty-five dollars for contempt of court." This was the crisis for which Whannell had caused all available officials and armed forces in the country to rush to his aid, braving arduous winter conditions, and incurring enormous expense. No blood had been shed, but Whannell and Perrier were soon pronounced "alike ignorant of the law, surrounded by evil counsellors, and carried away with the most unbounded ideas of the dignity of their office and themselves." The mining communities that had suffered their presence were soon to find themselves better served.

Characteristically, Ned McGowan did not long remain blameless. While still in Yale, he recognized an old enemy, Dr. M.W. Fifer, who had been a member of California's Vigilance Committee. McGowan promptly assaulted Fifer, and was arrested. Pleading guilty, he promised, publicly, to observe the laws in the future. Once more his persuasive charm caused him to be set free, and he soon returned to California.[10]

———

1. Parliamentary Papers Relating to British Columbia. Despatch, No. 6 (29), p. 20, item 14, Governor Douglas to Lord Stanley, July 1, 1858.

2. Correspondence, Wm. H. Bevis to Governor Douglas, January 1, 1859, in Frederic W. Howay, *The Early History of the Fraser River Mines* (Victoria: Archives of British Columbia, 1926), 23-24.

3. *New York Times*, June 21, 1858, reprinted in *The Times* (London), July 30, 1858. Also quoted in John Domer, *New British Gold Fields: A Guide to British Columbia and Vancouver Island, with Coloured Map, Showing the Gold and Coal Fields, Constructed from Authentic Sources* (London: W.H. Angel [1858]), 51-52.

4. Parliamentary Papers Relating to British Columbia. Despatch, No. 9 (35), p. 29, Governor Douglas to Lord Stanley, August 27, 1858.

5. Correspondence, Jas. H. Ross to C. Standish, Esq., Chief Commissioner of Police, Melbourne, May 9, 1859, in Howay, *The Early History of the Fraser River Mines*, 58-59.

6. Correspondence, Richard Hicks to Governor Douglas, November 9 and 17, 1858, in Ibid., 12, 16.

7. Correspondence, Richard Hicks to Governor Douglas, June 3, 1859, in Ibid., 22.

8. Correspondence, P.B. Whannel to Governor Douglas, December 31, 1858, in Ibid., 56-57.

9. Correspondence, Judge Begbie to Governor Douglas, January 1, 1859, in David Ricardo Williams, *The Man for a New Country: Sir Matthew Baillie Begbie* (Sydney, BC: Gray's, 1977), 43.

10. Howay, *The Early History of the Fraser River Mines*, xiv-vi, 35-37.

20
THE NEW COLONY, "A QUESTIONABLE INFANT"

DURING THE SUMMER OF 1858, Douglas remained unaware that the legality of the Company's charter and privileges was being questioned in Parliament, that its current licence for trade in New Caledonia would not be renewed, and that in the United States his own restrictions on shipping and trade in the Fraser River region had caused queries to be addressed to Her Majesty's Minister in Washington concerning the supposed jurisdiction of the HBC. The Company's tenuous situation was described by the British ambassador in Washington, Lord Napier, who, when writing to the British Foreign Secretary, the Earl of Malmesbury, in London, had observed:

> I have not assumed the responsibility of giving an official answer to questions involving the jurisdiction of the Hudson's Bay Company, a subject with which I am imperfectly acquainted. I have reserved these inquiries for the consideration and decision of Her Majesty's Government.
>
> Your Lordship has, probably, been informed from another quarter of the discovery of gold deposits in the basin of Fraser's River, and of the rush of labourers to this new field of enterprise.
>
> Should the reports of mineral wealth in the British territory prove to be well founded, a turbulent and adventurous population will shortly be collected, ill disposed to submit to the authority of the Hudson's Bay Company, and impatient to possess a share at least of those rights of property and self-government which they have exercised in their previous place of abode.
>
> The influx of consumers will be attended by the development of traffic, and the citizens of the neighbouring States will see with reluctance the profits of trade monopolized by a British corporation, though, I doubt not, those exclusive rights would be exercised liberally for the benefit of an improvident community.
>
> Finally, the immigration of large bodies of armed and reckless men can hardly fail to produce collisions with the Indians, and be

accompanied by injustice to that people, who have been reconciled to the Government of the Company by a long course of judicious treatment.

Should the abundance of precious metals fall below expectations, still the present emigration will probably lay the basis of an agricultural state, and open the country to progressive settlement.

In either case, it is apparent that the British Possessions cannot long be maintained as a preserve for the trade in furs, and that the jurisdiction of the Company must be dissolved, or restricted to regions less susceptible to profitable culture.[1]

The decision to create a new Crown Colony was referred to in a letter despatched in July from Downing Street on Lytton's behalf, for the attention of Major General Peel, the Under Secretary for War. After first addressing Douglas' request for military assistance, the letter continued: "The Crown will be advised to constitute immediately a Colonial Government for the Fraser's River District, in connexion, as far as may be practicable, with that already established in Vancouver's Island."[2]

Knowing nothing of these intentions, a careworn and overworked Douglas wrote to London in July:

I am not without cause looking forward most anxiously to receiving your instructions respecting the plan of Government for Fraser's River. The torrent of immigration is setting in with impetuous force, and to keep pace with the extraordinary circumstances of the times, and to maintain the authority of the laws, I have been compelled to assume an unusual amount of responsibility. I trust, however, from the present hasty reviews of the reasons which have influenced my public measures, that they will meet with the approval of Her Majesty's Government.[3]

This last, of course, was a reference by Douglas to his assumption of governmental authority on the mainland during the gold-rush emergency, and to his measures (reported fully in his despatches) both to preserve British sovereignty and to protect the interests of the Hudson's Bay Company. Clearly, from his forthright communications, Douglas had no idea that a new British Government would raise objections to those measures which he proposed on behalf of the Company. When, on June 10, for instance, he had suggested that to avoid unregulated takeover by squatters, "the whole country be immediately thrown open for settlement," he had added, as "the Hudson's Bay Company would in that case have to relinquish their exclusive rights of trade, compensation might be made to them for those rights, by an annual payment out of public Revenues of the country."[4]

Douglas must have been disagreeably surprised when, in due course, he was advised in no uncertain terms that the Company's "rights" in the mainland territory, which he was at pains to protect (and in which Governments heretofore had concurred), had, in this new Government's view, never existed on any legal basis. This advice was communicated to him in several strongly worded communications from Sir E.B. Lytton, who finally stated in summary:

> The Hudson's Bay Company have hitherto had an exclusive right to trade with Indians in the Fraser River territory, but they have had no other right whatever. They have had no right to exclude strangers. They have had no rights of Government, or of occupation of the soil. They have had no right to prevent or interfere with any kind of trading, except with Indians alone.[5]

In defence, Douglas replied: "We have always hitherto given a more extended application to these rights, believing, from the circumstances of the country being inhabited by Indians alone, and from its not being open for settlement to white men, that the intention of Parliament in granting the licence was to make over the whole trade of the country to the Hudson's Bay Company."[6] Douglas also defended the various measures he had taken "with the view of introducing public order and government into the Gold Region." These measures, he explained:

> were introduced under the pressure of necessity, without adequate means, and, therefore, necessarily imperfect; but in adopting them we had solely the great object in view of protecting British interests, and developing the resources of the Gold Regions.
>
> It was necessary for that purpose that we should maintain a proper control over the mixed multitude, that have literally forced an entrance into the British Possessions; that Americans and other foreigners should, on certain conditions, be admitted into the Gold Regions; that stocks of food should be thrown into those districts; that, for want of British ships, foreign vessels should, as a temporary measure, be allowed, under a sufferance renewable at the close of each voyage, to navigate the inland waters of Fraser's River, for the purpose of supplying the miners with food and clothing; that roads should be opened, to render the Gold Districts accessible to the miner and the merchant; that Courts of Law should be established, and officers appointed for the administration of justice, the punishment of offences, and the protection of life and property; and that the powerful native Indian Tribes who inhabit the Gold Regions should be at once conciliated and placed under proper restraint.

> All this I have attempted to do, and I trust that Her Majesty's Government will see in these attempts only a profound desire on my part to promote the interests of the Empire, without any admixture of other motives.[7]

But Douglas could not be aware that his connection with the Hudson's Bay Company had become a matter of serious concern to the British Government, which otherwise considered him to be the best choice to head the new government now planned for the mainland territory. The Colony of Vancouver Island, during his nine years as its governor, had become (in Douglas' own words) "self-supporting and defraying all the expenses of its own Government . . . a striking contrast to every other colony in the British Empire." And, had not Douglas, since the onset of the gold rush, shown exemplary initiative in protecting British sovereignty, while at the same time gaining revenues for the Crown? And, no man knew the country and its peoples, both white and native, better than "the old fur trader."

Lytton's personal regard for Douglas later was evident in the final paragraph of an October 16 despatch: "I cannot conclude without a cordial expression of my sympathy in the difficulties you have encountered, and of my sense of the ability, the readiness of resource, the wise and manly temper of conciliation, which you have so signally displayed; and I doubt not that you will continue to show the same vigour, and the same discretion in its exercise; and you may rely with confidence on whatever support and aid Her Majesty's Government can afford you."[8]

But Douglas' detractors in London had raised questions of divided loyalty, so that Lytton, in several of his despatches, stressed the importance of avoiding any act in connection either with appointments or with sales of land which could possibly be construed as conferring favour upon the Hudson's Bay Company: "All claims and interests must be subordinated to that policy which is to be found in the peopling and opening up of the new country, with the intention of consolidating it as an integral and important part of the British Empire."

Hardly had Douglas received this latest advice than it was immediately followed by a separate (and confidential) letter dated July 16, with startling news from Lytton. Following as it did upon Lytton's several despatches containing strong admonitions from which Douglas may well have inferred a certain loss of Government approval, this communication must surely have come as a pleasant shock:

> I wish to inform you, confidentially, that a Bill is in progress through Parliament to get rid of certain legal obstacles which interpose to prevent

the Crown from constituting a Government suited to the exigencies of so peculiar a case, over the territory now resorted to, according to report, by the multitudes whom the gold diggings on Fraser's River have attracted.

It is proposed to appoint a Governor, with a salary of at least 1,000 pounds per annum, to be paid for the present out of a Parliamentary vote. And it is the desire of Her Majesty's Government to appoint you to that office, on the usual terms of a Governor's appointment; namely, for six years at least, your administration of the office continuing to merit the approval of Her Majesty's Government; this appointment to be held, for the present, in conjunction with your separate Commission as Governor of Vancouver's Island.[9]

Queen Victoria had by then decided that the mainland territory, now to become a colony, should no longer be called New Caledonia, since this name also applied to certain French islands in the southwest Pacific. The new colony, she decided, would be called British Columbia. It would comprise those territories bounded to the south by the United States, to the east by the Rocky Mountains, to the north by Simpson's River and the Finlay branch of the Peace River, and to the west by the Pacific Ocean; and it would include the Queen Charlotte Islands and all other adjacent islands excepting Vancouver Island. (Within a few years the northern boundary was extended still farther.)

The decision to create the new Colony of British Columbia was not well received by *The Times* editorial writer, who, staunchly loyal to the Hudson's Bay Company, likened the event to the birth of a questionable infant—perhaps better never conceived and certainly no fit cause for celebration. Strong in opinion, though somewhat luridly misinformed, he declared "this howling wilderness,"

is utterly destitute of civilized inhabitants, except a few factors of the Hudson's Bay Company, who traffic in furs with the native Indians. These Indians are described as peculiarly fierce and intractable . . . They have, however, imbibed so much of civilization as to be perfectly aware of the value of gold, and evince a most civilized anxiety to keep the shining mischief entirely to themselves.

Equally covetous, and far more able to obtain their prize, a horde of diggers from California, a mixed multitude of all nations, armed, of course, after the fashion of such men, have set forward to the banks of the Fraser River. They are described as the very dregs of society, and the present California press, not over-fastidious in such matters, congratulates the State on their departure. The land is desolate and can offer them nothing. There is as yet no authority, no police, except what these rude outcasts of society may institute among themselves, influenced by the instincts of self-preservation; and when they have reached the new Eldorado, there waits for them the crafty, bloodthirsty, and implacable savage, who never throws away a chance, never exposes himself to the weapon of an enemy, nor misses the opportunity of slaughter and revenge. We can anticipate nothing from this meeting between the least civilized of civilized men and the most savage of savages but a war of mutual extermination, in which the cunning, the ferocity, and the local knowledge of the Indian may turn out at least a match for the higher knowledge of the white man. Considering the remoteness of the situation, the extreme difficulty of access, the almost total impossibility of adequately discharging the duties of government under circumstances so untoward and amid elements so turbulent, it might have been perhaps better to allow this remote and isolated region to remain untouched a little longer until society has assumed a shape which admitted of something like a possibility of regular government. We have placed this country, which seems destined to be the seat of war before it has become the settled habitation of civilized man, under the direct sovereignty of the Crown, and the honour of the Crown and the Empire is now pledged to preserve in this savage wilderness the same peace and order as prevail in every other part of Her Majesty's dominions. At whatever cost, this must be done, and the cost, we fear, will be heavy indeed. We can only hope that the responsibility we have undertaken, magnanimously if not wisely, will be surrounded by fewer difficulties than we at present anticipate.[10]

Readers of *The Times*—especially those better acquainted with the facts—must have been astonished at that prestigious publication's unwonted recourse to such vivid writing. Far from "magnanimously" undertaking a dubious responsibility, Parliament was creating the new colony partly as a counterpoise to the fast-developing states and territories of the United States; and also in order to develop, through settlement, the land's rich resources. As Lytton stated in his July 31 letter to Governor Douglas:

I need hardly observe that British Columbia, for by that name the Queen has been graciously pleased that the country should be known, stands on a very different footing from many of our early colonial settlements. They possessed the chief elements of success in lands which afforded safe though not very immediate sources of prosperity. This territory combines, in a remarkable degree, the advantages of fertile lands, fine timber, adjacent harbours, rivers, together with rich mineral products. These last, which have led to the large immigration of which all accounts speak, furnish the Government with the means of raising a Revenue which will at once defray the necessary expenses of an establishment.

And Lytton confidently asserted, "Whilst the Imperial Parliament will cheerfully lend its assistance in the early establishment of this new Colony, it will expect that the Colony shall be self-supporting as soon as possible."[11]

1. Parliamentary Papers Relating to British Columbia. Sub-enclosure 1 in No. 23, p. 64, Lord Napier to the Earl of Malmesbury, July 12, 1858.
2. Ibid. Enclosure 1 in No. 16, p. 53, H. Merivale, Colonial Office, to the Under-Secretary for War, for attention Secretary Major General Peel, July 13, 1858.
3. Ibid. Despatch, July 26, 1858, p. 23, Governor Douglas to Sir E.B. Lytton.
4. Ibid. Despatch, No. 2 (21), p. 14, Governor Douglas to Lord Stanley, June 10, 1858.
5. Ibid. Despatch, No. 8 (8), pp. 47-48, Sir E.B. Lytton to Governor Douglas, August 14, 1858.
6. Ibid. Despatch, No. 13 (42), p. 36, Governor Douglas to Sir E.B. Lytton, September 30, 1858.
7. Ibid. Despatch, No. 11 (39), p. 34, Governor Douglas to Sir E.B. Lytton, from Fort Hope, September 9, 1858.
8. Ibid. Despatch, No. 30 (30), p. 71, item 12, Sir E.B. Lytton to Governor Douglas, October 16, 1858.
9. Ibid. Despatch, No. 3, p. 43, (Confidential) Sir E.B. Lytton to Governor Douglas, July 16, 1858.
10. *The Times* (London), July 26, 1858.
11. Parliamentary Papers Relating to British Columbia. Despatch, No. 6 (1), p. 45, Sir E.B. Lytton to Governor Douglas, July 31, 1858.

Colonel Richard Clement Moody, the Chief Commissioner of Lands and Works, and commander of the Royal Engineers, developed a strained relationship with Governor Douglas. *Provincial Archives of British Columbia, Victoria.*

21
THE FIRST CONTINGENTS

SUMMER WAS ENDING, and with it the first season of extensive mining on the Fraser River. By late August, the rush of miners through Victoria was considerably abated, with a consequent decline in land speculation and with considerable price reductions, by merchants, of goods now found to be overstocked. The falling off of activity in Victoria was perhaps due partly to the approach of Autumn, and also to the increasing use of overland trails to the upper gold regions, as more routes became accessible to gold seekers. Victoria, however, continued to grow, reflecting its faith in the mines and in its own future. Hundreds of new buildings had been built within a matter of weeks, and two fire engines were acquired from San Francisco for the protection of these wooden structures.

As the northward tide of immigration abated, reporters on both sides of the Atlantic turned their attention from the gold rush to the more immediate sensation—the completion of the trans-Atlantic telegraph line. The connection of the New World with the Old by the electric cord was being celebrated on both sides of the Atlantic, to the exclusion of every other topic. (The celebration of the first successful transmission on August 16, 1858, was to prove premature, however, as the system failed after only three weeks; but its viability was proven, and Cyrus Field set about raising new funds that would result in success in 1866 when the *Great Eastern* completed the laying of the trans-Atlantic cable.)

It was at about this time that the British government sent a special agent to British Columbia and Vancouver Island to inform the United States government about developments in the region. To the British government, it was by then quite clear that only by immigration and settlement could the rich resources of the new colony be developed, and that the foreign "intrusion" so long opposed by the Hudson's Bay Company not only was inevitable, but should be actively encouraged. Also at this time, various means whereby postal service could be established between

Great Britain and the new colony were the subject of extensive correspondence between the Colonial Office, the Admiralty, the Postmaster-General, and the Treasury.

As Secretary for the Colonies, Sir E.B. Lytton was taking a keen personal interest in this newest colony, the creation of which he had fostered, and the early development of which was to be greatly influenced by his policies and selection of civil personnel urgently needed to assist in its administration. As early as June 10, Douglas had written to London[1] proposing to appoint, as Surveyor-General of Fraser's River, Joseph D. Pemberton, the Surveyor-General of Vancouver Island, who had been brought out from Ireland by the Hudson's Bay Company in 1851. In his August reply, Lytton (apparently confirming his previous admonitions regarding "Company" appointments) stated his contrary intention "to send to the Colony a head of that department from England," and also, "it is my wish that all legal authorities connected with the Government should be sent from home, and thus freed of every suspicion of local partiality, prejudices and interests."[2]

On September 2, he wrote, further:

> You will furnish me, at your earliest convenience, with a list of such officers for Civil situations, together with the rates of pay which you think they should receive, as the circumstances of the Colony shall, in your opinion, render it desirable for me to send from England. I shall be happy to assist you to the best of my ability in making the proper selection; for I think that, considering the great number of foreigners who are resorting to British Columbia, it is on every account proper to give encouragement to Englishmen of character and respectability to go out to the Colony.[3]

A subsequent despatch from Lytton advised Douglas that Wymond Hamley (the first of several civil appointments) had been selected Collector of Customs "with a salary of 400 pounds per annum," and was being despatched aboard the *Thames City*. Lytton also informed Douglas:

> With respect to offices generally, which the public exigencies may compel you to create, and for which selections should be made in England, I have to observe that I consider it of great importance to the general social welfare and dignity of the Colony that gentlemen should be encouraged to come from this Kingdom, not as mere adventurers seeking employment, but in the hope of obtaining professional occupations for which they are calculated, such, for instance, as Stipendiary Magistrates or Gold Commissioners. You will, therefore, report to me, at your early convenience, whether there is any field for such

situations, and describe as accurately as you can the peculiar qualifications which are requisite, in order that I may assist you by making the best selection in my power.[4]

Plans were by then nearing completion for sending to British Columbia a detachment of Royal Engineers—an elite body, chosen for their particular skills. Lytton had written in late July to advise Douglas that:

A party of Royal Engineers will be despatched to the Colony immediately. It will devolve upon them to survey those parts of the country which may be considered most suitable for settlement, to mark out allotments of land for public purposes, to suggest a site for the seat of government, to point out where roads should be made, and to render you such assistance as may be in their power, on the distinct understanding however, that this force is to be maintained at Imperial cost for only a limited period, and that, if required afterwards, the Colony will have to defray the expense thereof.

(The offer to maintain the force "at Imperial cost," even temporarily, was soon withdrawn, and the supposedly gold-rich colony was required to pay the entire cost of the expedition.) Lytton continued:

I shall endeavour to secure, if possible, the services of an officer in command of the Engineers who will be capable of reporting on the value of the mineral resources. This force is sent for scientific and practical purposes, and not solely for military objects. As little display as possible should, therefore, be made of it. Its mere appearance, if prominently obtruded, might serve to irritate, rather than appease, the mixed population which will be collected in British Columbia.[5]

On September 2, Lytton again wrote to Douglas regarding the sending of the Royal Engineers, advising him that Colonel R.C. Moody had been appointed to this command (and also as Chief Commissioner of Lands and Works) and including a copy of Lytton's official instructions to Colonel Moody. The same despatch enclosed a copy of a letter, on Lytton's behalf, to Colonel Moody, advising him that "immediate steps should be taken for despatching" an expedition to include: 1 lieutenant-colonel, 2 captains, 3 subalterns, and 150 non-commissioned officers and men, accompanied by 20 women; also, "a medical officer should be sent." Lytton's September 2 despatch also advised Douglas:

A ship has been chartered, and is in course of preparation for the conveyance of the larger portion of this detachment by the Horn; but as the passage will consume nearly four months [actually it took six months] and it is desirable that you should have the assistance and support of a part of this body without delay, both to represent the military force of this country and to facilitate those surveying and engineering operations which it may be expedient to commence forthwith, I have made arrangements for the despatch of 20 men and an officer by the steamer which leaves this country for Panama on the 2nd of next month.[6]

So it was not until early September that the advance contingent of the Royal Engineers left England for the two-month journey by Panama. The main force, coming by the much longer route round the Horn, was even further delayed. As Lytton explained in his October 16 despatch:

I regret that this force has been delayed in its departure, notwithstanding the unceasing care and pains I have devoted to the hastening of the necessary preparations; but owing to arrangements with the different Departments of the Government, the necessity for due care in the selection of the officers and men for the expedition, and the time required for preparing the vessels for sea, a delay unavoidably occurred that must have caused you an anxiety in which I fully sympathized.

Instalments, however, of the force, consisting of twenty and twelve men respectively, under Captain Parsons and Captain Grant, were despatched to the Colony via Panama, on the 2nd and 17th of September.

With the first of these detachments I forwarded your Commission as Governor, having immediately on the return of the Queen from the Continent obtained Her Majesty's signature, and taken your Commission myself on board the vessel in which the instalment of Engineers under Captain Parsons sailed from Southampton.

Of the Royal Engineers to be included in the expedition, Lytton wrote:

The superior discipline and intelligence of this force, which afford ground for expecting that they will be far less likely than ordinary soldiers of the line to yield to the temptation to desertion offered by the gold fields, and their capacity at once to provide for themselves in a country without habitation, appear to me to render them especially suited for this duty, whilst by their services as pioneers in the work of civilization, in opening up the resources of the country, by the construction of roads and bridges, in laying the foundations of a future city or seaport, and in carrying out the numerous engineering works which in the earlier stages of colonization are so essential to the progress and welfare of the community, they will probably not only be preserved from the idleness that might corrupt the discipline of ordinary soldiers, but establish themselves in the popular goodwill of the emigrants by the civil benefits it will be in the regular nature of their occupation to confer.

Lytton also advised Douglas: "I am glad to be able now to inform you that the *Thames City* has recently left England, having on board 119 men of the expedition."[7] (The military personnel on this six-months voyage round the Horn, and the 31 women and 34 children who were included in the expedition, were to experience Christmas at sea, New Year's Eve in the Falklands, cramped shipboard quarters, winds, storms, tropical heat, deaths, births, and even, in the Falklands, a wedding. It was not until the spring of the following year that their ship at last arrived at the harbour of Esquimalt.[8])

Lytton's October 16 despatch continued: "This vessel *[Thames City]* will be followed in a few days by the Briseis, laden with stores, &c belonging to the party; and a small number of men and some additional stores will be sent in the Euphrates which is expected to sail in about a month's time. Colonel Moody, who commands the expedition, will proceed to British Columbia via Panama on the 10th instant, to be in readiness to receive the main body of Engineers on their arrival."

The first contingent of twenty men under Captain R.M. Parsons, having left England on September 2, arrived at Vancouver Island on November 16. Captain Parsons brought with him Lytton's letter of introduction to Governor Douglas:

> Dear Sir: I have the honour to introduce to you Captain Parsons, the bearer of this Despatch, who, in pursuance of the intention which I have already communicated to you, has been directed to repair to British Columbia, accompanied by twenty non-commissioned officers and men of the Royal Engineers.
>
> I need scarcely observe to you that the object for which this officer and his party have been detached to British Columbia is for the exclusive service of that Colony. You will, therefore, afford him every assistance in your power for enabling him to commence immediately such operations as it shall appear to him to be necessary in anticipation of the arrival of his commanding officer, Colonel Moody, R.E., who will follow him with as much rapidity as is practicable. And I trust that if Captain Parsons should require the temporary occupation for his party of the trading posts up the country which belong to the Hudson's Bay Company, you will take measures for affording him such accommodation. I have, &c, E.B.L.[9]

Lytton had in due course received copies of Douglas' May letter to Rear-Admiral R.L. Baynes appealing for additional naval support and of the Rear-Admiral's negative response. Consequently, Baynes, then stationed at Valparaiso, Chile, received a letter from the Admiralty stating: "My Lords desire me to inform you that the presence of a force, as referred to in the

Colonial Office letter, herewith forwarded to you, is to be considered by you as a more pressing and important service than any other on your station of which they are cognizant."[10]

So it was that Rear-Admiral Baynes, diverted from the Britannic policing of Argentinian revolution, was hastening in his flagship the *Ganges* to Vancouver Island, where he would arrive just in time to attend the mainland ceremonies establishing British Columbia as a Crown Colony and James Douglas as its Governor.

Following the *Ganges* were two frigates, regarding which Lytton explained to Douglas:

> Indeed the First Lord of the Admiralty assures me, in reply to a letter I addressed to him, that Admiral Baynes "will be followed as quickly as possible by two frigates from China . . . This was the quickest mode of reinforcement we could possibly adopt, and in one case I sent a new captain overland to take command of a ship in China which had become vacant, and proceed at once to the Pacific."

And Lytton added: "I request that you will report to me what vessels at the time this despatch is received may be actually in your harbour designed for the special support of the Civil Government; and should you deem a still larger force to be requisite for the purpose, your representation to that effect shall have my immediate attention."[11] Douglas also had received a letter earlier from Lytton informing him,

> that the officers commanding Her Majesty's vessels at Vancouver Island will be directed to give you all the support in their power, and to render their crews, and more especially the Marines, serviceable, as far as circumstances will allow, if the Civil Government should require a force to maintain order among the adventurers resorting to the Gold Fields. But it will be necessary to be very cautious in employing them, on account of the obvious danger of desertion.
>
> Her Majesty's Government, feeling the difficulties and the critical nature of your present circumstances, have not hesitated to place these considerable powers in your hands; but they rely upon your forbearance, judgment, and conciliation to avoid all resort to military or naval force which may lead to conflict and loss of life, except under the pressure of extreme necessity.[12]

---

1. Parliamentary Papers Relating to British Columbia. Despatch, No. 2 (24), p. 14, item 25, Governor Douglas to Lord Stanley, June 10, 1858.
2. Ibid., No. 8 (8), p. 47, item 4, Sir E.B. Lytton to Governor Douglas, August 14, 1858.

3. Ibid., No. 21 (14), Sir E.B. Lytton to Governor Douglas, September 2, 1858.

4. Ibid., No. 25, p. 66, Sir E.B. Lytton to Governor Douglas, September 2, 1858.

5. Ibid., No. 6 (6), p. 45, Sir E.B. Lytton to Governor Douglas, July 31, 1858.

6. Ibid., No. 16 (7), p. 52, Sir E.B. Lytton to Governor Douglas, September 2, 1858.

7. Ibid., No. 30 (30), p. 69, Sir E.B. Lytton to Governor Douglas, October 16, 1858.

8. Beth Hill, *Sappers: The Royal Engineers in British Columbia* (Ganges, BC: Horsdal and Schubert, 1987), 35-41.

9. Parliamentary Papers Relating to British Columbia. Despatch, No. 10, p. 50, Sir E.B. Lytton to Governor Douglas, September 1, 1858.

10. Ibid., No. 14, p. 52, Sir E.B. Lytton to Governor Douglas; sub-enclosure 2, letter, W.G. Romaine, Admiralty, to Rear-Admiral Baynes, Valparaiso, August 16, 1858.

11. Ibid., No. 3 (36), p. 69, item 2, Sir E.B. Lytton to Governor Douglas, October 16, 1858.

12. Ibid., No. 41 (1), Sir E.B. Lytton to Governor Douglas, July 1, 1858.

The wide-travelling Judge Matthew Baillie Begbie worked in harmony with Governor Douglas in establishing new policies and laws for the vast colony. *Provincial Archives of British Columbia, Victoria.*

22
JUDGE BEGBIE AND COLONEL MOODY

O F ALL LYTTON'S CONCERNS regarding the new colony none was more important to him than the establishment and enforcement of British law. Writing from Downing Street on September 2, he instructed Douglas to issue a proclamation, "of the same date with your assumption of Government," declaring the law of England prevalent throughout the colony; and he went on: "Almost the first point to which your attention will be directed will be the establishment of a Court or Courts of Justice, with the necessary machinery for the maintenance of law and order. Her Majesty has issued a Commission to Mr. Begbie, who will proceed by this or next packet, as Judge of British Columbia."[1]

What is remarkable is that Lytton had managed to find a candidate who could meet the unique requirements of this appointment. The right man for the job had to be a capable and experienced lawyer, of impeccable character, and capable of filling a key role in the development of a new society. But what lawyer would be willing to forego a comfortable professional and social life in London for the arduous prospects of a lone frontier judge? Who in the legal profession would have endurance enough to travel in the gold region, on foot and on horseback, under the severe conditions imposed by its climate and geography; and the presence, and physical strength, to prevail in any hostile situation likely to be encountered?

At the suggestion of the Solicitor-General, Sir Hugh Cairns, Lytton interviewed Matthew Baillie Begbie, a Cambridge-educated London barrister, and knew that he had found his man. Begbie had the necessary professional qualifications, being an experienced chancery lawyer at the time of his appointment.[2] He also had the necessary physical strength and presence, being an all-round athlete and uncommonly tall. The 39-year-old Begbie was widely accomplished—skilled in science and mathematics, fluent in French, German, and Greek, and a master of the English language, well travelled, brilliant of intellect, witty and gregarious; remarkably he was, and remained, a bachelor.

Begbie, who already had contemplated a career in the colonies,[3] welcomed the challenge offered by Lytton, whose September 2 letter further informed Douglas: "Mr. Begbie has been fully instructed that, although invested with the very important office of Judge, he will nevertheless have the kindness, for the present at least, to lend you his general aid for the compilation of the necessary laws and other legal business." In a later despatch dated October 11, Lytton added: "I have to inform you that Mr. Begbie's salary as Judge of British Columbia is fixed at 800 pounds per annum, payable from the Revenue of the Colony."[4]

Leaving Liverpool on September 11, Begbie arrived in New York after a thirteen-day voyage; he next embarked for the Isthmus of Panama; thence to San Francisco, by a vessel of the Pacific Mail steamship line; and from San Francisco to Vancouver Island, where he arrived on November 16, 1858. Begbie was to become a most valuable friend and colleague to Governor Douglas, advising him on policy besides drafting legislation. Sincerely devoted to the public service, Judge Begbie held regular court sittings at Fort Langley, and also travelled, on horseback or on foot, to bring to the gold camps the laws which he assisted Governor Douglas in compiling. During these early expeditions he expressed marvel and wonder at the beauty of the wild, mountainous landscape, while observing, to Douglas, "the lack of all means of communication, except by foaming torrents and canoes, or over goat tracks on foot."[5] Begbie's early travelling companions included his registrar, Arthur Bushby (who had been an acquaintance of his in London), Sheriff Nicol, Martin the interpreter, a servant, and Indian packers. According to Bushby's diary:

> Begbie was the best of travelling and camping companions: hardy, adaptable and, better still, useful. He had with him all the necessary camping supplies: tents, straps, knives, frying pans, axes, teapots and other basic equipment. He chopped wood, baked bread, cut tent-pegs, shot game and caught fish. Until fairly late in his life, in fact, when on circuit he lived off the country by fishing or shooting, and could steer or paddle a canoe down a swift river as well as anyone. At night around the campfires, his conversational wit and learning led everyone hearing him to express astonishment at the contrast between his intellectual attainments and the rigorous backdrop against which they were so effortlessly displayed.[6]

While traversing the new territory Begbie, as a service to Douglas, filled his notebooks with observations of the country's topography, weather conditions, and agricultural potential, and with maps to which he would add useful notes concerning possible sites for roads, bridges, town sites, and other improvements. In the early days of his law career in London, Begbie had become expert in the Gurney system of shorthand writing, so that, like Charles Dickens, he had been able to augment his earnings by working as a court reporter for *The Times;* he also was competent in sketching and cartography. These skills were to serve him well in British Columbia.

On his circuits he would, besides holding court, receive deputations of Indian chiefs. According to his biographer: "From his first contact with the Indians he liked them; he got on well with them and, what is more important, they respected him. He had not been long in British Columbia before he could speak Chinook . . . but also the dialects of the Chilcotin and Shuswap areas, and, possibly, a Vancouver Island dialect as well."[7]

Begbie, over the years, was also to be in sympathy with the Chinese, whom he admired and whose part he took against prejudice and discrimination.[8]

Begbie's court circuit was to grow ever wider as, in successive spring and summer seasons, the miners moved on from the lower Fraser sandbars to various rich "strikes" on the upper river and on into the Cariboo. For wherever an abundance of gold was discovered, there another lively, ram-shackle mining town would be established, with the usual hotels, bars, stores, livery stables, and all the sundry initiatives, lawful and otherwise, by means of which gold might be acquired without digging. In these mining communities, all major crimes and conflicts came before Judge Begbie, while lesser crimes and minor litigation were dealt with, for his approval, by local Justices of the Peace, or Gold Commissioners, acting as magistrates. Be his "court room" a tent, a shack, or in the open air, Begbie would always appear in court wearing the impressive garb of an English judge, and the requisite solemn demeanour. Meticulous in his proceedings, he could be thunderously and theatrically scathing toward evil-doers, and occasionally toward juries whose verdicts displeased him. His reputation for severe sentencing caused many a criminal to flee the country rather than face Begbie in court. Yet he was humane, as in his habit of seeking extenuating circumstances where a death penalty might seem appropriate; for it was his deep aversion to the taking of life that had caused Begbie to choose the law rather than, like his father, a military career.

"Able, active, energetic and highly talented," wrote Douglas:

> Mr. Begbie is a most valuable public servant. I feel greatly indebted to him for the zealous discharge of his official duties, and for many services

beyond the strict line of official duty. It would be impossible, I think, to find a person better qualified for the position he fills.[9]

On Vancouver Island, since before the gold rush, justice had been administered for the very small and law-abiding population by a few magistrates under the authority of David Cameron (Douglas' brother-in-law), who in 1853 had been named Judge of the Supreme Court of Civil Justice of Vancouver Island. Though without formal training in law, Cameron filled the position creditably until 1865. In 1865 he was succeeded by Joseph Needham, upon whose retirement, in 1870, the position was filled by Henry Crease until 1871, at which time, after Confederation, Begbie became the sole Chief Justice of Canada's new province. In later years he was knighted for his services to the Crown.

For thirty-six years, to the end of his life, Begbie was honoured as the Chief Justice and as a most prominent and popular participant in the social and cultural life of Victoria, where he made his home. And he still is honoured, in memory, as one of that small, colourful band of colonial officials, who from the gold rush days of 1858 helped to build and guide a new country. At Begbie's funeral in 1894, his grieving colleague Judge Henry Crease said in formal tribute: "He was one of those great men, raised up by Providence, at a critical period in our history, to break in a new and wild country to order, law and civilization."[10]

In a despatch dated September 2, 1858 (and received by Douglas in November), Lytton advised Douglas that the officer chosen by the War Office to command the Royal Engineers was Colonel Richard Clement Moody. Born of a military family, Moody was a career soldier and a former Governor of the Falkland Islands. Lytton wrote: "Colonel Moody has been appointed to this command, and also has been selected for the office of Chief Commissioner of Lands and Works in British Columbia; and I transmit a copy of the Instructions which have been addressed to Colonel Moody with reference to the discharge of his duties in that capacity."[11]

The list of instructions to Moody was long and comprehensive, and in general summarized policies already outlined by Lytton in earlier despatches to Douglas. It also specified the various works to be undertaken by the Royal Engineers, and it included two important instructions to Colonel Moody, which were destined not to be observed as effectively as Lytton must have hoped. (The Colonial Office had learned too late that Moody had extravagant tastes and lacked caution in handling his accounts.[12])

The first of these instructions concerned expenditures: "You will not forget the caution I have so strenuously impressed on you in our conversations, viz., that it is the duty we owe to the Colony itself to hazard no large outlays and incur no unnecessary expenses until an adequate Revenue be raised and secured." Despite Lytton's concern, so clearly stated, Colonel Moody's grandiose undertakings, impractical expenditures, and erratic accounting were to cause serious problems for Governor Douglas.

The second special instruction focused on Moody's relations with Governor Douglas: "I trust that you will work in perfect harmony with the Governor; and that his experience of the localities, and of the character of the native population, with your own professional science, will combine to expedite the progress and develop the resources of the Colony."

Emphasizing Douglas' "many high qualities which will ensure your esteem, and add to the satisfaction with which you will co-operate with his efforts," Lytton added:

> On this subject I am bound, in justice to both parties, to guard against any risk of misapprehension as to your respective duties and powers. Whilst I feel assured that the Governor will receive with all attention the counsel or suggestions which your military and scientific experience so well fit you to offer, I would be distinctly understood when I say that he is, not merely in a civil point of view, the first magistrate in the State, but I feel it to be essential for the public interests that all powers and responsibilities should centre in him exclusively. Nothing could be more prejudicial to the prosperity of the Colony than a conflict between the principal officers of Government.

It is an interesting comparison that in appointing Begbie, Lytton apparently saw no necessity to emphasize the need for harmonious relations, yet Begbie and the governor achieved excellent rapport from the outset. Between Douglas and Moody, on the other hand, it was not long before serious differences became evident. Though sternly rebuked for the practice both by Douglas and the Colonial Secretary, Moody persisted in using his advantage as Chief Commissioner of Lands and Works to acquire extensive land holdings for himself; this despite clear directives from Douglas (obeyed by other officials) forbidding this practice. At the time that the Royal Engineers were recalled to England, Moody had purchased more than 3,750 acres at an average cost of less than $2 an acre.[13]

The administrative costs which Moody incurred were, in Douglas' opinion, excessive, some of them being "peculiar to the R.E. [Royal Engineers] & of no benefit to the Colony."[14] Douglas also wrote: "The services of the troops are I admit most useful to the Colony; but as the portion of those services devoted to civilian pursuits, really amounts to no more than the service of 80 men for 5 months in the year, I conceive they will be dearly purchased at the cost of [11,000 pounds] per annum."[15] Moody also very early forfeited the friendship of Judge Begbie by disdainfully rejecting, as "the work of an amateur,"[16] one of the field sketches that Begbie had made and submitted for the benefit of others who might travel the same trails.

By their magnificent feats of road and bridge building, and their admirable work in exploration, surveying, town planning, construction, and even printing and publishing (theirs was the first printing press in British Columbia), the Royal Engineers made contributions of incalculable value to the developing colony. Sadly, the friction between Moody and Douglas, and the insupportable drain on revenue, caused Douglas to welcome their recall to England in 1863. Happily, however, most of the non-commissioned officers and sappers of the Columbia Detachment (and also several of the Boundary Commission[17]) accepted the free land grants offered upon their discharge, and, to the lasting benefit of the country, remained to make British Columbia their home.

1. Parliamentary Papers Relating to British Columbia. Despatch, No. 22 (16), pp. 61-62, Sir E.B. Lytton to Governor Douglas, September 2, 1858.
2. David Ricardo Williams, *The Man for a New Country: Sir Matthew Baillie Begbie* (Sydney, BC: Gray's, 1977), 19.
3. Ibid., 30.
4. Parliamentary Papers Relating to British Columbia. Despatch, No. 27 (29), p. 67, Sir E.B. Lytton to Governor Douglas, October 11, 1858.
5. Williams, *The Man for a New Country*, 48.
6. Ibid., 47.
7. Ibid.
8. Ibid., 119.
9. Parliamentary Papers Relating to British Columbia. Despatch, No. 16 (7), pp. 52-53, Sir E.B. Lytton to Governor Douglas, September 2, 1858.
10. Williams, *The Man for a New Country*, 273.
11. Parliamentary Papers Relating to British Columbia. Despatch, No. 16 (7), pp. 52-53, Sir E.B. Lytton to Governor Douglas, September 2, 1858.
12. Margaret A. Ormsby, *British Columbia: A History* (Toronto: MacMillans in Canada, 1958), 172.
13. Beth Hill, *Sappers: The Royal Engineers in British Columbia* (Ganges, BC: Horsdal and Schubert, 1987), 126.
14. Governor Douglas to H.P.C. Newcastle, August 2, 1862, quoted in Ormsby, *British Columbia*, 193.
15. Governor Douglas to H.P.C. Newcastle, May 13, 1862, quoted in Ibid., 192.
16. Williams, *The Man for a New Country*, 54.
17. Hill, *Sappers*, 123.

NEW BRITISH GOLD FIELDS.

A GUIDE

TO

BRITISH COLUMBIA

AND

VANCOUVER ISLAND,

WITH COLOURED MAP,

SHOWING

THE GOLD AND COAL FIELDS,

CONSTRUCTED FROM AUTHENTIC SOURCES.

BY

JOHN DOMER, F.R.G.S.

LONDON:

WILLIAM HENRY ANGEL, 11, LOVELL'S COURT,

PATERNOSTER ROW;

Domer's 52-page hand-book appeared in London, summer 1858.

PRICE ONE DOLLAR AND FIFTY CENTS.

HAND-BOOK

AND

MAP

TO

THE GOLD REGION

OF

Frazer's and Thompson's Rivers,

WITH

TABLE OF DISTANCES.

By ALEXANDER C. ANDERSON,

Late Chief Trader Hudson Bay Co's Service.

TO WHICH IS APPENDED

CHINOOK JARGON—LANGUAGE USED

Etc., Etc.

PUBLISHED BY J. J. LE COUNT,

SAN FRANCISCO.

Entered according to Act of Congress, in the year 1858, by Alexander C. Anderson, in the Clerk's Office of the District Court of the Northern District of California.

Anderson's useful 31-page guidebook was published in San Francisco sometime after May 1858.

23
THE FIRST TOWNSHIPS

B Y SEPTEMBER, ON HIS second trip to the mines, Douglas had been able to convey important information to the mining population concerning prospects for settlement in the country. Earlier, in June, he had written to Lord Stanley regarding the richness and extent of the gold fields, and had raised the question of government policy that might be deemed advisable in the circumstances:

> My own opinion is that the stream of immigration is setting in so powerfully towards Fraser's River that it is impossible to arrest its course, and that the population thus formed will occupy the land as squatters, if they cannot obtain a title by legal means. I think it therefore a measure of obvious necessity that the whole country be immediately thrown open for settlement, and that the land be surveyed, and sold at a fixed rate not to exceed twenty shillings an acre. By that means, together with the imposition of a Customs duty on imports, a duty on licence to miners, and other taxes, a large revenue might be collected for the service of Government.
>
> Either that plan, or some other better calculated to maintain the rights of the Crown and the authority of the laws, should, in my opinion, be adopted with as little delay as possible, otherwise the country will be filled with lawless crowds, the public lands unlawfully occupied by squatters of every description, and the authority of Government will ultimately be set at naught.[1]

The British government's response was sent by Sir E.B. Lytton in his July 1 despatch, and received by Douglas early in September. Consequently, at the public meeting at Fort Yale on September 12, Douglas addressed the local inhabitants about this matter. First extending his government's welcome to people of every nationality, he then assured the miners that all might dig for gold, and that all would be protected by British law, as long as they would "obey those laws and pay the Queen's dues like honest men"; and he went on:

Now for a word about the country. Colonies cannot be established without the consent of Parliament . . . but we learn by last accounts from England that the subject was before Parliament, and, as public opinion is strongly in favour of colonizing the country, there is little doubt that the measure will pass. In the meantime what is to be done? Many of you, I know, wish to settle in the country, and wish to build and to make yourselves comfortable before the winter sets in. I have therefore adopted a plan which will meet the prospective views of Government, and your wants at the same time, by giving you the necessary amount of protection.

I have decided, entirely on my own responsibility, to give you the only title that can be granted for land at present.

I have given orders to Mr. Hicks, the Commissioner for Crown Lands, to have a townsite surveyed here, and to dispose of building lots to any person wishing to hold them under lease, with a pre-emption right when the land is sold by the Crown. This will give confidence and security to everyone.

In the same manner I have given Mr. Hicks instructions to lay out the farming lands near the town in convenient lots of 20 acres and to make grants of them under the same tenure.

I have also given him instructions to permit the building of sawmills, to establish ferries, to open roads, and generally to carry out the views of Government in the manner best calculated to give development to the resources of this glorious country. [It was not until later that "Mr. Hicks" was to be found less than reliable in following these instructions.]

I have now said all that relates to your individual interests, and have further to assure you that the laws will be administered with justice and impartiality; and I have to exhort you all to aid and support the civil officers in the discharge of their duties.

Every wise man and every good man knows the value of good laws, and every man who expects to receive their protection when he himself gets into trouble must be ready at all times to come out manfully in support of those laws.

Let all do so, and there will not be a better or more quiet community in any part of Her Majesty's dominions than will be found at Yale.

On our way up the river we stopped at nearly all the mining bars, and found the people healthy, happy, and prosperous, and I am proud to say what is much more to their honour, I found among the miners a degree of probity, of good order—aye, and intelligence, that I was not prepared to expect.

Gentlemen, I have now done and I have only further to wish you all well.[2]

Subsequent to this announcement, Douglas, in a despatch to Lytton dated October 11, wrote:

> The disposal of public lands and also of town lots, as suggested in your Despatch, will, I think, prove a prolific source of revenue, besides having the effect of opening the country for permanent settlement. In my late excursion to Fraser's River, of which I will soon forward an account, the most urgent appeals were made to me by intending settlers, on the prospect of approaching winter, for the purchase of town lots at Fort Yale and Fort Hope; but having no legal authority to make sales of land, or to grant sufficient titles, I could only meet their wishes by giving leases of the desired lots, at a monthly rent of 41 shillings, to be continued, with a pre-emption right to the holder, until the land is finally sold.
>
> Since the arrival of your Despatch, I have sent Mr. Pemberton, the Surveyor General, to lay out three several town sites on Fraser's River, namely, at Old Fort Langley, Fort Hope, Fort Yale, there being a demand at each of these places for town lots, in consequence of their position at important trading points of the river, which gives them a peculiar value in the estimation of the public.
>
> The surveyor has advertised a public sale at this place of town lots 64 x 120 feet in extent, at old Fort Langley, for the 20th of this month, October, the upset price to be 100 dollars for each lot of that size, and not to be sold for less than the upset price. Though this is not a propitious time for the disposal of town lots, it is expected that the Government will realize a considerable sum from that sale.[3]

Later, the new town of Port Douglas was similarly established.

------

1. Parliamentary Papers Relating to British Columbia. Despatch, No. 2 (24), p. 14, items 20-23, Governor Douglas to Lord Stanley, June 10, 1858.
2. "Address of His Excellency the Governor to the Inhabitants at Fort Yale, September 12th, 1858," in Frederic W. Howay, *The Early History of the Fraser River Mines* (Victoria: Archives of British Columbia, 1926), 1-3.
3. Parliamentary Papers Relating to British Columbia. Despatch, No. 11 (39) p. 38, items 8-10, Governor Douglas to Sir E.B. Lytton, October 11, 1858.

Police Inspector Chartres Brew led an eventful, adventure-filled life. He was decorated for bravery in the Crimean War, served in the Royal Irish Constabulary and as a Police Inspector in Cork, survived the burning of the *Austria* en route to North America, and policed the widespread mining communities of British Columbia. *Provincial Archives of British Columbia, Victoria.*

24
THE TRAGEDY OF
THE STEAMER *AUSTRIA*

IN ADDITION TO HIS APPOINTMENT of Begbie as Judge, Lytton suggested in his September 2 despatch to Douglas: "It would seem desirable to appoint, if you have not already done so, Gold Commissioners armed with the power of magistrates. I submit this suggestion to your local experience, and I feel it must be unnecessary to add the self-evident caution, to form at once a Police at the diggings."[1] In other letters, also, Lytton expressed to Douglas his view that a well trained police force was essential to the development of a stable society.

Contrary to Douglas' stated view—that a military force was needed to maintain law and order—Lytton's advice based upon his extensive experience in colonial administration and on his study of the reports of colonial officers in the Australian gold fields was that:

> Military force should be considered primarily as intended for the purpose of resisting foreign aggression. Its employment in the internal control of the community must be regarded as strictly subsidiary to the ordinary means of enforcing obedience to the orders of the civil power.
>
> On the other hand, nothing is so important to the peace and progress of the Colony as a well organized and effective Police; and I find that a Police is always feeble in Colonies that have been accustomed in every disturbance to rely upon soldiers. It is by the establishment of this Civil Constabulary, with a sufficient staff of Stipendiary Magistrates, that I would wish the Colonists to co-operate with the Government in the requisite protection of life and property.
>
> Hence I have sent to you the most experienced and trustworthy person I could select among the Irish Constabulary (a body of men peculiarly distinguished for efficiency) to serve as Inspector of Police, and to carry out your Instructions for the formation of a civil force of that character.[2]

Lytton was here referring to an admirable Irishman named Chartres Brew, decorated hero of the Crimean War, veteran of the Royal Irish Constabulary, and lately Police Inspector in the City of Cork. Chartres Brew was—as may be read on his tombstone—*A man imperturbable in courage and temper, endowed with a great and varied administrative capacity, a most ready wit, a most pure integrity and a most humane heart.* In the years that passed between Lytton's words of praise and those on Brew's tombstone (written by his friend, Judge Begbie) many were to speak warmly of Chartres Brew.

Brew was about forty-three years old when, on an early autumn day in 1858, he boarded the ship *Austria* for the long journey to Vancouver Island; and of all the personnel who sailed at about that same time bound for British Columbia, none other could have experienced a more eventful voyage. Eight days out of Southampton, the *Austria* (from Hamburg), was destroyed by fire, and Brew was among a pitifully few survivors fighting for their lives in the cold Atlantic.

After five hours in the water, Brew was rescued along with other survivors by the French bark *Maurice*, bound from Newfoundland. Later, the *Maurice* fell in with the bark *Lotus*, bound from Liverpool to Halifax, and Brew, being "anxious to get on British territory," was among a dozen survivors taken aboard the *Lotus* for Halifax, while the majority of the survivors, bound for New York, remained aboard the *Maurice*.

When the *Lotus* arrived at Halifax, an agent of the Associated Press boarded her and interviewed Inspector Brew and others. His report subsequently was published in the *New York Herald* [3] of September 20. As for those survivors who had proceeded to New York, an account of their experiences published in the *New York Times* [4] agreed substantially with that given by Brew in Halifax.

Brew related how, at about two o'clock in the afternoon while walking on the quarter deck, he saw dense smoke burst from the aft entrance of the steerage, while some women ran aft screaming that the ship was on fire. Shortly thereafter the magazine exploded, and Brew inferred "the engineers were instantly suffocated." Flames then broke through the lights amidships, and "as the ship was head to the wind, the fire travelled with fearful rapidity." Brew ordered the man at the wheel to put the vessel with her side to the wind, but the man, being German, did not understand him. Brew found a German gentleman to speak to him. He then noticed some passengers trying to let down a lifeboat:

What became of the boat I don't know, but think she was crushed under the screw. I then went to let a boat over from the starboard side of the quarter-deck, but the moment we laid our hands on the rope there were so many people who crowded into it that we could not lift it off the blocks. We therefore left it for a few minutes until the people got out, when we returned and launched it over the side of the ship, when, the people all rushing into it again, it descended with great violence into the water, and was instantly swamped, all the people being washed out excepting three, who held on to the sides. We then let down a rope and pulled up one person, who proved to be the steward. Another, in the act of being hauled up, was strangled by the rope.

By now most of the passengers were on the poop deck, except for a few first cabin passengers who must have been smothered in the smoking room, and a number of second cabin passengers who were trapped in their quarters. A few were pulled up through the ventilator, but most could not be; the last woman so rescued said six people already had suffocated.

Head to the wind, flames coming over the quarter-deck, the ship plowed on. Trying to fight his way through the crowd to the wheelhouse, Brew was told that the helmsman had deserted his post, leaving the vessel out of control. Brew described the scene on the quarter-deck at this time as

truly heartrending. Passengers were rushing frantically to and fro, husbands seeking their wives, wives in search of their husbands, relatives looking after relatives, mothers lamenting the loss of their children, some wholly paralyzed by fear, others madly crying to be saved, but a few perfectly calm and collected. The flames pressed so closely upon them that many jumped into the sea.

By now Brew was leaning out from the ship to avoid the flames. Standing outside the bulwarks and holding on by the davits, he saw beneath him a swamped boat spinning by a rope attached to the ship with the oars still tied to it:

I thought that if I could get to her I would be enabled to save myself and others. I let myself down by a rope, passing over a man who was clinging to it, but who refused to come with me. I took out a penknife and cut the tackle; the large blade broke, and I then severed it with the small blade. The ship passed ahead. As the screw approached I found the boat drawn towards it. I tried to keep the boat off, but the screw caught and capsized the boat over me. I dived away from the ship and came to the surface near a boat which was keel upwards; I got on her, and by pressing on one side, with the assistance of a wave, she righted but was still swamped. The oars had been knocked out by the screw;

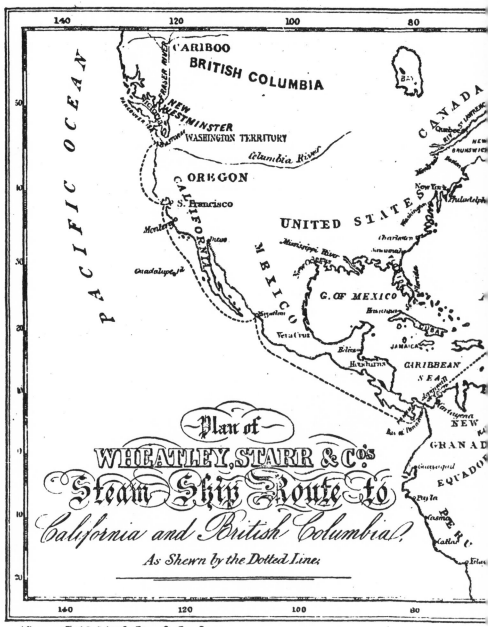

Map, from the *Guide Book for British Columbia, &c., by a Successful Digger* . . . (London, 1862).

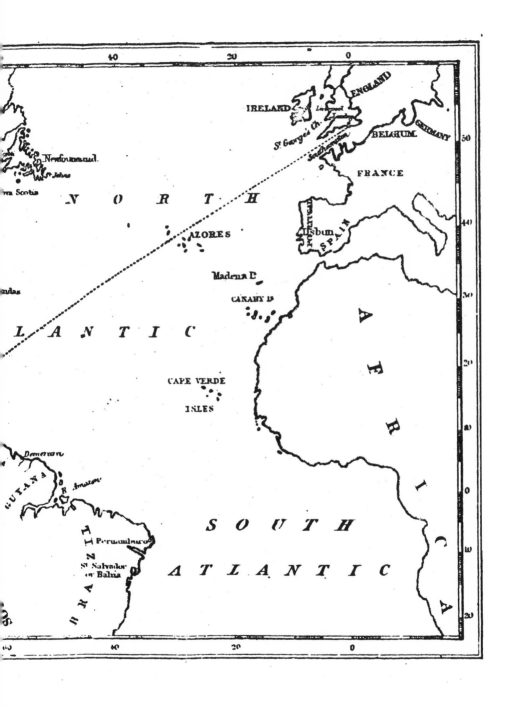

the only thing I could find in her to paddle with was some lathe nailed together as sheathing for the sides.

When I looked around the ship was a quarter of a mile away from me. I could see the ladies and gentlemen jumping off the poop into the water, in twos and threes, some of the ladies in flames. Several hesitated to jump from the burning ship until the last moment, as the height was 22 feet, and were only at length compelled to throw themselves off to avoid a more painful death. In half an hour not a soul was to be seen on the poop.

Brew came alongside a German who was swimming strongly and managed to pull him into the boat. On the horizon now appeared a ship—too far, until much later, to hear cries for help; too late, in arriving, to save more than a few lives. This vessel, the *Maurice*, reached the *Austria* at about five p.m. At about half past seven, Brew, having been five hours in the water, was within hailing distance of the *Maurice*, which had up to that time already rescued forty passengers from the burning ship. Later, about eight o'clock, one of the lifeboats with about 23 survivors came up; and three or four men, floating on a piece of wreckage, were also rescued. Brew added:

> The second officer was taken up, having been swimming with nothing to float him for six hours. The second and third officers were severely burnt; one male passenger was burnt frightfully . . . There were but six women saved, three of whom were burnt, one in a shocking manner.
>
> Captain Renaud acted with the utmost kindness. He gave clothes as far as he could furnish them to the suffering passengers, and acted as nurse, doctor and surgeon to the burnt people, dressing the wounds of the females with a delicacy and tenderness that evinced a benevolent and amiable disposition.

The *Maurice* searched throughout the night without success for a lifeboat that had drifted out of sight. With morning light, she returned to the smouldering *Austria*, but found no more survivors—only two corpses hanging to the ship by ropes. Of 560 passengers, most had perished. Only 68 were rescued—many of these had lost their loved ones, and all, of course, had lost their possessions.

Those survivors who were interviewed by the press were consistent in their opinion that the German officers and crew of the *Austria* had been negligent, deficient in basic emergency training, undisciplined, and lacking in humane responsibility for their passengers. The ship had lacked sufficient life preservers and lifeboats—of eight lifeboats on board, four were of wood and burned before they could be used.

The fire had started from an attempt to fumigate the steerage with smoke. A chain was to be heated and one end dipped in tar to produce smoke. However, the other end of the chain became too hot to hold and was dropped upon the deck which caught fire. The tar was upset and the flames that sprang up could not be extinguished, there being nothing at hand to meet such an emergency. The captain and crew were the first to make for the lifeboats to save themselves. Brew stated:

> I did not see an officer of the ship during the fire and am certain there was not one of them or the crew on the poop, except a man at the wheel for a short time. I understood that when the captain heard of the fire he rushed on deck without a cap, and when he saw the flames exclaimed, "We are all lost!." He tried to get out a boat, which, when let down, was swamped, and he fell into the sea and was soon left far behind. The fourth officer was in this boat. He cut loose from the davits; she was carried under the screw and smashed, and several in her drowned . . . About the same time one metallic lifeboat was let down from the port bow and swamped, but got cleared away with about 33 persons in her, including the first and third officers and several women.

Much later, this boat was one of those that managed to reach the rescue ship, *Maurice*, but not before it had capsized two or three times and several people had been lost. The boat did, however, pick up two or three others.

Resuming his journey from Halifax to British Columbia, Brew at last reached Victoria on November 8, and his first written report to Governor Douglas on November 11 told of his adventure:

> Sir,—I have the honor to inform your Excellency that, having been appointed Head of the Police Department in British Columbia by the Right Honourable Sir E.B. Lytton, Bart., Secretary of State for the British Colonies, I embarked on the 4th of September last at Southampton in the steamship "Austria" for New York to proceed across the Isthmus of Panama to Victoria. I arrived here on the 8th inst., on which day I had the honor of presenting myself to your Excellency . . .
>
> The steamer in which I left Southampton was burned at sea on the 13th of September, 4 days' sail from New York. By this disaster I lost all my property, all my money, and all my papers—amongst the last a despatch from the Colonial Office addressed to your Excellency. I escaped from the burning ship with nothing but the clothes on my person, and these were torn to shreds in my struggles to save myself. I was rescued by a French ship and on the following day got on board a vessel bound for Halifax, N.S., at which port we landed on the 27th of September.

In the absence of the Governor the Executive Council in Halifax advanced me [100 pounds], for which sum I gave my acknowledgment. This seasonable loan enabled me to start immediately for my destination, and notwithstanding the misfortune with which I met, and that after my escape I was 14 days in a sailing-ship and was taken out of my way to Halifax, I arrived here only 10 days later than the party of the Royal Engineers which sailed from England on the 2nd of September, two days before I left . . .[5]

1. Parliamentary Papers Relating to British Columbia. Despatch, No. 24, p. 65, Sir E.B. Lytton to Governor Douglas, September 2, 1858.
2. Ibid. No. 30 (30), p. 70, item 6, Sir E.B. Lytton to Governor Douglas, October 16, 1858.
3. *New York Herald*, September 28, 1858; reprinted in *The Times* (London), October 11, 1858.
4. *New York Times*, September 30, 1858; reprinted in *The Times* (London), October 14, 1858.
5. Correspondence, Chartres Brew to Governor Douglas, November 11, 1858, in Frederic W. Howay, *The Early History of the Fraser River Mines* (Victoria: Archives of British Columbia, 1926), 60-61.

25
THE POLICE FORCE THAT NEVER WAS

IF INSPECTOR BREW'S VOYAGE to British Columbia was a test of his endurance, so also, perhaps, were his initial experiences in the colony. His agreed salary of 500 pounds—seemingly generous enough in Britain—was quite inadequate in the colony where, as he promptly discovered, all costs were very much higher and any request of his for extra allowances or for reimbursements was to be refused. He was to be frustrated, too, in his reasonable expectation of being allowed to assume the duties for which he had been appointed—for, like Richard Blanshard, the first Governor of Vancouver Island, Brew had the misfortune of receiving an appointment which did not have Douglas' support. Governor Douglas, apparently content for the present to maintain order with the assistance of military sappers and naval marines, remained unconvinced of the necessity for a civil police force such as that mandated by Lytton.[1]

Immediately after his November 8 arrival in Victoria, Brew visited Fort Langley and Fort Yale, to observe the mining operations and to estimate policing requirements. Douglas, however, apparently found little time to respond to Brew's subsequent reports and recommendations, or to instruct him regarding his duties. Finally, on December 11, more than a month after his arrival, Brew wrote to Douglas:

> Sir,—I have the honor to state that, having been informed that the steamer "Beaver" will proceed on this day to British Columbia, I have to request Your Excellency's permission to proceed in her to Langley and there await until I shall receive Your Excellency's orders to commence the duties of my office.
>
> I beg leave to take the liberty of saying that if it be expected to have a Police Force in some working order next spring, when a great influx of people into British Columbia is anticipated, no time ought to be lost in commencing to erect barracks and in taking measures to provide clothes, arms, and accoutrements for the men.

If Your Excellency conceive that the strength of the Force I propose to raise is too great at present, one-half, a third, or a fourth of the
officers and men might be embodied in the first instance, and afterwards, if circumstances required, the number might be increased to
any extent.

I have the honor to be, Sir, Your Excellency's obedient servant.
(signed) C. Brew, *Chief Inspector of Police, British Columbia.*[2]

To Brew's initial request for a force of 150 men from the Irish Constabulary, Douglas withheld his consent, considering that the expense would
be too great and that a force of only 60 men would suffice. Apparently he
thought better of this when, just a few weeks later, the Whannell-Hicks
"crisis" at Fort Yale necessitated the mid-winter expedition under Brew's
command. Subsequently, Douglas did support Brew's request for 150 men
of the Irish Constabulary—but to no avail, since the British Government
now insisted that the cost be borne by the colony, out of its own revenue.
The assumption in London was that a colony so rich in gold could support
the expense; the fact was that to collect revenues in taxes and mining fees,
without the necessary numbers of enforcing officers, was usually difficult
and often impossible. Obtainable revenues could support no more than a
few constables, even if suitable candidates could be found.

Fortunately, Brew responded to his disappointed expectations by com-
municating with friends and colleagues in Ireland and, on his own initiative, attracting to the service several fine young men. It was the custom in
Victorian Britain for young men of good families and education to seek
careers in the colonies—and some were eager enough to pay their own
way. The prospect of a long sea voyage to an unknown land, where adventure, challenge, and opportunity awaited, was irresistible to just such young
men as were most needed in the new colony.

Typical of Brew's initiatives was a letter he wrote to Governor Douglas, dated December 29, 1858:

Sir,—I have the honor to inform Your Excellency that the bearer of
this communication, Mr. John Carmichael Haynes, a young gentleman from Ireland, arrived in Victoria on the 25th inst. and applied to
me for an appointment in the Police Force which he believed was
being organized in British Columbia.

I beg leave to submit to Your Excellency a strong testimonial
which he produced to me signed by the Mayor and Magistrates of
Cork, and I also beg leave to send attached two letters to me in his
behalf from two gentlemen of my acquaintance who are Magistrates
for the County and City of Cork.

I have the honor to be, Sir, Your Excellency's obedient servant,
(signed) C. Brew, *Chief Inspector of Police, British Columbia.*[3]

Haynes was but one of several Irishmen, and Englishmen, who arrived under similar circumstances (some bearing introductory letters from Lytton) and who served in various official capacities with notable ability and good humour—and with, at times, an unorthodoxy happily appropriate to immediate circumstances. Their character, resourcefulness, and stamina were equal to the multiple demands made of them in the understaffed new colony. It was on these men (many of whom went on to achieve long and distinguished careers in the public service) that Governor Douglas came to rely to keep peace and order as Gold Commissioners and Magistrates in the mining communities, and this they did, winning the respect and cooperation of the general population.

Brew's sister, Jane, came out from Ireland to keep house for Chartres—but not for long, for soon she met and married a handsome Irishman, Augustus F. Pemberton, Magistrate and Commissioner of Police at Vancouver Island. Augustus had been appointed by Douglas at the start of the gold rush to keep order among Victoria's inflated population. He was the youngest son of Joseph Pemberton, a former Lord Mayor of Dublin, and also was related to Joseph Despard Pemberton, Vancouver Island's Surveyor-General. Tomkins Brew, Chartres' brother, also came to British Columbia. He became a Revenue Officer and Constable of Burrard Inlet.

For several months, Brew continued attempting to communicate with Douglas in order to clarify his status in the colony. Douglas' terse responses came via his Colonial Secretary, William A.G. Young, to whom therefore Brew necessarily addressed his queries:

> *[April 10, 1859, Brew to Young, from Fort Yale]* Sir,—With reference to your letter of the 2nd Inst., stating that you were desired by His Excellency the Governor of British Columbia to acquaint me that I am to act as Collector or Sub-Treasurer in my District, I have the honor to state that as my appointment as Chief Inspector of Police was for the whole of British Columbia, and as the appointment which His Excellency did me the honor of conferring on me was Chief Gold Commissioner for British Columbia, and as I was under the impression that the Assist. Commissioner's duties at Fort Yale were only temporarily to be carried on under my superintendence until an Assist. Commissioner should be appointed, I do not know what the limits of my District are, unless I am to assume that it is intended that the range of my duties is not to extend beyond the District of Fort Yale . . .

[Answer—Douglas' response to Young] The duties alluded to were not inforced with reference to either of the appointments held, but were allotted to him [Brew] for the time being as the principal and most responsible public officer at Yale, and these particular duties are confined to the Yale District.

[April 11, 1859, Brew to Young] Sir,—As a step towards entering upon the task to accomplish which I was appointed to the office of Chief Inspector of Police for the Colony of British Columbia—the organization of a uniform system of police in the Colony—I have the honor to request that His Excellency the Governor will be pleased to permit me to take under my exclusive management and control the whole Body of Constables at present in the Colony. This step appears to be the more necessary as it is now determined that the financial arrangements of the several departments are to be conducted distinctly of each other with the Colonial Treasurer by the head of each department.

I am satisfied that the superintendence of the colonial police and the conducting of the financial branch of the department will occupy my time to an extent that will render it impracticable for me to hold with advantage to the public service the supervision of another department.

If His Excellency be pleased to allow me to assume this charge, I have to beg His Excellency's orders to proceed without delay to the seat of Government [Victoria] to prepare and submit for His Excellency's consideration a plan for conducting the police duties of the Colony, and to enable me to confer with the Colonial Treasurer respecting the system of police accounts which should be established.

[Answer—Douglas' response to Young] The Police Force of British Col. is now under Mr. Brew's superintendence. It is not proposed to increase that force on account of the great expense to which it puts the country, and for the reason that the Royal Marines now serving in British Columbia may in emergencies be employed as a Police force.

[April 16, 1859, Brew to Young] Sir,—I have the honor to state that I have been called upon by the Colonial Treasurer to furnish returns showing the probable income and expenditure of the Gold and Police Department from the 1st of April to the 31st December, 1859.

As I am at present advised, any estimate of probable expenses I could give would be merely a wild guess, for I do not know what staff His Excellency the Governor will appoint to the Gold Department, and I am not informed of what determination has been arrived at with regard to the formation of a police. I have never taken charge of the constables at present under pay in the Colony; they are under the control of the Magistrate of the districts in which they are stationed.

I beg leave to ask His Excellency's orders for me to proceed to Victoria for a few days, as I have to request the honor of being permitted to have an interview with His Excellency on these matters, and I should be most anxious to have an opportunity of consulting with the Colonial Treasurer.

I shall arrange to have all the duties here carried on during my absence just as well as if I were present . . .

[April 23, 1859, Brew to Young, while submitting two letters received by him from Assist. Commissioner Travaillot, indicating need for law enforcement at Lytton]. . . As I have not been placed in charge of the Body of police Constables in the Colony, I presume I have nothing to do with the appointment of any Constables in the Lytton District . . . *[and in a separate letter of the same date Brew offered his polite resignation of his apparently powerless position as Chief Gold Commissioner]*

[Answer—Douglas' response to Young] Let instructions be forwarded to Mr. Brew, directing him to take charge of the police constables in the Colony and to make such distribution thereof as may be requisite for the public safety and convenience.[4]

Thus, nearly six months after Brew's arrival, did Douglas finally acknowledge him as head of British Columbia's police force—while still denying him the courtesy of any written or personal contact. (In contrast, Brew became one of Begbie's group of good friends and card-playing companions; and it is Begbie's heart-felt tribute that graces Brew's gravestone.)

Though Vancouver Island continued to have its own police force under Commissioner Pemberton (appointed by Douglas in 1858), Brew's continuing efforts to have a police corps organized for the mainland colony met with no success—the very few constables permitted to be employed were selected by the magistrates of the various gold districts. Though his "police force" was virtually non-existent, Brew was to prove himself to be a capable, reliable, and universally respected choice to fill any official vacancy—Chief Magistrate of New Westminster, Chief Gold Commissioner, Justice of the Peace, County Court Judge, and, as needed, various important positions in an "acting" capacity. In 1864 he was to become a member of British Columbia's first Legislative Assembly. It was not until the spring of 1864 that the then Governor, Frederick Seymour, concerned about native peace-keeping, formed a centralized police under his own control.

It is interesting to note that in later years the famous British Columbia Provincial Police—romantically renowned for their dedication to duty and for their many courageous exploits in policing the wild outer regions of the province—still claimed the name of Chartres Brew and the year 1858 for the founding of their force.[5] This tradition has been upheld even since 1950 when the "B.C. Police" was absorbed into the Royal Canadian Mounted Police.

A few months after Brew's appointment as Chief Gold Commissioner, eighty miners at Hill's Bar (who heretofore had suffered from the administrative deficiencies of George Perrier and Richard Hicks) wrote to him, in grateful tribute:

> Your discriminating judgment and practical sagacity have been evinced in many exciting questions wherein the rights of miners have conflicted. In their settlement, honesty and common sense were the predominant characteristics of your decisions, and for them, sir, we desire to thank you. The habits and customs of immigrants to new countries—particularly gold-bearing countries—are so diversified, that it is indeed one of the most difficult things for those in power to mete out justice for all, and not to incur the enmity of some. To do so is the act of no ordinary mind, and evinces an intimate knowledge of human nature. You have done the first, sir, and not only avoided the latter, but have retained the kind feelings and respect of all.[6]

Some years later, Governor Frederick Seymour, who had joined in Brew's expedition during the Chilcotin Indian war of 1864, wrote: "I shall always look back with satisfaction to the time when I had the honor to serve under him as one of the New Westminster Volunteers."[7] In all his years of service to men who sought for gold, such tributes, from the humble and the mighty, and the respect and affection which prompted them, were the only wealth that Chartres Brew ever accumulated.

---

1. Parliamentary Papers Relating to British Columbia. Despatch, No. 11 (39), p. 39, Governor Douglas to Sir E.B. Lytton, September 9, 1858.
2. Correspondence, Inspector Brew to Governor Douglas, December 11, 1858, in Frederic W. Howay, *The Early History of the Fraser River Mines* (Victoria: Archives of British Columbia, 1926), 61-62.
3. Ibid., pp. 62-63, Inspector Brew to Governor Douglas, December 29, 1858.
4. Ibid., pp. 105-7, 115, various correspondence.
5. See, Royal Canadian Mounted Police Veterans' Association, *92 Years of Pride, 1858-1950: The British Columbia Provincial Police* (Kelowna, BC: Royal Canadian Mounted Police Veterans' Association, 1983).
6. C. Brew correspondence; G.B. Colonial Office, despatches to B.C., no. 11, 2 Sept. 1859, enclosure, C. Brew, testimonials. See also University of Toronto, *Dictionary of Canadian Biography*, vol. 9 (Toronto: University of Toronto Press, 1976), 81-82.
7. From Parliamentary Papers, letter, Seymour to Cardwell, September 9, 1864, quoted in Margaret A. Ormsby, *British Columbia: A History* (Toronto: MacMillans in Canada, 1958), 207.

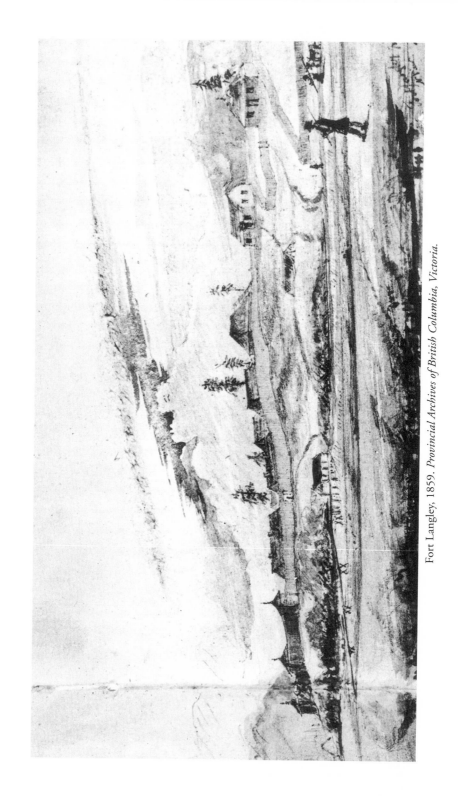

Fort Langley, 1859. *Provincial Archives of British Columbia, Victoria.*

26
CEREMONY, CELEBRATION, AND YEAR'S END

T HE DOCUMENTS PERTAINING to the establishment of the new colony and the appointments of Governor Douglas and Judge Begbie, having been signed by Queen Victoria, were delivered by Sir E.B. Lytton personally on board ship on the day of the departure from England of Judge Begbie. Arriving at Esquimalt on November 16, 1858, Begbie proceeded to Victoria, and thence to the mainland for the swearing-in ceremonies, which were to be held with appropriate pomp (supported by the newly arrived Royal Engineers) at Fort Langley. This was Douglas' third trip to the Fraser River in 1858. The historic occasion was reported in the following day's issue of the *Victoria Gazette:*

> On Friday, the 19th inst., His Excellency, accompanied by his suite, and received by a guard of honour commanded by Captain Grant, disembarked on the wet, loamy bank under the Fort, and the procession proceeded up the steep bank which leads to the palisade. Arrived there, a salute of eighteen guns commenced pealing from the *Beaver*, awakening all the echoes of the opposite mountains. In another moment the flag of Britain was floating, or to speak the truth, dripping over the principal entrance. Owing to the unpropitious state of the weather, the meeting, which was intended to have been held in the open air, was convened in the large room at the principal building. About 100 persons were present.[1]

Included in the momentous gathering were Rear-Admiral Baynes, Chief Justice Cameron of Vancouver Island, captains Grant and Parsons of the Royal Engineers together with some troops, Police Inspector Chartres Brew, and numerous other government officials.

Also among those present, inconspicuous among the throng, was Murray Yale, the small but lion-hearted man, who in the service of the Hudson's Bay Company had overseen the development of old Fort

Langley—struggling in the early days to protect it from hostile Indians; rebuilding it after destruction by fire in 1840; and developing its farms, fisheries, and cooperage, whereby the export of produce and dried salmon had brought profits to the company. For Murray Yale, the end had begun when, in the spring of this year, the first hordes of gold miners had swarmed into Fort Langley and throughout the land. Today's ceremonies marked an end for him, the company, and the place which had been his life for thirty years.[2] The *Victoria Gazette* report continued:

> The ceremonies were commenced by His Excellency addressing Mr. Begbie, and delivering to him Her Majesty's commission as Judge in the Colony of British Columbia. Mr. Begbie then took the oath of allegiance, and the usual oaths on taking office, and then, addressing his Excellency, took up Her Majesty's commission appointing the Governor, and proceeded to read it at length. Mr. Begbie then administered to Governor Douglas the usual oaths of office—viz., allegiance, abjurations, etc. His Excellency being thus duly appointed and sworn in, proceeded to issue the Proclamations of the same date (19th instant)—viz., one proclaiming the Act; a second indemnifying all the officers of the Government from any irregularities which may have been committed in the interval before the proclamation of the Act; and a third proclaiming English law to be the law of the Colony. The reading of these was preceded by His Excellency's Proclamation of the 3rd inst., setting forth the revocation by Her Majesty of all the exclusive privileges of the Hudson's Bay Company. The proceedings then terminated.
>
> On leaving the Fort, which His Excellency did not finally do until today, another salute of seventeen guns was fired from the battlements, with even grander effect than the salute of the previous day.
>
> On leaving the river-side in front of the town, a number of the inhabitants were assembled with whom His Excellency entered into conversation previous to embarking on board the *Beaver*, and by whom he was loudly cheered in very good style as he was on his way to the steamer.[3]

Thus, on November 19, 1858, was the Colony of British Columbia officially established. This day was the beginning. Soon new roads would be built—first to the gold mines, and then to open up this new country to profitable enterprise of all kinds and to the development of new communities.

On this bleak November day, however, Governor Douglas and his party probably were content to board ship and depart for the established comforts of Victoria. In fact, Victoria was to remain the effective seat of government, and the chosen place of residence for most of the chief officials. The city had the advantage not only of close proximity to the important harbour and naval base at Esquimalt, but also it had the well established, comfortable homes of the few prominent families and a convivial social life, which was much enhanced by Douglas' own hospitable house and by the presence of his five pretty daughters and son James William.[4] Despite New Westminster's early status as the capital (until 1868), Victoria was destined to become the capital of British Columbia.

Reporting on the Fort Langley events in a despatch to Lytton, Douglas concluded: "I returned to this place (Victoria) on the 21st instant, and Rear-Admiral Baynes and all the other Gentlemen who accompanied me to Fort Langley except Captains Grant and Parsons, who were left with the Royal Engineers at old Fort Langley."[5]

It was not until Christmas Day that Colonel and Mrs. Moody, and their four children, arrived with their entourage in Victoria. As Douglas reported in a December 27 letter to London:

> Colonel Moody and party arrived here on the 25th, not in time, I regret to say, to take part in our Christmas festivities, which would have been all the gayer for his presence. Our quarters are rather crowded at this moment, in consequence of so many official arrivals, and the want of official residences, but we have contrived through the kindness of friends to procure temporary house accommodation for the whole party.[6]

For those advance personnel newly arrived from England, what a joy it must have been for them after a long sea voyage, just to be arrived on land, enjoying the season's good cheer among new friends and colleagues, and contemplating, with them, prospects of new homes and an adventurous future. Even the weather smiled for this season, for, in Douglas' words: "The opposite hills still retain their hue of green; a single Castile rose, somewhat faded, was picked yesterday, and the humble Daisy-heart's Ease, and wall flower, growing exposed in my garden, have not yet entirely lost their bloom."[7]

The words seem to reflect a tranquil mood, as Douglas perhaps contemplated the year that was ending. Since early spring, extraordinary events had demanded all of his time, energies, and abilities, but at last help had arrived and, as he now knew, more was on the way. For many years past he had celebrated Christmas as chief of the Hudson's Bay Company's vast western territory and as governor of the few colonists on Vancouver Island.

He had not welcomed the gold rush, and surely could not have wished for its great success, knowing as he did that it would mean the end, in that region, of the fur-trading company to whose services he had been committed since boyhood. But, faced with the fact, he had done his best, and now by an unexpected quirk of fortune he might even be said to be among those who had "struck it rich." Now, his company days ended, he was governor of a new country of unlimited potential—and his salary as governor of the new colony was besides that as Governor of Vancouver Island, partly to compensate for his loss of Hudson's Bay Company pay. (Until his retirement in 1864, Douglas remained governor of the two separate colonies. In that year, Arthur E. Kennedy became Governor of Vancouver Island, and Frederick Seymour was appointed Governor of British Columbia. When the two colonies finally merged in 1866, Seymour took over as governor of the united Colony of British Columbia, and New Westminster was named the capital.)

Many of the gold miners, some with new-found wealth, left the gold fields to spend the Christmas season and the winter months in California, Oregon, or Washington. Of those who remained, some preferred not to leave their claims, some found accommodation and festivity in Victoria, and some, lacking the means for passage home, were obliged to stay and depend on charity or casual employment to see them through the winter.

The Royal Engineers of the Boundary Commission had settled into their barracks at Esquimalt for the winter; while, on the mainland, the men of the advance contingent of the Columbia Detachment spent that first Christmas in tents and unfinished log buildings at Derby (old Fort Langley), where they were to prepare the barracks for the later arrival of the main force with the women and children. (As it happened, Colonel Moody was to veto this site, choosing to locate at a place which he named Queensborough—later New Westminster.)

Along the lower Fraser, some 3,000 miners spent the winter in the mining camps or on their claims. Some, perhaps, had laid in supplies and fuel enough, but many underestimated the severity of the climate and were to endure the winter months in flimsy log cabins—small, dark, and often damp—inadequately heated by woodstoves. The monotonous daily diet consisted mainly of flour, beans, and bacon, together with tea and coffee. For some, comfort and companionship could be had, for a price, at the drinking and gambling establishments at Fort Hope and Fort Yale. Boredom might be relieved by hunting, when weather permitted, and chopping firewood; and hours must have been spent in exchanging yarns about past adventures and discussing plans for an affluent future. Along the riverbanks, there may well have been heard, sometimes, the sound of voices raised in song. Days with gray skies and chilling rain would be followed by weeks of snow, creating, on bright days, a scenic wonderland. But the picturesque setting would be little comfort to many a lonely miner, sustained only by thoughts of home, and of spring, and of the new gold finds (that would prove to be among the richest in history) that lay beyond the lower river and along the innumerable tributary streams of the Cariboo region's lakes and rivers.

By the early 1860s, Yale, the head of navigation on the Fraser, was to become the starting point for the building of the Cariboo Wagon Road. Today, telling as history what was then in the future, there stands at Yale a Historic Sites plaque bearing the words:

> *Here began the Cariboo Wagon Road which extended four hundred miles to the northward to the gold of Cariboo. Built in 1862-1865. In the golden days of Cariboo, over this great highway, passed thousands of miners and millions of treasure.*

And at Barkerville, where the Cariboo Wagon Road ended, there also is a Historic Sites plaque, which proclaims its location to be:

> *The centre of old Cariboo, whose gold fields, discovered in 1861, have added over forty million to the wealth of the world. Here was the terminus of the great wagon road from Yale, completed in 1865. The story of the Cariboo gold mines and the Cariboo Road is the epic of British Columbia.*

As news of the Fraser River and then the Cariboo gold rush spread throughout the world, more adventurers arrived from Europe, Britain, and the eastern United States and Canada. As in California, however, prospecting was quickly to reach its peak and then decline. Within a few years, gold mining in British Columbia demanded capital investment, and many former gold seekers had become the pioneer farmers, traders, and builders who laid the foundations for the country's development.

Epilogue

For several years British Columbia remained an isolated colony, not becoming part of Canada until, in 1871, the promise of a Canadian Pacific Railway link with the east persuaded her to join the Canadian

Confederation. Since then, as a proud province of Canada, British Columbia has become, as Sir Edward Bulwer Lytton envisioned, "a magnificent abode for the human race."

Its two major cities—Victoria and Vancouver—are counted high among the world's most beautiful and livable cities. Friendly "invaders" still come from below the border and from overseas, seeking now the gold of commerce, and finding also a wealth of recreational activities, exciting urban venues, and abundant natural beauty. Since the days of the gold rush, railways, highways, airways, and modern communications have defeated distance, bringing British Columbia into the world community and bringing the world to British Columbia. Today, British Columbia's fast-growing population includes people from many nations, just as did her very first non-native population—the gold miners of 1858.

———

1. *Victoria Gazette,* November 20, 1858.
2. B.A. McKelvie, *Fort Langley: Outpost of Empire* (Vancouver: Vancouver Daily Province, 1947), 87.
3. *Victoria Gazette,* November 20, 1858.
4. Jan Gould, *Women of British Columbia* (Saanichton, BC: Hancock House, 1975), 53-55.
5. McKelvie, *Fort Langley,* 86.
6. Parliamentary Papers Relating to British Columbia. Governor Douglas to Sir E.B. Lytton, December 27, 1858.
7. Correspondence, James Douglas to Mr. Blackwood, December 27, 1858, in Frederic W. Howay, *The Early History of the Fraser River Mines* (Victoria: Archives of British Columbia, 1926), 3.

SELECT BIBLIOGRAPHY

Primary Sources

Archives and Special Collections
(original despatches, letters, documents, etc.)

British Columbia Provincial Archives, Victoria
British Library, London
California Historical Society, San Francisco
California State Library, Sacramento
National Maritime Museum, Greenwich, London
Scottish National Library, Edinburgh
University of British Columbia Library, Vancouver
U.S. National Archives, Pacific Sierra Region, San Bruno, California
Vancouver Public Library (BC), Northwest History Reading Room and Special Collections

Contemporary Newspapers, 1858

Daily Alta California (San Francisco)
Daily Scotsman (Edinburgh)
New York Times (New York)
Pioneer and Democrat (Olympia, Wash. Terr.)
Puget Sound Herald (Steilacoom, Wash. Terr.)
San Francisco Bulletin (San Francisco)
San Francisco Herald (San Francisco)
The Times (London)
Victoria Gazette (Victoria)

Selected Contemporary Guidebooks and Descriptive Works
(the great gold strikes era; Fraser to Cariboo, 1858-62)

1858

Anderson, Alexander C. *Hand-Book and Map to the Gold Region of Frazer's and Thompson's Rivers, with Table of Distances.* San Francisco: J.J. LeCount, 1858.
Ballantyne, Robert M., ed. *Handbook to the New Gold Fields: A Full Account of the Richness and Extent of the Fraser and Thompson River Gold Mines.* Edinburgh: A. Strahan; and London: Hamilton, Adams, 1858.

Cornwallis, Kinahan. *The New El Dorado; or British Columbia.* London: T.C. Newby, 1858.

Domer, John. *New British Gold Fields: A Guide to British Columbia and Vancouver Island, with Coloured Map, Showing the Gold and Coal Fields, Constructed from Authentic Sources.* London: W.H. Angel [1858].

[?Hazlitt, William Carew.] *British Columbia and Vancouver's Island: A Complete Hand-Book, Replete with the Latest Information Concerning the Newly-Discovered Gold Fields.* London: W. Penny, 1858.

Waddington, Alfred. *The Fraser Mines Vindicated, or, The History of Four Months.* Victoria: P. DeGarro, 1858.

1859

DeGroot, Henry. *British Columbia; Its Conditions and Prospects, Soil, Climate, and Mineral Resources, Considered.* San Francisco: Alta California, 1859 [a series of 1858-59 *Daily Alta California* newspaper columns by an on-the-scene reporter, presented "in a collected shape"].

1861

Begbie, Matthew B. "Journey into the Interior of British Columbia," *Journal of the Royal Geographic Society* 31 (1861): 237-48.

1862

[Anon.] *Cariboo, the Newly Discovered Gold Fields of British Columbia, Fully Described by a Returned Digger, Who Has Made His Own Fortune There, and Advises Others to Go and Do Likewise.* London: Darton, 1862.

[Anon.] *Guide Book for British Columbia, &c., by a Successful Digger, Containing Practical Information for the Emigrant, and other Useful Matter* [London: n.p., 1862].

[Anon.] *The Handbook of British Columbia, and Emigrant's Guide to the Gold Fields, with Map and Two Illustrations from Photographs by M. Claudet.* London: Oliver, 1862.

Barrett-Lennard, C.E. *Travels in British Columbia, with the Narrative of a Yacht Voyage round Vancouver's Island.* London: Hurst and Blackett, 1862.

Hazlitt, William Carew. *The Great Gold Fields of Cariboo; with an Authentic Description, Brought Down to the Latest Period, of British Columbia and Vancouver Island.* London: Routledge, Warne, and Routledge, 1862.

MacDonald, D.G.F. *British Columbia and Vancouver's Island: Comprising a Description of These Dependencies . . . also an Account of the Manners and Customs of the Native Indians.* London: Longman, Green, Longman, Roberts, and Green, 1862.

Mayne, R.C. *Four Years in British Columbia and Vancouver Island.* London: J. Murray, 1862.

Rattray, Alexander. *Vancouver Island and British Columbia: Where They Are, What They Are, and What May Become: A Sketch of Their History, Topography, Climate, Resources, Capabilities, and Advantages, Especially as Colonies for Settlement.* London: Smith, Elder, 1862.

Other Selected Primary Source Materials

Brown, R.C. Lundin. *British Columbia: An Essay.* New Westminster: Royal Engineer Press, 1863.

Forbes, Charles. *Prize Essay. Vancouver Island: Its Resources and Capabilities, as a Colony.* [Victoria:] The Colonial Government, 1862.

Howay, Frederic W., ed. *The Early History of the Fraser River Mines.* Victoria: Archives of British Columbia, 1926 ["official correspondence taken from the original documents in the Provincial Archives . . . annotated by His Honour Judge Howay"].

Papers Relative to the Affairs of British Columbia. London: Queen's Printer, 1859 [also 1860 and 1862].

Journal Articles

Genini, R. "The Fraser-Cariboo Gold Rushes: Comparisons and Contrasts with the California Gold Rush," *Journal of the West* 2 (July 1972): 470-87.

Ireland, Willard E., ed. "First Impressions: Letter of Colonel Richard Clement Moody, R.E., to Arthur Blackwood, February 1, 1859," *British Columbia Historical Quarterly* 15 (January/April 1951): 85-107.

Lamb, W. Kaye. "British Columbia Official Records: The Crown Colony Period," *Pacific Northwest Quarterly* 29 (January 1938): 17-25.

_____. "The Governorship of Richard Blanshard," *British Columbia Historical Quarterly* 14 (January/April 1950): 1-40.

Ormsby, Margaret A. "Some Irish Figures in Colonial Days," *British Columbia Historical Quarterly* 14 (January/April 1950): 61-82.

Pettit, Sydney G. "Dear Sir Matthew: A Glimpse of Judge Begbie," *British Columbia Historical Quarterly* 11 (January 1947): 1-14.

Sage, Walter N., ed. "Peter Skene Ogden's Notes on Western Caledonia," *British Columbia Historical Quarterly* 1 (January 1937): 48-56.

White, Hester E. "John Carmichael Haynes," *British Columbia Historical Quarterly* 4 (July 1940): 195-96.

Books (Secondary Sources)

Akrigg, G.P.V. and Helen B. *British Columbia Place Names.* Victoria: Sono Nis Press, 1988.

Anglin, Ron. *Forgotten Trails: Historical Sources of the Columbia's Big Bend Country,* ed. with contributions by Glen W. Lindeman. Pullman: Washington State University Press, 1995.

Bancroft, Hubert H. *History of British Columbia.* San Francisco: History Company, 1887.

_____. *History of the Northwest Coast.* New York: History Company, 1884.

Barman, Jean. *The West beyond the West: A History of British Columbia.* Toronto: University of Toronto Press, 1991.

Duff, Wilson. *The Indian History of British Columbia, Volume 1: The Impact of the White Man.* Victoria: Provincial Museum of British Columbia, 1969.

Fraser, Simon. *[Journal of a Voyage from the Rocky Mountains to the Pacific Coast, 1808] Les Bourgeois de la Compagnie du Norde-Ouest . . . ,* ed. by L.R. Masson. Quebec, 1889.

Gough, Barry M. *Gunboat Frontier: British Maritime Authority and Northwest Coast Indians, 1846-90.* Vancouver: University of British Columbia Press, 1984.

Gould, Jan. *Women of British Columbia.* Saanichton, BC: Hancock House, 1975.

Gunn, Angus M. *British Columbia: Landforms and Settlement.* Richmond, BC: Smith Lithograph, 1968.

Hill, Beth. *Sappers: The Royal Engineers in British Columbia.* Ganges, BC: Horsdal and Schubert, 1987.

Howay, Frederic W. *British Columbia: The Making of a Province.* Toronto: Ryerson, 1928.

————, W.N. Sage, and H.F. Angus. *British Columbia and the United States: The North Pacific Slope from Fur Trade to Aviation,* ed. by H.F. Angus. New York: Russell and Russell, 1942 [1970].

Hudson's Bay Company. *A Brief History of the Hudson's Bay Company.* Winnipeg: Hudson's Bay Company, 1958.

Kerr, J.B. *Biographical Dictionary of Well-Known British Columbians.* Vancouver: Kerr and Begg, 1890.

McKelvie, B.A. *Fort Langley: Outpost of Empire.* Vancouver: Vancouver Daily Province, 1947.

————. *Pageant of B.C.* Toronto: Thomas Nelson and Sons, 1955.

Meeker, Ezra. *Pioneer Remembrances of Puget Sound.* Seattle: Lowman and Hanford, 1905.

Ormsby, Margaret A. *British Columbia: A History.* Toronto: MacMillans in Canada, 1958.

Paterson, T.W. *British Columbia: The Pioneer Years.* Langley, BC: Stagecoach, 1977.

Pethick, Derek. *Men of British Columbia.* Saanichton, BC: Hancock House, 1975.

Plasterer, Herbert P. *Fort Victoria: From Fur Trading Post to Capital City of British Columbia.* Victoria: n.p., n.d.

Robinson, J. Lewis, and Walter G. Hardwick. *British Columbia: One Hundred Years of Geographical Change.* Vancouver: Talonbooks, 1973.

Royal Canadian Mounted Police Veterans' Association. *92 Years of Pride, 1858-1950: The British Columbia Provincial Police.* Kelowna, BC: Royal Canadian Mounted Police Veterans' Association, 1983.

Ruby, Robert H., and John A. Brown. *Indian Slavery in the Pacific Northwest.* Spokane: Arthur H. Clark, 1993.

Ryerson, Stanley B. *Unequal Union: Roots of Crisis in the Canadas, 1815-1873.* Toronto: Progress Books, 1973.

Sage, Walter N. *Sir James Douglas and British Columbia.* Toronto: University of Toronto Press, 1930.

Scholefield, E.O.S., and R.E Gosnell. *A History of British Columbia, Volume 2, Biography.* Vancouver: British Columbia Historical Association, 1913.

Stenzel, Franz. *James Madison Alden: Yankee Artist of the Pacific Coast, 1854-1860.* Fort Worth, TX: Amon Carter Museum, 1975.

University of Toronto. *Dictionary of Canadian Biography.* Toronto: University of Toronto Press, 1976.

Walkem, W. Wymond. *Stories of Early British Columbia.* Vancouver, 1914.

Williams, David Ricardo. *The Man for a New Country: Sir Matthew Baillie Begbie.* Sydney, BC: Gray's, 1977.

INDEX

CHEESE

CHEESE

a comprehensive guide to cheeses of the world

Juliet Harbutt

LORENZ BOOKS

This edition is published by Lorenz Books

Lorenz Books is an imprint of Anness Publishing Ltd
Hermes House, 88–89 Blackfriars Road, London SE1 8HA
tel. 020 7401 2077; fax 020 7633 9499
www.lorenzbooks.com; info@anness.com

Published in the USA by Lorenz Books, Anness Publishing Inc.
27 West 20th Street, New York, NY 10011; fax 212 807 6813

Published in Australia by Lorenz Books, Anness Publishing Pty Ltd
Level 1, Rugby House, 12 Mount Street, North Sydney, NSW 2060
tel. (02) 8920 8622; fax (02) 8920 8633

This edition distributed in the UK by Aurum Press Ltd
25 Bedford Avenue, London WC1B 3AT
tel. 020 7637 3225; fax 020 7580 2469

This edition distributed in the USA by National Book Network
4720 Boston Way, Lanham, MD 20706
tel. 301 459 3366; fax 301 459 1705; www.nbnbooks.com

This edition distributed in Canada by General Publishing
895 Don Mills Road, 400–402 Park Centre, Toronto, Ontario M3C 1W3
tel. 416 445 3333; fax 416 445 5991; www.genpub.com

This edition distributed in New Zealand by David Bateman Ltd
30 Tarndale Grove, Off Bush Road, Albany, Auckland
tel. (09) 415 7664; fax (09) 415 8892

PUBLISHER: Joanna Lorenz
SENIOR EDITOR: Linda Fraser
COPY EDITOR: Jenni Fleetwood
DESIGNER: Nigel Partridge

Previously published as *A Complete Illustrated Guide to the Cheeses of the World*

1 3 5 7 9 10 8 6 4 2

PHOTOGRAPHY ACKNOWLEDGEMENTS

Pictures are by William Lingwood, except for the following: p6 Sopexa; p7
The Italian Trade Centre; p9 Sopexa; p10 (tl) Cheeses from Switzerland, (tr)
J.P. Quicke, (b) Italian Trade Centre; p11 (tl) CS, (tr/b) Sopexa; p12 and 13 Sopexa;
pp130 (bl), 131, 132, 133, 135, 136, 137, 138 (t/bl), 139, 140 and 141 Walt Chrynwski;
p142 Gabriella Kervella; p150 Russ McCallum

CONTENTS

—

INTRODUCTION

—

In shops and markets around the world, thousands of cheeses tempt our eyes and challenge our tastebuds. Wrinkled and mouldy, smooth and sunshine yellow, orange and smelly or brilliant white, they are all labelled cheese, and their shapes and sizes, flavours and textures range from the sublime to the truly extraordinary. Yet they are all made from the same basic raw material – milk. What changes this simple product into something so complex and diverse?

DIFFERENT KINDS OF MILK

First, the type of animal yielding milk makes a difference. The cow's milk we drink is slightly sweet, mild and subtle in flavour. Most of it comes from Friesian cows, yet there are more than 50 different breeds whose milk is suitable for cheesemaking. Milk from Guernsey cows, for instance, is rich and pale yellow with larger fat globules than most other types, so this milk tastes smoother and fuller. Water buffalo's milk – used in Italy for making mozzarella – is ivory white, earthy and slightly nutty.

Sheep's milk is also mild but has undertones of roast lamb and lanolin. It is slightly sweeter than cow's milk. As sheep's milk cheese matures, these characteristics are intensified, as exemplified in the hard mature sheep's milk cheeses like the famous Pecorinos of Italy or the Basque and Pyrenees cheeses of France and Spain. Typically they are very nutty – as if fresh milk has been infused with crushed walnuts or brazil nuts – and the sweetness comes through to suggest burnt caramel, sweet fudge or caramelized onions. The aroma of lanolin, like the smell of wet wool, also adds its own distinct personality to the final cheese.

The most misunderstood of all cheeses are those made from goat's milk. There's an explanation for the negative way it is often perceived: if the milk, which is mild with a slightly aromatic background, is handled badly, the microscopic globules of fat suspended in the milk burst and release their contents. These impart a

ABOVE: The milk from cows has a mild, subtle, slightly sweet flavour

bitter, nasty, "billy goat" flavour to the milk. If you have ever been close to a billy or male goat, it is a smell you are unlikely to forget. However, if the milk is handled with care, those same fat globules will gradually break down and will contribute to the delicious, herbaceous taste of the cheese. A good goat's milk cheese tastes as though the milk has absorbed the oils and aromas of tarragon, thyme or marjoram, set against a background of dry, crisp white wine.

There are as many different breeds of goat and sheep as there are cows. In some countries, cheese is made from the milk of llamas, camels or even reindeer, adding yet another dimension to the cheese.

Milk is not produced all year round but only after the animal has given birth. Unlike humans, animals come into season only once a year. Although farmers can control and manipulate their animals' natural urges, sheep and goats are more difficult to persuade to mate out of season than cows. Added to this, they have a shorter lactation period than cows, so there are times when their milk is not available. Some producers freeze goat's or sheep's milk for these times and continue to make excellent cheeses. Others believe

in the old ways and simply stop milking their animals. Their cheeses are therefore seasonal. But the type of animal is only one factor that affects the flavour.

THE GRAZING, THE SOIL AND THE SEASONS

Of equal significance is what the animals eat. Even the most unobservant amongst us cannot fail to see and smell the difference between fresh grass, wild clover and unspoilt meadows compared with compacted feed, silage, turnips and straw.

You only have to taste the great mountain cheeses of Europe (where, by law, the herds can only graze on natural pastures or sweet hay cut from Alpine meadows), to appreciate the difference. The amount of milk these cows give may be lower than that yielded by animals fed on lush green pastures or carefully prepared balanced diets of dried food supplement and vitamins, but the milk is rich and thick and the flavour is concentrated.

The seasons will also affect the taste and even the texture of cheeses from animals that seek their own grazing and do not rely on their keepers. In spring, the herbage is sweet, moist and green as the young shoots come through; in early summer the grazing is bountiful and varied compared with mid- to late summer when the earth becomes parched and dry and only hardy grasses survive. With the autumn rains comes another burst of new growth before the winter forces many animals inside to become reliant during the winter months on the hay the farmer has cut. The flavour of the milk reflects these differences and changes with the seasons.

The soil and geology of an area will also affect the flavour of the milk and may even govern the type of cheese that can be made. Clay and limestone will support different grasses to volcanic soils and granite. The grasses that grow will absorb different minerals, each making a minute but significant impact on the flavour of the milk. Rainfall, humidity and temperature also affect what will grow and which animals will thrive where.

MAKING CHEESE

—

Once the milk has been obtained, the skill of the cheesemaker is needed to convert it into a form that will last for days or even years. To achieve this, the cheese-maker must first separate the milk into the solids, protein and fats (known collectively as curds) and the liquid or whey (that consists mainly of water). This process is known as coagulation.

THE STARTER

If left in a warm place, milk will sour and coagulate or curdle by itself. This souring process is due to the action of millions of tiny bacteria who "eat" lactose (milk sugars), turning them into lactic acid or sour milk. To speed up the process and to stop the milk becoming bitter and unpleasantly sour, a little warm "matured" or slightly sour milk, taken from the previous evening's milk, is added to the new, fresh batch of unpasteurized milk. This speeds up or starts the process of coagulating the milk and is known as a starter or starter culture. It is not unlike adding the culture to yogurt – and in fact some cheesemakers use home-made yogurt as their starter.

If the milk is pasteurized, all these bacteria will have been lost and must be

BELOW: The cheesemaker stirring a vat of coagulating milk for Parmesan

replaced in order for the milk to sour and curdle. The replacements consist of a combination of cultures grown in laboratories. Some the cheesemaker can just tip into the vat of milk; others are a blend specifically requested by the cheesemaker and must be grown in an incubator before they can be added to the milk. These cultures are valuable, but they will never replace the myriad different bacteria naturally present in unpasteurized milk.

Certain types of cheese must use specific cultures if the desired result is to be obtained. Invisible to the naked eye, these cultures work alongside the numerous enzymes on the lactose, protein and fat through all the stages of cheesemaking. Each thrives at a specific range of temperatures and degree of acidity and contributes to the final flavour and texture of the cheese. As the level of acidity changes in the milk (and later in the young curd), some die off or become dormant, while others, preferring the new climate, will spring into action. Their unique characteristics combine to create a kaleidoscope of flavours that no amount of copying can emulate.

THE RENNET

Although the starter culture speeds up the process of souring the milk and would eventually cause it to curdle, it produces quite a sharp, acidic cheese, so it is only suitable when making a cheese that will be eaten young. The use of rennet significantly improves cheesemaking techniques, and it was its discovery centuries ago that allowed shepherds to make harder cheeses that lasted through the winter months when their animals and the land were barren.

All milk-fed animals are born with an enzyme in their stomachs that attacks the milk and converts it into solids (which they can digest) and liquid (which is mainly waste). The travelling herdsman probably discovered the effects of the enzyme – rennet – when they stored their milk in sacks made from the stomach of a young kid or lamb and found the warm

ABOVE: Lifting newly formed Parmesan out of the whey using cheesecloth

milk had soured slightly and separated into curds and whey.

If too much rennet is used, there is a risk that the finished cheese will be hard, dry and friable, and have a pronounced bitter taste, especially if acidification is insufficient. When preparing cheese with a rapid coagulation rate, the dosage of the rennet is higher than for cheeses that coagulate slowly.

Rennet also helps to break down the curd into a smooth, even consistency, contributing to the texture and flavour.

The use of this animal product means that many vegetarians are reluctant to eat cheese. Fortunately, manufacturers and chemists recognized that vegetarianism was not a passing fad but represented an increasingly significant proportion of the population and have created non-animal alternatives. Over 85 per cent of cheeses made in Britain and 60 per cent in New Zealand use a rennet substitute suitable for vegetarians. Some traditional cheeses dating back thousands of years use vegetable or fungal alternatives to trigger coagulation. These include the juices or tissues of certain plants, such as thistle and Lady's Bed Straw. Fig juice has also been used to start coagulation.

THE TYPES OF CHEESE AND HOW THEY ARE MADE

The type of cheese that is produced by the cheesemaker is determined by the amount of moisture he eliminates from the curd and the size of cheese that he wants to make. The amount of moisture in the curd will also determine what sort of rind or mould will grow on the cheese. The presence of rind is a huge advantage for the consumer. You may not be able to judge a wine by its bottle or a book by its cover, but the essential characteristics of a cheese can certainly be judged by a glance at the rind.

From just a brief glance at the rind and texture of a hitherto unknown cheese you can tell roughly what sort of texture, taste and strength of flavour you can expect. With practice – and the occasional squeeze and sniff – you can even learn to determine the condition and maturity of a cheese. Using the "rind" as a guide gives you an insight into the character, background and probable traits and foibles of virtually any cheese you encounter and enables you to dazzle your friends and family with your expertise.

LOW-FAT CHEESES

Traditional cheeses, such as Parmesan and Single Gloucester, were made with skimmed milk. The cream was skimmed off to use for cooking or to make butter. Today, with the growing obsession with low-fat foods, increasing numbers of cheeses are being made in low-fat versions. The fat, however, is what gives the cheese its texture and depth of the flavour. Consequently low-fat versions of traditional cheeses tend to lack both body and texture. It is far better to use a smaller amount of a traditional cheese than a large quantity of a bland, low-fat substitute.

Try using a soft cheese as they have a higher moisture content and therefore a lower percentage of fat than a harder cheese. Or, simply use less of a more mature, stronger-tasting hard cheese.

FRESH CHEESES

(NO VISIBLE RIND OR GROWTH OF MOULD)

EXAMPLES: *ricotta, feta, Myzlthra, mozzarella, cream cheese, fresh chèvre*

The milk is warmed, the starter culture is added and the acidity starts to increase. For some cheeses, like fromage frais, the starter is sufficient. These are called LACTIC CHEESES. Most cheeses, however, require the addition of rennet. This is stirred into the milk, then left for a few hours until it coagulates and resembles a very floppy milk jelly. The amount of moisture remaining with the whey will determine how soft or hard the final cheese will be.

Fresh cheeses are high in moisture. The young curd is carefully placed in sacks or small perforated containers and drained slowly without pressure for a few hours so that the curd retains much of the whey. Once sufficient whey has been drained off, the curds are either mixed or sprinkled with salt. They are now ready to be eaten. Some fresh cheeses are allowed to mature and grow either a white or bluish-grey mould, which places them in a different category.

Milk was a precious commodity to the herdsmen and their families. It was vital that none should be wasted, so some cheesemakers made cheeses from the whey, which contains small amounts of fat, vitamins and proteins. The most famous of these WHEY CHEESES is ricotta. This is made by boiling the whey, thus causing the small solid particles to float to the top. These are then scooped off, put in basket moulds to drain and sold within a few days. Whey cheeses tend to be used for cooking rather than eating fresh, as are most of these fresh cheeses. Scandinavian cheesemakers boil the whey slowly for hours, reducing it to a sticky toffee-like substance known as Gjetost or Mesost.

The other style of fresh cheeses are STRETCHED CURD CHEESES, with their irresistible stringy, impossible-to-control texture. These came originally from the Middle East, but the best known example today is mozzarella. The young curd is

heated in the whey before being stretched or kneaded until the strings do not break when stretched. The pliant curd is then "spun" into balls or plaited and tossed in hot water to seal the cheese.

COMMON CHARACTERISTICS: Fresh cheeses are always mild and high in moisture and therefore low in fat. They have a slightly acidic or lactic taste. Most are used for cooking but some may be wrapped in leaves or dusted with paprika, charcoal or fresh herbs for serving as a table cheese.

WATCH POINTS: A slightly bitter smell, normally accompanied by a greyish brown or thin opaque mould, indicates the cheese is no longer fresh and will taste bitter.

SOFT-WHITE CHEESES

(WHITE, FUZZY PENICILLIUM CANDIDUM RIND)

EXAMPLES: *Camembert, Brie, Bonchester, Pencarreg, Chaource*

The floppy curd is ladled gently into moulds and left to drain in perforated moulds in an atmosphere of high humidity so that the curd does not lose too much whey. After a few hours, the cheeses are turned out of their moulds and left to mature for a few weeks. Their high moisture content, coupled with the high humidity, attracts and encourages the growth of the classic white penicillium mould seen on Bries and Camemberts around the world.

The penicillium moulds help to break down the curd and contribute to the flavour and texture of the cheese. The result is a creamy, smooth, voluptuous interior that when perfect looks as though it is almost ready to run.

Originally, the mould would have existed naturally in the atmosphere, along with other wild moulds and yeasts. Today, these need to be introduced into the cheesemakers' ripening rooms. Artisan cheesemakers encourage the growth of these wild moulds. On their cheeses, the white rinds tend to be dusted or impregnated with red, yellow, grey or pink moulds, all of which add to the depth and uniqueness of flavour. The wild moulds, however, do not stand up to the modern hygiene conditions that exist in factories. Here the mould spores have to be continually sprayed into the ripening rooms or even injected into the cheeses, producing a rather one-dimensional flavour.

COMMON CHARACTERISTICS: Brie is a classic example of a soft-white cheese, with its rich, runny, creamy texture. The taste is reminiscent of soup made from wild mushrooms, with just a dash of sherry. Pasteurized Bries remain white, and smell more like hay and button mushrooms and have a buttery, mushroom taste.

WATCH POINTS: A strong smell of ammonia indicates that the cheese has entered second fermentation or has been kept too damp. Soft-white cheeses with long shelf lives have been stabilized to prevent them running. They will consequently taste sweeter and more buttery and will be elastic rather than runny. Soft-white cheeses made with milk that has been enriched with cream before being coagulated will be higher in fat, more solid and have the richness of cream but will seldom develop a great depth of flavour. However, they will feel like melted butter or ice cream in the mouth and will taste delicious.

EXCEPTIONS: Blue Bries and other flavoured Brie-type cheeses belong in this category as the classification relates to the *rind* first rather than the cheese's interior. Thus, by looking at a soft flat Brie-type cheese you can tell that its overall character will be that of a soft-white cheese even though only a label or a sharp knife will tell you what is inside.

NATURAL-RIND CHEESES

(BLUE-GREY MOULDED RIND, USUALLY GOAT)

EXAMPLES: *Crottin de Chavignol, Saint-Marcellin, Selles-sur-Cher*

The majority of French farmhouse goat's milk cheeses belong in this category, which applies to fresh cheeses that have been left to drain for longer and in a drier atmosphere than the fresh cheeses. These are the cheeses you see piled on wooden trestles in French markets. When young, they have a slightly wrinkled, cream-coloured rind. In time they dry out, the wrinkles become more pronounced and the character and flavour increases, along with the growth of bluish grey mould.

ABOVE: Shelves of unpasteurized Brie de Meaux in a special ripening room where the cheeses will gradually develop their distinctive rind

COMMON CHARACTERISTICS: Initially, the taste is fresh, almost fruity, with undertones of goat; as the cheeses dry out the flavours intensify, becoming rich and nutty and acquiring a decidedly goaty taste. The mould starts as a discrete hue on the surface, gradually covering the entire cheese in greyish-blue blotches. There are few examples of this variety made in Britain, America or Australasia as the majority of consumers are dubious about moulds.

WATCH POINTS: To mature and ripen, these cheeses must be kept dry. Any wetness on the surface should be patted dry immediately or the cheese will become damp and lose its sharp, clean taste.

WASHED-RIND CHEESES

(ORANGEY-BROWN STICKY RIND)

EXAMPLES: *Epoisses, Herve, Milleens, Stinking Bishop, Munster*

The curd, which may or may not be cut depending on how soft the final cheese should be, is scooped into moulds and left to drain. The high moisture of the curd and the humidity of the maturing rooms attracts a bitter-tasting, grey, hairy mould called "cat fur". To discourage this, the newly formed cheese is rubbed with or dunked in baths of salty water, wine or a similar alcoholic liquid. This produces a rather robust cheese and encourages the development of orange, sticky bacteria that help to break down the curd from the outside, gradually becoming an integral part of the interior, rather than just a skin.

Invented by Trappist monks to enhance their otherwise rather meagre diet on fast days, these cheeses are found right across Europe, but mainly in France, Belgium and (more recently) Ireland.

COMMON CHARACTERISTICS: Ranging from rather spicy to outrageously piquant in taste and aroma (and once banned on French public transport for that very reason), they can smell yeasty or can be almost meaty. The interior may resemble Brie or be more supple and elastic.

WATCH POINTS: A dull brownish rind may indicate that the cheese has been kept too long or has been allowed to dry out. Cracking, if noticed early, can be arrested by wrapping the cheese in clear film to conserve the moisture.

SEMI-SOFT CHEESES

(PINKISH/BROWN TO DARK GREY RIND WITH SUPPLE, ELASTIC "FEEL")

EXAMPLES: *Raclette, Desmond, Gubbeens, Edam, Sonoma Jack, Fontina*

To obtain a firmer cheese, the curd is cut up to release some of the whey before the curd is placed in moulds. It is then often lightly pressed to speed up the draining. After a day or so, the cheese is turned out of its mould and washed in brine. This

ABOVE: Fresh, cloth-wrapped Gruyère curd is placed in the massive, traditional, round wooden hoop

ABOVE: Hundred's of Quicke's Cheddars maturing on ceiling-high shelves in the ripening rooms at their farm in Devon

seals the rind before the cheese is placed in cellars or ripening rooms, where other moulds are encouraged to grow. To eliminate the formation of the rind, the cheeses may be sealed in plastic; otherwise the moulds that form are frequently brushed off, gradually building up a leathery rind that may be fine and barely perceptible from the interior, thin orange brown like the rind on raclette or thick grey-brown and leathery like the rind on Tomme de Savoie.

COMMON CHARACTERISTICS: The lower moisture content means the fermentation process is slower, producing cheeses with a round, full-bodied, rather than strong, flavour. Their taste often seems to be embodied with the oils and esters of the wild mountain flowers of Europe. When young, semi-soft cheeses have a firm yet springy, school eraser texture, becoming elastic and supple.

WATCH POINTS: Cheeses that have been dipped in wax to prevent dehydration and splitting may sweat, causing mould to develop under the rind.

EXCEPTIONS: Some semi-soft cheeses are only very lightly pressed and can be eaten within a few days or the cheese may be encouraged to grow a soft-white rind, although this will slowly be corrupted by the more virulent moulds common to this type of cheese.

HARD CHEESES

(THICK RIND, OFTEN WAXED, OILED OR CLOTHBOUND)

EXAMPLES: *Cheddar, Manchego, Cantal, Gruyèye, Cheshire, Parmigiano-Reggiano, Pecorino*

To make a hard cheese the curd must be cut more finely – from small cubes to rice-size pieces – the smaller the pieces, the more whey will be lost from the curd. The curds are then gently heated in a vat to force out more moisture before the whey is drained off. Salt is then added to the curds, which now resemble rubbery, lumpy, cottage cheese. They may be cut again (the process differs for various types of hard cheeses) before being placed in large perforated moulds that are frequently engraved with a unique symbol, logo, pattern or name to identify the finished cheese or its maker.

Most traditional, hard British cheeses are wrapped in cloth, sealed with lard and left to mature for weeks or even years. Hard European cheeses tend to be left in brine overnight (or, in the case of Parmigiano-Reggiano, for up to 21 days) to seal the rind. Then they, like their British counterparts, are placed in "caves" or ripening rooms to mature. Most hard cheeses require at least a

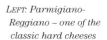

LEFT: Parmigiano-Reggiano – one of the classic hard cheeses

ABOVE: Bleu d'Auvergne curds draining in their stainless steel moulds – they are left for one or two weeks

the flavourings tended to be cumin, cloves or herbs but in the last five years, particularly in Britain, flavoured cheeses have become a significant growth area of the market. Some combinations are successful, others sublime and a few positively ridiculous.

THE ART OF CHEESE TASTING

The most effective way of putting your new knowledge to the test is to taste a selection of cheeses – preferably one of each of the different types. Buy some cheese, wine and bread, then invite a few friends round to compare the flavours and textures of the cheeses against each other. The categories here are roughly in order of strength so use them as a guide, starting from mild to strong, though as with all rules, there are exceptions and reasons for breaking them. Don't lose sight of the object of the exercise, however, which is to enjoy the gentle art of learning that one "lives to eat, not eats to live".

BELOW: Once Bleu d'Auvergne cheeses are removed from the moulds, they are rubbed with salt

BLUE CHEESES

(THE RIND VARIES FROM A FINE BLOOM TO A THICK GRITTY RIND LIKE THAT ON STILTON, BUT GENERALLY BLUE CHEESES ARE WRAPPED IN FOIL)

EXAMPLES: *Stilton, Roquefort, Gorgonzola, Cabrales, Maytag Blue, Danish Blue*

Blue cheeses are neither pressed nor cooked. Most frequently the curd is crumbled, eliminating much of the whey, then scooped into stainless steel cylindrical moulds, each with a wooden disk on the top. The curd remains in the moulds for 1–2 weeks and is turned frequently to let the weight of the curds press out more of the whey. Once the cheeses can stand up on their own, they are removed from the moulds, rubbed with salt, then returned to the cellars.

The blue mould is a strain of penicillium that is added to the milk before the rennet is added either in liquid or powder form. The cheese will not turn blue, however, unless it is given air to breathe. This is done by piercing the cheese with rods. The blue then grows along the tunnels and into the nooks and crannies between the loose curd, producing the shattered porcelain look that typifies blue cheese.

Those that are made like Brie have the blue injected into the young curd as the moisture content is so high that any holes made in the cheese would immediately close up, preventing air from penetrating the curd.

WATCH POINTS: Most blue cheeses are normally wrapped in foil to prevent them from drying out. This causes the moisture pumped out by the bacteria during fermentation to gather on the rind. Scrape this off before serving.

SPECIALITY CHEESE

(SIMILAR TO THE ORIGINAL CHEESE USED AS A BASE)

EXAMPLES: *Gouda with Cumin, Sage Derby, Cheddar with Date & Walnut, Red Leicester with Pecans, Raclette with Peppercorns*

These are made from familiar semi-soft or hard cheeses to which flavourings or other ingredients – nuts, fruit, spices, herbs, even fish – have been added . Traditionally

---

ABOVE: A newly-formed Gruyère cheese is frequently pressed and turned, then it is left in the press overnight

few weeks to mature, if not years, as is the case with good farmhouse Cheddar, Emmental or Cantal.

Hard block cheeses are pressed into shape and then matured in special plastic wrap that allows the cheese to age without the development of either moulds or rind. The moisture that would normally be lost during maturation is also retained. The cheese will mature faster but its texture will be softer than traditionally matured, clothbound cheeses. However, the method for block cheeses is more economical as a hard cheese like Cheddar can lose up to 15 per cent of its original weight if not wrapped.

WATCH POINTS: Hard cheeses are user-friendly. They may grow some surface mould, but this can easily be scraped off. The important thing to remember is to keep the cut surfaces of hard cheese tightly covered with foil or clear film (leaving an opening for the rind to breathe) to prevent the cheese from absorbing any taints from the fridge. Fatty substances, particularly cheeses and fat, absorb smells very easily, which is an advantage when the aroma is acquired intentionally, but a drawback if not.

WINE AND CHEESE: THE PERFECT MARRIAGE

As a very general rule, the whiter and fresher the cheese the crisper and fruitier the wine should be. The heavier, richer soft cheeses can be partnered with a big white like a Chardonnay or a light red. The harder and darker the cheese, the heavier and richer the style of wine can be. Most blue cheeses, on the other hand, go superbly with sweet wines.

Perfumed or floral reds are too over-powering. So are heavy tannic wines – the tannin tends to steal the nutty richness of the cheese. If asked to select one grape variety over any other to have with a cheeseboard, the author would go for a Pinot Noir from the New World or a soft Burgundian Pinot Noir. However, white wines are often unexpectedly good part-ners, allowing the cheese and the wine a chance to show their character in a way that a red wine may often fail to do.

FRESH CHEESES

Try fresh light, crisp white wines like Sauvignon or Chenin Blanc; also try Frascati, Soave or Loire whites. Red wines are too heavy, unless the cheese is part of a spicy dish like a pizza.

BELOW: Red wine, especially those made with Pinot Noir grapes, makes an ideal accompaniment to cheese

SOFT-WHITE CHEESES

With the mild, slightly sharp, salty style try a slightly sweet wine. Those with a richer, sweeter and more creamy taste need a fruitier wine with a good balance of fruit and acidity. A New Zealand or Chilean Sauvignon Blanc would be ideal. The more meaty Bries prefer a full-bodied, fruity red like a Pinot Noir or even a rich white, such as Chardonnay.

SEMI-SOFT CHEESES

Try a full-bodied gutsy white or a light fruity, red. The firmer, more distinctly flavoured semi-soft cheeses need a Chianti, Rioja or Merlot.

WASHED-RIND CHEESES

The strong, pungent, washed rind cheeses respond well to beer. If you serve wine, make it a spicy Gewurztraminer or a robust red.

HARD CHEESES

They range from the mild to the outra-geously tangy, so almost any wine can be a potential match. However a general rule is the stronger the cheese the bigger the wine required.
MILD: something red and fruity – Fitou, Merlot or Chilean reds
MEDIUM: try Côtes du Rhône or a New Zealand Cabernet Sauvignon
STRONG: Californian Cabernet Sauvignon or even an Australian Shiraz
EXTRA STRONG: these can handle the rich sweetness of fortified wines, such as Port or Madeira

BLUE CHEESES

Milder blues need a light fruity white like a Vouvray, Chenin Blanc or a Rosé, while the more piquant blues prefer robust, spicy reds like the Rhônes or a Shiraz. Better still, serve a sweet wine like Monbazillac or some of the sweeter wines from the New World. The classic marriage is of Roquefort with a Sauterne. The sharp, salty tang of the cheese is softened by the wine, while the sweetness of the sheep's milk is underlined.

CREATING THE PERFECT CHEESEBOARD

U se the list of cheese types outlined in the introduction as a guide next time you buy your cheeses. Learn to determine which category you prefer and how to offer a balanced cheeseboard. You should have not only a selection from several categories, but also take care to offer a combination of shapes and provide at least one goat's or sheep's milk cheese.

ACCOMPANIMENTS TO YOUR CHEESEBOARD

BREAD: There are almost as many breads as there are cheeses. The best are home-made or country-style breads. Walnut and raisin breads are favoured by some, but plain breads are often better with cheese.

NUTS: The Europeans often serve their cheese with fresh walnuts, almonds or hazelnuts in the shell. Pre-shelled nuts rarely have the same sweetness.

PICKLES: Serving pickles or chutney with cheese is a very English habit. these accompaniments are suitable for hard, mature cheeses, such as Cheddar, but they can overpower. The best are home-made and sweet, rather than hot and spicy.

FRESH FRUIT: Serve seasonal fruit, preferably local. Citrus is too sharp, and tropical fruit generally too sweet – apples, pears and figs are perfect.

DRIED FRUIT: Dried figs, prunes and raisins are delicious with all style of cheese. The Spanish make a number of delicious fruit pastes or "cheeses" from quinces, figs, almonds and raisins. These are delicious with all their cheeses, particularly the hard cheeses made from sheep's milk.

SAVOURY TOUCHES: Spring onions, olives, celery, fresh beans and crisp greens like rocket (arugula)or long leaf lettuces can be served with, but not on, the cheeseboard.

HONEY: Drizzling blue cheeses lightly with a little wild honey heightens their flavour.

ABOVE: Choose a selection of different cheeses for your cheeseboard and accompany them with bread and fruit

◆ The best cheese board is the one chosen with care and enthusiasm and served on a rough board with chunks of bread, copious quantities of wine and good friends to share it with.

◆ One superb cheese is better than three or four small wedges.

◆ Choosing several cheeses from different categories means you will have a variety of textures. The colours of the rinds will differ, as will the interior of the cheeses.

◆ Colour should come from the rinds of the cheeses and not come from a bunch of grapes or similar fruit. If you want to decorate the board, use chestnut or oak leaves, fresh herbs or wild flowers. Add several different breads.

◆ Biscuits tend to take away from the texture of the cheeses and are often very salty. Try fresh, crusty country-style breads instead.

◆ Serve fresh fruit separately.

◆ There are some wonderful alternatives to the basic round wooden or marble cheeseboard. Experiment with wicker trays, shallow baskets, a piece of driftwood or a tray covered with a linen napkin and grape leaves.

◆ Shapes add interest to your cheeseboard. Where possible avoid having all the shapes of the cheeses the same. Instead, offer pyramids, logs, squares or cylinders. Alternatively, cut the cheese into irregular shapes.

◆ The habit of serving cheese before dessert is practised by the French for the simple reason that this enables the red wine from the main course to be finished with the cheese. The sweet wine can then be served with the blue cheeses (which, because they have the strongest flavour, should be eaten last) and follows through to accompany the dessert.

◆ A cheese board can also be served as a main course for lunch. Serve a selection of cheeses with a lightly dressed mixed leaf salad, pickles or chutney, fresh fruit and nuts and country-style bread. If you like, serve a selection of wines.

CHEESES OF THE WORLD

To taste and record the cheeses of the world would be an impossible, if infinitely pleasurable task. Instead, this reference section includes a cross-section of the world's cheeses. A few are made in huge creameries, but most come from small co-operatives or family-owned farms. Some, such as Roquefort and Cheddar, are found all over the world; others, such as Aorangi from New Zealand, Yerba Santa Shepherd's Cheese from the USA and Cooleeney from Ireland, are recently created, while others use recipes that have remained unchanged for centuries and are rarely found outside the village in which they were first made.

FRENCH CHEESES

France has many of the most fascinating cheeses in the world; over 750 of them. Most are traditional cheeses, cherished and fiercely protected.

The earliest recorded French cheese was Roquefort. Pliny, writing in the first century BC, described it as "the cheese that bears away the prize at Rome where they are always ready to compare and appreciate good things from every land". Roquefort continues to be appreciated to this day – all over the world.

During the Middle Ages the cheese-making tradition was kept alive in the monasteries of France. Monks taught the farmers how to keep their animals healthy and their milk clean. It was they who showed the farmers how to mature cheese, usually the peasants' major source of protein. Their numerous fast days gave them the motivation to invent new recipes and in 960AD the first of the monastery cheeses, Maroilles, was created at an abbey in the Thiérache region of northern France. The monks discovered that rubbing the surface of small, soft cheeses with salt created a pungent and quite meaty aroma and taste. The first of the famous Trappist cheeses was born. Munster, Pont l'Evêque, Epoisses and others were to follow.

French cheeses have retained their individual character, allowing the vagaries

ABOVE: Chevrotin des Aravis (left) and Chèvre Feuille (right)
BELOW RIGHT: Carré de l'Est

of nature, combined with the ingenuity of man, to dictate their type, size and final flavour. In the valleys and on the plains small, fresh cheeses were made that could either be eaten by the family or swiftly sold; in the mountains, where cheeses had to be stored until the shepherds could get them to market, large wheels of cheese were made that would not mature for many months or even years. The numerous limestone caves, like those at Cambalou, where Roquefort is made, proved perfect for the making of blue cheeses.

Most of the vast number of cheeses made in France today are traditional varieties, but even the French have been unable to resist the temptation to create new cheeses. Most of the new cheeses have emerged from the huge dairy companies that now dominate the French market. Some are dismal, bland variations on traditional cheeses, particularly the standardized, pasteurized Bries and Camemberts; others, such as Chaumes, Saint-Agur and Le Roulé, have been made by adapting traditional methods to the modern factory environment, and offer the consumer a stepping stone to the more complex artisan cheeses they might otherwise shy away from trying.

Surprisingly, it is not Camembert that is the most popular cheese in France. That honour goes to Comté (or Comté Jura), the wonderful, hard, fruity mountain cheese from the northwest corner of France. Second favourite is Roquefort. Camembert owes its place as the best-known French cheese outside France to two apparently unrelated events. The first was the manufacture of small wooden boxes that proved perfect for packing the soft, fragile cheeses of Normandy, and the second was the invention of the train. Properly packed and rapidly transported to Paris, and beyond, Camembert soon became a best-seller.

The finest way to discover French cheeses is to travel through France, stopping at markets and fromageries to taste. Failing that, find a good cheesemonger and eat your way to an education.

BELOW: Vignotte

ABBAYE DE BELLOC (AOC)

REGION: *Pays Basque*
TYPE: *Traditional, farmhouse, unpasteurized, hard cheese*
SOURCE: *Sheep's milk (Manech and others)*
DESCRIPTION: *5kg/11lb fat wheel with natural, crusty, brownish rind with patches of red, orange and yellow. The rind is marked with tiny craters*
CULINARY USES: *Table cheese, grating, grilling, sauces*

The Abbaye de Notre-Dame de Belloc was founded by Benedictine monks. For centuries they have made their cheese from milk produced in the locality. In summer, the shepherds follow the ancient tradition of taking their flocks to mountain pastures. Along with other hard sheep's milk cheeses of the area, Abbaye de Belloc comes under the Ossau-Iraty AOC banner. The cheese has a firm, dense, rich and creamy texture. The taste resembles burnt caramel and there is a distinctive lanolin aroma.

AISY CENDRÉ

REGION: *Burgundy*
TYPE: *Traditional, farmhouse, unpasteurized, semi-soft cheese*
SOURCE: *Cow's milk*
DESCRIPTION: *200–250g/7–9oz round cheese with natural rind covered with a thick coating of ash*
CULINARY USE: *Table cheese*

To make this speciality, a local cheese (usually a young Epoisses) is immersed in a bed of ashes for at least one month. The best the author tasted was made by a winemaker who washed the cheese in his own marc de bourgogne before burying it in ashes. A few days before serving, the winemaker would brush off the ash, soak the cheese overnight in his precious eau-de-vie, then present it along with the rest of the bottle. Slow to ripen, Aisy Cendré has a white, salty, chalky centre surrounded by a softer, earthy-tasting outer layer. Unless you are the sort of person who likes sand with your picnic, you should brush off the layer of ashes before serving the cheese.

Olivet Cendré is a similar cheese.

ARDI-GASNA

REGION: *Pays Basque*
TYPE: *Traditional, farmhouse, unpasteurized, hard cheese*
SOURCE: *Sheep's milk*
DESCRIPTION: *3–5kg/6½–11lb wheel with natural, crusty, yellow rind with greyish moulds*
CULINARY USES: *Table cheese, grating, snacks, desserts*

Ardi-Gasna means "sheep's cheese" in Basque, and this cheese has remained virtually unchanged for centuries. There are still a few local shepherds who make the long journey with their flocks up to the high mountain pastures. Here they make their cheese in stone huts in late spring and early summer. Seldom found outside the region, Ardi-Gasna cheeses are highly prized. The cheese has a hard texture, but feels rich in the mouth. The flavour is clean and fresh with the sweetness of mountain flowers and a nuttiness born of age. The finish has a touch of sharpness that increases as the cheese matures.

Similar cheeses include Laruns and Esbareich.

ARÔMES AU GÈNE DE MARC

REGION: *Lyonnais*
TYPE: *Traditional, farmhouse, unpasteurized, natural-rind cheese*
SOURCE: *Cow's and goat's milk*
DESCRIPTION: *80–120g/3¼–4¼oz small, round cheeses. The whitish rind has some mould. The fermenting lees of the marc are pressed into it*
CULINARY USE: *Table cheese*

Made in various wine-making areas, some two to three months after the grapes have been pressed, these are the result of small immature cheeses such as Rigotte or St Marcellin being macerated or cured in vats of marc (fermenting grape skins and pips). They are then rolled in the marc before being sold. Definitely not for the faint-hearted, the cheeses have a strong, bittersweet, yeasty taste and aroma. When young, the moist, creamy taste of the cheese offers a balance; with age, the cheese becomes hard and flaky, with a formidable pungent taste – not necessarily appreciated by the uninitiated.

Similar cheeses are produced by other villages in the area.

AOC

To preserve and protect the traditions and experience of centuries of French cheesemaking, the AOC (Appellation d'Origine Contrôlée) system was established, as it had been for wine. Each cheese protected by the system must comply with strictly enforced rules that govern the following:

◆ the area where cattle may graze
◆ the origin and type of feed provided
◆ the breed of cattle that furnish the milk
◆ when the cheese is made (what season)
◆ how the cheese is made
◆ the shape and size of the cheese
◆ how the cheese is stored

The regulations often mean that cattle may only graze on permanent pastures that are organically managed, rather than ploughed and re-sown every year. The use of silage or other fermented or man-made feed is prohibited.

The AOC rules guarantee the quality of France's famous cheeses, protecting them against copies and giving the consumer the confidence to buy raw milk cheeses. Some AOC cheeses are made in huge factories, others on tiny farms, but all proudly respect and uphold the traditions of the area.

BELOW: Abbaye de Belloc

ABOVE: Banon

BELOW RIGHT: Beaufort

BAGUETTE LAONNAISE
REGION: *Ile-de-France*
TYPE: *Traditional, creamery,
washed-rind cheese*
SOURCE: *Cow's milk*
DESCRIPTION: *500g/1¼lb oblong loaf
with glossy but crusty,
orange-brown rind*
CULINARY USE: *Table cheese*

Created after the Second World War, Baguette Laonnaise has become a favourite with lovers of strong cheese. The sticky, ridged, orange-brown rind hides a supple, yet dense interior.

As the cheese ages it develops a very pungent, spicy nose and taste, and a finish that is reminiscent of the farmyard. In the wrong hands (or a cold fridge) the rind may dry out and the cheese will become quite bitter and unpleasant to eat.

Similar cheeses include Maroilles, Herve and Limburger.

BANON
REGION: *Provence*
TYPE: *Traditional, farmhouse and
creamery, unpasteurized, natural-
rind cheese*
SOURCE: *Cow's, sheep's or goat's milk,
or a combination*
DESCRIPTION: *100g/3¾oz small, round
cheese, traditionally sold wrapped in
chestnut leaves and tied with raffia*
CULINARY USES: *Table cheese*

This cheese takes its name from the market-town of Banon, where cobbled paths wind up past old, stone cottages to the church. Chestnut trees provide welcome shade and also provide the leaves used for wrapping the cheese. The leaves keep the young, slightly acidic cheese moist and impart a fresh vegetable flavour with a hint of wine. As the cheese ages, blue and grey moulds and yeasts are produced on and under the leaves, which contribute to the taste. Banon cheeses range from firm, mild and lactic to soft, creamy and tart, with a nutty flavour. Although traditionally produced from goat's, sheep's or mixed milks, most are today produced in large creameries, from cow's milk. At the weekly market in Banon, you can buy fresh and aged local cheeses.

The local speciality, Fromage Fort du Mont Ventoux, is produced by placing a young Banon cheese (minus chestnut leaves) in an earthenware crock, seasoning it liberally with salt and pepper and pouring over vinegar or local eau-de-vie. The crock is then placed in a cool cellar and the cheese left to ferment, with just the occasional stir. The longer it is left, the more ferocious it becomes.

BEAUFORT (AOC)
REGION: *Savoie*
TYPE: *Traditional, farmhouse,
unpasteurized, hard cheese*
SOURCE: *Cow's milk*
DESCRIPTION: *Large, concave cartwheel,
about 60cm/24in in diameter and
weighing up to 75kg/165lb. The hard,
brownish-yellow, natural, brushed
rind is slightly rough*
CULINARY USES: *Table cheese, snacks,
fondues, grated, in pies*

A member of the Gruyère family, but with a higher fat content, this ancient cheese dates back to the time of the Roman Empire. Made in mountain chalets, it has an irresistible smoothness, despite its hard appearance. It owes its superb flavour to the flowers, sweet grasses and herbs of the high pastures, where, by AOC rules, the cows must graze. Gruyère gets its name from the time when kings sent their tax collectors, known as "agents gruyers", to collect taxes from the cheesemakers. Also known as Gruyère de Beaufort.

BLEU D'AUVERGNE (AOC)

REGION: *Auvergne*
TYPE: *Traditional, farmhouse and
creamery, blue cheese*
SOURCE: *Cow's milk*
DESCRIPTION: *1–3kg/2¹/₄–6¹/₂ lb short
cylinder. The moist, natural rind has
grey and blue moulds*
CULINARY USES: *Table cheese, crumbled
in salads (with nuts)*

Named after the magnificent mountain-ous region where it is made, this is a moist, creamy cheese that resembles Roquefort, although it is made with cow's milk, not sheep's milk. It has a piquant smell and sharp, clean taste with a hint of herbs and melted butter. The cheese is composed of pockets and broken threads of bluish-grey mould. With age, the crust becomes sticky and reddish-orange moulds start to develop. These help to break down the interior, which gradually collapses, intensifying the spicy flavour.

Although Bleu d'Auvergne is now made by large creameries, the AOC regulations ensure that tradition and craftsmanship are retained. Some examples of this cheese are still made in farmhouses from raw milk, but they are seldom found out-side the region.

Similar cheeses include Bleu des Causses and Bleu de Laqueuille.

BLEU DE HAUT JURA (AOC)

REGION: *Franche-Comté*
TYPE: *Traditional, farmhouse and
co-operative, unpasteurized,
blue cheese*
SOURCE: *Cow's milk*
DESCRIPTION: *7.5kg/16¹/₂lb wheel with
convex edges. The natural rind is
dry, rough and thin, with powdery
yellow to red moulds*
CULINARY USES: *Table cheese, salads*

Unlike most blue cheeses, this is made in the shape of a large, flat wheel, which speeds the ripening process. The result is a cheese that is more supple and less creamy than other blues, with a mild taste that hints of mushrooms, tarragon and fresh milk. The AOC was granted in 1977. Other blues made in the region, such as Bleu de Gex and Bleu de Septomoncel, are now named Bleu de Haut Jura.

BLEU DE LAQUEUILLE

REGION: *Auvergne*
TYPE: *Traditional, creamery,
unpasteurized, blue cheese*
SOURCE: *Cow's milk*
DESCRIPTION: *800g–2.5kg/1³/₄–5¹/₂lb
cylinder with natural, pale orange
rind, on which the more dominant,
white penicillium mould battles it out
with the greyish moulds common to
blue cheeses*
CULINARY USE: *Table cheese*

A statue in Laqueuille reminds visitors to the village that Antoine Roussel created this cheese in 1850 after sprinkling young curd with blue moulds he found growing on rye bread. It rapidly became popular, both locally and in Paris. Like a smaller version of Fourme d'Ambert, it tends to develop a soft, white mould on some or all of the rind. The consistency leans towards that of Brie. The blue is chunky rather than in streaks and the flavour is spicy, fresh and creamy, with a slightly salty tang. The smaller version makes an attrac-tive addition to a cheeseboard.

*BELOW: Clockwise from bottom left, Bleu
de Laqueuille , Bleu d'Auvergne, Bleu
des Causses and Bleu de Gex*

BLEU DES CAUSSES (AOC)

REGION: *Auvergne*
TYPE: *Traditional, creamery,
unpasteurized, blue cheese*
SOURCE: *Cow's milk*
DESCRIPTION: *2.25–3kg/5–6¹/₂lb flat
cylinder. The sticky, ivory rind has
fine reddish-orange and grey moulds*
CULINARY USES: *Table cheese, salads*

For centuries, this pungent cheese was made in the Rouergue and surrounding areas, using cow's or sheep's milk. However, since 1947 AOC rules have decreed that it must be made with cow's milk to differentiate it from Roquefort, which is made in the same area. Bleu des Causses, like Roquefort, is matured in limestone caves with natural fissures that allow fresh air currents or "fleurines" to circulate and move the natural moulds through the ripening cheese. The result is a cheese that is firm-textured, but more moist and spicy in flavour than other French blues. Fresh-tasting, with a sharp finish, it is an excellent, less salty alter-native to Roquefort.

Bleu des Causses cheeses that attain the required standards of quality are stamped with the AOC symbol before being wrapped in silver foil.

BOUGON

REGION: *Poitou-Charentes*
TYPE: *Traditional, creamery,*
soft-white cheese
SOURCE: *Goat's milk*
DESCRIPTION: *80g/3¹/₄oz round with*
fine, white penicillium mould rind
CULINARY USE: *Table cheese*

Although similar cheeses have been made in various forms in France for generations, Bougon was only recently made commercially. Although *bougon* means "grumpy" in French, this is no reflection on the cheese – it is simply named after the town where it is made. It is a smooth and voluptuous cheese with a taste that has been likened to a blend of tarragon, thyme and white wine. The Camembert shape is the most popular, but it also comes in pyramids, cylindrical logs and mini rounds.

BOULETTE D'AVESNES

REGION: *Nord-Pas-de-Calais*
TYPE: *Traditional, farmhouse and*
creamery, fresh cheese
SOURCE: *Cow's milk*
DESCRIPTION: *150–180g/5–6¹/₄oz cone*
with natural rind given a dark red
colour by the use of annatto
or paprika
CULINARY USE: *Table cheese*

This unusual cheese was originally produced from buttermilk and was made on farms as a by-product of buttermaking. Today, creameries use underripe or less-than-perfect Maroilles or Dauphine cheeses. The soft curd is kneaded and mashed with parsley, tarragon, pepper and paprika. The cheese has a fairly doughy texture and a quite outrageously spicy flavour.

ABOVE: Boulette d'Avesnes

BOURSAULT

REGION: *Ile-de-France*
TYPE: *Modern, creamery,*
soft-white cheese
SOURCE: *Cow's milk*
DESCRIPTION: *200g/7oz small*
half-cylinder with light, white
penicillium mould rind with
pinkish tones
CULINARY USES: *Table cheese, canapés*

Invented by Henri Boursault in 1953, about the same time as Boursin, this soft-white-rinded cheese became successful almost overnight. The company is now owned by the cheese giant Van den Berg. The method resembles that used for Brie, but Boursault has a softer and thinner rind. This helps to ripen the cheese, giving off a sweet, mushroomy aroma. The high cream content means that the taste is smooth and almost buttery. The interior is solid rather than supple or runny and the finish is nutty and it has a refreshing citrus tang to balance the richness of the cream. One of the best enriched cheeses, Boursault is also known as Lucullus. Délice de Saint-Cyr is a larger version.

BOURSIN

REGION: *Ile-de-France and Normandy*
TYPE: *Modern, creamery, fresh cheese*
SOURCE: *Cow's milk*
DESCRIPTION: *80g/3¹/₄oz small half-*
cylinder without rind, sold in an
attractive, corrugated-foil wrapper
CULINARY USES: *Table cheese,*
baking, spreading

Founded in 1957 by a Monsieur Boursin and now produced by one of the major French cheese companies (Van den Bergh), this is a moist, yet creamy cheese with a sweet, rich flavour with a hint of acidity. It melts in the mouth like ice cream. The quality has remained consistently good, both as regards the original cheese and the two well-known variations, one with garlic and herbs and the other rolled in fiery cracked peppercorns.

Boursin was the first cheese advertised on French TV and became a sensational success. The wacky, off-the-wall advertisement showed a famous actor being driven from his bed by his desire for the Boursin that was waiting elegantly in his fridge. Boursin – and the catch phrase "*du pain, du vin, du Boursin*" – became part of French culture.

Made only from rich Normandy milk and cream, the cheese is produced without rennet. Only a starter culture is used and much of the processing is still only semi-automated, to ensure that the texture and quality are maintained. Since Van den Bergh took over, it has invented three more exotic variations, but these are nowhere near as good, or as authentic, as the famous three.

ABOVE: Boursin

LEFT: Boursault

ABOVE: Bresse Bleu

BRESSE BLEU
REGION: *Rhône-Alpes*
TYPE: *Modern, creamery, blue cheese*
SOURCE: *Cow's milk*
DESCRIPTION: *125–500g/4¹/₂oz–1¹/₄lb cylinder with soft-white rind with penicillium mould*
CULINARY USE: *Table cheese*

Developed during the Second World War and now owned by the milk processing giant Bongrain, Bresse Bleu became increasingly popular in the 1950s as an alternative to stronger blue cheeses. The interior is rich and buttery. Like Brie, it melts in the mouth, with a sweet, slightly spicy tang. The smooth, white rind has the aroma of button mushrooms. Because of the dense, creamy nature of the cheese, the blue mould must be injected into it, rather than being added to the milk before coagulation. It forms pockets of blue-grey mould rather than fine streaks. Tiny mould spores from the rind may be carried into the cheese when it is injected, forming patches of fluffy, white mould within the cheese.

Individual cheeses are small, so can be sold whole rather than in slices. This fact, together with convenient packaging, means that Bresse Bleu travels well and is therefore widely available outside its country of origin.

Similar cheeses include Blue Brie and Cambazola.

BRIE DE MEAUX (AOC)
REGION: *Ile-de-France*
TYPE: *Traditional, farmhouse, unpasteurized, soft-white cheese*
SOURCE: *Cow's milk*
DESCRIPTION: *2.5–3kg/5¹/₂–6¹/₂lb wheel. The white penicillium mould rind has reddish-brown ferments. The marks of the straw mat on which the cheese matures are visible*
CULINARY USE: *Table cheese*

The father of all soft-white or bloomy-rind cheeses. Brie de Meaux was first recorded in AD774 when the gourmet and soldier Charlemagne tasted it in Brie and ordered two batches to be sent to him annually in Aix.

You will know when you have found the perfect Meaux – it is smooth, voluptuous and not quite runny. The aroma is that of mushrooms with the merest hint of ammonia and the taste is of creamy wild mushroom soup with a dash of sherry.

Although the cheese is now protected by AOC regulations, some critics claim these do not go far enough. Regrettably, the Friesian-Holstein cow continues to replace the old indigenous cattle. The richness and character of the milk is therefore not always what it should be. Fortunately, there remain some superb farm-produced Meaux brought to the point of perfection by talented affineurs.

BRIE DE MELUN (AOC)
REGION: *Ile-de-France*
TYPE: *Traditional, farmhouse, unpasteurized, soft-white cheese*
SOURCE: *Cow's milk*
DESCRIPTION: *1.5–8kg/3–18lb wheel with white penicillium mould forming a fine, white crust with a mix of yellow and red ferments*
CULINARY USE: *Table cheese*

Produced in the same region as Brie de Meaux, Brie de Melun is sharper and more salty. Whereas rennet is used to coagulate Meaux, Melun relies entirely on the action of lactose-loving bacteria. The art of bringing the cheeses to the point of perfection belongs to the affineur. He will watch over row upon row of Bries in various stages of ripeness, each of them sitting on a well-worn wooden shelf lined with a straw mat. The cheese is judged to be ripe when the yellow mould dominates, with just a touch of the red. To attain the perfect balance, the affineur and his team turn as many as 18,000 cheeses twice a week for about two months. They take care not to leave fingermarks and to ensure that no bacteria from their hands are permitted to pass to the cheeses.

A perfect Melun has a supple texture with meadow scents and flavours – quite like an unripe Brie, but with more depth.

BELOW: Brie de Meaux

BELOW: Butte

BRILLAT-SAVARIN
REGION: *Normandy*
TYPE: *Modern, creamery, fresh or soft-white cheese*
SOURCE: *Cow's milk*
DESCRIPTION: *450–500g/1–1¼lb round cheese. There may be a soft-white rind. The cheese will eventually grow a thick, velvety, white crust*
CULINARY USES: *Table cheese, canapés*

Named after the French magistrate, born in 1755, who published a gastronomic tome: *La Physiologie du Goût*. This book bore witness to a lifetime committed to good food. Brillat-Savarin would have approved of this rich triple cream cheese.

Other triple cream cheeses include Le Saulieu, Lucullus and Boursault.

BROCCIU/BROCCIO (AOC)
REGION: *Corsica*
TYPE: *Traditional, farmhouse, unpasteurized, whey cheese*
SOURCE: *Sheep's and goat's milk*
DESCRIPTION: *500g–1kg/1¼–2¼lb cheeses in various shapes, without rind*
CULINARY USES: *Served with herbs as a snack or with fruit for breakfast*

This fresh cheese is made with sheep's milk in winter and goat's milk in summer. Traditionally made from whey, although skimmed milk is often used today. The cheese is drained in woven baskets and has a mild flavour. Some cheeses are salted and dried for six months, when the flavour becomes very sharp and pronounced.

BÛCHETTE D'ANJOU
REGION: *Loire*
TYPE: *Traditional, farmhouse, unpasteurized, natural-rind cheese*
SOURCE: *Goat's milk*
DESCRIPTION: *80–100g/3¼–3¾oz log with natural rind dusted with salt and charcoal*
CULINARY USES: *Table cheese, slicing and grilling, in salads*

These delightful, plain or ash-covered cheeses have been made in the Loire area for centuries. When young they are firm and grainy, with a mild, fresh, citrus taste. Under the watchful gaze of a talented affineur, the interior softens to melting point and the taste becomes redolent of fresh asparagus and wild herbs.

Bûchette de Banon is a similar cheese.

BUTTE
REGION: *Ile-de-France*
TYPE: *Modern, creamery, soft-white cheese*
SOURCE: *Cow's milk*
DESCRIPTION: *350g/12oz brick with thick, smooth, velvety, white penicillium rind*
CULINARY USE: *Table cheese*

This takes its name from the shape, which resembles a small hillock. The cheese owes its buttery texture to cream, which is added to the milk before it is coagulated. The fresh cheese melts in the mouth and has a mushroomy aroma and a salty, bitter tang. If allowed to ripen, the rind develops reddish pigmentation, the interior becomes runny around the edges, the aroma becomes acrid and the taste sharper and (to some) more delicious.

Similar cheeses include Grand Vatel and Explorateur.

RIGHT: From the top, Cabécou de Rocamadour, Camembert and Brillat-Savarin

CABÉCOU DE ROCAMADOUR (AOC)
REGION: *Midi-Pyrénées*
TYPE: *Traditional, farmhouse, unpasteurized, natural-rind cheese*
SOURCE: *Sheep's and goat's milk*
DESCRIPTION: *30–40g/1¼–1½oz disc. The natural, soft rind is cream-coloured and wrinkly. It develops pale blue moulds*
CULINARY USES: *Table cheese, baking, grilling*

These tiny, round discs, with their creamy white rind, have been made in the area for centuries, ever since the locals domesticated the herds of goats and sheep that once roamed wild on the mountainsides. Today, at the height of the season, the cheeses are sold in flat, wooden, slatted trays, which are piled high on market stalls decked with chestnut boughs. The cheeses are sometimes decorated with tiny sprigs of wild herbs, or sold wrapped in bacon strips, ready for grilling and tossing into a salad of frisée lettuce. When the dense, creamy cheese is grilled (perhaps on a crusty baguette), the nutty taste and distinctly goaty aroma intensify – wonderful when washed down with a bottle or two of local wine. Sometimes the cheese is made with sheep's milk, which gives a nuttier taste with a hint of butterscotch.

The cheese is also known simply as Rocamadour.

CAMEMBERT DE NORMANDIE (AOC)

REGION: *Normandy*
TYPE: *Traditional, farmhouse and
creamery, unpasteurized,
soft-white cheese*
SOURCE: *Cow's milk*
DESCRIPTION: *250g/9oz round
with thin, white penicillium
mould crust that becomes
impregnated with red, brown
and yellow pigments as it matures*
CULINARY USES: *Table cheese. Anything
else would be sacrilege*

Camembert started life towards the end of the eighteenth century as a dry, yellow-brown cheese made for her family by Marie Harel, a farmer's wife. This was around the time of the French Revolution, and the family gave shelter to a priest from the Brie region. Having often talked to his parishioners while they made their cheeses, he was able to repay the Harels' kindness by imparting his knowledge. As a result, the cheese became softer and more earthy, but it would be some years before it acquired the name by which we know it today.

In 1855, one of Marie Harel's daughters presented Napoleon with one of the cheeses and told him that it came from Camembert. The name stuck, but the cheese might still have remained relatively unknown had it not been for three factors. First, the expansion of the railways opened up new markets. Second, small, wooden cheeseboxes proved perfect for protecting the cheeses on their long journeys. Finally, in the 1920s came the discovery of how to isolate and introduce into the ripening rooms the white penicillium moulds. These virulent moulds were capable of fighting off the less aggressive grey and blue moulds that had previously tainted the young cheeses. As a bonus, they prevented the interior from drying out. The voluptuous texture and mushroom aroma of a classic Camembert was finally achieved.

Today, hundreds of producers in Normandy are permitted to make AOC Camembert. The finest have a fragrant aroma and taste of wild mushroom soup, with a slightly yeasty, almost meaty taste.

ABOVE: Cantal

BELOW: Caprice des Dieux

CANTAL (AOC)

REGION: *Auvergne*
TYPE: *Traditional, farmhouse and
creamery, unpasteurized, hard cheese*
SOURCE: *Cow's milk*
DESCRIPTION: *35–45kg/80–100lb tall
cylinder with natural, straw-yellow to
grey crust, dusted with grey and
red pigments*
CULINARY USES: *Table cheese, grating, in
soups and in sauces*

One of the oldest French cheeses, Cantal was originally produced by putting the curd into *le formage*, the wooden cylinder that is believed to be the origin of the French word for cheese – *fromage*. Cantal Fermier is produced in mountain chalets during the summer months, while Cantal Laitier is a pasteurized cheese made all year round, using milk from nearby farms in accordance with the AOC regulations. Each cheese has a metal badge embedded in the rind, and is stamped with the official AOC logo.

When young, Cantal is moist, open-textured and springy, with a cheese sauce tang not unlike Lancashire. With age, it becomes more like a mature Cheddar. The cheese is sold as *jeune* when it is at least 30 days old. When it is over six months old and has developed a robust personality, it is categorized as *vieux*. Between two and six months old, the cheese is sold as *entre-deux* (between the two).

CAPRICE DES DIEUX

REGION: *Champagne-Ardenne*
TYPE: *Modern, creamery, soft-white
cheese*
SOURCE: *Cow's milk*
DESCRIPTION: *120g/4¹/₄oz oval,
with a smooth, velvety, pure
white penicillium rind*
CULINARY USE: *Table cheese*

Milky and rather bland, this cheese looks rather more interesting than it tastes. The texture, too, is somewhat disappointing, being more elastic than supple. However, demand has kept the small, oval boxes on the supermarket shelves and no doubt has provided a stepping stone for many would-be cheese connoisseurs.

CARRÉ DE L'EST

REGION: *Champagne and Lorraine*
TYPE: *Traditional, farmhouse, and
creamery, washed-rind or
soft-white cheese*
SOURCE: *Cow's milk*
DESCRIPTION: *300g/11oz square with
either an orange-red, washed-rind or
a penicillium mould crust*
CULINARY USE: *Table cheese*

Made in the area for generations, Carré de l'Est is ripened in cellars and encouraged to grow either a soft-white crust or washed in brine and eau-de-vie to produce a pungent, ridged orange rind. Each cheese is turned and washed by hand to spread the colourful bacteria over the cheese. The washed-rind cheeses have a runny interior with a smoky-bacon flavour. The white cheeses have a Camembert-like rind and a flavour reminiscent of melted butter and warm mushrooms.

ABOVE: *Chaource*

CHABICHOU DU POITOU (AOC)

REGION: *Poitou-Charentes*
TYPE: *Traditional, farmhouse and creamery, unpasteurized, natural-rind cheese*
SOURCE: *Goat's milk*
DESCRIPTION: *120g/4¼oz cylinder with a beautiful, bluish-grey mould that overlays the thin, white mould when mature*
CULINARY USES: *Table cheese, grilling*
The texture is firm and creamy rather than grainy or gluggy, and the cheese has a fresh ground-nut flavour. Mothais, Saint-Maixent and Sainte-Maure are similar.

CHAOURCE (AOC)

REGION: *Champagne*
TYPE: *Traditional, creamery, soft-white cheese*
SOURCE: *Cow's milk*
DESCRIPTION: *250–450g/9oz–1lb cylinder with downy, white penicillium rind*
CULINARY USE: *Table cheese*
Some people prefer the cheese young, when the rind has barely formed and is milky, slightly tart and salty. At this stage, the interior is grainy and coarse, rather than smooth. Other cheese-lovers prefer to wait for the rind to thicken and develop red ferments. The rind of the mature cheese has a slightly bitter flavour with a hint of mushrooms, and the interior is buttery and quite piquant, fruity and sharp. Similar cheeses include Ervy-le-Châtel, and Neufchâtel.

CHAUMES

REGION: *Dordogne*
TYPE: *Modern, creamery, washed-rind cheese*
SOURCE: *Cow's milk*
DESCRIPTION: *2kg/4½lb flattened wheel. The soft, thin rind is deep tangerine in colour with a thin, orange-paper cover*
CULINARY USES: *Table cheese, grilling*
Based upon traditional Trappist-style cheeses, this has proved to be one of the most popular of the modern French varieties. The soft rind is bright tangerine-orange and the interior is smooth, supple and quite rubbery. Although it looks as though it is about to run, the cheese is actually fairly dense and feels wonderfully rich and creamy on the tongue. The nutty, almost meaty taste and aroma are milder than you might suspect. Port Salut is a similar cheese.

LEFT: *Chabichou du Poitou – an unpasteurized natural-rind cheese made with goat's milk*

ABOVE: *Chaumes*

CHÈVRE LOG

REGION: *Loire*
TYPE: *Modern, creamery, soft-white cheese*
SOURCE: *Goat's milk*
DESCRIPTION: *3kg/6½lb log with white, velvety rind, which can become damp, acrid and separate from the cheese*
CULINARY USES: *Table cheese, hors d'oeuvres*
First made by a large co-operative in Poitiers and now sold under various brand names, chèvre log, or Bûcheron, is now available throughout Europe. At two days old, it has a lovely, sweet-sour, fruity taste, with just a touch of the almondy character of goat's milk, when the texture is dense with a fine grain. By 10 days, it is firm yet breakable and feels slightly sticky in the mouth. It retains fresh acidity and the aromatic, goaty taste intensifies. It slices easily, so is ideal for grilling.

BELOW: *Chèvre log*

CHEVROTIN DES ARAVIS

REGION: *Rhône-Alpes*

TYPE: *Traditional, farmhouse, unpasteurized, washed-rind cheese*

SOURCE: *Cow's and goat's milk*

DESCRIPTION: *250–350g/9–12oz round with yellowish-orange, floury-washed rind*

CULINARY USES: *Table cheese, snacks*

One of the few washed-rind goat's cheeses, Chevrotin is produced in the same way as Reblochon, which it resembles in appearance and texture – smooth, melting, rich and sensuous. It has a mild, goaty aroma and a wonderful complexity of character. The taste is nutty and quite savoury.

CÎTEAUX/ABBAYE DE CÎTEAUX

REGION: *Burgundy*

TYPE: *Traditional, farmhouse, unpasteurized, washed-rind cheese*

SOURCE: *Cow's milk (Montbéliard)*

DESCRIPTION: *700g/1lb 9oz wheel. The fine, leathery crust is pale yellow-orange with a dusting of various moulds*

CULINARY USE: *Table cheese*

L'Abbaye de Notre Dame at Cîteaux, near Beaune, was founded in 1098 by the Benedictine monks and became the birthplace of the Cistercian movement. The term "Trappist" was not introduced until the 18th century, and it is now used to describe the monastic-type cheeses.

Set in the heart of wine country, the abbey has a herd of around 200 red and white Montbéliard cows and prefers to keep production small, selling most of its cheese locally. The cheese resembles Reblochon, but because the soil and pastures are very different, so is the taste of the cheese. That great 20th-century cheese-lover Patrick Rance describes it as follows: "Cîteaux has a delicious, melt-in-the-mouth, refreshing character all its own, set off by its fine crust, more even in patina than that of Reblochon. Like the crust of the good bread with which it deserves to be paired, it is an important part of the cheese's savour and consistency against the palate, and should never be cut away and wasted."

COEUR DE CAMEMBERT AU CALVADOS

REGION: *Normandy*

TYPE: *Modern, farmhouse, soft-white cheese*

SOURCE: *Cow's milk*

DESCRIPTION: *250g/9oz round with washed rind covered with fine breadcrumbs soaked in Calvados and decorated with a half walnut*

CULINARY USE: *Table cheese*

For those not satisfied with the delicious taste of a ripe Camembert, there is this variation. The rind is removed from a semi-cured Camembert, which is then soaked in Calvados. Fresh breadcrumbs are then pressed into the cheese and a walnut garnish is added. The cheese absorbs the heady spirit. The faint apple aroma seems to complement the rich, creamy texture of the cheese.

COMTÉ/GRUYÈRE DE COMTÉ (AOC)

REGION: *Franche-Comté*

TYPE: *Traditional, creamery, unpasteurized, hard cheese*

SOURCE: *Cow's milk*

DESCRIPTION: *35–55kg/80–120lb wheel with convex sides. The natural, hard, thick rind is golden-yellow to brown*

CULINARY USES: *Table cheese, snacks, canapés, fondues, gratins*

The French make two Gruyères – Beaufort and Comté, both wonderfully large, impressive wheels. Comté is sweeter than Beaufort and has a convex rather than a concave rind. As with their Swiss counterparts, the quality can be judged by the size,

shape and condition of the holes. An experienced affineur, with a gentle tap of a special hammer, can detect their condition by the resonance of the cheese. If you find one with a tiny drop or "tear" in one of the holes, it will be as near perfect as you can get.

Comté is a magnificent, unspoilt, mountain chalet cheese. It is very creamy and has a piquant yet sweet, fruity flavour. The bite is firm, dry and slightly granular, while the acidity is fruity and slightly fizzy – like fermenting pears.

These huge cheeses have been made in co-operatives in the Franche-Comté for centuries. Shepherds, with their small herds, have always spent the summer months in remote mountain huts. Due to their distance from the nearest markets, they needed to make a cheese that required months to mature. So they pooled their milk, creating huge cheeses that were often only taken down the mountain at the end of the season.

When the cattle return to the valleys at the end of summer all production of Comté ceases. Instead, they make the equally delicious but very different Vacherin Mont d'Or, now known as Mont d'Or. Both cheeses are governed by the rules of the AOC.

Similar cheeses include Gruyère, Emmental and Beaufort.

ABOVE: *Coeur de Camembert au Calvados*

CRÈME FRAÎCHE

REGION: *Various*
TYPE: *Traditional, farmhouse and creamery, matured cream*
SOURCE: *Cow's milk*
DESCRIPTION: *Matured cream, rather than cheese, sold in pots*
CULINARY USE: *Wonderful to cook with as it curdles less easily than double (heavy) cream when heated*

Crème fraîche isn't a true cheese. It is a matured cream made by adding a culture to fresh cream. The bacteria, similar to those used to make yogurt, thicken and ripen the cream. The result is a truly delicious and exceedingly smooth cream that is rich and nutty with just a hint of lemony sourness.

ABOVE LEFT: Crème fraîche

ABOVE RIGHT: Crottin de Chavignol

COULOMMIERS

REGION: *Ile-de-France*
TYPE: *Traditional, farmhouse, unpasteurized, soft-white cheese*
SOURCE: *Cow's milk*
DESCRIPTION: *400–500g/14oz–1¹/₄lb disc with white penicillium mould*
CULINARY USES: *Table cheese, canapés*

Smaller than Brie, Coulommiers ripens more quickly. Some prefer to eat it when the white mould is barely discernible, while others prefer it *affiné* (when the aroma is stronger and more like that of ripe Brie). Commercial versions are pleasant, but lack the depth of an unpasteurized cheese, which can be as good as farmhouse Camembert.

The cheese is also known as Brie de Coulommiers or Petit Brie.

CROTTIN DE CHAVIGNOL (AOC)

REGION: *Loire*
TYPE: *Traditional, farmhouse and creamery, unpasteurized, natural-rind cheese*
SOURCE: *Goat's milk*
DESCRIPTION: *60–100g/2¹/₄–3³/₄oz cylinder with natural rind that ranges from pale ivory to almost black*
CULINARY USES: *Table cheese, snacks, grilling, in salads*

The young cheese has an off-white, slightly wrinkled rind with a mere suggestion of white and blue moulds. At eight days, the cheese has a gentle, aromatic, yeasty taste and a fine, moist texture. At 11 days, the interior softens; the taste is nuttier and full-bodied. At 20 days, the cheese is denser and creamier and there is a fruity tinge to the taste. The flavour intensifies when the cheese is grilled, as it often is. Grilled crottin is the basis of a delicious chévre salad that is popular all over France. If the cheese is allowed to mature further, blue and grey moulds will cover the rind, drawing out the moisture. The result is a small, hard, dark grey disc that justifies the name: Crottin de Chavignol means "horse droppings". The interior develops a fruity, bitter taste. Most crottins are, however, sold young.

ABOVE: Coulommiers

DAUPHIN

REGION: *Nord-Pas-de-Calais*
TYPE: *Traditional, farmhouse and creamery, unpasteurized, semi-soft cheese*
SOURCE: *Goat's milk*
DESCRIPTION: *300–350g/11–12oz dolphin- or brick-shaped cheese with brick-red, washed rind*
CULINARY USE: *Table cheese*

The cheese is said to derive its name from the unusual shape. Usually this resembles a dolphin or fish, although some are small rectangles. A more likely explanation is that when Louis XIV and the Dauphin visited the region and praised the local cheese, the inhabitants settled on both name and shape accordingly.

The brick-red rind gives way to the firm, yet supple interior. Tarragon and pepper are added to the fresh curd, which is then drained and matured. The cheese has a spicy flavour with a yeasty aroma.

DREUX À LA FEUILLE

REGION: *Ile-de-France*
TYPE: *Traditional, farmhouse, unpasteurized, soft-white cheese*
SOURCE: *Cow's milk*
DESCRIPTION: *300–350g/11–12oz round with white penicillium mould rind, enclosed in a chestnut leaf*
CULINARY USE: *Table cheese*

In size and texture, this cheese, being supple and almost runny when ripe, resembles Coulommiers. The chestnut leaf wrapping imparts a nutty, slightly aromatic taste to the cheese, which is generally a good buy.

EPOISSES DE BOURGOGNE (AOC)

REGION: *Burgundy*
TYPE: *Traditional, farmhouse, unpasteurized, washed-rind cheese*
SOURCE: *Cow's milk*
DESCRIPTION: *250g/9oz round cheese with smooth, shiny, brick-red, washed rind*
CULINARY USE: *Table cheese*

Each cheese is "washed" by hand, using a small brush to spread the bacteria over and into the rind. The final wash is alcohol – usually marc de Bourgogne.

Like many of France's best-loved cheeses, Epoisses are enjoyed at different stages of their maturation by different people. Epoisse Frais (30 days) is a mere shadow of its aged counterpart, being firm, moist and grainy, yet still creamy with a fresh acidity and mild yeasty tang.

At 40 days the rind is orange-brown in colour and very sticky. When the outer edges of the cheese are close to collapse, the interior is not far behind. The pungent, spicy aroma is matched by the strong and strangely meaty taste. Unbelievably good, the cheese deserves to be served with a fine Burgundy or a spicy aromatic white wine. Carré de l'Est, Chambertin, Langres and Sou-maintrain are all similar cheeses.

ABOVE: Epoisses de Bourgogne

BELOW: Dauphin

ABOVE: Etorki

ETORKI

REGION: *Aquitaine*
TYPE: *Modern, creamery, hard cheese*
SOURCE: *Sheep's milk*
DESCRIPTION: *4kg/9lb fat wheel with reddish-brown, thin, natural rind*
CULINARY USES: *Table cheese, grating, melting*

Until 1984, most of the sheep's milk in this region went to the makers of Roquefort. However, to comply with the strict AOC rules governing the grazing area and the breed of sheep, the region's milk was excluded after that date. Fortunately, the situation was anticipated by Fromagerie des Chaumes (best known for the cheese of the same name). In 1979, they built a factory that now processes most of the sheep's milk in the area into Etorki. The recipe is based on a cheese that has for centuries been made by the local shepherds.

This factory-made cheese has a bright yellow interior, rich texture and a nutty finish and is more close-textured and supple than the hand-made original, but it is nevertheless good, with the burnt-caramel sweetness and creamy texture typical of sheep's milk cheeses. As sheep's milk is abundant only from winter to early summer, the factory makes cow's milk cheese – Lou Palou – for the rest of the year.

ABOVE: Explorateur

EXPLORATEUR

REGION: *Ile-de-France*
TYPE: *Modern, creamery,
soft-white cheese*
SOURCE: *Cow's milk*
DESCRIPTION: *250g/9oz cylinder with
soft-white rind*
CULINARY USE: *Table cheese*

Invented in the 1950s and named in honour of the first US satellite – Explorer. Explorateur is a firm, creamy cheese with a grainy feel. It has a delicate aroma and a slightly salty, mushroomy tang.

Similar cheeses include Excelsior, Boursault, Brillat-Savarin and Magnum.

FIGUE

REGION: *Aquitaine*
TYPE: *Traditional, farmhouse,
unpasteurized, fresh cheese*
SOURCE: *Goat's milk*
DESCRIPTION: *160–200g/5¹/₄–7oz fresh
hemispherical cheese*
CULINARY USES: *Table cheese, grilling*

Named for its fig shape, this is similar in taste and texture to the wonderful chèvre cheeses found in the Loire, Aquitaine and Périgord areas of France. Mild and pure with a lemony acidity, it is normally dusted with salt and ash, paprika or herbs.

FLEUR DU MAQUIS

REGION: *Corsica*
TYPE: *Traditional, farmhouse,
unpasteurized, fresh or
natural-rind cheese*
SOURCE: *Sheep's milk*
DESCRIPTION: *575–675g/1¹/₄–1¹/₂lb
square cheese with rounded corners.
The natural rind is covered with
chillies, juniper berries, savory
and rosemary*
CULINARY USE: *Table cheese*

If the author were asked to identify her favourite cheese, Fleur du Maquis would be near the top of her list. Not merely because it looks so desirable with its covering of wild herbs, peppers and juniper berries, nor because of its aromatic scent, but largely because it is never the same.

Most Corsican cheeses are superb, thanks to the diverse breeds of sheep and goats and the natural grazing. The island is covered with wild thyme, marjoram and the maquis, a scrubby, aromatic bush on which the sheep graze and which gave its name to this exceptional cheese.

When young, Fleur du Maquis is mild, sweet and lemony. Age brings a richness of character (and a string of superlatives): sweet, nutty, aromatic and creamy. The cheese has a melt-in-the-mouth texture.

BELOW: Figue

ABOVE: Fleur du Maquis

FOUGERUS, LE

REGION: *Ile-de-France*
TYPE: *Traditional, farmhouse,
unpasteurized, soft-white cheese*
SOURCE: *Cow's milk*
DESCRIPTION: *1kg/2¹/₄lb thick disc with
white penicillium mould rind. It is
decorated with a piece of bracken
or fern*
CULINARY USE: *Table cheese*

Similar in both size and texture to Coulommiers, this cheese is supple, almost runny when ripe and resembles Dreux à la Feuille. The fern or bracken *fougerus* used to decorate it imparts an earthy charm to the cheese.

FOURME D'AMBERT
REGION: *Auvergne*
TYPE: *Traditional, farmhouse and co-operative, blue cheese*
SOURCE: *Cow's milk*
DESCRIPTION: *1.5–2kg/3¹/₄–4¹/₂lb cylinder. The natural, white crust develops patches of red and blue moulds*
CULINARY USE: *Table cheese*

Fourme d'Ambert ("cheese of Ambert") is more supple and dense than most blues. The mould gathers in erratic patches rather than the more usual streaks and the flavour is savoury and nutty. The cheese is easily recognized by its unusually tall, cylindrical shape.

Similar cheeses include Fourme de Montbrison, Bleu de Montbrison, Bleu de Gex and Bleu de Septmoncel.

FRINAULT
REGION: *Orléanais*
TYPE: *Traditional, creamery, unpasteurized, soft-white cheese*
SOURCE: *Cow's milk*
DESCRIPTION: *120–150g/4¹/₄–5oz round with natural rind covered with ash*
CULINARY USE: *Table cheese*

Invented by Monsieur Frinault in 1848 at Chécy, this cheese is similar to a Camembert, but matured in wood ash. It has a slightly firmer, less voluptuous texture and a strong, rather spicy taste. The quality varies, however, and the cheese can be bitter if it is allowed to dry out too much. It is quite difficult to obtain. Also known as Chécy, it is similar to Olivet Cendré.

LEFT: Fourme d'Ambert

RIGHT: Fromage frais

FROMAGE CORSE
REGION: *Corsica*
TYPE: *Traditional, farmhouse, unpasteurized, semi-soft cheese*
SOURCE: *Sheep's and goat's milk*
DESCRIPTION: *500g/1¹/₄lb round. The crusty, washed rind has orange and yellow moulds*
CULINARY USE: *Table cheese*

Made by the local people for the local people, and thus it has remained for centuries. Even the rennet is still obtained by drying the stomach of a young goat, then slicing it and soaking it in water for two days before it is required. This ancient practice, first discovered by nomadic tribes over 2,000 years ago, gives the cheese added depth.

The rough exterior is pungent, with orange and yellow ferments on a pale beige-yellow background. The interior is supple, sometimes almost runny, with small holes. It has a robust flavour redolent of the wild maquis and herbs that grow on the rugged mountains of the island. The cheese is seldom found outside Corsica, except in Paris. It resembles Niolo.

RIGHT: Fromage Corse

FROMAGE FRAIS
REGION: *Various*
TYPE: *Traditional, farmhouse and creamery, fresh cheese*
SOURCE: *Cow's, goat's and sheep's milk*
DESCRIPTION: *Moist, creamy, white, fresh cheese sold in pots*
CULINARY USES: *On fresh fruit, for breakfast, as a spread*

One of the first cheeses made by man, fromage frais is simply milk that has been coagulated using a bacteria culture rather than rennet. High in moisture, it varies little except for the fat content, which ranges from *maigre* (very low) to *allégé* (double) and *triple crème*. The culture used is similar to that for yogurt, but, because it is slower-acting, it produces a citrus tingle rather than an acidic taste. The milk is left for around 12 hours to coagulate, the whey is then drained and the fromage frais is strained for two hours before being potted.

GAPERON
REGION: *Auvergne*
TYPE: *Traditional, farmhouse and co-operative, soft-white cheese*
SOURCE: *Cow's milk*
DESCRIPTION: *250–350g/9–12oz cheese shaped like a small, upturned basin and tied with raffia. It has a soft-white rind dusted with white mould.*
CULINARY USES: *Table cheese, snacks*

Traditionally, this cheese and others like it were made in homes, rather than by cheesemakers. Buttermilk was originally used, although skimmed milk is more often used today. The curds were kneaded with garlic and peppercorns before being pressed into the bowl-shaped moulds, tied with raffia and hung in the kitchen or cellar to dry.

Mild and milky, the cheese has a gentle acidity and spongy, texture. The aroma of the garlic and peppercorns dominate the flavour.

GRATARON D'ARÈCHES
REGION: *Savoie*
TYPE: *Traditional, farmhouse, unpasteurized, washed-rind cheese*
SOURCE: *Goat's milk*
DESCRIPTION: *300–400g/11–14oz thick cylinder with smooth, beige, washed rind*
CULINARY USE: *Table cheese*

Grataron d'Arèches is one of the few washed-rind goat's cheeses of the Savoie, and it is worth looking out for. The leathery, pale beige rind covers an open-textured, white interior with a wonderful scent of almonds and flowers.

RIGHT: Gris de Lille

GRATTE-PAILLE
REGION: *Ile-de-France*
TYPE: *Modern, farmhouse, soft-white cheese*
SOURCE: *Cow's milk*
DESCRIPTION: *300–350g/ 11–12oz brick with natural white mould rind*
CULINARY USES: *Cheeseboards, baked in pastries with chicken and vegetables*

Invented in the 1970s by a creamery in Seine-et-Marne, this cheese takes its name from *gratte* (to scratch) and *paille* (straw), marking the fact that when bales of straw were carried through the narrow streets in summer, pieces of the straw would become wedged in the walls along the way. Some of the cheeses are sold on small straw mats. The cheese is very good. Rich and exceedingly creamy, it has a pleasant mushroomy flavour. With age comes a slight sharpness.

LEFT: Gaperon

RIGHT: Gratte-Paille

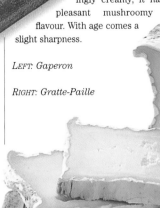

GRIS DE LILLE
REGION: *Nord-Pas-de-Calais*
TYPE: *Traditional, farmhouse, and creamery, unpasteurized, washed-rind cheese*
SOURCE: *Cow's milk*
DESCRIPTION: *700g–1kg/1lb 9oz–2¼lb square with sticky, pinkish-grey, washed rind*
CULINARY USES: *Table cheese, snacks*

Gris de Lille is also known as Puant de Lille or Puant Macéré. The word *puant* means obnoxious or stinking – a term of endearment to those who love the rich flavour of this pungent cheese with its distinctive farmyard aroma. The cheese is similar to Maroilles, although the curing process is different.

LA TAUPINIÈRE

REGION: *Poitou-Charentes*
TYPE: *Traditional, farmhouse,
unpasteurized, natural-rind cheese*
SOURCE: *Goat's milk*
DESCRIPTION: *225–250g/8–9oz dome-
shaped cheese. The wrinkled, natural
rind has a delicate, blue mould*
CULINARY USES: *Table cheese, grilling*

La Taupinière means molehill, which aptly describes this unusually shaped cheese. Quite dense, it is ripened for two to three weeks and is deliciously nutty, with a fresh, lemony tang.

LA VACHE QUI RIT

REGION: *Various*
TYPE: *Modern, creamery,
processed cheese*
SOURCE: *Cow's milk*
DESCRIPTION: *Small disc with bright
red, waxed rind*
CULINARY USES: *Snacks, lunch boxes*

The slightly supercilious face of La Vache qui Rit – the laughing cow – is seen on the walls of the Metro, and in supermarkets across France. It may well laugh, for it seems so unlikely that this sweet, bland, buttery, processed cheese should have become a household name in a country famous for its magnificent, pungent cheeses. The tiny discs are a favourite snack with children and adults alike.

LAGUIOLE (AOC)

REGION: *Auvergne*
TYPE: *Traditional, farmhouse,
unpasteurized, hard cheese*
SOURCE: *Cow's milk*
DESCRIPTION: *30–50kg/65–110lb
cylinder. The hard, mottled brown-
grey, natural rind carries the
distinctive, red lettering proclaiming
its AOC status*
CULINARY USES: *Table cheese, snacks,
grating, grilling*

With an ancient pedigree (the cheese was certainly made in the fourth century BC and was earlier described by Pliny the Elder), Laguiole has a supple to firm texture. Not as compact as the classic English Cheddar, it has a light, musty aroma that can be quite penetrating when the cheese is fully aged. The straw-yellow interior has

ABOVE: Laguiole

a creamy feel and a taste reminiscent of cheese and onion quiche.

Over the years, economics and the disinclination of sons to follow in the footsteps of their cheesemaking fathers have led to changes in the production of the cheese. The Holstein cow, a prolific milker, was brought in to replace the native Aubrac breed. The number of traditional cheesemakers or *buronniers* has dramatically reduced. At the beginning of this century there were more than a thousand *buronniers*; today there are only four or five producing the cheese.

Laguiole is still a great cheese, especially if you buy one made from *transhumance* milk (produced between late May and mid October, when cows are taken up to the mountain pastures that are covered in gentians, violets, broom and wild herbs). Many people hope that a growing awareness of the need to retain the old ways, coupled with a little assistance from the AOC, will mean that the character of this wonderful, old French cheese will not be lost in the race for progress.

RIGHT: Langres

LANGRES (AOC)

REGION: *Champagne-Ardennes*
TYPE: *Traditional, farmhouse, and
co-operative, unpasteurized,
washed-rind cheese*
SOURCE: *Cow's milk*
DESCRIPTION: *180g or 800g/6¼oz or
1³/₄lb concave cone or cylinder with
washed rind ranging from orange
and sticky to brick-red and dry*
CULINARY USES: *Table cheese, also baked
and used as a dip for vegetables*

Monks who passed through the region during the Middle Ages probably introduced this cheese. The shape is unusual – a cone or cylinder with a hollow in the top. To form the hollow, the curd is turned only twice during draining. The weight of the whey, and its movement through the curd, causes the centre to subside.

The brightly coloured rind is the result of continual washing; orange bacteria grow on the surface, as well as some white flora or yeasts.

The cheese is notable for its pungent, smoky-bacon aroma. When young, the texture is firm and grainy. With age, the rind starts to break down and becomes smooth-flowing and creamy. The flavour intensifies. Some affineurs pour eau-de-vie into the crater. This gradually seeps into the cheese, adding a new dimension to an already powerful flavour.

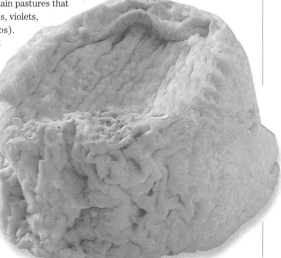

ABOVE: *Laruns*

LARUNS
REGION: *Pyrénées*
TYPE: *Traditional, farmhouse, unpasteurized, hard cheese*
SOURCE: *Sheep's milk*
DESCRIPTION: *5–6kg/11–13lb flattened round loaf with smooth, thin, yellow to ochre, natural rind*
CULINARY USES: *Table cheese, snacks, cooking (when aged)*

Named after the local market town, this cheese has been made by shepherds in mountain huts for generations and is now produced by Ossau Valley. When young, it has a supple texture and is mild and nutty; as it ages it becomes hard and brittle, with a sharper flavour. At six months it is best for grating and cooking.

LE FIUM'ORBO
REGION: *Corsica*
TYPE: *Traditional, farmhouse, unpasteurized, semi-soft cheese*
SOURCE: *Sheep's and goat's milk*
DESCRIPTION: *400–450g/ 14oz–1lb round cheese with natural rind*
CULINARY USE: *Table cheese*

A farmhouse version of Fromage Corse, this has a pungent nose but a more delicate taste, suggesting herbs and flowers. It is an ancient cheese, which has been made by the shepherds for centuries.

LE BRIN
REGION: *Savoie*
TYPE: *Modern, creamery, semi-soft, vegetarian cheese*
SOURCE: *Cow's milk*
DESCRIPTION: *150g/5oz small, hexagonal cheese with natural, thin, reddish-orange rind dusted with white penicillium mould*
CULINARY USE: *Table cheese*

Le Brin was created by Fromagerie Guilloteau in the 1980s as a milder version of the traditional French washed-rind cheeses. It is made by the ultrafiltration method rather than by using rennet to separate the curd from the whey. This gives a higher yield of solids per litre of milk, which means the production costs are lower than when traditional cheese-making methods are employed. *Brin* means a wisp, a breath or a twig – something small or light. The cheese is velvety smooth, like English custard, and has a mild, sweet, almost perfumed aroma and taste. It resembles its soft-white-rinded cousin, Pavé d'Affinois.

Le Terroir is a similar cheese.

ABOVE: *Le Roulé*

ABOVE: *Le Brin*

LE ROULÉ
REGION: *Loire*
TYPE: *Modern, creamery, fresh cheese*
SOURCE: *Cow's milk*
DESCRIPTION: *Logs of various sizes, rolled in fresh herbs*
CULINARY USES: *Table cheese, baking, spreading*

The now familiar logs of Le Roulé with their distinctive green swirl of herbs and garlic, were first introduced in the mid-1980s by Fromagerie Triballat, with the aim of attracting attention to cheese counters in supermarket delicatessens. An overnight success, Le Roulé was rapidly joined by Roulé Light and miniature Roulé logs with numerous exotic combinations: salmon and dill; chives and even strawberry. These may not be to everyone's taste, but attention to quality and an excellent marketing campaign have ensured the success of this new cheese. Its melt-in-the-mouth texture and refreshing herb and garlic layer practically guarantees that first-time consumers will come back for more.

RIGHT: Livarot

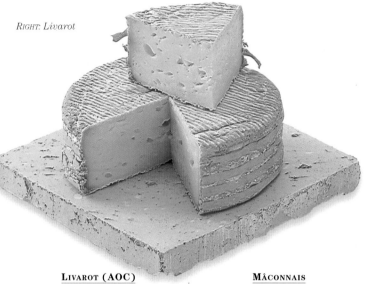

MAMIROLLE

REGION: *Franche-Comté*
TYPE: *Modern, creamery, washed-rind cheese*
SOURCE: *Cow's milk*
DESCRIPTION: *500–675g/1¼–1½lb brick. The finely ridged, orange, washed rind can be slightly damp*
CULINARY USES: *Table cheese, grilling*

The author first tasted Mamirolle at Besançon, where she shared it with the cheesemaker, one of the students at the Ecole Nationale d'Industrie Laitière de Besançon-Mamirolle, where it is made as part of their hands-on experience. She reports as follows: "The supple, smooth interior is encased with a fine, orange rind with a sweet-sour, faintly smoked aroma and taste, although the occasional batch can be as robust and enthusiastic as the students, particularly if it is made towards the end of their academic year!"

The cheese is produced in the depart-ment of Doubs and is similar to Limburger.

MAROILLES (AOC)

REGION: *Flanders*
TYPE: *Traditional, farmhouse and creamery, unpasteurized, semi-soft cheese*
SOURCE: *Cow's milk*
DESCRIPTION: *700g/1lb 9oz square cheese with brick-red, smooth, washed rind*
CULINARY USES: *Table cheese, snacks and pies, especially the local goyère*

This is regarded as the forefather of all the Trappist cheeses. It was first made in the tenth century at the Abbaye de Maroilles in northern France, where St Hubert, the patron saint of cheese, is buried.

The cheese has a thickish, damp, brick-red rind with fine ridges. The interior is pale yellow, bouncy and porous, not sup-ple and dense like many similar cheeses. The aroma – powerful and aromatic, with a suggestion of fermenting fruit – is stronger than the flavour, which is sweet-sour in character, with perhaps a hint of smoky bacon. The cheeses can be ripened for up to four months, although many are sold too young, when they are still chalky in the centre and have bitter rinds.

Similar cheeses include Baguette Laonnaise, Dauphin and Gris de Lille.

LIVAROT (AOC)

REGION: *Normandy*
TYPE: *Traditional, farmhouse and creamery, unpasteurized, semi-soft cheese*
SOURCE: *Cow's milk*
DESCRIPTION: *250g/9oz or 450g/1lb round cheese. The smooth, glossy, brown, washed rind has some white and occasional bluish moulds*
CULINARY USES: *Table cheese, snacks*

This smooth, supple-textured cheese is washed to encourage the orange ferments to grow. These days the wash is a flavour-less natural dye, annatto, which may be one of the reasons the cheese is less pun-gent than it used to be. Heavy in the mouth, it leaves a spicy taste on the finish.

Livarot is jokingly called "the colonel" because of the stripes of sedge grass (today, more often orange plastic) that encircle the cheese. Originally made by the monks in the area, nowa-days most Livarot is prod-uced in factories, but the AOC regulations should help to maintain its ancestry.

MÂCONNAIS

REGION: *Burgundy*
TYPE: *Traditional, farmhouse and co-operative, unpasteurized, natural-rind cheese*
SOURCE: *Cow's and goat's milk*
DESCRIPTION: *50–60g/2–2¼oz truncated cone with natural, fine white to pale blue rind*
CULINARY USES: *Table cheese, grilling, in salads*

Small and elegant, this cheese can be made from cow's or goat's milk – or a mix-ture – depending on the season. When young, it has a dense, flaky interior with a rind of blue and white moulds. The sub-tle hint of tarragon in the flavour recalls the fruitiness of a young Chardonnay, and the cheese is the perfect partner for a Mâcon white wine. The locals prefer the cheese when it is brittle, almost rancid, savouring it with a generous glass of the local Burgundy or a Beaujolais.

RIGHT: Maroilles

MIMOLETTE FRANÇAISE

REGION: *Flanders*
TYPE: *Traditional, creamery,*
hard cheese
SOURCE: *Cow's milk*
DESCRIPTION: *2–4kg/4¹/₂–9lb sphere.*
The natural rind ranges in
colour from yellow-orange to
light brown, and is pitted, dry
and hard
CULINARY USES: *Table cheese, snacks,*
canapés, grating

This cheese originated in Holland and was probably introduced into France when Flanders was part of that country. Basically, it is a matured Edam that is allowed to ripen for around six to nine months, by which time it becomes so hard and brittle that pieces have to be chiselled off in granite-like chunks. Intensely fruity, with a mouth-puckering tang, it is popular as a cooking cheese, and as a snack to eat with a glass of beer. When young (four to six months), the cheese is firm, compact and slightly oily, with a subtle, fruity aroma and a mellow, nutty taste. Most Mimolette is, however, eaten when aged (*vieux* or *étuvé*).The bright, deep tangerine colour of the cheese is due to the natural dye, annatto.

Mimolette Française is also known as Boule de Lille.

BELOW: Mimolette

MONT D'OR/VACHERIN HAUT-DOUBS (AOC)

REGION: *Franche-Comté*
TYPE: *Traditional, farmhouse and*
co-operative, unpasteurized, washed-
rind cheese
SOURCE: *Cow's milk (Montbéliard and*
Pie Rouge de l'Est)
DESCRIPTION: *500g–1kg/1¹/₄–2¹/₄lb*
round with a wrinkled, pale-
brownish pink, washed rind, dusted
with fine, white mould. The cheese is
encircled with a band of spruce bark
and set in a wooden box
CULINARY USE: *Table cheese*

In the days when the borders of France and Switzerland were less well defined, the local soft, washed cheese was called Vacherin Mont d'Or, regardless of which side of the mountain it came from. Later, the Swiss (who produce the pasteurized version) laid claim to the name, and the unpasteurized French Vacherin became simply Mont d'Or or Vacherin Haut-Doubs.

A good Mont d'Or has an aroma of chopped wood and mountain flowers, with a faint hint of fermentation and resin. The texture is full and creamy and the flavour suggests wild herbs. Production begins on 15 August, when the cows return from the mountain pastures. The cheese is available only from the end of September through to 31 March. At the moment it may not be exported. Summer milk is taken to one of the local co-operatives to create another great French cheese – Gruyère de Comté.

To check if the cheese is ripe, press gently on the rind. As the soft, runny cheese flows away from the pressure you should see a gentle wave. Carefully remove the "lid" or rind using a sharp knife, then carefully fold back the "lid", scraping off any soft cheese attached. Scoop a dollop of cheese on to a chunk of country bread, and enjoy a superb treat, preferably with a glass of good wine.

Other French Vacherin cheeses include d'Abondance and des Beauges.

BELOW: Morbier

MORBIER

REGION: *Franche-Comté*
TYPE: *Traditional, farmhouse and*
creamery, unpasteurized,
semi-soft cheese
SOURCE: *Cow's milk*
DESCRIPTION: *5–9kg/11–20lb wheel. The*
yellow-brown or pale grey rind is
thick, moist and leathery
CULINARY USES: *Table cheese, snacks,*
grilling, slicing

Made during the winter months on the lower reaches of the Jura Mountains, Morbier has a horizontal band of wood ash and salt through its centre. The mixture was originally sprinkled over the fresh curds made from the morning milking, left during the day, then covered with the curds from the evening milking. Nowadays the ash layer is more likely to be food colouring, and is purely decorative.

The cheese is elastic and springy, with a pungent, yeasty aroma and a sweet, fruity taste. Traditionally, a half-wheel of Morbier would be propped up by the fire. As it started to melt, the cheese would be scraped on to crusty bread or hot potatoes.

Factory-made versions tend to be bland and odourless, but are excellent for melting.

RIGHT: Münster (bottom) and the smaller, Münster Géromé (top)

MUNSTER/MUNSTER GÉROMÉ (AOC)
REGION: *Alsace*
TYPE: *Traditional, farmhouse and creamery, unpasteurized, washed-rind cheese*
SOURCE: *Cow's milk (Vosgiennes)*
DESCRIPTION: *120g/4¹/₄oz; 450g/1lb; 1.5kg/3–3¹/₂lb rounds. The sticky, washed rind ranges in colour from yellow-orange to russet*
CULINARY USES: *Table cheese, snacks, grilling*

The Vosges mountains are the backbone of Alsace and home to one of the smelliest and most delicious cheeses on earth. Those made in Alsace are called Munster, while the smaller versions from Lorraine are known as Géromé.

The cheese owes its unique character to the unspoilt pastures of Alsace and the Vosgiennes cows, renowned for giving high-protein milk.

The cheese is constantly rubbed with brine over a period of two to three months. This causes the rind to develop its rich colour and the aroma to intensify.

Don't let the smell put you off. The cheese is wonderful – supple, with a flavour that is both sweet and savoury (almost yeasty), and an intense, spicy, aromatic finish. It is traditional to enjoy the cheese with boiled potatoes, cumin seeds and a glass of local wine.

Munster au Cumin is a popular variation. Langres is a similar cheese, as of course is Géromé.

MUROL
REGION: *Auvergne*
TYPE: *Traditional, creamery, semi-soft cheese*
SOURCE: *Cow's milk*
DESCRIPTION: *450–500g/1–1¹/₄lb ring. The thin, smooth, washed rind is mottled pinkish-yellow*
CULINARY USES: *Table cheese, cheese puffs*

This cheese was invented by Monsieur Jules Bérioux, a local affineur. In the 1930s, M Bérioux decided to stamp out a central hole from several young Saint-Nectaire cheeses, ripen the rings and call them Grand Murols, after one of the villages in the area. The cheese is simple and uncomplicated. Supple, creamy and very smooth, it has the sweetness of fresh milk with a delicious, nutty aroma and taste. The unique shape adds a little *je ne sais quoi* to any cheeseboard and the taste appeals to every palate.

The stamped-out holes are not wasted, but are made into Murolait or Le Trou de Murol. These tiny, cork-shaped treats are very soft, but are held in check by a coating of bright red wax. They resemble La Vache qui Rit, but have more flavour.

NANTAIS
REGION: *Brittany*
TYPE: *Traditional, creamery, washed-rind cheese*
SOURCE: *Cow's milk*
DESCRIPTION: *175–200g/6–7oz square cheese with smooth, straw to ochre, washed rind*
CULINARY USE: *Table cheese*

Brittany has no native cheeses and had to wait until the early 1790s for a young priest who was on the run from the French Revolution to introduce cheese-making. This cheese, also known as Curé de Nantais or Fromage de Curé, celebrates that fact. A small, sticky, washed-rind cheese, it has a pungent, yeasty rind. The voluptuous, creamy interior has a rich, smoky-bacon taste and spicy finish. Nantais can be rather good and deserves a weighty Pinot Noir or a strong-tasting Gewurztraminer wine for company.

Carré de l'Est Lavée is a similar cheese.

NEUFCHÂTEL (AOC)
REGION: *Normandy*
TYPE: *Traditional, farmhouse and creamery, soft-white cheese*
SOURCE: *Cow's milk*
DESCRIPTION: *100–200g/3³/₄–7oz cheeses in various shapes, with natural, downy, white rind, which develops reddish pigmentation*
CULINARY USES: *Table cheese, snacks*

Unlike other soft-white-rinded cheeses, Neufchâtel has a grainy texture. Although it has the aroma and taste of mushrooms, it is also quite sharp and salty. Some lovers of this cheese prefer it when it has been kept until the rind develops reddish pigmentation and a smell of ammonia. At this stage the taste is bitter, salty and acrid.

Neufchâtel is available in various shapes, such as squares, rounds, logs, hearts, loaves and cylinders. Some are available unpasteurized. Gournay is a similar cheese.

LEFT: Neufchâtel – a soft-white cheese with a pleasant, grainy texture

OLIVET AU FOIN
REGION: *Orléanais*
TYPE: *Modern, farmhouse, unpasteurized, soft-white cheese*
SOURCE: *Cow's milk*
DESCRIPTION: *250g/9oz round with soft, dry rind decorated with fine strands of hay*
CULINARY USE: *Table cheese*
Similar to Camembert, but milder and not as soft when ripe, Olivet au Foin is decorated with fine strands of hay *(foin)*, whose scent is absorbed into the cheese.

OLIVET BLEU
REGION: *Orléanais*
TYPE: *Traditional, farmhouse, unpasteurized, blue cheese*
SOURCE: *Cow's milk*
DESCRIPTION: *300g/11oz disc with blue-white, natural rind*
CULINARY USE: *Table cheese*
Slightly grainy, with a distinct aroma and taste of mushrooms and a salty finish, Olivet Bleu resembles a mild Camembert. "Bleu" refers to the rind, which is so white that it has a blue tinge – like whiter-than-white washing!

OLIVET CENDRÉ
REGION: *Orléanais*
TYPE: *Traditional, farmhouse, unpasteurized, soft-white cheese*
SOURCE: *Cow's milk*
DESCRIPTION: *250–300g/9–11oz round with ash-grey, natural rind*
CULINARY USES: *Table cheese, snacks*
Olivet Cendré resembles Olivet au Foin, but is cured for three months in wood ash from vines. This gives it a more supple texture and a fairly pungent, spicy aroma. Similar cheeses include Vendôme Cendré and the Cendrés of Champagne and the Ardennes.

OSSAU-IRATY-BREBIS PYRÉNÉES (AOC)
REGION: *Pyrénées*
TYPE: *Traditional, farmhouse, unpasteurized, semi-soft cheeses*
SOURCE: *Sheep's milk*
DESCRIPTION: *2–7kg/4¹/₂–15¹/₄lb wheels with natural rind*
CULINARY USES: *Table cheese, grating, soups*
A number of *fermier* (farmhouse), artisan, co-operative and industrial cheeses made in the rugged and majestic Béarn and Basque regions come under this AOC umbrella. The regulations state that the affinage for the mountain sheep's milk cheeses must be at least 60 days for the small and 90 days for the larger ones. Coagulation can only be from rennet, and no milk may be used until 20 days after lambing. These and other conditions must be met before any cheese can carry the AOC label. Those that do not conform must be sold as simple Fromage de Brebis.

Transhumance (the moving of cows in summer to mountain pastures) is still a way of life for the shepherds of this region. The cheeses are still made in small mountain chalets – *kaiolar* – and the hills ring with the sound of the bells worn by the black-faced Manech sheep as they wander across landscapes of spectacular natural beauty.

Other cheeses in this group include Matocq, Ardi-Gasna and Abbaye de Belloc.

ABOVE: Ossau-Iraty-Brebis Pyrénées

PALET DE BABLIGNY
REGION: *Loire*
TYPE: *Traditional, farmhouse, unpasteurized, soft-white cheese*
SOURCE: *Cow's milk*
DESCRIPTION: *100g/3³/₄oz oval with fine, white penicillium mould rind*
CULINARY USE: *Table cheese*
This tiny cheese packs a lot of punch for its size. Hard and flaky in texture, it has a flavour like that of a fruity, mature Cheddar, yet it melts like chocolate in the mouth and has a hint of chèvre.

ABOVE: Olivet au Foin (left) and Olivet Cendré (right)

ABOVE: Pavé d'Affinois

RIGHT: Pélardon

PAVÉ D'AFFINOIS
REGION: *Lyonnais*
TYPE: *Modern, creamery, soft-white,*
vegetarian cheese
SOURCE: *Cow's milk*
DESCRIPTION: *150g/5oz square with*
ridged penicillium rind
CULINARY USE: *Table cheese*

This was one of the first cheeses to be made commercially using ultrafiltration – a method of extracting the solids from liquid milk, which gives a much higher yield of solids than when traditional means are used. No rennet is required for the cheese-making process, only a culture to encourage the lactic fermentation. The technique, together with the packaging and promotion of Pavé d'Affinois and its stablemates Le Brin and Chèvre d'Affinois, has led to excellent sales, but it is to be hoped that this method of preparation is not adopted for the traditional cheeses of Europe.

When young, Pavé d'Affinois is grainy, mildly scented and virtually tasteless apart from a slight hint of mushrooms from the rind. However, if it is allowed to ripen in a warm, humid cellar for two to three weeks, the interior of the cheese literally melts, retaining a firm, slightly chalky centre the size of a quail's egg. The taste is similar to Brie and has hints of Granny Smith apples.

RIGHT: Pavé d'Auge – so-named
because it is shaped like "pavé", the
squarish French cobble stones

PAVÉ D'AUGE
REGION: *Normandy*
TYPE: *Traditional, farmhouse,*
unpasteurized, semi-soft cheese
SOURCE: *Cow's milk*
DESCRIPTION: *675–800g/1½–1¾lb*
square cheese. The russet-yellow rind
can be dry or washed. It is sometimes
covered with a white mould
CULINARY USE: *Table cheese*

Pavé is the name given to the roughly square cobblestones you still see in old marketplaces in France. It is a charming name for this supple, creamy cheese, with its reddish rind. The aroma suggests cool cellars. The flavour is earthy and spicy, but it can be a little bitter.

PÉLARDON
REGION: *Languedoc-Roussillon*
TYPE: *Traditional, farmhouse,*
unpasteurized, fresh cheese
SOURCE: *Goat's milk*
DESCRIPTION: *60–100g/2¼–3¾oz disc.*
The thin, wrinkled, natural rind
has white and pale
blue moulds
CULINARY USES: *Table cheese, grilling*

Softer and more mousse-like than most goat's milk cheeses when young, the flavour of Pélardon suggests sour cream infused with walnut oil, balanced by a gentle, salty finish. When aged, the wrinkled, mould-covered rind has a distinct goaty aroma and an intense, Brazil-nut sweetness. The texture is somewhat drier, but the cheese is still very creamy in the mouth.

Pélardon is made in several areas in the Languedoc region and is currently being considered for inclusion among the AOC cheeses of France.

Similar cheeses include Pélardon des Cevennes, Pélardon d'Altières and Pélardon des Corbières.

BELOW: Pérail

PÉRAIL

REGION: *Rouergue*
TYPE: *Traditional, farmhouse, unpasteurized, natural-rind cheese*
SOURCE: *Sheep's milk*
DESCRIPTION: *80–120g/3¼–4¼oz disc. The soft, wrinkled, natural rind is a pale straw colour with a pinkish tinge*
CULINARY USE: *Table cheese*

This *fermier* (farmhouse) or artisan cheese has the softest, most delicate of rinds with a nutty aroma. Inside is an even softer, toffee-like centre with the freshness of meadow flowers. The sweet taste of the sheep's milk makes you wish you had bought two – or even three.

BELOW: Picodon

PETIT-SUISSE

REGION: *Various*
TYPE: *Traditional, farmhouse and creamery, fresh cheese*
SOURCE: *Cow's milk*
DESCRIPTION: *30g/1¼oz cylinder without rind*
CULINARY USES: *Eaten as a snack with fruit, honey or nuts; also used as the basis of several traditional French desserts*

Normally sold in trays of six, this mousse-like fresh cheese was invented in the late nineteenth century by Charles Gervais, a Swiss cheesemaker. He decided to make a variation on the local cheese, Neufchâtel, by adding cream to the fresh curd and selling the result before the soft white rind could develop.

The light, yet creamy texture and charming shape made Petit-Suisse a major success. It is now produced throughout France, although the fat content and quality vary as much as the recipe.

PICODON DE L'ARDÈCHE/PICODON DE LA DRÔME (AOC)

REGION: *Rhône-Alpes*
TYPE: *Traditional, farmhouse and creamery, unpasteurized, natural-rind cheese*
SOURCE: *Goat's milk*
DESCRIPTION: *50–100g/2–3¾oz round with natural rind that ranges in colour from pale ivory to soft white or pale blue-grey*
CULINARY USES: *Table cheese, grilling, baking, fromage fort*

The lower end of the Rhône Valley is too dry for the cultivation of vines, but is ideal for the hardy goats, which attack the tufts of grass and scented scrub with the sort of enthusiasm we might reserve for a gastronomic feast. The milk they yield is the basis of a cheese that varies from area to area, but seldom disappoints. The thin rind has the scent of stone cellars and the hard, compact interior is aromatic. The cheeses are occasionally packed with herbs in jars of the local green olive oil.

Picodon cheeses are very similar to the Pélardon cheeses of the Languedoc-Roussillon region further south.

ABOVE: Pithiviers

PITHIVIERS AU FOIN

REGION: *Orléanais*
TYPE: *Traditional, farmhouse, unpasteurized, soft-white cheese*
SOURCE: *Cow's milk*
DESCRIPTION: *300g/11oz round cheese with soft-white rind rolled in strands of hay or grass*
CULINARY USE: *Table cheese*

Similar to Camembert, Pithiviers au Foin has a mild, milky, caramel flavour. The fine, white rind is delicately rolled in wisps of hay or grass. As such, it resembles Olivet au Foin.

POIVRE D'ANE

REGION: *Provence–Alpes–Côte d'Azur*
TYPE: *Traditional, farmhouse, unpasteurized, natural-rind cheese*
SOURCE: *Cow's, sheep's or goat's milk*
DESCRIPTION: *100–120g/3¾–4¼oz round cheese. The natural rind is white with a hint of blue or yellow. It is traditionally covered with a sprig of wild savory*
CULINARY USES: *Table cheese, grilling, fromage fort*

This dense, fine-grained cheese has a lovely, aromatic scent and flavour. Any variation comes from the source of the milk: sheep's milk in spring and early summer; goat's milk from the end of spring to the start of autumn; cow's milk virtually all year round.

Banon is a similar cheese.

PONT L'EVÊQUE (AOC)

REGION: *Normandy*
TYPE: *Traditional, farmhouse and creamery, unpasteurized, semi-soft cheese*
SOURCE: *Cow's milk*
DESCRIPTION: *350–400g/12–14oz finely ridged square with greyish-yellow, washed rind*
CULINARY USE: *Table cheese*

This is probably one of the oldest cheeses of Normandy, an area

RIGHT: Pouligny-Saint-Pierre – due to its shape, this elegant, traditional goat's cheese has earned several nicknames. The two most often used are "the pyramid" or "Eiffel Tower"

renowned for the lushness of its pastures. The small Normandy cow has produced some of the greatest French cheeses, including Camembert, Livarot, Pavé d'Auge and Boursin.

Pont l'Evêque is said to have originated in an abbey, though there appears to be no evidence to substantiate this. Despite being granted its AOC status in 1976 to protect its history and good name, only around 2 or 3 per cent of the cheese is *fermier* (farmhouse) made; the majority comes from just two large producers. To comply with AOC regulations and achieve the authentic taste and texture, the cheese must be regularly washed, brushed and turned to encourage the special bacteria to grow on the rind. The milk used for Pont l'Evêque must come from the local area and the curd must be kneaded before it is drained.

The aroma of the cheese has been likened to damp washing, mouldy cellars and farmyards, but the taste is deliciously savoury and piquant, with just a trace of sweetness and a robust tang on the finish. The texture is springy and open and the cheese glistens, thanks to the richness of the milk.

POULIGNY-SAINT-PIERRE (AOC)

REGION: *Berry*
TYPE: *Traditional, farmhouse and creamery, unpasteurized, natural-rind cheese*
SOURCE: *Goat's milk*
DESCRIPTION: *250g/9oz truncated pyramid with soft, wrinkled, ivory-coloured, natural rind. When this dries out, the wrinkles deepen and grey, white and blue moulds gather. A red label indicates that it is made in a dairy, while a green label means it is farmhouse-made*
CULINARY USES: *Table cheese, grilling, in salads*

Named after the eponymous village, this cheese has earned various nicknames because of its shape, the most common of which is "the pyramid". To many people it epitomizes chèvre: wonderfully rustic, yet elegant. The rind is soft and ivory-coloured when the cheese is young. As it ages and dries, the rind becomes reddish-orange and acquires an array of beautiful moulds, providing a magnificent contrast to the firm, pure white, slightly grainy interior.

The first impression is a heady mix of goat, fresh hay and mould. Tasting reveals a complexity of flavours, including herbaceous plants (especially tarragon) and white wine, and a texture that is both creamy and nutty. Like a fine wine, once tasted Pouligny-Saint-Pierre is never forgotten.

ABOVE: Pont l'Evêque

RACLETTE

REGION: *Savoie*
TYPE: *Traditional, farmhouse and creamery, unpasteurized, semi-soft cheese*
SOURCE: *Cow's milk*
DESCRIPTION: *7–8kg/15¼–18lb round or square cheese with smooth pink to deep orange, slightly sticky, natural rind*
CULINARY USES: *Sliced and grilled on potatoes or blanched vegetables*

Raclette is an ancient mountain cheese common to the Savoie region in France and the canton of Valais in Switzerland. Although the cheese has a pleasant enough flavour, it is not particularly special until it is heated in front of a fire or under a hot grill. Then the full, nutty, sweet and slightly fruity aroma intensifies and the stringy elasticity of the melting cheese makes it truly magnificent. The rind has a farmyard aroma. When grilled it becomes really crunchy and has a wonderful savoury flavour.

Traditionally, a large cheese was cut in half and leant against a stone with the cut surface facing the open fire. The outer layer of the supple interior was allowed to heat up gradually. As soon as it started to crinkle and change colour, a bowl of steaming potatoes would appear, to be smothered in an avalanche of bubbling cheese. The aroma was irresistible and the rich, nutty, sweet flavour of the cheese was the perfect partner for the potatoes. Nowadays, the dish can be created by heating slices of cheese under the grill.

Bagnes and Conches are similar.

Above: Raclette

RIGHT: Rigotte

RIGHT: Reblochon

REBLOCHON (AOC)

REGION: *Haute-Savoie*
TYPE: *Traditional, farmhouse and creamery, unpasteurized, semi-soft cheese*
SOURCE: *Cow's milk*
DESCRIPTION: *240g/8½oz or 550g/1¼lb round cheese. The yellow to orange, natural rind has fine, white, powdery mould*
CULINARY USES: *Table cheese, melting*

Not unlike Saint-Nectaire or Tamie, Reblochon has a supple, creamy texture that flows over and caresses the palate. The cheese, made in the factories or by co-operatives (*fruitières*), has a warm, yeasty aroma, with the sweet flavour of freshly crushed walnuts, whereas the farm- (*fermier*-) made cheese is both more intense and more complex, and has a distinct savour of fresh spring grass and wild alpine flowers. Do not be deterred by the farmyard aroma of the rind.

RIGOTTE

REGION: *Auvergne and Lyonnais*
TYPE: *Traditional, creamery, unpasteurized, fresh cheese*
SOURCE: *Cow's or goat's milk*
DESCRIPTION: *70–90g/2¾–3½oz cylinder. The rind is very lightly coloured with annatto*
CULINARY USES: *Table cheese, grilling, in salads, fromage fort*

Firm and grainy when a few weeks old, with a mild, lemony freshness and slightly bitter finish, Rigotte becomes quite tart if allowed to dry. Some dry cheeses are marinated in aromatic oils flavoured with peppers and fresh herbs. The cheese absorbs the flavours while becoming creamier, and the result is strangely reminiscent of *saucisson* (sausages) or salami.

Rigottes that are matured in humid conditions develop the classic pale blue moulds. They acquire a more nutty character, but still retain a slight bitterness of taste.

ROQUEFORT (AOC)
REGION: *Rouergue*
TYPE: *Traditional, farmhouse and creamery, unpasteurized, blue cheese*
SOURCE: *Sheep's milk (Lacaune, Manech, Baso-bernaise; also Corsican breeds)*
DESCRIPTION: *2.5–3kg/5¹/₂–6¹/₂lb cylinder with sticky, pale ivory, natural rind. Sold wrapped in foil*
CULINARY USES: *Table cheese, blue cheese dressings, in salads*

For over 2,000 years, shepherds have been maturing their cheeses in the deep limestone caves of Cambalou, which are famous for the blue moulds that exist naturally in the air.

The traditional way of introducing the mould was to allow it to grow on loaves of rye bread placed beside the cheeses in the caves, and a version of this method is still practised by some cheesemakers today. Loaves of the local rye bread are baked especially for the purpose at the start of the season. The bread is left for 70 days to dry and become mouldy, then it is ground to a powder and tiny amounts are sprinkled on the curds before they are placed in the moulds.

Roquefort has a distinct bouquet and a flavour that combines the sweet, burnt-caramel taste of sheep's milk with the sharp, metallic tang of the blue mould. Crumbly, melt-in-the-mouth, refreshing, clean – all these adjectives and more have been used to describe this great cheese.

ROUY
REGION: *Burgundy*
TYPE: *Modern, creamery, washed-rind cheese*
SOURCE: *Cow's milk*
DESCRIPTION: *250g/9oz square cheese with rounded corners. The smooth, terracotta-coloured rind is slightly sticky and may have some white mould*
CULINARY USE: *Table cheese*

This is a commercially made copy of the stronger, more pungent, traditional French washed-rind cheeses like Langres or Epoisses. Nevertheless, it is a good buy.

SALERS (AOC)
REGION: *Auvergne*
TYPE: *Traditional, farmhouse, unpasteurized, hard cheese*
SOURCE: *Cow's milk*
DESCRIPTION: *30–50g/1¹/₄–2oz cylinder with hard, brown, natural rind that becomes rough and crusty with age*
CULINARY USES: *Table cheese, grating, grilling, sauces*

Salers or Fourme de Salers is the *fermier* version of Cantal. Thousands of cheese mites – the sign of a truly great cheese – colonize the thick, brownish-yellow rind, creating a craggy, rock-like surface. The aroma is very meaty, and the rich yellow interior is redolent of wild flowers, including dandelions, and fresh green grass. There is an overlying nutty taste and a strong, savoury, raw-onion bite. Languiole is a similar cheese.

ABOVE: Salers

SANCERRE
REGION: *Loire*
TYPE: *Traditional, farmhouse, unpasteurized, natural-rind cheese*
SOURCE: *Goat's milk*
DESCRIPTION: *120–150g/4¹/₄–5oz round. The natural rind is cream in colour, with soft wrinkles*
CULINARY USES: *Table cheese, grilling, in salads*

This classic chèvre has a fine, wrinkled rind that hardens over time. It has a light, goaty smell and a slightly grainy texture that becomes dense and smooth. There is a fresh "white wine" fruitiness to the young Sancerre and a strong, nutty, goaty taste when aged. The white wine of the region is a perfect partner for the cheese. Similar cheeses include Crottin de Chavignol and Santranges.

ABOVE: Rollot

ROLLOT
REGION: *Picardy*
TYPE: *Traditional, farmhouse and creamery, unpasteurized, semi-soft cheese*
SOURCE: *Cow's milk*
DESCRIPTION: *280–300g/10¹/₄–11oz round or heart-shaped cheese with grainy, burnt orange, washed rind*
CULINARY USE: *Table cheese*

The cheese takes its name from the village of Rollot. Under the tough, sticky rind, the pale yellow interior is firm yet supple, with a rather pungent, yeasty aroma and taste with a fruity bite on the finish. It can be quite salty and bitter if the rind is allowed to dry out.

BELOW: Roquefort

SELLES-SUR-CHER (AOC)
REGION: *Loire*
TYPE: *Traditional, farmhouse and creamery, unpasteurized, natural-rind cheese*
SOURCE: *Goat's milk*
DESCRIPTION: *150–200g/5–7oz round cheese. The ash-covered rind gradually develops blotches of grey and blue moulds*
CULINARY USES: *Table cheese, grilling, in salads*

The Loire is famous for its goat's milk cheeses. They come in a wide array of shapes – pyramids, rounds, truncated cones, hearts, logs and cylinders – but all have the same natural, blue-grey rind and many are lightly dusted with wood ash.

Selles-sur-Cher is a classic example. The ash, mixed with coarsely ground salt, is sprinkled over the cheese, adding to its visual appeal while facilitating the draining of the whey. The concept was probably introduced to the Loire in the eighth century, when the Saracen invaders from Spain reached its southern banks. Most of the invaders were later repelled, but some remained with their goats to provide the foundation for these famous chèvres.

SOUMAINTRAIN
REGION: *Burgundy*
TYPE: *Traditional, farmhouse and creamery, unpasteurized, washed-rind cheese*
SOURCE: *Cow's milk*
DESCRIPTION: *350g/12oz round cheese with washed rind. The white of the curd can be seen through the shiny, reddish-brown moulds*
CULINARY USES: *Table cheese, fromage fort*

Quite grainy and moist when young, Soumaintrain has a mild, refreshing lemony flavour. After six weeks in a humid cellar, where it is frequently washed in brine, it begins to resemble its more outspoken cousin, Epoisses. The rind becomes more pungent and it develops a strong, spicy tang and a creamier feel. Soumaintrain is sometimes immersed in ash to make Aisy Cendré, a local speciality. Saint-Florentin is a similar cheese.

BELOW: Sancerre (left) and Selles-sur-Cher (right)

ABOVE: Soumaintrain is often used to make a traditional delicacy called "fromage fort" (strong cheese) – the cheese is steeped in the local wine before if is eaten

SAINT-AGUR
REGION: *Auvergne*
TYPE: *Modern, creamery, blue cheese*
SOURCE: *Cow's milk*
DESCRIPTION: *2kg/4 1/2lb octagonal cylinder with cream-yellow, natural rind with blue-grey moulds*
CULINARY USES: *Table cheese, in salads and dressings*

Created in 1986 by the huge French cheese company Bongrain, Saint-Agur is made from pasteurized milk and has a moist, creamy texture and spicy, blue cheese taste. It is far milder than most other French blue cheeses, with the blue mould evenly spread in patches throughout the cheese. The unique octagonal shape makes this cheese very easy to cut into wedges.

ABOVE:
Saint-Agur

ABOVE: Saint-Marcellin

SAINT-NECTAIRE (AOC)
REGION: *Auvergne*
TYPE: *Traditional, farmhouse and creamery, unpasteurized, semi-soft cheese*
SOURCE: *Cow's milk (Salers)*
DESCRIPTION: *1.5kg/3–3¹/₂lb round cheese. The leathery, natural rind is pinkish, with a covering of pale grey mould*
CULINARY USE: *Table cheese*

This soft, voluptuous cheese is cured on a bed of straw for eight weeks, and seems to absorb some of its earthy, pastoral aroma. Like a large version of Reblochon, a cheese from the Savoie, Saint-Nectaire is creamy and rich, redolent of freshly cut grass, sweet hay, wild flowers and herbs.

When selecting a Saint-Nectaire, look out for an oval, green label that declares it to be a *fermier* (farmhouse) cheese made from raw milk. A square, green label is used on factory-made cheeses, which are usually pasteurized.

BELOW: Saint-Nectaire

SAINT-ALBRAY
REGION: *Aquitaine*
TYPE: *Modern, creamery, soft-white cheese*
SOURCE: *Cow's milk*
DESCRIPTION: *2kg/4¹/₂lb round cheese with a hole in the centre. The rind is reddish-brown, overlaid with white penicillium mould*
CULINARY USES: *Table cheese, snacks*

Saint-Albray was invented in 1976 to appeal to those who found the flavour of Camembert too strong, but liked that type of cheese. Twenty years later, it is still found in supermarkets around the world. The stable nature of the cheese means that it can survive the rigours of long journeys and cold cabinets.

Ripened for only two weeks, Saint-Albray develops a moist, rubbery texture and has a mild, creamy, undemanding flavour. The shape makes it very practical for serving: round, with a hole in the middle, it is marked into neat sections by indentations in the rind.

ABOVE: Saint-Albray

SAINT-MARCELLIN
REGION: *Rhône-Alpes*
TYPE: *Traditional, farmhouse and creamery, unpasteurized, natural-rind cheese*
SOURCE: *Cow's or goat's milk*
DESCRIPTION: *80g/3¹/₄oz round with wrinkly, natural rind dusted with a coating of white yeast. With age, a delicate, blue mould and red and yellow pigments develop*
CULINARY USES: *Table cheese, fromage fort à la Lyonnaise*

Saint-Marcellin is known to have been served to royalty as early as 1461. In those days it would probably have been made from goat's milk, although cow's milk is often used today. The texture of the young cheese varies from firm to very runny, and it has a mild, slightly salty flavour. When ripe, it is irresistible, with a slightly yeasty taste.

SAINT-PAULIN
REGION: *Various*
TYPE: *Modern, farmhouse and creamery, semi-soft cheese*
SOURCE: *Cow's milk*
DESCRIPTION: *500g–1.5kg/1¼–3½lb or 1.8–2kg/4–4½lb wheel. The thin, washed rind is smooth and leathery. It ranges in colour from pale yellow to bright mandarin orange*
CULINARY USES: *Table cheese, melting, snacks*

Based on the Trappist cheese Port-du-Salut, Saint-Paulin has remained a popular cheese since it was first made in 1930. It was the first French cheese produced from pasteurized milk and has remained so, although one producer decided to buck the trend in 1990 and is making a version made with raw milk. Saint-Paulin has a slightly smoky, sweet-sour aroma and taste.

SAINTE-MAURE DE TOURAINE (AOC)
REGION: *Loire*
TYPE: *Traditional, farmhouse, unpasteurized, fresh or natural-rind cheese*
SOURCE: *Goat's milk*
DESCRIPTION: *250g/9oz log rolled in black wood ash. It develops a blotchy, blue-grey rind with age*
CULINARY USES: *Table cheese, grilling, baking*

Saint-Maure is made both on small farms and in large factories throughout Touraine, but the protection afforded by the AOC regulations ensures that the quality is always good. The freshly formed curd is scooped by hand into log-shaped moulds. Farmhouse cheeses have a piece of straw running through the centre. In theory, this makes them easier to pick up; in practice, pulling or lifting the straw often makes the cheese collapse in large chunks.

The ash coating provides a wonderful contrast when the cheese is cut to reveal the stark white interior. Young cheeses are moist and grainy, but as the mould develops the cheese dries, hardens and becomes more dense. Saint-Maure has a lovely musty, citrus flavour that intensifies with age.

ABOVE: *Tomme d'Abondance*

TAMIE
REGION: *Haute-Savoie*
TYPE: *Traditional, farmhouse, unpasteurized, semi-soft cheese*
SOURCE: *Cow's milk (Montbéliard, La Tarine)*
DESCRIPTION: *500g/1¼lb or 1.3kg/2¾lb round. The fine, leathery, washed rind ranges in colour from pinkish-brown to orange-pink*
CULINARY USE: *Table cheese*

Tamie, made by the monks of the Abbaye de Tamie, has an attractive rind with a sweet, earthy aroma. Underneath, the cheese is a creamy colour. Initially, the taste is sweet, herbaceous and vaguely nutty, followed by a more powerful tang. The rind should be soft and supple; if it is hard and unyielding, the cheese has probably been kept for too long at too low a temperature and will be past its prime. Such a cheese is liable to be highly acidic without the balancing sweetness.

Similar cheeses include Reblochon and Chambarand.

TOMME D'ABONDANCE (AOC)
REGION: *Savoie*
TYPE: *Traditional, farmhouse, unpasteurized, hard cheese*
SOURCE: *Cow's milk*
DESCRIPTION: *5–15kg/11–33lb wheel with brushed, natural, grey rind*
CULINARY USES: *Table cheese, melting*

For centuries, this deep golden cheese has been made in mountain chalets near the border between France and Switzerland. The cheese has a distinct, fruity tang with a hint of yeast. Firm, but supple and slightly grainy, it is made from skimmed milk.

ABOVE: *Tamie*

TOMME DE ROMANS
REGION: *Dauphine*
TYPE: *Traditional, farmhouse and creamery, unpasteurized, natural-rind cheese*
SOURCE: *Cow's milk*
DESCRIPTION: *200–300g/7–11oz round. The natural rind has fluffy, white and blue-grey mould*
CULINARY USE: *Table cheese*

These attractive little cheeses are traditionally sold in wooden trays lined with straw. They have a slightly sour, grassy flavour with a delicate, nutty finish.

TOMME DE SAVOIE
REGION: *Savoie*
TYPE: *Traditional, farmhouse and creamery, unpasteurized, semi-soft cheese*
SOURCE: *Cow's milk*
DESCRIPTION: *1.5–3kg/3–6¹/₂lb wheel. The thick, furry, grey, natural rind has yellow and orange blotches*
CULINARY USES: *Table cheese, grating, grilling*

An ancient mountain cheese from the Savoie, made in winter when the herdsmen have returned from the summer pastures. In summer, the milk goes with the milk from other herds to become Beaufort, but when the weather worsens and yield drops, the herdsman makes his cheese at home. When searching out the best Tomme, look for *"lait cru"* on the label, the numbers 73 or 74 on an oval, red, casein plaque and the logo of four red hearts and the word "Savoie". Don't be put off by the appearance of the rind. Inside, the pale yellow cheese with its few small holes will be firm, yet supple with a gentle flavour hinting at meadow flowers, milk and walnuts.

ABOVE:
Valençay

ABOVE: Tourée de l'Aubier

TOURÉE DE L'AUBIER
REGION: *Normandy*
TYPE: *Modern, creamery, washed-rind cheese*
SOURCE: *Cow's milk*
DESCRIPTION: *200g/7oz or 2kg/4¹/₂lb round. Sticky, leathery, washed rind with powdery, white mould on its orange red surface*
CULINARY USE: *Table cheese*

The spruce bark belt gives this washed-rind cheese a unique flavour. Creamy, sweet, yet pungent, it becomes almost runny when mature. Created as a pasteurized copy of the great French Mont d'Or, it is passable as long as it is ripe.

LEFT: Tomme de Savoie

VALENÇAY
REGION: *Berry*
TYPE: *Traditional, farmhouse and creamery, unpasteurized, natural-rind cheese*
SOURCE: *Goat's milk*
DESCRIPTION: *200–250g/7–9oz truncated pyramid with natural, white rind dusted with charcoal ash. With age, the rind develops blue-grey moulds*
CULINARY USE: *Table cheese*

This elegant pyramid is dusted with fine, black charcoal. When young, the white cheese can be seen through the ash. Gradually, however, the colours merge and blue-grey moulds appear. The taste is at first fresh and citrus-like, but age gives the cheese a nuttier flavour and a distinctly goaty character. The commercially produced version is known as Pyramide.

VIGNOTTE/LES VIGNOTTES
REGION: *Champagne or Lorraine*
TYPE: *Traditional, creamery, soft-white cheese*
SOURCE: *Cow's milk*
DESCRIPTION: *150g/5oz cylinder or 2kg/4¹/₂lb thick disc with thick, velvety, smooth penicillium rind*
CULINARY USES: *Table cheese, grilling*

This very popular, triple-cream cheese has a light, almost mousse-like texture, thanks to the careful ladling of the young curd into the moulds. The flavour is fresh and creamy, slightly lemony and salty.

ITALIAN CHEESES

For more than six centuries Europe was dominated by the Romans. What began as a few farming settlements in the eighth century BC grew into the city of Rome. In the sixth century BC Rome became a republic, governed by a senate, which was made up of representatives from the influential families of the day. The Romans set about conquering the world as they knew it, and by the second century AD the Roman Empire included all the countries that encircled the Mediterranean, stretching as far as the Persian Gulf in the east, to England, France and Spain in the west, and the countries of North Africa.

Cheese played a major role in the diet of the Romans, as it was convenient, compact and travelled well – even in the knapsacks of the legionnaires – and came in numerous forms. One of the earliest mentions of cheeses was by Pliny the Elder, when he referred to the cheese-making techniques used by shepherds on the outskirts of Rome to make the sheep's milk cheese that was the forefather of Pecorino Romano. In his writings, Columella also referred to cheese and cheesemaking, demonstrating his understanding of the use of rennet, a significant breakthrough in the art.

Cheesemaking skills were recorded and communicated to shepherds and farmers across Europe who, until the arrival of the Romans, had only a rudimentary understanding of the process, and made mainly soft, fermented cheeses preserved in oil or salt.

It was the legions of Julius Caesar who brought the knowledge of how to make hard cheeses to Switzerland in 400BC, laying the foundation for what were to become some of the world's finest cheeses. Some of the classic English and French hard cheeses also owe their origins to Roman cheesemaking skills.

Roquefort was among the earliest cheeses from the provinces to be mentioned by Pliny in around AD40. The stretched curd *(pasta filata)* cheeses, such as Provolone and mozzarella, are thought to have originated, not in Italy, but with the Bedouin tribes of Persia.

LEFT: Bel Paese, one of Italy's most famous semi-soft cheeses, is now also made under licence in the USA

In a recent survey, nearly 400 Italian cheeses were identified. Some have been given the protection of the DOC (a system of control and protection), while others are yet to be included. They rate in quality and diversity alongside the cheeses of France, but whereas in France cheese tends to be served as a separate course, the great Italian cheeses have found fame for the flavour, style and character they give to Italian food. Enormous volumes of Grana Padano, Parmigiano-Reggiano, Provolone and Pecorino are sent around the world.

It is a shame that most consumers use these wonderful hard cheeses purely for cooking. Once you have eaten a freshly cut chunk of Parmigiano-Reggiano or Pecorino Toscano with fresh figs and Parma ham or simply solo, with a glass of Barolo, you will understand why Italians like to refer to these as table cheeses – the implication being that they should be kept on the table to be eaten whenever wanted.

Many of Italy's greatest cheeses are seldom found outside the areas where they are made, let alone beyond Italy's borders, so the best way to discover them is to take a trip through this wonderful country.

LEFT: Parmigiano-Reggiano

Asiago (DOC)

REGION: *Vicenza & Trento*
TYPE: *Traditional, farmhouse and creamery, unpasteurized, hard cheese*
SOURCE: *Cow's milk*
DESCRIPTION: *8–20kg/18–44lb wheel. The natural rind is smooth and glossy. Yellow when young, it deepens to burnt orange*
CULINARY USES: *Table cheese, grating, as a condiment*

Centuries ago, this was a sheep's milk cheese, made by shepherds from the Asiago plateau. However, as sheep gave way to cattle (with their higher milk yields), cow's milk came to be used. There are two distinct types of Asiago. The first is a lightly pressed cheese made from whole milk in small dairies. It is sometimes incorrectly referred to or mistaken for Pressato – a fact that irritates the Asiago producers – and it ripens within 20–30 days. Pale yellow and springy, with a delicate, sweet, undemanding flavour and fragrance, it has achieved

RIGHT: Asiago

significant commercial success with the modern consumer.

Asiago d'Allevo is the mature cheese, and, according to locals, the better form. Although it is made with skimmed milk, the long, slow maturation process creates a fruity, slightly sharp cheese with a compact, granular interior full of small holes. After 12 months it is the colour of liquid honey; after two years it acquires a toffee colour and becomes brittle and intensely flavoured. Like Parmesan cheese, Asiago can, when grated, be used as a condiment.

BEL PAESE

REGION: *Lombardy*
TYPE: *Modern, creamery, semi-soft cheese*
SOURCE: *Cow's milk*
DESCRIPTION: *2kg/4½lb wheel with shiny, golden, waxed rind*
CULINARY USES: *Table cheese, melting; can be used instead of mozzarella*

Dante referred to Italy as "bel paese" – beautiful land. This later became the title of a book, which in turn proved the inspiration for Egidio Galbani when he sought a name for his soft and yielding cheese. Bel Paese is ivory in colour and has a delicately sweet flavour that has won the hearts of thousands around the world. The cheese ripens in one to three months. A version is made in the USA under licence.

BRA (DOC)

REGION: *Piedmont*
TYPE: *Traditional, farmhouse and co-operative, unpasteurized, hard cheese*
SOURCE: *Cow's milk*
DESCRIPTION: *8kg/18lb round. The natural rind ranges in colour from pale straw yellow to deep brownish-yellow and has some surface moulds*
CULINARY USES: *Table cheese, grating, melting*

Like Stilton, Bra is named not for where it is made, but for the place where it was originally sold. The people of Bra (in Cuneo, Piedmont) used to buy young cheeses from the herdsmen of the Alpine valleys. These they matured in their own cellars, either for their own consumption or for selling on. If the cheeses were matured for long enough, they could be substituted for the more expensive and less readily available Pecorino.

Today there are two types of Bra, both similar in appearance but cured in different ways. The traditional, hard version is still the most popular. It is matured for three to six months, when the colour darkens and the flavour intensifies.

The cheese is also sold young, at 45 days, when the paste is still soft. This version is made in small dairies, almost always from pasteurized milk; it is disapproved of by traditional producers.

DOC

Like France, Italy operates a system to protect certain indigenous cheeses. It goes under the acronym DOC (Denominazione di Origine Controllata). In 1955 the Ministry of Agriculture and Forestry, in conjunction with a consortium of cheesemakers, set out to identify suitable candidates for DOC regulation. They agreed standards of production and determined areas where the cheeses in question could be made. So far 26 cheeses have been given the DOC classification, and more will undoubtedly follow.

Identifying and promoting indigenous cheeses in this way helps to protect them from being copied, while guaranteeing the consumer a level of quality. It also brings to the attention of the public artisan cheeses that might otherwise have become extinct.

Inspectors regularly visit the cheesemakers. If a cheese sold under the DOC label fails to comply with the regulations, the producer can be heavily fined and legal action may be taken. The DOC symbol is more than a legal requirement, however. It recognizes that indigenous cheeses and their makers have an important role to play in the nation's history. It also acknowledges the places where the cheeses are traditionally made. DOC status is a matter of pride.

What DOC status does not do is guarantee that every cheese that carries the symbol is perfect (or identical with every other cheese of the same type). The character of an individual cheese will depend upon the grazing, the season and the skills of the cheesemaker. DOC status, however, guarantees an overall standard.

CACIOCAVALLO
REGION: *Southern Italy*
TYPE: *Traditional, farmhouse and creamery, stretched curd cheese*
SOURCE: *Cow's milk*
DESCRIPTION: *2–3kg/4¹/2–6¹/2lb fat, gourd-shaped cheese, tied at the thin end with a cord for hanging. The rind is oily and smooth*
CULINARY USES: *Table cheese, grating, grilling, melting*

This stretched curd (*pasta filata*) cheese is typical of the south of Italy. The origin of the name has long been debated. *Cavallo* means "horse" in Italian, and some say the cheese was originally made from mare's milk. A more logical, but less romantic, explanation is that the name comes from the method of hanging pairs of cheeses over a pole, as if on horseback.

Usually farm-made, the curd is pulled and stretched until it is stringy but no longer breaks. It is then divided into portions, kneaded into shape and matured. At three months the Caciocavallo is sweet and supple and eaten as a table cheese. Some though are matured for up to two years, when they can be grated. The interior is golden-yellow and close-textured, the aroma is intense and lingering, and the taste is full but mellow. Caciocavallo is sometimes made with a lump of butter in the middle, which oozes out when the cheese is cut. There are also smoked versions.

CANESTRATO PUGLIESE (DOC)
REGION: *Foggia*
TYPE: *Traditional, farmhouse, unpasteurized, hard cheese*
SOURCE: *Sheep's milk (Merino or Apulian Gentile)*
DESCRIPTION: *7–14kg/15¹/4–31lb cylinder. The natural, beige to gold rind is embossed with the intricate pattern of the basket in which it is drained*
CULINARY USES: *Table cheese, grating*

Named after the simple, hand-woven reed basket in which it is pressed and drained, Canestrato Pugliese is a flavoursome Pecorino. After being allowed to mature on a wooden shelf for a month or two, the cheese has an aroma reminiscent of wet wool, lanolin and mould. Although hard and grainy, the texture retains the rich, creamy feel and burnt-caramel taste characteristic of sheep's milk cheeses. The cheese can be left to mature for up to a year, and has a fat content of 45 per cent.

BELOW: Casciotta di Urbino

ABOVE: Caciocavallo

CASCIOTTA DI URBINO (DOC)
REGION: *Tuscany and Umbria*
TYPE: *Traditional, farmhouse, unpasteurized, semi-soft cheese*
SOURCE: *Sheep's milk (Sardinian and Appennine Brown) plus some cow's milk*
DESCRIPTION: *1.2kg/2¹/2lb round-edged cylinder with thin, polished, yellow to orange, natural rind*
CULINARY USES: *Table cheese, snacks, cooking, in salads*

Casciotta is the name used to describe the many small, artisan cheeses made all over central Italy and in some parts of the south. They can be made with cow's, goat's or sheep's milk (or a mixture) and are popular with both locals and tourists alike. Some have smooth, firm, oiled rinds; others have the basket imprint typical of Pecorinos.

Casciotta di Urbino is said to be one of the best. The yellow rind gives way to a deliciously compact, friable, straw-coloured interior. Sweet-tasting and moist, with the aroma and flavour of warm milk, it is a delicate, subtle cheese with underlying flavours of fresh green grass, nuts and wild flowers.

The makers of Casciotta di Urbino use raw milk and make their cheese only between April and September. It ripens in 15–30 days and has a fat content of 45 per cent. The cheese may be flavoured with garlic, onion or truffles.

CASTELMAGNO (DOC)

REGION: *Cuneo*
TYPE: *Traditional, farmhouse and co-operative, unpasteurized, hard cheese*
SOURCE: *Cow's milk (with goat's or sheep's milk)*
DESCRIPTION: *5–7kg/11–15¼lb cylinder. The reddish-yellow, natural rind is crusty, with some grey moulds and yeasts*
CULINARY USES: *After-dinner cheese; also used to make gnocchi*

The first official record of Castelmagno was in 1277, when it was mentioned as a unit of exchange. Production remained steady for centuries and some even found its way to Paris and London, but by the early 1950s demand had dropped significantly. Recognizing the importance of preserving a part of local history, an association to protect Castelmagno was formed and formalized under the DOC system in 1982.

Castelmagno is made from partially skimmed cow's milk, with some goat's or sheep's milk added. The evening milk is left to ripen overnight. Next day, the morning milk is added, which contributes to its strong taste and unusual texture. This has been described as resembling cotton wool, but lovers of Castelmagno prefer to describe it as flaky or compact, but not dense, not unlike young Lancashire.

The cheeses are left to ripen in damp cellars and drying rooms, occasionally being turned and washed to encourage the development of the natural micro-flora that contribute to the pungent, yeasty aroma. Blue moulds, present in the cellars, some- times penetrate the rind to form fine, blue streaks that impart a more spicy flavour to the cheese. It ripens in two to five months (today's consumers tend to prefer it younger and milder).

CRESCENZA

REGION: *Lombardy*
TYPE: *Traditional, farmhouse and creamery, fresh cheese*
SOURCE: *Cow's milk*
DESCRIPTION: *1–2kg/2¼–4½lb white square or rectangle*
CULINARY USES: *Baking, grilling, in sauces*

The texture of this Stracchino-style cheese varies considerably from one brand to the next and according to the percentage of fat. The best examples are reputed to come from around Milan or Pavia. Sold within a few days of making, they come wrapped in simple, white, greaseproof paper and are quite luscious. Squidgy and so moist as to be almost wet, they have a fresh, clean acidity not unlike that of yogurt. Other Crescenzas are more rubbery, jelly-like or mushy, with a sour, synthetic taste. Low-fat varieties can be grainy.

Crescenza should be ripened for no longer than 10 days and eaten as soon as possible after that. The fat content varies between 48 and 50 per cent.

BELOW: Dolcelatte

DOLCELATTE

REGION: *Lombardy*
TYPE: *Modern, creamery, blue cheese*
SOURCE: *Cow's milk*
DESCRIPTION: *1–2kg/2¼–4½lb wheel. The moist, natural rind is white, blotched with blue and grey mould*
CULINARY USES: *Table cheese, dressings, in salads and on pasta*

The name means "sweet milk" and the cheese has a luscious, sweet taste. Deliciously soft, it melts like ice cream in the mouth. Created by Galbani, a company already famous for Bel Paese, Dolcelatte appeals to those who find the more traditional blue cheeses, such as Gorgonzola and Roquefort, too strongly flavoured, robust and spicy.

The cheesemaking method is similar to that used for Gorgonzola, except that Dolcelatte is made from the curd of only one milking. Produced in factories, the cheese ripens in two to three months and has a fat content of around 50 per cent. It may also be labelled Gorgonzola Dolce. Similar cheeses include Dolceverde and Torta Gaudenzio.

LEFT: Dolcelatte Torta

FONTINA (DOC)
REGION: *Valle d'Aosta*
TYPE: *Traditional, farmhouse and creamery, unpasteurized, semi-soft cheese*
SOURCE: *Cow's milk*
DESCRIPTION: *8–18kg/18–40lb wheel. The thin, uneven, light brown to terracotta rind is lightly oiled*
CULINARY USES: *Table cheese, melting, grilling*

In the pastures of the Valle d'Aosta, dominated by the highest mountains in Europe, the very dry summers result in a wide variety of high-quality fodder. There has been a cheese industry here since the eleventh century, when the local cheese was known simply as "caseus" to indicate that it was made from cow's milk.

Today, the name Fontina is used exclusively and proudly to identify cheeses produced in the Valle d'Aosta. The best of these are made in mountain chalets between May and September, when the herds graze the alpine meadows.

Fontina is dense, smooth and slightly elastic. The straw-coloured interior, with its small, round holes, has a delicate nuttiness with a hint of mild honey. When melted, as it frequently is (Fontina being the foundation for that superb fondue-style dish, fonduta), the flavour is earthy, with a suggestion of mushrooms and a fresh acidity.

Each cheesemaker has his own favourite location for ripening his cheeses – caves, tunnels, former military bunkers and even an abandoned copper mine. Fontina ripens in about three months and has a fat content of 45 per cent.

ABOVE: Fontina

DOLCELATTE TORTA
REGION: *Various*
TYPE: *Modern, creamery, blue cheese*
SOURCE: *Cow's milk*
DESCRIPTION: *2–3kg/4½–6½lb rectangle with moist, natural rind covered in grey and blue moulds*
CULINARY USES: *Table cheese; also used in dips and spreads and over pasta*

Created in the 1960s, this cheese consists of thick layers of mascarpone cream alternating with the mild, Italian blue cheese, Dolcelatte. The cream mellows the blue cheese and the feel in the mouth is soft and gentle, more like ice cream than cheese. Spread it on warm toast, melt it over pasta or keep it for a private feast. Dolcelatte Torta is really too rich – the fat content is a hefty 75 per cent – to serve with ordinary wine, but it is delicious accompanied by a smooth fortified wine, such as Madeira, or even a sweet Italian dessert wine to cut the richness.

In the USA it may also be labelled Gorgonzola Torta.

The success of this cheese has led to the creation of other *tortas*, some good, some almost inedible. One of the best has layers of lightly toasted pine nuts and pesto alternating with the mascarpone – a few chunks of this *torta* melted into hot pasta and sprinkled with fresh chopped basil makes an irresistible starter.

FIORE SARDO (DOC)
REGION: *Sardinia*
TYPE: *Traditional, farmhouse and co-operative, unpasteurized, hard cheese*
SOURCE: *Sheep's milk*
DESCRIPTION: *1.5–4kg/3–9lb cylindrical wheel. The hard, ridged, natural rind is golden-yellow to dark brown*
CULINARY USES: *Table cheese, grating, cooking, snacks*

Don't be put off by the sour, damp smell of the rind. This is the sweetest of the Pecorinos. Straw-coloured and compact, this hard and grainy cheese has a wonderfully rich flavour, with a caramel sweetness, a mouthwatering, salty tang and a hint of fruit.

Rennet from lamb or kid (goat) is used to coagulate the milk. The method differs from that used for traditional Pecorino in that the curds are not "cooked" or heated in the whey. Once drained, the curds are scalded in hot water to seal the rind. They are then stored on a woven reed shelf, which hangs over the family hearth, absorbing the sweet smoke as they dry. Ripening continues in another room or the attic and the cheeses are periodically rubbed with olive oil and sheep fat to keep them moist and prevent moulds from forming. Fiore Sardo ripens in three to six months and has a fat content of 45 per cent.

GORGONZOLA (DOC)

REGION: *Lombardy*
TYPE: *Traditional, creamery and co-operative, blue cheese*
SOURCE: *Cow's milk*
DESCRIPTION: *6–12 kg/13–26lb drum with red to orange rind covered with powdery patches of grey and blue moulds*
CULINARY USES: *Table cheese, dressings, salads, on pasta or gnocchi*

There are several folk legends to explain how what was originally a winter-made Stracchino cheese became one of the world's first blue cheeses. According to some, it was discovered inadvertently by an innkeeper in Gorgonzola, who found that his young Stracchino cheese had turned "blue" after a few weeks in his cool, damp cellars. Conscious of his profit margin, he decided to dish it up to some passing customers. Far from protesting, they demanded more.

The greenish-blue penicillium mould imparts a sharp, spicy flavour and provides an excellent contrast to the rich, creamy cheese. Gorgonzola is made by over 80 producers – large and small – in the north of Italy. Some use unpasteurized milk and follow the traditional method of allowing the curd to hang overnight so that it can become exposed to the mould naturally, but most Gorgonzola is made with

pasteurized milk, to which the mould is added. At about four weeks the cheeses are pierced with thick needles to encourage the spread of the mould. Some are still ripened in the caves at Valsassina and Lodi, which provide ideal conditions for the formation of the mould.

Gorgonzola ripens in three to six months and has a fat content of 48 per cent. The cheese is usually wrapped in foil to keep it moist.

LEFT: Grana Padano

GRANA (DOC)

REGION: *Po Valley*
TYPE: *Traditional, creamery, unpasteurized, hard cheese*
SOURCE: *Cow's milk*
DESCRIPTION: *24–40kg/52–88lb drum with rock-hard, polished, yellow to brown, natural rind*
CULINARY USES: *Table cheese, grating, in sauces, as a condiment*

Grana is the generic name for the hard, grainy cheeses that originated in the Po Valley in Roman times. Magnificent, fruity and full of flavour, Grana must be matured for at least 12 months (longer, if covered by DOC controls).

The most famous examples of Grana are Grana Padano and Parmigiano-Reggiano, which are listed separately in this book. Grana Lodigiano is characterized by a slightly greenish tinge and the flavour is very strong, even bitter. It is unbelievably expensive to buy.

LEFT: Gorgonzola

GRANA PADANO (DOC)

REGION: *Specified parts of Piedmont, Lombardy, Emilia Romagna, Veneto and Trentino*
TYPE: *Traditional, co-operative, unpasteurized, hard cheese*
SOURCE: *Cow's milk*
DESCRIPTION: *24–40kg/52–88lb drum. The smooth, natural rind is extremely hard and thick. Deep yellow and often oily, it carries the official logo*
CULINARY USES: *Table cheese, grating, in starters and sauces, on pasta and salads*

Both Grana Padano and Parmigiano-Reggiano are known to many of us as simply "Parmesan". The cheese should taste fresh, fruity and sweet, with a hint of pineapple; never sour or dull. The pale yellow interior should be hard, grainy and crumbly. Although they are expensive, a little goes a long way. These cheeses freeze very well, you can either grate the cheese first and pack in a freezer container, or simply freeze the piece. It can be grated straight from the freezer – a far better convenience food than the unpleasant-tasting pre-packed pots of grated Parmesan that are available.

Grana Padano ripens in 12–48 months and has a fat content of 32 per cent.

MASCARPONE
REGION: *Various*
TYPE: *Traditional, farmhouse
and creamery, vegetarian,
matured cream*
SOURCE: *Cow's milk*
DESCRIPTION: *Pale cream and shiny,
sold in pots*
CULINARY USES: *Desserts, baking, with
pasta, in savoury dishes*

Technically speaking, mascarpone is not a cheese at all, but rather the result of a culture being added to the cream skimmed off the milk used in the production of Parmesan. It is, however, often described as a curd cheese although it is made in much the same way as yogurt.

After the culture has been added, the cream is gently heated, then allowed to mature and thicken. It develops a magnificent, thick, spoonable texture and is extremely versatile.

Famous as the main ingredient of that most sensuous of all Italian desserts, tiramisù, it also makes an excellent alternative to double (heavy) cream in both sweet and savoury dishes. In southern Italy mascarpone is sometimes made from buffalo's milk. It takes only a few days to ripen and has a fat content of 75 per cent.

BELOW: Mascarpone

MONTASIO (DOC)
REGION: *Friuli and Veneto*
TYPE: *Traditional, farmhouse
and creamery,
unpasteurized, hard cheese*
SOURCE: *Cow's milk (with
some sheep's milk)*
DESCRIPTION: *5–10kg/11–22lb
wheel. The yellow-brown rind is
smooth and springy at first, becomes
harder and a darker brown with age*
CULINARY USES: *Table cheese, grating,
in sauces*

Developed in the thirteenth century at the monastery of Maggio, Montasio was originally made wholly from sheep's milk. Cow's milk is used today. The evening milk is partially skimmed (the cream being used to make mascarpone) and then mixed with the morning milk. The cheese is the same shape as Fontina, but in texture it resembles a young Asiago. Pale yellow or straw-coloured, the body is firm, with small holes. A good Montasio is creamy, rich and fruity, with a hint of pineapple. It should be quite tangy at the finish – not unlike a medium Cheddar. As it matures, the rind becomes very hard and the interior quite granular, even brittle. The fruity taste intensifies.

Montasio ripens in three to 18 months and has a fat content of 30–40 per cent.

ABOVE: Mozzarella

MOZZARELLA DI BUFALA
REGION: *Various*
TYPE: *Traditional, farmhouse and
creamery, stretched curd cheese*
SOURCE: *Water buffalo's milk*
DESCRIPTION: *Spherical or oval cheeses
in various sizes – wet, shiny and
pure white*
CULINARY USES: *Freshly sliced in salads,
baked on pizzas, also grilled*

Like most fresh cheeses, mozzarella is used to add texture rather than a specific taste to a dish. The juices, oils and flavours of the other ingredients are absorbed and intensified by the mild, moist, open layers of spun curd. It is this characteristic, together with the fact that mozzarella melts to become wonderfully elastic, that has made the cheese so popular.

The cheese is sold swimming in whey. It should be floppy rather than rubbery and have moisture trapped between the layers of springy curd. Cow's milk mozzarella is not as delicately flavoured as that from water buffalo's milk, nor as soft in texture, but it can be exceptional if well made. A fresh cheese, it should be eaten within a few days of being made.

If the cheese is lightly smoked, it is called mozzarella affumicata. If the cheese is more heavily smoked (a process that dries it out), it is referred to as scamorza. The hard, rubbery "pizza" cheese sold as mozzarella outside Italy may be perfect for pizzas in terms of texture, but will never equal fresh mozzarella in taste. In Italy, the commercial "block" mozzarella is usually called pizzaiola.

MURAZZANO (DOC)

REGION: *Cuneo*
TYPE: *Traditional, farmhouse and creamery, unpasteurized, fresh cheese*
SOURCE: *Cow's and sheep's milk in 60:40 ratio*
DESCRIPTION: *150–250g/5–9oz round with fine, smooth, yellow rind*
CULINARY USES: *Table cheese, grilling*

Named for the village where it is made, this is a typical Piedmontese *robiola* – a soft, round cheese made from a mixture of cow's and sheep's milk. The texture is delicate and supple and the taste fresh and milky, with a hint of the caramel characteristic of sheep's milk cheese. Although it is delicious as it is, it is usually melted on pizzas or crostini or used in sauces or pastries. Murazzano ripens in four to five days and has a fat content of 45 per cent.

ABOVE: Parmigiano-Reggiano

PARMIGIANO-REGGIANO (DOC)

REGION: *Modena, Parma, Reggio Emilia, parts of Bologna and Mantua*
TYPE: *Traditional, co-operative, unpasteurized, hard cheese*
SOURCE: *Cow's milk*
DESCRIPTION: *24–40kg/52–88lb drum with thick, hard, yellow to orange rind*
CULINARY USES: *Table cheese, grating, in sauces and salads, over pasta and risotto*

In Italy, this wonderful cheese is sold in large, rough, grainy chunks chiselled from the shiny drum that carries its name emblazoned on the rind. The aroma is sweet and fruity, the colour fresh yellow and the taste exquisite – fruity (like fresh pineapple), strong and rich, but never overpowering or vicious. It will keep for months in the fridge, but the rough surface may grow some mould. If you have bought a large chunk and use it infrequently – an unthinkable possibility – freeze it. You can grate it straight from the freezer. In 1955 the rules relating to where Parmigiano-Reggiano could be made were tightened and the method of manufacture strictly specified. The cows whose milk goes into the cheese may have only fresh grass, hay or alfalfa. Enforcing these rules adds to the production cost, but the result is a cheese whose flavour and quality are guaranteed.

The secret of the continuing success of Parmigiano-Reggiano is the determination of the regulating body to maintain the 800 or so local dairy farms producing it. Only on small farms, where the milk does not have far to travel to the cheesemaker, can the close relationship between each batch of milk and its transformation into cheese be maintained.

A surprising feature of this delicious, robust and full-bodied cheese is that it is made from partially skimmed milk. The evening milk is left to rest in vats overnight. Next morning, the slightly soured cream is skimmed off to make mascarpone and the skimmed milk is combined with the fresh morning milk. It is then poured into conical, copper cauldrons so that the cheesemaking process can begin.

To seal the rind, and protect it from drying out over the next 18–48 months, the cheeses are floated in enormous brine baths for around 21 days, then they are moved to the storerooms. Throughout the maturation process, the huge cheeses are carefully brushed, turned, checked and rechecked before being graded by an official representative of the consortium responsible for determining the quality of each one.

The trademark, Parmigiano-Reggiano, is branded all over the rind, so that even a small piece of the cheese can easily be identified. It is one of the finest cheeses in the world.

RIGHT: Murazzano

PECORINO ROMANO (DOC)

REGION: *Lazio and Sardinia*
TYPE: *Traditional, farmhouse and creamery, hard cheese*
SOURCE: *Sheep's milk*
DESCRIPTION: *22–33kg/48–72lb drum. The smooth, hard rind is pale straw to dark brown in colour*
CULINARY USES: *Table cheese, grating, in sauces, on pasta*

Pecorino is the generic name for cheeses made from sheep's milk. Each is characteristic of a specific area and of a particular breed of sheep. For centuries, Pecorino Romano was made in the countryside around Rome, and it remains virtually unchanged to this day.

Since the first century AD the cheese has been widely exported, thanks to its excellent keeping qualities. It was issued to Roman legionaries as part of their rations. Demand continued to grow until the Roman producers could no longer keep up. At that point production spread to Sardinia, where there are now more than 60 factories or dairies compared with only 10 in the area around Rome.

The cheese is made between November and late June, when the sheep graze freely on the natural pastures. Pecorino Romano is larger than most cheeses of this type and must be pressed. It takes eight to 12 months to mature, during which time it develops its characteristic flavour – salty, with a fruity tang that becomes steadily more robust. The rind varies in colour, depending on the age of the cheese, and may have a protective coating of lard or oil. The compact interior is white to pale yellow, with irregular, small eyes. It should feel moist, yet granular and it is a superb grating cheese.

Other Romanos are Caprino Romano made with goat's milk and Vaccino Romano made with cow's milk. Both are hard and have their own individual character.

PECORINO SARDO (DOC)

REGION: *Sardinia*
TYPE: *Traditional, farmhouse, unpasteurized, hard cheese*
SOURCE: *Sheep's milk*
DESCRIPTION: *1–4kg/2¼–9lb cylinder. The natural rind varies in colour from pale straw yellow to deep russet*
CULINARY USES: *Table cheese, grating, in snacks, salads and sauces, on pasta*

Only recently brought under the protective umbrella of the DOC system, this cheese has two distinct styles. The delicate and sweet Pecorino Sardo Dolce is matured for 20–60 days and weighs 1–2.3kg/2¼–5lb. The body is white and firm, with a few scattered eyes.

Pecorino Sardo Maturo is matured for up to 12 months and becomes hard, granular and dry. It develops a robust sharpness and a salty tang. A cornucopia of flavours – sweet, nutty and herbaceous – is released when the cheese is grated on to hot foods such as pasta.

Each season can bring a subtle difference in the flavour of the cheese, depending on the flowers, grasses and herbs favoured by the native Sardinian sheep – the *mouflon* – that range over the rocky hillsides of the island.

BELOW: Pecorino Romano (left), Sardo (top) and Toscano (right)

PECORINO TOSCANO (DOC)

REGION: *Tuscany*
TYPE: *Traditional, farmhouse and co-operative, unpasteurized, hard cheese*
SOURCE: *Sheep's milk*
DESCRIPTION: *1–3kg/2¼–6½lb wheel. The natural rind ranges in colour from pale straw to brown or black*
CULINARY USES: *Pared or grated on pasta or risotto, in sauces and salads*

A young Pecorino Toscano is supple, fruity and aromatic; the complex flavour suggests walnuts and rich, burnt caramel.

Until recently, the name was used to describe any cheese made in Tuscany from sheep's milk or a mixture of milks. New regulations mean that the name is now protected and reserved only for pure sheep's milk cheeses. Mixed milk cheeses are sold as Caciotta.

Generally smaller than other Pecorinos, Toscano ripens more quickly. Those sold young have a yellow rind and are firm, but not hard. The rind darkens to a brownish-red after two to three months. The black-rinded cheese (Pecorino Toscano Crosta Nero) is matured for at least six months and has an intense flavour.

PRESSATO (DOC)

REGION: *Vicenza and Trento*
TYPE: *Traditional, co-operative, hard cheese*
SOURCE: *Cow's milk*
DESCRIPTION: *Various sizes and shapes with pale straw to golden-yellow rind*
CULINARY USES: *Table cheese, melting*

Pressato simply means "pressed" and is a generic name for a family of lightly pressed cheeses made from either skimmed or semi-skimmed milk. These sweet-sour, milky cheeses are sold young, when they are supple and open-textured. Asiago (to the annoyance of the producers) is sometimes wrongly referred to as Pressato.

ABOVE: Provolone

PROVOLONE (DOC)

REGION: *Lombardy*
TYPE: *Traditional creamery stretched curd cheese*
SOURCE: *Cow's milk*
DESCRIPTION: *200g–5kg/7oz–11lb cheeses in various shapes. The thin, hard rind is golden-yellow and shiny. It is sometimes waxed*
CULINARY USES: *Table cheese, grilling, melting*

No one knows precisely where or how this cheese originated, but it was certainly among the earliest cheeses known by the Romans. Local names for Provolone usually reflect the shape or size, which can vary considerably. The cheese can be spherical, pear-shaped, cylindrical or even plaited and the weight depends on the mood of the cheesemaker. The Giganti (monster cheeses), often made for special occasions or trade fairs, can be over 3m/3¼yd long, but the most familiar shape, often found hanging in Italian delicatessens, is the sausage tied with cord.

Dolce (mild Provolone) is aged for two to three months, and it is supple and smooth, with a thin, waxed rind. It is generally used as a table cheese. Picante (piquant) is coagulated with kid's rennet, which gives it a stronger flavour. Aged for six months to two years, it is darker, with small eyes, a hard rind and a strong, spicy flavour. It is often grated as a condiment.

QUARTIROLO LOMBARDO

REGION: *Lombardy*
TYPE: *Traditional, farmhouse and creamery, semi-soft cheese*
SOURCE: *Cow's milk*
DESCRIPTION: *1–3kg/2¼–6½lb square cheese. The tender, pale pink rind hardens with age and acquires reddish-grey moulds*
CULINARY USES: *Table cheese, served with salads and cold meats*

In summer, the abundant grass in the Lombardy valleys was traditionally mown three times. After the final mowing, the cattle would be brought from the mountain pastures to graze on the sweet, new grass (*erba quartirola*) before being turned into the barns for the winter. The cheese made from the rich milk yielded at this time was called Quartirolo Lombardo. Skimmed milk was used (the cream being turned into butter).

Today, the cheese is made all year round, usually from full-cream milk. It looks like a young Taleggio, and has a slightly crumbly, lumpy centre. If eaten within the first few weeks, it has a lemon-fresh acidity and delicate fragrance; after two months it becomes dense, almost runny, and its fruity character is more distinctive. Cheese lovers seek out those made in the mountains – Quartirolo di Monte – which are unpasteurized and slowly ripened. Producers are currently attempting to have the cheese brought under the control of the DOC system to protect its quality and character.

BELOW:
Raschera

RAGUSANO (DOC)

REGION: *Sicily*
TYPE: *Traditional, farmhouse and co-operative, unpasteurized, hard cheese*
SOURCE: *Cow's milk (Modicana)*
DESCRIPTION: *10–12kg/22–26lb brick. The thin, smooth, natural, yellow rind is polished*
CULINARY USES: *Table cheese, grilling*

In local dialect, Ragusano (or Caciocavallo Ragusano) is described as a *scaluni* or step. The curd is heated and stretched until it is rubbery. It is then pressed into special rectangular moulds. Once draining is complete, the cheeses are rubbed with salt and left to mature in cellars for up to six months. To stave off insects, they are regularly rubbed with a mixture of oil and vinegar. The pale yellow interior is soft and supple, with a savoury taste that becomes stronger as the cheese hardens and ages beyond six months.

RASCHERA (DOC)

REGION: *Cuneo*
TYPE: *Traditional, farmhouse and co-operative, semi-soft cheese*
SOURCE: *Cow's milk (with sheep's or goat's milk)*
DESCRIPTION: *7–10kg/15¼–22lb round or square. The thin, reddish-yellow crust with white or grey moulds*
CULINARY USES: *Table cheese, grilling*

Named after Lake Raschera, which lies at the foot of Mt Mongioie, this cheese resembles Toma, but is square, the practical shape having been determined in the days when it was transported by mule.

Generally made with the sweet milk of the Piedmontese cow, Raschera has a pale ivory interior scattered with tiny holes which occasionally have a bluish tinge. When young, the cheese is supple and elastic, with a delicate sweet taste that becomes richer, more aromatic and slightly tart. The flavour changes from season to season. Spring and summer cheeses are sweet and fresh, whereas those made in winter tend to be more solid and vibrant. The best is reckoned to be that which comes from the alpine pastures – look for the words "*di alpessio*" on the label.

RICOTTA

REGION: *Various*
TYPE: *Traditional, farmhouse and creamery, whey cheese*
SOURCE: *Cow's milk*
DESCRIPTION: *1–2kg/2¹/₄–4¹/₂lb basin-shaped cheese, pure white and wet, but not sticky*
CULINARY USES: *As a dessert cheese with sugar and fruit; also baked in ravioli or pastries*

When cheese is made, the solids in the milk are separated from the liquid by coagulation. Yet, however careful the cheesemaker, some solids are lost to the whey. To retrieve these, the milk is heated until the solids come to the surface as small, white lumps. These are skimmed off and drained in woven baskets until the curd is solid enough to stick together and can be turned out. The result is a soft, moist, basin-shaped cheese.

Good ricotta should be firm, not solid, and consist of a mass of fine, moist, delicate grains, neither salted nor ripened. One of the finest, Fior di Maggio, has a texture not unlike delicate bread and butter pudding. Only vaguely grainy, it melts in the mouth. Unfortunately, much of the ricotta made today uses semi-skimmed milk instead of whey and the texture can vary tremendously. It can be gritty, lumpy or even wet, causing havoc for those trying to use it in a traditional recipe.

In Italy, ricotta appears in a number of guises. Ricotta Romano is made from sheep's milk and is available only from November to June. Ricotta Salata is a salted and dried version that resembles feta, while Ricotta Infornata is a Sicilian speciality that is baked until it is lightly browned. Northern Italians like their ricotta smoked.

Ricotta ripens in one to five days and has a fat content of around 20 per cent.

RIGHT: Ricotta Salata (left) and fresh Ricotta (right)

ROBIOLA DI ROCCAVERANO (DOC)

REGION: *Lombardy*
TYPE: *Traditional, farmhouse and co-operative, fresh cheese*
SOURCE: *Cow's and goat's milk*
DESCRIPTION: *200g/7oz round or square cheese. Pure white when fresh, it becomes pink to orange with reddish ferments if aged*
CULINARY USES: *Table cheese, baking, spreading, in sauces*

Roccaverano is a small, typically Italian hillside town. The local cheese was once made exclusively from goat's milk, but a mixture of milks is now permitted and cow's milk can account for as much as 85 per cent. Some Robiola di Roccaverano is still made on farms for family consumption, but the majority is made in small co-operatives, using pasteurized milk.

The cheese can be eaten fresh, at just a few days old, when it is sweet and very moist. Others prefer it once it has matured for up to 20 days. The mature cheese is sharper, but still retains the subtle, taste characteristic of goat's milk. The pasteurized cheese is spreadable, with a smooth texture. It has a sweet-sour aroma and a taste that resembles melted butter, but can be quite salty. The unpasteurized cheese has a much more complex flavour. Rich and meaty, it has a piquant, yeasty aroma.

ABOVE: Scamorza Affumicate

SCAMORZA

REGION: *Various*
TYPE: *Traditional, farmhouse and creamery, stretched curd cheese*
SOURCE: *Cow's milk*
DESCRIPTION: *Smooth, shiny, white cheese traditionally made in a money-bag shape*
CULINARY USE: *Cooking*

The producers of Caciocavallo make this cheese when milk is abundant. It matures within a few days and it thus provides a good way to boost their income while waiting for the Caciocavallo to ripen.

A stretched curd cheese, Scamorza resembles Provolone. It is rubbery, with a stringy texture, and is drier than mozzarella. Sold young, within two to three days of making, it has a bland, vaguely milky taste. The smoked version, Scamorza Affumicate, is more popular than the plain and is often used in pasta dishes. It is also served with ham, mushrooms or chargrilled vegetables.

STRACCHINO

REGION: *Lombardy*
TYPE: *Traditional, farmhouse and creamery, semi-soft cheese*
SOURCE: *Cow's milk*
DESCRIPTION: *Made in various sizes and shapes (usually square). The thin, natural rind ranges from pale cream to reddish-brown, and can be sticky*
CULINARY USES: *Table cheese, melting, grilling*

Stracchino is a generic term, used to describe a style of soft cheese that has been made in Lombardy since the twelfth century. The quality varies considerably, so it is wise to taste before you buy. A good Stracchino will have a supple, yielding texture and a deliciously fruity flavour.

Well-known Stracchino-style cheeses include Crescenza, Quartirolo, Taleggio and Robiola.

TALEGGIO (DOC)

REGION: *Lombardy*
TYPE: *Traditional, farmhouse and creamery, semi-soft cheese*
SOURCE: *Cow's milk*
DESCRIPTION: *2kg/4¹/₂lb square with distinctive markings. The rough, rosy crust is imprinted with the official stamp of the consortium*
CULINARY USES: *Table cheese, grilling, melting (popular over polenta)*

Taleggio was originally only one of several cheeses referred to as "Stracchino", a term still used to describe the soft, square cheeses of Lombardy. Today, DOC regulations govern both how and where Taleggio is made, and the quality is maintained (as are the basic shape and method of production) despite the fact that the majority of the cheese is now produced in factories from pasteurized milk.

Traditionally, the cheeses were matured in natural caves, which had deep crevices that provided natural air-conditioning and encouraged the spread of the moulds and ferments essential to create Taleggio's unique aroma and taste. Over 30 per cent of the cheeses sold today continue to be matured in these

ABOVE: Stracchino

caves, which undoubtedly makes a difference to their flavour.

By the time Taleggio reaches your favourite cheese shop it will have developed its rosy crust. The curd will be very nearly at melting point, while the centre will be elastic, with some eyes. The aroma will be gentle, but insistent, redolent of almonds and sweet hay.

In the hands of a talented affineur, the rind will harden and the ivory interior will reveal its magic – to experience it is like smelling and then eating a rich cream of asparagus soup.

Taleggio ripens in 25–50 days and has a fat content of 48 per cent.

ABOVE: Taleggio, which is still matured in caves

TOMA (DOC)

REGION: *Piedmont*
TYPE: *Traditional, farmhouse, semi-hard cheese*
SOURCE: *Cow's milk (or mixed milk)*
DESCRIPTION: *Made in various shapes and sizes. The natural rind ranges from thin and pale yellow to thick, grey and crusty*
CULINARY USES: *Table cheese, cooking*

Toma has been made in the mountains of Piedmont in various shapes and sizes for generations. Although it now comes under the DOC umbrella, there are as many variations as there are small dairy farms in the Valle d'Aosta, where the finest Toma is said to be made. The young cheese is sweet and milky, but if it is allowed to mature for up to 12 months, the flavour becomes more tangy, often sharp. The Toma Piedmontese available in Britain has a soft, leathery rind and supple texture. It tastes fresh and creamy, with a hint of meadow flavours.

UBRIACO

REGION: *Vicenza and Trento*
TYPE: *Traditional, farmhouse, unpasteurized, hard cheese*
SOURCE: *Cow's milk*
DESCRIPTION: *8–12kg/18–26lb wheel. The deep burgundy, natural rind is rough and hard*
CULINARY USES: *Table cheese, grating*

Ubriaco means "drunken" in Italian, and it isn't difficult to see how the cheese got its name. Following local custom, the young cheese is soaked in wine, covered with the crushed grape skins left after pressing and allowed to mature for six to 10 months. The result is a cheese with the heady aroma of fermenting fruit. Ubriaco has a firm, crumbly but open texture that is fairly wet (the moisture tastes distinctly alcoholic and salty) and has a mouth-puckering bite that is reminiscent of ripe pineapple.

ENGLISH CHEESES

Simple cheesemaking implements dating back to the Iron Age have been found in England, but it was the arrival of the Romans in the first century AD – and the sweeping agricultural changes that ensued – that resulted in the introduction of harder, longer-lasting cheeses.

It is possible that Celtic monks from Wales and Ireland introduced the Trappist cheeses, but no records exist until the arrival of William the Conqueror in 1066. William brought with him Cistercian monks from Cîteaux in Burgundy, who taught the shepherds of the Yorkshire Dales how to make sheep's milk cheeses.

The dissolution of the monasteries during the reign of Henry VIII, meant that the monks were forced to find shelter and employment on local farms. Their cheesemaking skills spread further afield. Gradually sheep were replaced by cattle, which yielded far more milk and had longer lactation periods.

England is well suited to dairy farming, and by the sixteenth century nearly every county had its own cheese. Sadly, few of these cheeses exist today. Those that do are known as "territorials", with the best-known example being Cheddar.

The unique texture is obtained by using the traditional "cheddaring" process, whereby the curds are drained, cut into bricks, then pressed numerous times until the texture satisfies the cheesemaker. It is this laborious task that makes farmhouse Cheddar unique.

Unlike the other great cheeses of Europe, neither the name of Cheddar nor its method of production is protected, and the cheese has been copied the world over. The "cheddaring" performed in giant factories means that a generation of Cheddar eaters have grown up without the slightest clue as to what this great cheese should really taste like.

Although the origin of its name is still hotly disputed, it was unquestionably the landlord of the Bell Inn in the village of Stilton who put Stilton on the world map in the 1800s by serving the cheese to travellers journeying on the Great North Road from London to Scotland.

Cheshire, mentioned in the Domesday Book, is one of Britain's oldest cheeses. It derives its distinct character from the salt marshes on which the cattle graze. Port records from 1770 show that over 5,000 tons of Cheshire were shipped to London that year. It was considered to be one of Britain's finest cheeses, and by the 1930s there were more than 400 farms producing Cheshire.

Both Double and Single Gloucester have been made in Gloucestershire since the sixteenth century, originally from the milk of the native Old Gloucester cows.

Although still popular in the north of England, Lancashire has all but lost its way since the last century, when it was considered to be one of England's finest cheeses. Leicester – or Red Leicester as it is now known – was, until the late 1700s, produced in volume. However, the production of farmhouse versions of this russet cheese all but ceased before the Second World War. The same can be said of most of England's farmhouse cheeses, which are made only in limited volume and farmhouse varieties rarely exist.

LEFT: Today, Cheddar accounts for about 70 per cent of all cheese consumed in Britain

ABOVE: Stilton is one of England's best-loved cheeses

Several factors led to the decline and almost fall of these great cheeses. First was the cattle epidemic of 1860, when thousands of cows were slaughtered and tons of mass-produced American Cheddar was imported, paving the way for the industrialization of the cheese industry.

With the increasing demand for milk, many farmers found it easier to sell their milk rather than make cheese, and the number of cheesemakers declined further.

The ravages of the Second World War devastated the industry. With few men to run the farms and severe food shortages, the Ministry of Food ruled that any excess milk be used to make fast-ripening "National Cheese". When rationing ended in 1954 many farming families were without their menfolk and cheesemaking skills had been lost. Before the war there had been 15,000 cheesemakers; by the time it ended, only 126 remained.

In the past 15 years there has been a revolution. Block cheeses have improved, farmhouse cheesemakers are on the increase, old recipes are being revived and old breeds of cow are on the increase. Sheep's and goat's milk cheeses are making their way on to supermarket shelves.

England can now boast over 300 artisan cheeses. At the recent British Cheese Awards, 507 cheeses were entered. Of these, 44 were sheep's milk and 64 were goat's milk – as diverse and distinctive as those found in Europe.

ABOVE: Bath Cheese – one of the many recently created British cheeses that is based on an old recipe

BASING

REGION: *Kent*
TYPE: *Modern, farmhouse, unpasteurized, organic, vegetarian, hard cheese*
SOURCE: *Goat's milk*
DESCRIPTION: *4kg/9lb truckle cheese. The fine natural rind has some moulding*
CULINARY USES: *Table cheese, grating*

Maureen and Bill Browning make this Caerphilly-type cheese with milk from their own goats at Lower Basing Farm. It is lightly pressed, moist and crumbly. The mild and pleasant acidity, with just a hint of the herbaceous goat's milk, becomes smooth and more creamy as it matures. It ripens within two months and has a fat content of 45 per cent.

Basing has been a silver medal winner at the British Cheese Awards.

BATH CHEESE

REGION: *Avon*
TYPE: *Modern, farmhouse, unpasteurized, soft-white cheese*
SOURCE: *Cow's milk (Friesian and Ayrshire)*
DESCRIPTION: *225g/8oz square with smooth, white penicillium rind*
CULINARY USE: *Table cheese*

When young, Bath Cheese has a slightly grainy texture, while the flavour is mild and slightly tart, with a salty finish. When aged, the soft, furry, white rind yields to a soft interior, which oozes on to the plate as it reaches perfection. The flavour has hints of mushroom and warm milk balanced with a peppery, dandelion bite.

The producers, G. and P. Padfield, who also make York Cheese, developed the cheese after reading Patrick Rance's description of a similar cheese made in Bath a century ago.

Bath Cheese ripens in three to four weeks. It has twice been a silver medal winner at the British Cheese Awards.

BEENLEIGH BLUE

REGION: *Devon*
TYPE: *Modern, farmhouse, unpasteurized, organic, vegetarian, blue cheese*
SOURCE: *Sheep's milk*
DESCRIPTION: *3kg/6½lb cylinder. The rough, crusty, natural rind is slightly sticky and has some patches of blue, grey and white moulds*
CULINARY USE: *Table cheese*

Robin Congdon and Sari Cooper of Ticklemore Cheese are gifted cheesemakers. Their Beenleigh Blue is one of only three blue sheep's milk cheeses made in Britain. A consistent gold medal winner at the British Cheese Awards, it is moist yet crumbly, with the blue appearing as bold blue-green streaks through the white interior. The flavour is steely blue, with the burnt-caramel sweetness characteristic of fine sheep's milk cheese. It melts on the palate, disclosing its strong, spicy character. Don't cook it – eat it. It is wonderful with mead or sweet cider. Beenleigh Blue ripens in six months and has a fat content of 45–50 per cent. It is available from August to January.

Robin and Sari also produce Harbourne – a blue, goat's milk cheese – and Devon Blue, made from cow's milk. Ticklemore, their hard, goat's milk cheese, has a smooth texture and herbaceous character. These cheeses – and others from all over the country – are available from their cheese shop in Totnes.

BELOW: Beenleigh Blue

BERKSWELL

REGION: *West Midlands*
TYPE: *Modern, farmhouse, unpasteurized, vegetarian, hard cheese*
SOURCE: *Sheep's milk (Friesland)*
DESCRIPTION: *3.25kg/7lb flattened round. The deep russet-red, natural rind bears the intricate marks of the basket mould in which it is made*
CULINARY USES: *Table cheese, grating, in soups*

Stephen Fletcher and his mother make their magnificent-looking cheese at Ram Hall, an Elizabethan house in Berkswell, near the Forest of Arden. The milk comes from their flock of East Friesland sheep.

Berkswell is sold at around four months, when the hard, crusty, ridged rind has an aroma of lanolin and damp wool. The cheese is hard and chewy, almost granular, with a fat content of 48 per cent. Each bite reveals more of its complex flavours – roasted nuts, caramelized onions and meadow flowers with a prickly tang.

This is truly one of the great modern British cheeses.

ABOVE: Berkswell

BLUE CHESHIRE

REGION: *Cheshire*
TYPE: *Traditional, farmhouse and creamery, vegetarian, blue cheese*
SOURCE: *Cow's milk*
DESCRIPTION: *9kg/20lb truckle cheese. The natural rind is rough and crusty*
CULINARY USE: *Table cheese*

Traditionally, because of its open, crumbly texture, some Cheshire cheese would develop fine threads of blue during the months spent maturing in cellars. As this occurred naturally it was referred to as "blue fade" and came to be highly prized.

In recent years, the old idea has been revived, particularly by some of the Stilton makers. To guarantee that the blueing occurs, however, the mould is added to the milk before curdling. The young cheese is pierced, which allows in air and encourages the blueing to spread so that it provides an attractive contrast to the orange interior. A dry, dense and crumbly cheese, Blue Cheshire tends to be quite sharp, with a hint of green grass and salt balanced by the creaminess of the milk. The colour, which was originally obtained from carrots or marigolds, is now provided by annatto, a natural dye. Blue Cheshire ripens in two to three months.

LEFT: Blue Wensleydale (front) and Blue Vinny (back)

BLUE VINNY

REGION: *Dorset*
TYPE: *Traditional, farmhouse, unpasteurized, vegetarian, blue cheese*
SOURCE: *Cow's milk*
DESCRIPTION: *2–7kg/4¹⁄₂–15¹⁄₄lb cylinder. The natural, hard and crusty rind is reddish, with a dusting of white mould*
CULINARY USE: *Table cheese*

In 1982 Mike Davies set out to revive the old Dorset blue cheese, Blue Vinny, which had all but disappeared, yet about which there were a host of rumours. One claimed the cheese acquired its spidery, blue veining from having had old leather boots placed beside the vats.

Like most rumours, this had little foundation. "Vinny" is the old English word for "veining", and the blue comes from the family of penicillium moulds that occur naturally in the air. These invade the young, moist, open-textured, skimmed milk curd to create what is known as "blue fade". The same mould is attracted to old leather, hence the tall tale.

Today the blueing is not left to chance, and the penicillium mould is added directly to the milk.

Blue Vinny ripens in three to five months. The fat content is 40 per cent.

BLUE WENSLEYDALE

REGION: *North Yorkshire*
TYPE: *Traditional, creamery, vegetarian, blue cheese*
SOURCE: *Cow's milk*
DESCRIPTION: *4kg/9lb clothbound cylinder with hard, dry, brown-orange, rough rind*
CULINARY USE: *Table cheese*

Based on an original recipe that dates back to the eleventh century, this cheese has recently been revived by several creameries in the Yorkshire Dales. Firmer than most blues and slightly crumbly, Blue Wensleydale has a spicy, blue tang with a slightly bitter, dark chocolate and chicory finish. It takes nine to 12 weeks to mature and has a fat content of 45 per cent.

BOSWORTH

REGION: *Staffordshire*
TYPE: *Modern, farmhouse,*
unpasteurized, vegetarian,
soft-white cheese
SOURCE: *Goat's milk*
DESCRIPTION: *150g/5oz round cheese*
with very thin, velvety, penicillium
rind dusted with a fine layer of ash
CULINARY USE: *Table cheese*

Made by Hugh Lillington of Innes Cheese, this elegant, soft-white cheese has an unexpectedly firm, breakable texture rather than the usual Brie-like softness. It melts in the mouth like fudge, yielding up its sweet, nutty flavours with just a suggestion of goat's milk. It matures in three to four weeks and has a fat content of 45 per cent.

Hugh and his team at High Fields Dairy make various unpasteurized goat's milk cheeses, including Bosworth Leaf, so called because of the chestnut leaf wrapping that contrasts beautifully with the fluffy, white rind of the cheese. Bosworth Leaf has a fine, grained texture that softens to a velvety smoothness. The taste is reminiscent of vanilla and butterscotch, with a subtle but distinct, almost almondy finish.

BUFFALO

REGION: *Hereford and Worcester*
TYPE: *Modern, farmhouse,*
unpasteurized, vegetarian,
hard cheese
SOURCE: *Water buffalo's milk*
DESCRIPTION: *2kg/4 1/2lb wheel with*
thin, leathery, polished,
natural rind
CULINARY USES: *Table cheese, grilling*

The sight of water buffalo in the rolling Cotswold Hills is an incongruous one, yet these animals have adapted to their new home exceedingly well. Buffalo was released on the market in 1996 and won the British Cheese Awards' Best New or Experimental Cheese that same year. Not surprisingly, it is the only hard buffalo's milk cheese made in Britain, where the smooth, soft, Italian cheese – mozzarella – is better known. Firm yet supple, with a creamy feel, Buffalo has a flavour that hints of almonds and has a citrus tang.

RIGHT: Buffalo is the only hard buffalo's milk cheese made in Britain

BUTTON/INNES

REGION: *Staffordshire*
TYPE: *Modern, farmhouse,*
unpasteurized, vegetarian,
fresh cheese
SOURCE: *Goat's milk*
DESCRIPTION: *50g/2oz round*
CULINARY USE: *Table cheese*

Voted Supreme Champion at the British Cheese Awards in 1994, Button, or Innes Button, is soft, mousse-like and fragile. It simply dissolves on the palate, trailing a hint of almonds, honey, lemon, white wine and tangerine. One of Britain's finest goat's milk cheeses, it is also available dusted with ash, pink peppercorns, chopped nuts or herbs. Button ripens in five to 10 days and has a fat content of 45 per cent. Like Bosworth it is made by Hugh Lillington of Innes Cheese in Staffordshire.

BUXTON BLUE

REGION: *Derbyshire*
TYPE: *Modern, creamery,*
vegetarian, blue cheese
SOURCE: *Cow's milk*
DESCRIPTION: *8kg/18lb*
clothbound cylinder. The
rind is orange-brown
and crusty
CULINARY USES: *Table cheese,*
crumbled into soups or
salads, also blended with
soft cheese to make
a spread

The Duke of Devonshire established one of the first creameries in England at Hartington in Derbyshire in the 1870s, using milk from his tenant farmers. The building was virtually destroyed by fire towards the end of the nineteenth century and lay abandoned until Thomas Nuttall, a successful Stilton maker, took it over. The creamery, now part of Mendip Dairy Crest, still concentrates on making Stilton, but created Buxton Blue in 1994 to meet the growing demand from consumers and supermarkets for new cheeses.

Buxton Blue is firmer than Stilton, with fine, blue streaks in the pale orange interior. More crumbly than hard, it is milder than most blues and has a hint of dark chocolate and burnt onions on the finish. It ripens in 10–12 weeks and has a fat content of 45 per cent. The factory also makes Dovedale Blue.

ABOVE: Buxton Blue is one of only nine British cheeses that has been granted PDO status by the EC

CAPRICORN GOAT
REGION: *Somerset*
TYPE: *Modern, creamery, vegetarian, soft-white cheese*
SOURCE: *Goat's milk*
DESCRIPTION: *125g/4¹/₂oz cylinder or 1.2kg/2¹/₂lb square cutting cheese with pure white, soft rind*
CULINARY USE: *Table cheese*

Lubborn Cheese is best known for its Somerset Camembert and Brie cheeses, but Capricorn Goat has made giant strides in convincing the British public that goat's milk cheese can be mild, not vicious, and can have a distinct character without being overwhelming.

The smaller version of this cheese is an attractive cylinder with a delicate, soft-white rind. Slightly chalky, like unripe Camembert when young, it becomes softer around the edges and is sometimes almost runny. The fresh, creamy feel with a background of chicory and nuts is very appealing. The cheese ripens in four to six weeks and has a fat content of 26 per cent. It has twice won bronze medals at the British Cheese Awards.

CERNEY
REGION: *Gloucestershire*
TYPE: *Modern, farmhouse, unpasteurized, vegetarian, fresh cheese*
SOURCE: *Goat's milk*
DESCRIPTION: *240g/8¹/₂oz pyramid dusted with oak ash and salt*
CULINARY USE: *Table cheese*

Like many of Britain's artisan cheese-makers, Lady Angus, creator of this distinctive cheese, maximizes the flavour by using unpasteurized milk. Her cheeses are named after the pretty village of Cerney where they are made. Each has a mild, zingy, citrus taste, with a delicate, goaty finish. The light, moist texture resembles that of fromage frais. Each of the small, truncated cones is hand-made, and over the years a number of interesting variations has emerged. Apart from the original, which is dusted with a fine layer of ash, there is Cerney Smoked, Cerney Pepper and Cerney Village. Cerney Ginger is particularly good, with freshly chopped, spicy, ginger pieces scattered throughout the soft curd. Cerney ripens in seven to 10 days and has a fat content of 43 per cent.

BELOW: Capricorn Goat

CHEDDAR
REGION: *Somerset*
TYPE: *Traditional, farmhouse, unpasteurized, hard cheese*
SOURCE: *Cow's milk*
DESCRIPTION: *26kg/57lb cylinder with natural rind, bound in cloth*
CULINARY USES: *Table cheese; also widely used for cooking in a host of traditional dishes*

Since the sixteenth century, the hard cow's milk cheese made in the Mendip Hills near the Cheddar Gorge has been known as Cheddar. The cheese undoubtedly goes back to earlier centuries, perhaps even to the Romans, who first introduced the people of England to hard cheeses.

Over the centuries, the recipe for this West Country cheese has been taken by emigrants to Canada, the USA, Australia, South Africa and New Zealand. More than any other British cheese, it has been copied and emulated, but it is not really Cheddar unless it comes from the verdant hills of Somerset, Devon and Dorset.

To taste a hand-made, unpasteurized, clothbound Cheddar, made from the milk of cows whose daily diet is fresh green grass, buttercups and daisies, is to taste a piece of magic. The bite is like chocolate, firm and yielding; the aroma is fresh, nutty and slightly savoury. The flavour differs from farm to farm, but there is always the rich sweetness of the milk, a classic acid tang and a long-lingering kaleidoscope of flavours. Cheddar is generally matured for between nine and 24 months, and has a fat content of 50 per cent (34.4 per cent in the dry matter).

Unlike the great cheeses of Europe, Cheddar's name is not protected, so it has been used and abused. Hundreds of tasteless tonnes are churned out in giant factories around the world. Even in Britain, both the consumers and the market have conspired against the farmhouse Cheddar makers. Today there are only six cheesemakers who still make traditional, clothbound Cheddars:

CHEWTON (Chewton, Somerset): Firm and biteable, the cheese has a flavour that

ABOVE: Traditional clothbound Cheddars from top right, Green's, Keen's, Quicke's and Montgomery's

CHESHIRE

REGION: *Cheshire*
TYPE: *Traditional, farmhouse, unpasteurized, hard cheese*
SOURCE: *Cow's milk*
DESCRIPTION: *900g/2lb, 8kg/18lb or 20kg/44lb tall cylinders with natural rind with grey moulding, tightly wrapped in cloth*
CULINARY USES: *Table cheese, grilling, snacks, grating*

Fewer than a handful of cheesemakers still make the traditional clothbound Cheshire, using raw milk. Most of the cheeses are factory-made today and lack any real depth of character. The fine, moist texture that is the hallmark of a good Cheshire (but which also renders the cheese susceptible to cracking, crumbling or blueing) is rejected by many supermarkets in favour of cheeses that are creamier and more solid. Changes are afoot, however, and smaller producers are now being encouraged to return to a more traditional style.

Clothbound Cheshire is produced by several traditional cheesemakers, including the Applebys, H. S. Bourne and V. J. Hares. The Appleby's have been making Cheshire for generations. The current cheesemaker, Mrs Appleby, now in her 70s, is particularly highly regarded. Her Cheshire has a crumbly, flaky texture and a sea-breeze freshness with the tang of orange zest.

Cheshire requires two to six months to mature.

BELOW: Cheshire

explodes on the palate. The rind is nutty, the interior suggests cheese and onion with a hint of butter. The mature, unpasteurized Chewton has twice won the accolade of Best Cheddar at the British Cheese Awards. Both pasteurized and unpasteurized cheeses are available.

DENHAY (Bridport, Devon): Hand-made and matured on the farm, Denhay is nutty, and rich with a strong, savoury tang. All the milk comes from the farm's own herd.

GREEN'S (Glastonbury, Somerset): Made by three generations on the same farm, Green's is matured for 12 months or more. Each cheese is hand turned until all reach their peak. Twice winner of a gold medal at the British Cheese Awards, the cheese is savoury (redolent of cheese and onion) and tangy.

KEEN'S (Wincanton, Somerset): Made on the farm since the turn of the century, using only milk from its own herd, Keen's

has a full-bodied flavour. It is complex, with hints of liquorice and a fresh, green tang. Nutty, smooth and creamy, it melts in the mouth. A past winner of a silver medal in the British Cheese Awards, it is both clothbound and larded.

MONTGOMERY'S (Yeovil, Somerset): Twice voted Best Cheddar at the British Cheese Awards, this has a superb richness, a spicy acidity and real depth to the fruity finish. Montgomery's makes only eight or nine cheeses a day.

QUICKE'S (Exeter, Devon): The only traditional cheddarmakers in Devon, the Quicke family have been farming at Newton St Cyres for over 450 years. Their Cheddar is a regular medal winner at the British Cheese Awards. Firm and chewy, with a buttery texture and tangy, nutty, complex aroma, the cheese, when tasted, suggests green grass and fresh hay. Pasteurized and unpasteurized versions are available.

COQUETDALE

REGION: *Northumberland*
TYPE: *Traditional, farmhouse,
vegetarian, hard cheese*
SOURCE: *Cow's milk*
DESCRIPTION: *650g/1¹/₂lb or 2.2kg/5lb
round cheese. The fine, leathery,
natural rind has yellowish-
grey mould*
CULINARY USE: *Table cheese*

Mark Robinson's cheesemaking urge came in 1985 after he read a book about sheep and their cheeses. At the time he had over 600 ewes on his farm in Northumberland. Over the following five years he built up the herd, changing over to Friesland sheep, then diversifying into cow's milk as well.

On a trip to France, he visited the makers of Saint-Nectaire and decided to develop a similar cheese at home in Northumberland. Once the cheese was placed in his wonderful old caves, however, and came into contact with the natural flora and moulds that live on the walls and roofs, the original recipe began to change. The result is a soft, supple cheese with a wonderful balance of sweet-savoury flavours and a nutty, slightly salty finish.

Coquetdale ripens in 10–12 weeks and has a fat content of 55 per cent. Mark Robinson's Northumberland Cheese Company also produces Northumberland and Redesdale.

ABOVE: Cornish Yarg

CORNISH PEPPER

REGION: *Cornwall*
TYPE: *Modern, farmhouse, vegetarian,
fresh cheese*
SOURCE: *Cow's milk*
DESCRIPTION: *500g/1¹/₄lb round cheese
coated in cracked peppercorns*
CULINARY USES: *Table cheese; also
spread or grilled on country-style
bread*

Lynher Valley Dairies produces two soft cheeses, Cornish Pepper and Cornish Herb and Garlic. Both are rich, moist cream cheeses. The former is liberally sprinkled with cracked peppercorns; the latter is mixed with herbs and garlic before being rolled in chopped parsley. The cheeses ripen in four to six weeks and have a fat content of 45 per cent. The dairy also produces Cornish Yarg.

*ABOVE: Coquetdale is ripened in old
caves at the dairy in Northumberland*

CORNISH YARG

REGION: *Cornwall*
TYPE: *Modern, farmhouse, vegetarian,
hard cheese*
SOURCE: *Cow's milk (Friesian)*
DESCRIPTION: *900g/2lb and 2.75kg/6lb
circular cheeses. The natural rind is
covered in fresh nettles*
CULINARY USE: *Table cheese*

Cornish Yarg is a hand-made cheese produced from a traditional seventeenth-century recipe discovered and initially made by a couple called Gray. When they were trying to find an authentic Cornish name for it, someone pointed out that Gray spelt backwards had a very Cornish ring to it and so Yarg it became.

Michael Horrell of Lynher Dairies now produces this delicious cheese. The nettle wrapping provides an unusual and attractive contrast to the white interior, and gives a slight flavouring to the cheese. Moist but crumbly, Cornish Yarg is not unlike Caerphilly, and has a lovely freshness. As it matures, a greyish hue covers the nettles, the interior softens and the taste is reminiscent of meadow flowers and creamed spinach. Other cheeses made by Michael Horrell include Cornish Pepper and Cornish Herb and Garlic. Cornish Yarg won a silver medal in the British Cheese Awards of 1995. It matures in 10–15 weeks and has a fat content of 45 per cent.

COTHERSTONE

REGION: *Durham*
TYPE: *Traditional, farmhouse,
unpasteurized, hard cheese*
SOURCE: *Cow's milk*
DESCRIPTION: *900g/2lb or 3.5kg/8lb
round. The cream-coloured, natural
rind has some white or grey moulds*
CULINARY USES: *Table cheese, grilling*

Made by Joan and Alwyn Cross in Teesdale from an old Dales recipe, Cotherstone is a hard, crumbly, open-textured cheese. Yeasty, with a crisp, white wine acidity and a fresh, citrus tang, it is one of the few traditional Dale cheeses still being made in the wild and beautiful Pennines.

Cotherstone matures in two to 10 weeks and has a fat content of 45 per cent.

COVERDALE

REGION: *North Yorkshire*
TYPE: *Traditional, creamery, vegetarian, hard cheese*
SOURCE: *Cow's milk*
DESCRIPTION: *1.5kg/3¼lb clothbound truckle cheese with pale yellow rind*
CULINARY USE: *Table cheese*

A mild, buttery cheese, Coverdale has a sharp, clean taste. The texture is firm and open. In recent years many of the old cheese recipes have been revived and new cheeses created in the same style. Coverdale is one such. It reappeared in 1987 after an absence of 50 years. Originally made in Coverdale, it is now produced in nearby Fountains Dairy. Coverdale matures in four to five weeks.

CURWORTHY

REGION: *Devon*
TYPE: *Traditional, farmhouse, unpasteurized, vegetarian, hard cheese*
SOURCE: *Cow's milk (Friesian)*
DESCRIPTION: *450g/1lb and 1.4kg/3lb truckle cheese with natural, firm, grey rind*
CULINARY USES: *Table cheese, grilling, grating*

In the heart of Devon is Stockbearne Farm. Here Rachel Stevens makes cheeses by hand, using milk from the farm's own Friesian cows. Curworthy, her first cheese, is based on a seventeenth-century recipe. It has a creamy interior with a supple, open texture. The delicate, melted butter taste becomes more rounded with age. Curworthy Cheeses also produce two variations on Curworthy: Meldon (flavoured with Chiltern ale and whole-grain mustard) and Belston. Curworthy is matured for three to four months and has a fat content of 48 per cent. Devon Oke is larger than the Curworthy. Aged for up to six months, it has a richer, more full-bodied flavour.

DENHAY DORSET DRUM

REGION: *Dorset*
TYPE: *Traditional, farmhouse, vegetarian, hard cheese*
SOURCE: *Cow's milk*
DESCRIPTION: *2kg/4½lb clothbound truckle cheese with natural rind*
CULINARY USES: *Table cheese, grilling, grating*

A smaller version of the traditional Denhay Cheddar, Denhay Dorset Drum matures more quickly and has a dense, chewy texture and a delicious, mellow nuttiness. The small size of cylinder, known as a truckle, makes this cheese an excellent gift.

Denhay Dorset Drum is a past silver medal winner at the British Cheese Awards. It matures in six to nine months and has a fat content of 50 per cent.

BELOW: Curworthy is an unpasteurized vegetarian cheese

BELOW: Coverdale – one of the newly revived old cheeses

DERBY

REGION: *Derbyshire*
TYPE: *Traditional, creamery, hard cheese*
SOURCE: *Cow's milk*
DESCRIPTION: *4–13.5kg/9lb–30lb cylinder with natural, pale primrose yellow rind*
CULINARY USES: *Table cheese, grilling*

Originally made on small farms, in 1870 Derby became the first cheese in Britain to be made in a factory, which was tantamount to signing its death warrant. However, the growing interest in Britain's old cheeses may well see a resurgence in its popularity.

Similar in texture to Cheddar, but more open, Derby has a softer, flakier curd and a melted-butter taste . Few, if any, farmhouse examples exist, and those that are sold tend to be too young and lacking in flavour.

Derby ripens in one to six months and has a fat content of 45 per cent More commonly available is Sage Derby, a herb-flavoured version.

DEVON BLUE
REGION: *Devon*
TYPE: *Modern, farmhouse, unpasteurized, vegetarian, blue cheese*
SOURCE: *Cow's milk (Ayrshire)*
DESCRIPTION: *3kg/6¹/₂lb cylinder with rough, crusty, natural rind mottled with grey, white and brown moulds*
CULINARY USE: *Table cheese*

Ticklemore Cheeses make three excellent blues, one each from cow's milk, goat's milk and sheep's milk. Available all year round, Devon Blue is milder than the others and has a subtle flavour of new leather overlaid by the spicy blue tang. Smooth, creamy and deliciously herbaceous, it is aged for four to six months, then wrapped in foil to prevent it from drying out.

DEVON GARLAND
REGION: *Devon*
TYPE: *Modern, farmhouse, unpasteurized, vegetarian, speciality cheese*
SOURCE: *Cow's milk*
DESCRIPTION: *4kg/9lb wheel. The natural rind is firm and smooth, with a grey-brown crust*
CULINARY USES: *Table cheese, grilling, grating*

This old West Country cheese was revived by Hilary Charnely and is now made by the Peverstone Cheese Company Limited at Cullompton, near Exeter. When young, it resembles Caerphilly. The "garland", or layer of fresh herbs, from which it gets its name, is added to the cheese before it is placed in cellars to mature for up to eight weeks. The aroma of the herbs permeates the loosely packed, lemon-fresh curds and the resultant taste is fresh, clean and savoury. Devon Garland matures in six to eight weeks and has a fat content of 45 per cent.

DOUBLE GLOUCESTER
REGION: *Gloucestershire*
TYPE: *Traditional, farmhouse and creamery, unpasteurized, hard cheese*
SOURCE: *Cow's milk*
DESCRIPTION: *3.5–8kg/8–18lb deep round. The hard, natural rind has some grey-blue moulds and bears the marks of the cloth in which it is matured*
CULINARY USES: *Table cheese, grating, grilling, sauces*

Both Double and Single Gloucester have been made in Gloucestershire since the sixteenth century and were originally clothbound, round cheeses made from the milk of the native Old Gloucester cows. Single Gloucester is smaller, made from skimmed milk and meant to be eaten young. The full-cream milk in Double Gloucester gives it its characteristic, rich, buttery taste and flaky texture. It is firm and biteable, like hard chocolate. The colour is a pale tangerine. It has a wonderful, savoury flavour of cheese and onions. Not as firm as Cheddar, it has a mellow, nutty character with a delicious, orange-zest tang.

Few of these cheeses are made by traditional methods today, but those that are are well worth trying. Traditional makers include Appleby, Quicke and Smart.

ABOVE: Devon Blue (back) and Devon Garland (front)

DOUBLE WORCESTER
REGION: *Worcester*
TYPE: *Modern, farmhouse, unpasteurized, hard cheese*
SOURCE: *Cow's milk (Holstein/Friesian)*
DESCRIPTION: *4kg/9lb cylinder. The hard, natural rind is yellow with some moulding*
CULINARY USES: *Table cheese, grilling, sauces*

A smaller version of Double Gloucester, this is made by Anstey's in the neighbouring county of Worcester. It develops a firm, breakable, flaky texture and deep tangerine-orange interior with a rounded, mellow character and a flavour that is reminiscent of citrus zest. Hand milking contributes to its unique flavour.

The farm on which the cheese is made has been in the Anstey family for four generations. Colin and Alyson Anstey decided to diversify into cheesemaking in 1995 and won a silver medal at the British Cheese Awards that same year. Their Double Worcester matures in five to seven months and has a fat content of 45 per cent.

Another cheese created by the Ansteys is Old Worcester, flavoured with Worcestershire sauce. They have a farm shop and mail order service.

ABOVE: Mellow and nutty Double Gloucester

DUDDLESWELL

REGION: *East Sussex*
TYPE: *Modern, farmhouse, unpasteurized, vegetarian, hard cheese*
SOURCE: *Sheep's milk*
DESCRIPTION: *2kg/4¹/₂lb truckle cheese with hard, finely ridged, polished, natural rind*
CULINARY USES: *Table cheese, grating (can be substituted for Pecorino)*

The producers of this cheese, Sussex High Weald Dairy, are based at Putlands Farm in the heart of Ashdown Forest, the hunting ground of the kings of England since 1372. Mark Hardy and his father Guy have been making a range of sheep's products for over 10 years, including yogurt and a fresh cheese called Sussex Slipcote that comes in various flavours.

Duddleswell is a cheerful-looking truckle whose firm, almost flaky texture seems to melt in the mouth, releasing a sweet, caramel flavour with a hint of Brazil nuts and fresh hay. It is a past winner of a silver medal at the British Cheese Awards. The cheese ripens in 10–12 weeks and has a fat content of 45 per cent. Sussex High Weald Dairy also produces halloumi and feta cheeses.

EMLETT

REGION: *Avon*
TYPE: *Modern, farmhouse, unpasteurized, soft-white cheese*
SOURCE: *Sheep's milk*
DESCRIPTION: *150g/5oz disc with fine crusty penicillium rind dotted with reddish-brown ferments*
CULINARY USE: *Table cheese*

Emlett is a firm, smooth and cream cheese produced by Mary Holbrook of Sleight Farm. As it ages, the cheese softens like ice cream. Quite earthy, it has a delicious, yeasty aroma that penetrates the cheese and enhances the sweet acidity and characteristic nuttiness. The cheese requires four to six weeks to mature.

Little Rydings, another of Mary Holbrook's cheeses, is made from the same curd, but because it is bigger, it drains and matures at a different rate to produce a cheese that is distinctly different. Also in the Sleight Farm range are Tyning, Tymsboro and feta.

ABOVE: Exmoor Blue

EXMOOR BLUE

REGION: *Somerset*
TYPE: *Modern, farmhouse, unpasteurized, vegetarian, blue cheeses*
SOURCE: *Cow's, goat's or sheep's milk*
DESCRIPTION: *Various sizes and shapes, all with natural rind*
CULINARY USE: *Table cheeses*

Alan Duffield makes five blue cheeses from cow's, goat's and sheep's milk, each with its own unique character and style. The Jersey milk cheeses – Somerset Blue and Jersey Blue (a soft white) – are made with milk from two local herds. Both these cheeses are a distinctive, Monet yellow colour. The goat's milk comes from the same area, but the sheep's milk is from the Quantocks. Cheesemaking takes place in the original dairy at Willett Farm. All the cheeses are made with raw milk.

FINN

REGION: *Hereford and Worcester*
TYPE: *Modern, farmhouse, unpasteurized, vegetarian, soft-white cheese*
SOURCE: *Cow's milk*
DESCRIPTION: *225g/8oz round with thick, white penicillium rind*
CULINARY USES: *Table cheese, baking*

Produced by Charlie Westhead of Neal's Yard Creamery, this is the only triple cream cheese made in England. It is firm and amazingly rich, with a mild, fresh, creamy acidity and just a hint of mushrooms. Finn ripens in two to four weeks and has a fat content of 75 per cent.

LEFT: Duddleswell (bottom) and Emlett (top)

FLOWER MARIE
REGION: *East Sussex*
TYPE: *Modern, farmhouse, unpasteurized, vegetarian, soft-white cheese*
SOURCE: *Sheep's milk*
DESCRIPTION: *200g/7oz or 1.5kg/3¼lb square cheese. The thin, soft-white rind has a mushroomy-pink tint*
CULINARY USE: *Table cheese*
Produced by Kevin and Alison Blunt at Greenacres Farm, Flower Marie has a gentle fragrance like that of fresh mushrooms and a soft rind that envelops the firm yet moist interior. It melts like ice cream in the mouth to reveal a lemony freshness under the characteristic sweetness of the sheep's milk. It ripens in five to six weeks.

FRIESLA
REGION: *Devon*
TYPE: *Modern, farmhouse, vegetarian, hard cheese*
SOURCE: *Sheep's milk*
DESCRIPTION: *2.5kg/5½lb boulder-shaped cheese. Hard natural rind*
CULINARY USE: *Table cheese*
Friesla is an excellent hard sheep's milk cheese. Sweet and fragrant, the flavour suggests elderflowers with a hint of blackcurrants and a delicious almond finish. Its creamy, melt-in-the-mouth feel appeals to a wide range of palates and it provides the perfect introduction to sheep's milk cheeses. Based on the original Gouda recipe, it takes its name from the Friesland Islands, where both the world's finest milking sheep and this cheese originate. Friesla matures in six to 10 weeks and has a fat content of 45 per cent.

GOLDEN CROSS
REGION: *East Sussex*
TYPE: *Modern, farmhouse, unpasteurized, vegetarian, soft-white cheese*
SOURCE: *Goat's milk*
DESCRIPTION: *225g/8oz log with mould-ripened rind dusted with salted ash*
CULINARY USE: *Table cheese*
Based on the traditional, French, artisan cheese Sainte-Maure, Golden Cross is lightly dusted with ash. At first firm and slightly grainy, the cheese softens with age to a texture more like ice cream. The flavour is a careful blend of sweetness and acidity: vanilla and caramel combine with the bitterness of celery and green grass, and there is a barely detectable goaty finish.

Produced by Kevin and Alison Blunt, Golden Cross ripens in four to six weeks.

ABOVE LEFT: Flower Marie

BELOW: Gospel Green (back) and Golden Cross (front)

GOSPEL GREEN
REGION: *Surrey*
TYPE: *Modern, farmhouse, unpasteurized, vegetarian, hard cheese*
SOURCE: *Cow's milk*
DESCRIPTION: *900g–3.25kg/2–7lb clothbound truckle cheese. The fascinating range of moulds that impregnate the fine, leathery crust are essential to the final flavour*
CULINARY USES: *Table cheese, grilling, grating, sauces*
A small, Cheddar-style cheese, Gospel Green is slightly softer and less dense than classic Cheddar, with a taste reminiscent of meadow flowers and lush grass. The name comes from the hamlet where it is made by James and Cathy Lane. The cheese is left to mature for four to eight weeks. Its flavour and texture reflect unashamedly the seasonal changes; some suggest that in late summer, the cheese absorbs the fruity aroma of apples crushed in the old cider press outside the dairy.

Gospel Green has a fat content of 48 per cent.

HARBOURNE BLUE
REGION: *Devon*
TYPE: *Modern, farmhouse, unpasteurized, vegetarian, blue cheese*
SOURCE: *Goat's milk*
DESCRIPTION: *5kg/11lb round. Crusty, natural rind with some moulding*
CULINARY USE: *Table cheese*

This smooth, yet crumbly blue is one of the great, modern, British cheeses. Like Beenleigh Blue, it is made by Robin Congdon and Sari Cooper of Ticklemore Cheeses and has twice won medals at the British Cheese Awards.

Available all year round, Harbourne Blue is one of only three English, hard, blue, goat's milk cheeses. The aroma suggests tropical fruit, and it finishes with the hot, spicy tang associated with blues. Harbourne Blue needs three to four months to ripen and has a fat content of 48 per cent.

HEREFORD HOP
REGION: *Gloucestershire*
TYPE: *Traditional, farmhouse, vegetarian, speciality cheese*
SOURCE: *Cow's milk*
DESCRIPTION: *2.2kg/5lb round cheese. The flaky, natural rind of toasted hops is yellow to brown*
CULINARY USE: *Table cheese*

Charles Martell, a cheesemaker renowned for his love of tradition and local history, revived this old Hereford cheese in 1988. The recipe came from local archives and is made using Hereford hops and milk from his own herd. Supple and Caerphilly-like, with the unusual rind of lightly toasted hops, the cheese makes an attractive addition to any cheeseboard. The hops are crunchy, with the slightly yeasty taste associated with beer, while the cheese is mellow, sweet and buttery. It requires one to three months to mature and has a fat content of 45 per cent.

Hereford Hop is also produced by Malvern Cheesewrights, although each cheese has its own distinct style.

HERRIOT FARMHOUSE
REGION: *North Yorkshire*
TYPE: *Modern, farmhouse, vegetarian, hard cheese*
SOURCE: *Sheep's milk*
DESCRIPTION: *1.4kg/3lb and 3.25kg/7lb truckle cheese. The rough, dry rind has some moulds and yeasts*
CULINARY USE: *Table cheese*

Judy Bell and her husband Nigel decided to diversify from farming, and in 1988 turned to cheesemaking. They now make a range of sheep's milk cheeses, including Herriot Farmhouse, which is based on a nineteenth-century recipe. It is an unpressed "hard" cheese, firm, moist and crumbly, with a zesty taste and a soft sweetness that hints at misty hills. It is matured for eight to 12 weeks.

LANCASHIRE
REGION: *Lancashire*
TYPE: *Traditional, farmhouse and creamery, hard cheese*
SOURCE: *Cow's milk*
DESCRIPTION: *4–18kg/9–40lb clothbound cylinder. The hard, thin, natural rind is pale gold. It bears the marks of the cloth and has some grey-blue mould*
CULINARY USES: *Table cheese, snacks, grilling, grating (a superb melting cheese)*

Few of these historic cheeses are produced in Lancashire today – and fewer still are made on farms. During the Industrial Revolution, Lancashire cheese was the staple food of the mill workers. The first factory-made Lancashire appeared in 1913, and today most of this cheese comes from creameries that are scattered throughout Britain.

When young, the traditional cheese is described as "Creamy Lancashire". At this stage the texture is moist and crumbly – rather like scrambled egg – with a cheese and chive finish and an excellent balance of fat and acidity. As the cheese matures, the flavour intensifies and the cheese becomes known as "Tasty Lancashire".

One of the finest of these is Kirkham's Tasty Lancashire, which was declared Supreme Champion at the British Cheese Awards in 1995. A superb example of a genuine farmhouse Lancashire, it had been matured for nearly six months by Neal's Yard Dairy.

Mrs Kirkham's and Dew-Lay are the only two Lancashire makers who use a combination of three days' curd to give a unique, slightly mottled texture. As the curds ripen at different times, it acquires a three-dimensional flavour that is sharp and peppery, with a mouth-puckering finish.

Acid or "crumbly" Lancashire, introduced in the 1970s is a faster-ripening cheese that has the bite of true Lancashire, but lacks the depth.

ABOVE: Hereford Hop

LEFT: Mrs Kirkham's Tasty Lancashire

LEAFIELD
REGION: *Oxfordshire*
TYPE: *Modern, farmhouse, vegetarian, hard cheese*
SOURCE: *Sheep's milk*
DESCRIPTION: *2kg/4¹/₂lb wheel. The hard, natural rind is imprinted with a pattern that resembles the tread on a nineteenth-century steam wheel*
CULINARY USE: *Table cheese*

Before the dissolution of the monasteries in the 1530s by King Henry VIII, the monks of Abingdon Abbey owned the farm where Rodney Whitworth now produces his sheep's milk cheese. It was recorded that, at that time, the monks made three "ponders" (tons) of sheep's milk cheese a year.

The history of Abbey Farm obviously captured Rodney Whitworth's imagination and in the late 1980s he faithfully revived the sixteenth-century recipe for Leafield.

It is a hard, dense, chewy cheese, with a delightful medley of flavours. There is a certain fruitiness (rather like fresh pineapple) coupled with a nutty taste with hints of hawthorn and aniseed. The cheese matures in three to four months and has a fat content of 48 per cent.

Abbey Farm also produces Tubney, which is the size and shape of a cricket ball. Smooth and creamy, Tubney has a sweet aroma and a lemon-zest tang that balances the smoky background and the burnt-caramel flavour of the sheep's milk. These small cheeses are mainly made for the Christmas market.

BELOW: Lincolnshire Poacher (top) and Leafield (bottom)

LINCOLNSHIRE POACHER
REGION: *Lincolnshire*
TYPE: *Modern, farmhouse, unpasteurized, hard cheese*
SOURCE: *Cow's milk (Holstein)*
DESCRIPTION: *20kg/44lb cylinder. The brown rind resembles granite in appearance*
CULINARY USES: *Table cheese, grating, grilling*

Lincolnshire is not an area generally known for its dairy farming. This fact did not deter Simon Jones when he decided to turn the abundant spring milk from his herd of Holsteins into cheese. One morning the cheese legend, Dougal Campbell, arrived at Simon's farm with a bottle full of rennet. Together they made the first batch of Lincolnshire Poacher. On the following day, Simon found himself in charge of the cheesemaking. That was in 1992. A few years later, his cheese was declared to be the Supreme Champion at the British Cheese Awards. It had been chosen from a field of 480 entries.

LITTLE RYDINGS
REGION: *Avon*
TYPE: *Modern, farmhouse, unpasteurized, soft-white cheese*
SOURCE: *Sheep's milk*
DESCRIPTION: *250g/9oz round with fine, uneven, whitish penicillium rind covered with red-brown pigmentation*
CULINARY USE: *Table cheese*

This irresistible cheese is made from March to November by Mary Holbrook, one of Britain's leading cheesemakers. The slightly uneven Camembert-like rind encloses a unpasteurized, soft cheese that is deep creamy yellow around the edge. If young, it may be slightly chalky and white in the centre. Like good Camembert, Little Rydings simply melts in the mouth to reveal distinct yet subtle layers of flavour: the sweetness of caramel, a hint of Brazil nuts and a slightly "sheepy" taste that is reminiscent of soggy lambswool sweaters or lanolin. Little Rydings matures in three to five weeks and has a fat content of 48 per cent.

Mary Holbrook also produces Tyning, Emlett and Tymsboro.

ABOVE: Little Rydings

MALVERN

REGION: *Hereford and Worcester*
TYPE: *Modern, farmhouse,*
unpasteurized, vegetarian,
hard cheese
SOURCE: *Sheep's milk (Friesland)*
DESCRIPTION: *2.5kg/5¹/₂lb wheel with*
smooth, polished, yellow rind that is
slightly greasy
CULINARY USES: *Table cheese,*
grating, grilling

Malvern Cheesewrights were the first of
the new generation of English cheesemakers to make a sheep's milk cheese in
sufficient volume to sell in the supermarket. Cheesemaker Nick Hodgetts modified
the recipe for Wensleydale, which was
made with sheep's milk in the seventeenth
century. Malvern is ideal for people aller-
gic to cow's milk. Firm and dry, yet dense
and creamy in the mouth, it has a definite,
sweet, butterscotch taste infused with
a hint of thyme. The finish is salty and
the aroma is of wool or lanolin. Malvern
matures in 16 weeks and has a fat content
of 50 per cent. At the 1997 British Cheese
Awards it won a silver medal.

Malvern Cheesewrights also produce
Hereford Hop, Buffalo and Duchy
Originals Herb and Garlic.

RIGHT: Malvern

MENALLACK FARMHOUSE

REGION: *Cornwall*
TYPE: *Modern, farmhouse,*
unpasteurized, vegetarian,
hard cheese
SOURCE: *Cow's milk*
DESCRIPTION: *2kg/4¹/₂lb truckle cheese*
with hard, greyish-brown, natural,
crusty rind
CULINARY USES: *Table cheese,*
grilling, sauces

Menallack at two months old is mild,
smooth and creamy. At four months, the
texture is firm and biteable, the colour has
deepened to a golden yellow and there is
a wonderful, rich, savoury tang to balance
the acidity. It has a fat content of 45 per
cent. In 1995, Menallack Farmhouse won
a bronze medal at the British Cheese
Awards. Variations include Nanterrow and
Menallack with Chives and Garlic.

LODDISWELL AVONDALE

REGION: *Devon*
TYPE: *Modern, farmhouse,*
unpasteurized, vegetarian,
semi-soft cheese
SOURCE: *Goat's milk*
DESCRIPTION: *1.4kg/3lb round*
with brownish-orange,
washed rind
CULINARY USE: *Table cheese*

Jocelyn and Bill Martin won the British
Cheese Awards' 1994 Cheese
Lover's Trophy with this
impressive cheese.

Firm, almost dry, it has a fragrant,
almondy nose that carries through as it
melts in the mouth, leaving behind an
unusual hint of aniseed and a sweet, sher-
bet-like zing. It matures in two months
and has a fat content of 45 per cent.

Jocelyn and Bill make several goat's
milk cheeses, including Hazelwood and
the soft, fresh Loddiswell Bannon.

NORTHUMBERLAND

REGION: *Northumberland*
TYPE: *Modern, farmhouse, vegetarian,*
hard cheese
SOURCE: *Cow's milk*
DESCRIPTION: *2.2kg/5lb round. The*
firm, natural rind is pale yellow,
dusted with greyish mould
CULINARY USE: *Table cheese*

In 1987 Mark Robertson started making
Northumberland, basing it upon a
European washed curd recipe. It matures
slowly in the old, stone cellars of a farm
where cheesemaking has been going on
since 1296. Northumberland is a moist,
firm cheese with a sweet, fruity nose. The
flavour is robust, with a tart bite that lasts.
It matures in 10 weeks and has a fat
content of 50–55 per cent.

OLDE YORK

REGION: *North Yorkshire*
TYPE: *Modern, farmhouse, vegetarian,*
fresh cheese
SOURCE: *Sheep's milk*
DESCRIPTION: *450g/1lb round with*
waxed rind
CULINARY USES: *Table cheese, grilling,*
in salads and on baked potatoes

Loosely based upon an authentic York
recipe for a cheese originally made by
farmers' wives, Olde York resembles feta
without being salty. It is more moist than
feta – almost wet – coming apart in layers,
rather than crumbling. Creamy, soft and
high in "acid", it has a lemony zest offset
by the subtle sweetness of sheep's milk.
At the 1996 British Cheese Awards, Olde
York won a silver medal. The cheese
matures in 10–22 days and has a fat content of 45 per cent. Cheesemaker Judy
Bell of Shepherd's Purse makes several
medal-winning variations, including Green
Peppercorns, Garlic and Parsley, and Mint.

ORANGE GROVE
REGION: *Leicestershire*
TYPE: *Modern, creamery, vegetarian,
speciality cheese*
SOURCE: *Cow's milk*
DESCRIPTION: *2kg/4¹/₂lb round cheese.
It looks rather like a cheesecake,
with the surface decorated with
rings of candied orange*
CULINARY USE: *Table cheese/dessert*

Created in 1964 by Millway Foods, best
known for their Stilton, this is the answer
for those who are uncertain as to whether
to end a meal with dessert or cheese.
Decorated with candied orange rings,
Orange Grove has a layer of finely
chopped orange peel through the middle
of the slightly tart, creamy cheese. The
cheese matures in two to six weeks and
has a fat content of 50 per cent.

Orange Grove is a past winner of a
British Cheese Awards bronze medal. The
producer, Millway Foods, also makes
Pineapple Grove.

BELOW: Orange Grove

*BELOW: Perroche can be
plain (centre), or
flavoured with
dill (left) or
rosemary
(right)*

OXFORD BLUE
REGION: *Oxfordshire*
TYPE: *Modern, creamery, vegetarian,
blue cheese*
SOURCE: *Cow's milk*
DESCRIPTION: *2.5kg/5¹/₂lb round,
wrapped in silver foil. The moist rind
is cream-coloured and has some grey-
blue moulds*
CULINARY USE: *Table cheese*

Baron Robert Pouget is well known to visitors to Oxford's famous covered market,
where he has a wonderful, old-fashioned
cheese shop. Always searching for something new, he decided to create his own
cheese in the style of the French blues, as
a distinct alternative to Stilton. After
months of experimentation in conjunction
with a well-known blue cheesemaker,
Oxford Blue was born in 1993. Three
years later it won a silver medal at the
British Cheese Awards.

When ripe, the cheese is a luscious,
creamy blue with a distinct but not strong,
blue flavour. Aromatic and spicy, it has a
hint of dark chocolate and white wine,
with tarragon on the finish. It matures
in 14–16 weeks and has a fat content of
30 per cent.

PERROCHE
REGION: *Hereford and Worcester*
TYPE: *Modern, farmhouse,
unpasteurized, vegetarian,
fresh cheese*
SOURCE: *Goat's cheese*
DESCRIPTION: *150g/5oz round or
450–900g/1–2lb log*
CULINARY USES: *Table cheese,
toasting, grilling*

Perroche, produced by Charlie Westhead
of Neal's Yard Creamery, has a subtle,
goaty taste that is clean and slightly
almondy. The high moisture gives it a
light, almost fluffy feel, but a short shelf
life. It ripens in less than two weeks and
has a fat content of 45 per cent. It is also
made with herbs, such as tarragon, dill,
rosemary and thyme.

ABOVE: Ribblesdale Goat

ABOVE: Red Leicester

RED LEICESTER

REGION: *Leicestershire*
TYPE: *Traditional, farmhouse and creamery, hard cheese*
SOURCE: *Cow's milk*
DESCRIPTION: *4–18kg/9–40lb wheel. The bright orange-red rind has fine, powdery moulds*
CULINARY USES: *Table cheese, grilling, grating*

Leicester was produced in volume by the late eighteenth century. The cheese owed its bright orange-red colour to the natural dye, annatto. During the Second World War, however, all cheese producers had to make National Cheese, a moist, Cheddar-like variety, and the practice of adding annatto to Leicester was banned. When the colour was eventually returned to the pale, wartime version of Leicester cheese, it became known as Red Leicester to distinguish it from the tasteless imposter.

Traditional makers of Red Leicester include Quicke and Overton Hall. A good Red Leicester has a firm body and a close, flaky texture. The flavour is delicately sweet and improves with keeping. There is a mere suggestion of green-grass bitterness behind the more distinct butterscotch and nut flavours.

Red Leicester can be eaten young, but it should ideally be left to mature for six to nine months. It has a fat content of 48 per cent.

RIBBLESDALE GOAT

REGION: *North Yorkshire*
TYPE: *Modern, farmhouse, unpasteurized, vegetarian, hard cheese*
SOURCE: *Goat's milk*
DESCRIPTION: *2kg/4¹/₂lb wheel with smooth rind covered with white wax*
CULINARY USES: *Table cheese, grating, grilling*

Created in 1982 by Iain and Christine Hill, this cheese is sought after for its fresh, delicate flavour. The texture is rather like a young Gouda, and the taste suggests chicory and almonds, with a trace of misty hills and wild herbs. The sharp whiteness of the cheese is further enhanced by the distinctive, white, wax coating. Ribblesdale Goat won a bronze medal at the 1996 British Cheese Awards. It matures in six to eight weeks and has a fat content of 45 per cent. Ribblesdale is also made with cow's milk.

BELOW: Rosary Round (front right), Rosary Herb Log (back) and Rosary Dazel (front left)

ROSARY PLAIN

REGION: *Wiltshire*
TYPE: *Modern, farmhouse, vegetarian, fresh cheese*
SOURCE: *Goat's milk (Saanen)*
DESCRIPTION: *275g/10oz round or 1kg/2¹/₄lb log – stark white and decorated with a sprig of fresh herbs*
CULINARY USES: *Table cheese, melting, spreading*

Made by Claire Moody, Rosary Plain won a bronze medal at the 1996 British Cheese Awards. Delicate, moist, soft and creamy, the cheese is subtly flavoured by the sprig of fresh herbs that is used as a decoration. Rosary Plain matures in one to two weeks and has a fat content of 45 per cent. Flavoured versions, including Rosary Herb Log and Rosary Dazel, are also available.

ABOVE: Shropshire Blue

SHROPSHIRE BLUE

REGION: *Nottinghamshire*
TYPE: *Traditional, creamery, vegetarian, blue cheese*
SOURCE: *Cow's milk*
DESCRIPTION: *8kg/18lb cylinder. The deep orange-brown, natural rind has a cocktail of colourful moulds and yeasts*
CULINARY USE: *Table cheese*

Despite its name, this cheese was invented in Scotland earlier this century, and was then introduced to the Stilton makers. It is similar in style to Stilton, but is distinguished by the wonderful, orange colour, created by adding a few drops of annatto, a natural dye, to the vat. The royal blue of the mould provides a distinct colour contrast. The cheese maintains its wonderful blue taste, while the annatto seems to create an underlying hint of rich, buttery, burnt caramel. Shropshire Blue matures for 10 weeks and has a fat content of 34 per cent.

NOTE: When a blue cheese appears to be lopsided or is wider at the bottom than at the top, it has "soggy bottom". This indicates that it has not been turned often enough during the maturation process. The moisture has dropped to the bottom, leaving the top of the cheese to dry out. Avoid any cheese like this.

SAGE DERBY

REGION: *North Yorkshire*
TYPE: *Traditional, creamery, vegetarian, speciality cheese*
SOURCE: *Cow's milk*
DESCRIPTION: *4–13.5kg/9–30lb cylinder flecked with tiny flakes of sage*
CULINARY USES: *Table cheese, grilling*

In the seventeenth century, the custom of adding sage (a herb valued at the time for its health-giving properties) to Derby cheese was begun. As the cheese aged, the savour of the herbs was gradually incorporated. Today, however, most Sage Derby unfortunately consists of reconstituted cheese blended with spinach juice or green vegetable dye and colourless dried sage. The effect is to give the cheese a green-and-white-marbled appearance.

Sage Derby ripens in one to three months and has a fat content of 45 per cent.

SHARPHAM

REGION: *Devon*
TYPE: *Modern, farmhouse, unpasteurized, vegetarian, soft-white cheese*
SOURCE: *Cow's milk (Jersey)*
DESCRIPTION: *250g/9oz; 500g/1¼lb or 1kg/2¼lb round or square cheese with smooth, soft, velvety-white rind*
CULINARY USE: *Table cheese*

The Sharpham estate's permanent pastures undoubtedly give its Jersey milk a unique flavour. This Brie-type cheese is hand-ladled into moulds to retain the soft feel of the smooth Jersey milk, which is so thick that it feels more like clotted cream. It has just a hint of acidity and a whiff of mushrooms. The cheese is made from March to December, ripens in six to eight weeks and has a fat content of 45 per cent.

BELOW: Sage Derby – this version has a central layer of sage-speckled cheese

SINGLE GLOUCESTER
REGION: *Gloucestershire*
TYPE: *Traditional, farmhouse and creamery, unpasteurized, hard cheese*
SOURCE: *Cow's milk*
DESCRIPTION: *3.25kg–5.5kg/7–12lb millstone shapes or 1.4kg/3lb truckles. The hard, smooth, natural rind bears the marks of the cloth*
CULINARY USES: *Table cheese, grilling*
Traditionally made from skimmed milk from the evening milking, which was then mixed with the morning's whole milk, Single Gloucester is lighter, more crumbly and lower in fat than Double Gloucester. Only two traditional cheesemakers produce this firm, biteable cheese. The buttery flavour has hints of vanilla and ice cream. Mild, but with character, it has some sweetness on the finish to balance the slight acidity. Charles Martell's Single Gloucester is made from milk from a rare breed of cow – Old Gloucester. Smart's version is chewy, with the richness of cream toffee and just a hint of liquorice. Since 1997, Single Gloucester can only be made in Gloucester.

ABOVE: Spenwood

RIGHT: Somerset Brie

SOMERSET BRIE
REGION: *Somerset*
TYPE: *Modern, creamery, vegetarian, soft-white cheese*
SOURCE: *Cow's milk*
DESCRIPTION: *2.5kg/5¹/₂lb cylinder with soft, velvety, smooth, white rind*
CULINARY USE: *Table cheese*
Probably the best-selling British soft cheese, Somerset Brie has a delicious "set custard" texture. The aroma and taste suggest mushrooms with a hint of green grass, with some acidity to give the cheese depth. It does not pretend to be like a French Brie, which is richer and more robust, due to the differences in climate, soil, breed of cattle and production methods. Somerset Brie matures in six weeks, with a fat content of 50 per cent. It is made by Lubborn Cheese Ltd, which also produces Somerset Brie and Capricorn Goat.

SPENWOOD
REGION: *Berkshire*
TYPE: *Modern, farmhouse, unpasteurized, vegetarian, hard cheese*
SOURCE: *Sheep's milk*
DESCRIPTION: *2kg/4¹/₂lb round cheese. The natural rind is firm and crusty. The colour is yellowish-grey*
CULINARY USES: *Table cheese, grating, grilling*
Made by Anne Wigmore of Village Maid Cheese, Spenwood was not only awarded a gold medal at the 1996 British Cheese Awards, but also took the Cheese Lover's Trophy. Hard and seemingly dry, the cheese is creamy in the mouth, melting to release its distinct sweet, caramel flavour, which is superbly balanced with acidity. With age, the flavour of ground nuts becomes more pronounced. Spenwood ripens in six months and has a fat content of 50 per cent.

ABOVE: Staffordshire Organic

STAFFORDSHIRE ORGANIC

REGION: *Staffordshire*
TYPE: *Modern, farmhouse,
unpasteurized, vegetarian, organic,
speciality cheese*
SOURCE: *Cow's milk*
DESCRIPTION: *3.5–18kg/8–40lb cylinder
with firm, Cheddar-like rind*
CULINARY USES: *Table cheese, grilling,
grating*

Smooth and creamy, yet firm, this is one of the few hard, pressed, organic cheeses in the UK. Herb and Chive varieties are available, but the most interesting addition is wild garlic. Whereas some farmers scour their fields to remove any trace of wild garlic, Michael Deaville harvests his, then minces and freezes it so that it retains its zingy freshness when added to the cheese. Staffordshire Organic matures in six to eight weeks and has a fat content of 48 per cent.

RIGHT: The perfect Stilton will have blue mould spreading out to the rind

STILTON

REGION: *Nottinghamshire,
Derbyshire, Leicestershire*
TYPE: *Traditional,
creamery, vegetarian,
blue cheese*
SOURCE: *Cow's milk*
DESCRIPTION: *2.5kg/5¹/₂lb or
8kg/18lb drum. The rough,
crusty rind formed by a
multitude of moulds gives
the cheese the appearance
of a rock covered in lichen*
CULINARY USES: *Table cheese,
snacks, soups*

Who first made Stilton has been debated for centuries, but it remains one of Britain's best-loved cheeses, thanks to the foresight of the Stilton makers. In the early 1900s they formed themselves into an association to control how the cheese should be made. As with the AOC system in France, they also specified where Stilton could be made – only in the three counties of Nottinghamshire, Derbyshire and Leicestershire.

The rind of good Stilton exudes wonderful aromas of cellars, stone walls

and moulds. It is punctuated with tiny holes where it has been pierced by stainless-steel needles to allow air to penetrate the interior. The perfect Stilton should have the blue mould spreading out to the rind so that it looks like shattered porcelain, while the taste should suggest old leather, dark chocolate and an intense spicy "blue" quality, with a hint of white wine and herbs. It should be rich and creamy, not dry and crumbly, with a clean, lasting, tangy finish.

The mistake some producers and retailers make is to sell Stilton too young, when it can be bitter and dry. It matures in nine to 15 weeks, with a fat content of 55 per cent.

Over the years, some unusual rules of etiquette have developed around Stilton – especially the habit of "digging" pieces out with a spoon. This tradition arose when a whole Stilton used to be served at banquets, or in a pub, where it would be consumed quickly. If you are given a whole or even a half Stilton, don't dig into it unless you are planning to eat all of it within a week, or it will dry out. Instead, work your way down gradually, keeping the surface as flat as possible.

Stilton producers include Colston Bassett Dairy, Millway, Long Clawson, Websters, Cropwell Bishop, Mendip Dairy Crest and Tuxford & Tebbutt.

STINKING BISHOP

REGION: *Gloucestershire*
TYPE: *Modern, farmhouse, vegetarian, washed-rind cheese*
SOURCE: *Cow's milk*
DESCRIPTION: *1.8kg/4lb round with glistening, orange-yellow, slightly sticky rind washed in brine*
CULINARY USE: *Table cheese*

This wonderfully eccentric cheese was created by Charles Martell. It looks a little like Munster and is washed and rubbed with perry, an alcoholic drink made with a local variety of pear called "Stinking Bishop". Wonderfully aromatic, pungent, almost meaty and probably over-the-top for most people.

At the British Cheese Awards in 1994 and 1996 it was awarded gold and bronze medals respectively and at a recent tasting in France, this velvety-smooth, almost spoonable cheese was greeted with amazement. It seems the French still labour under the misconception that the only cheeses made in England are Cheddar and Stilton – a view unfortunately shared by many of the British.

Stinking Bishop requires six to eight weeks to mature and has a fat content of 48 per cent.

SUSSEX SLIPCOTE

REGION: *Sussex*
TYPE: *Modern, farmhouse, unpasteurized, vegetarian, fresh cheese*
SOURCE: *Sheep's milk*
DESCRIPTION: *115g/4oz round or 900g/2lb log. The pure white cheese may form a fine clear "skin"*
CULINARY USES: *Table cheese, baking, spreading*

The recipe is said to date back to the time of Shakespeare, when the young curd would mature too fast and slip out of its cheesecloth coat – hence the name. Today the curd is carefully ladled into moulds so that sufficient whey is retained to give the finished cheese its light, mousse-like texture and refreshing, citrus acidity. Light and creamy, with a suggestion of sweetness from the sheep's milk, Sussex Slipcote is available in three varieties: plain, garlic and herb, and cracked peppercorn. The cheese takes 10 days to mature and has a fat content of 45 per cent.

SWALEDALE

REGION: *North Yorkshire*
TYPE: *Modern, farmhouse, vegetarian, hard cheese*
SOURCE: *Cow's or sheep's milk*
DESCRIPTION: *2.5kg/5¹/₂lb round. The hard, natural rind has a blue-grey mould*
CULINARY USE: *Table cheese*

Swaledale is a classic Yorkshire cheese, made by David Reed in the valley of the Swale River. It is soaked in brine before being left to mature in humid cellars, where the rind acquires the attractive mould that prevents the interior from drying out. Softer than Wensleydale and a little more moist, it has the freshness of the misty Yorkshire Dales and wild bracken, along with the typical acidity associated with Dale cheeses.

A frequent medal winner at the British Cheese Awards, Swaledale matures in one month and has a fat content of 48 per cent. Variations of the cow's milk version include cheeses flavoured with fresh chives, garlic and apple mint, and another that is soaked in Old Peculiar ale.

TOP RIGHT:
Stinking Bishop

ABOVE: Swaledale Cow

TALA

REGION: *Cornwall*
TYPE: *Modern, farmhouse, unpasteurized, vegetarian, hard cheese*
SOURCE: *Sheep's milk (Dorset and Friesland cross)*
DESCRIPTION: *400g/14oz and 1.8kg/4lb drum. The smooth, hard, brushed rind is yellowish-grey and sometimes has beautiful pinkish moulds*
CULINARY USE: *Table cheese*

Hans and Heather White took up cheese-making in 1989 after Hans retired from teaching. Their delightful, small, drum cheese is a past bronze medal winner at the British Cheese Awards. Although firm, the cheese melts in the mouth. Creamy and full-bodied, it has the sweet, aromatic, burnt-caramel taste and suggestion of lanolin and aromatic rosemary that is so typical of sheep's milk. Gentle smoking seems to underscore the sweet caramel nature of the cheese, and the smoked version of Tala is a gold medal winner.

Tala matures in five months and has a fat content of 48 per cent.

ABOVE RIGHT: Tyning – a former "Best English Cheese"

RIGHT: At the 1997 British Cheese Awards, Tymsboro was voted Best Soft-white Cheese

TORVILLE

REGION: *Somerset*
TYPE: *Modern, farmhouse, unpasteurized, washed-rind cheese*
SOURCE: *Cow's milk*
DESCRIPTION: *3.25kg/7lb round with fine pink to orange, natural rind with speckles of chopped herbs*
CULINARY USE: *Table cheese*

Making traditional, farmhouse Caerphilly has been an integral part of the lives of the Duckett family for decades. The sweet, musty aroma of ripening cheese seems to envelop you as you step into their large, farmhouse kitchen. Ten years ago, Chris Duckett decided to turn his hand to something a little different and began washing some of the fresh Caerphilly in the local scrumpy cider and herbs. As the bacteria in the alcohol attack the young curd, the outer edge rapidly softens and absorbs some of the tart apple flavour – an excellent foil for the slightly salty, sweet Caerphilly. Torville can be difficult to find, but the search is well worth the trouble.

Torville ripens in 15–30 days and has a fat content of 45 per cent.

TYMSBORO

REGION: *Avon*
TYPE: *Modern, farmhouse, unpasteurized, vegetarian, soft-white cheese*
SOURCE: *Goat's milk*
DESCRIPTION: *250g/9oz flat-topped pyramid. The natural rind, dusted with black ash, is covered with a fine, white mould*
CULINARY USE: *Table cheese*

When Mary Holbrook's elegant-looking cheese is cut, a fine layer of black ash is revealed between the centre and the crust. The taste is of lemon sorbet, elder-flowers and apples; the finish suggests crisp, fresh fruit with a gentle, spicy tang. Tymsboro ripens in two to four weeks.

TYNING

REGION: *Avon*
TYPE: *Modern, farmhouse, unpasteurized, hard cheese*
SOURCE: *Sheep's milk*
DESCRIPTION: *2.25–3.25kg/5–7lb cheese shaped like a flying saucer and with a natural rind in various shades of brown and grey*
CULINARY USES: *Table cheese, grating*

Tyning is hard, almost brittle and slightly oily. Intensely fruity and spicy, and full of contrasting flavours, it seems to get better every year. Even when young, it has a burnt-caramel sweetness with a fresh, pineapple tang. Made by Mary Holbrook of Sleight Farm, Tyning was judged Best English Cheese and Best Modern British Cheese at the British Cheese Awards in 1995. It matures in three to 12 months and has a fat content of 45 per cent.

VULSCOMBE

REGION: *Devon*

TYPE: *Modern, farmhouse, unpasteurized, vegetarian, fresh cheese*

SOURCE: *Goat's milk*

DESCRIPTION: *170g/6oz round, decorated with a bay leaf or crushed peppercorns*

CULINARY USE: *Table cheese*

Twice winner of a bronze medal at the British Cheese Awards, Vulscombe is produced by Joyce and Graham Townsend. The cheese is unusual in that rennet is not used to separate the milk; coagulation occurs purely through the acidity of the curd. Vulscombe is small, round and elegantly packaged, its stark white appearance offset by a bay leaf or crushed peppercorns. Moist but creamy, it has a fresh, lemon-sorbet taste and just the merest hint of goat's milk. It matures in one to three weeks and has a fat content of 45 per cent. Vulscombe is available plain, with fresh herbs and garlic, or with crushed peppercorns and garlic.

WATERLOO

REGION: *Berkshire*

TYPE: *Modern, farmhouse, unpasteurized, vegetarian, semi-soft cheese*

SOURCE: *Cow's milk (Guernsey)*

DESCRIPTION: *900g/2lb round. The thick natural, pinkish rind is dusted with white moulds. With age it becomes grey, crusty and wrinkled*

CULINARY USE: *Table cheese*

Made by Anne and Andy Wigmore, Waterloo is a washed curd cheese: sweet, supple and smooth, it is full-bodied in flavour and a rich yellow colour. It starts life mellow and fruity, but time and nature break down the proteins and fat. As the interior reaches the point where it starts to run, the cheese acquires a vegetal taste like young celery leaves and dandelions. These somewhat peppery tastes are balanced by the richness of the milk.

Waterloo matures in four to 10 weeks and has a fat content of 45 per cent. It is a past silver medal winner at the British Cheese Awards.

ABOVE: Vulscombe, with fresh herbs and garlic (left), with crushed peppercorns and garlic (right), and plain (centre)

WELLINGTON

REGION: *Berkshire*

TYPE: *Modern, farmhouse, unpasteurized, vegetarian, hard cheese*

SOURCE: *Cow's milk (Guernsey)*

DESCRIPTION: *2kg/4½lb round. The natural, crusty rind has moulds in various shades of grey and brown*

CULINARY USES: *Table cheese, grating*

Wellington is a superb, modern, British cheese. Made in a similar way to a Cheddar, but much smaller, it owes its Monet-yellow colour to Guernsey milk. Initially smooth and creamy, the cheese progesses to a more intense, sharp, Cheddar bite and has a finish reminiscent of parsley, celery and chives. Wellington matures in six to 10 weeks and has a fat content of 45 per cent.

WHITE STILTON
REGION: *Leicestershire*
TYPE: *Traditional, creamery, vegetarian, hard cheese*
SOURCE: *Cow's milk*
DESCRIPTION: *8kg/18lb drum with pale primrose-yellow, natural rind*
CULINARY USES: *Table cheese, salads*

White Stilton is a younger version of the King of the Blues, Stilton, without the blue. It is mild and crumbly with a lemon-fresh acidity and none of the punch of its more mature, blue cousin. Pleasant but rather unexciting, it is made by most of the Stilton makers. It matures in six to eight weeks and has a fat content of 45 per cent.

WIGMORE
REGION: *Berkshire*
TYPE: *Modern, farmhouse, unpasteurized, vegetarian, semi-soft cheese*
SOURCE: *Sheep's milk*
DESCRIPTION: *500g/1¼lb or 2kg/4½lb round. The thick natural rind ranges from pink to grey-brown and is uneven and wrinkled*
CULINARY USE: *Table cheese*

This is produced by Anne Wigmore of Village Maid Cheese. The curd is washed to remove excess whey, then packed in moulds to drain. This creates a low-acid cheese, which retains the sweetness of the milk and develops a voluptuous consistency. The rind is washed and has a yeasty aroma that penetrates the supple interior of the cheese. The result is a taste sensation, combining floral flavours with burnt caramel, macadamia nuts and roast lamb. Wigmore, consistently wins gold medals at the British Cheese Awards.

WENSLEYDALE
REGION: *Yorkshire*
TYPE: *Traditional, farmhouse, hard cheese*
SOURCE: *Cow's milk*
DESCRIPTION: *4.5kg/10lb or 21kg/46lb clothbound cylinder with natural rind*
CULINARY USES: *Table cheese; also traditionally eaten with apple pie*

The most famous of all the Yorkshire Dales cheeses, Wensleydale is now made by several small creameries and cheesemakers, including some who have revived the tradition of using sheep's milk. Based on a recipe that can be traced back to the Cistercian monks who came over with William the Conqueror in the 11th century, it is wrapped in cheesecloth and matured in cellars.

The best-known example of this cheese is made by the Wensleydale Creamery in

ABOVE: Wensleydale (top), Wellington (left) and Baby Waterloo (right)

Hawes, where it has been produced for almost a century. Production almost ended in the mid-1990s when the owners decided to close down the creamery. They reckoned without the determination of the local community, workers and management, who fought the closure and have revitalized the company.

Good Wensleydale has a supple, crumbly, moist texture and resembles a young Caerphilly. The flavour suggests wild honey balanced with a fresh acidity. It matures in two to four months and has a fat content of 45 per cent.

RIGHT: White Stilton

THE BRITISH CHEESE AWARDS

The British Cheese Awards, sponsored by Tesco, is an annual event which rewards excellence within the British cheese industry. Created by the author, the awards are endorsed by the media, respected specialists and the dairy industry and aim to stimulate awareness of the diversity and quality of cheeses being produced in Britain.

Each year, British cheesemakers are invited to submit their cheeses to a carefully chosen panel of judges including food writers and experts from the cheese, hospitality, retail and food industries. In 1997, over 500 cheeses (including 64 goat's milk cheeses and 46 sheep's milk cheeses) were entered for the awards.

Each cheese is judged alongside others produced in the same way. There are no guaranteed prizes, only those cheeses that attain a level of excellence are awarded gold, silver or bronze medals. The award for Best of Category is chosen from the gold medal winners in each category, and a Supreme Champion is chosen from the 12 category winners.

A national compaign, The British Cheese Festival, runs for two weeks after the award announcements, not only to promote the winners, but also to increase awareness of all British cheese and its regional diversity.

Winners of the awards include: Peroche – Best Fresh Cheese; Tymsboro and St Killian – Best Soft-white Cheese; Croghan and Wigmore – Best Semi-soft Cheese; Montgomery's Cheddar and Chewton's Cheddar – Best Traditional British Cheese; Milway Shropshire Blue and Cropwell British Blue – Best Blue Cheese; and Hereford Hop – Best Speciality Cheese. Milleens, Mrs Kirkham's Lancashire and Lincolnshire Poacher have been Supreme Champion.

YORKSHIRE BLUE

REGION: *North Yorkshire*
TYPE: *Traditional, farmhouse, vegetarian, blue cheese*
SOURCE: *Sheep's milk*
DESCRIPTION: *3.5kg/8lb cylinder with moist, yellow-white, crusty, natural rind*
CULINARY USE: *Table cheese*

Judy Bell of Shepherd's Purse developed this excellent cheese using traditional methods dating back to the early Yorkshire cheeses of the eleventh century. It was introduced in 1995 and won a British Cheese Awards gold medal in 1997. A creamy, sweet, moist blue, it is mellow but not mild. When young, it is typical of a young Wensleydale – crumbly and flaky with a subtle "blue" flavour – but maturity brings softness and a more pronounced taste. It matures in eight to 10 weeks and has a fat content of 48 per cent.

BELOW: *Wigmore is one of only a handful of washed-rind cheeses made in Britain*

IRISH CHEESES

There is a certain magic in the hand-made cheeses of Ireland that is indefinable yet almost tangible. Perhaps it is the touch of the leprechaun or the passion of the Irish for life that comes through the soil. For despite all the past and present problems that are a part of Irish life, the land is still rich and green and fertile.

Since ancient times, the people of this natural dairy land have valued butter and milk, but, curiously, there is no early record of cheesemaking. Even the monks who were responsible for so many of the great European cheeses never inspired in the Irish a love of cheese nor much desire to make it. Most of what is produced today is rather unexciting block Cheddar, mainly made in large factories in Northern Ireland and exported.

The situation is changing, however. A new generation of cheesemakers has arisen, rediscovering old recipes and creating new ones.

There must be something in the West Cork air that has led four of Ireland's best-loved cheese-makers to produce the Trappist-style washed-rind cheese. Perhaps it is the rugged coastline battered by the Atlantic or the gentle mist and rain that have inspired Milleens, Gubbeen, Ardrahan and Durrus. Certainly the presence of Cashel Rock must have influenced the Grubbs to make their robust and spicy Cashel Blue.

The cheese revolution has barely crossed the border into Northern Ireland, where production remains highly industrialized. However, Blue Rathgore, a goat's milk cheese produced by Woodford Dairies in South Belfast is hope-fully the first of many modern specialist cheeses.

ARDRAHAN
REGION: *West Cork*
TYPE: *Modern, farmhouse, vegetarian, washed-rind cheese*
SOURCE: *Cow's milk*
DESCRIPTION: *400g/14oz and 1.5kg/3¹/₄lb wheel. The ridged, brine-washed rind is encrusted with brown, ochre, grey and yellow moulds*
CULINARY USE: *Table cheese*

A silver medal winner at the 1995 British Cheese Awards, Ardrahan is made by Eugene and Mary Burns. It has a distinctive, earthy aroma. Beneath the brine-washed rind, the deep yellow interior is firm and slightly chalky. It exudes a wonderful complexity of flavours, the zesty acidity underscoring the buttery, savoury, meaty character. The finish is reminiscent of a young Gruyère. Ardrahan matures in four to eight weeks.

ABOVE: Coolea

CASHEL BLUE
REGION: *Tipperary*
TYPE: *Modern, farmhouse, blue cheese*
SOURCE: *Cow's milk*
DESCRIPTION: *1.5kg/3¹/₄lb cylinder. The wet, crusty rind has rampant, grey moulds*
CULINARY USES: *Table cheese; also excellent spread thickly on warm walnut bread*

Jane and Louis Grubb are descendants of buttermakers and millers expelled from England in the seventeenth century. Ten years ago they started making the only Irish blue cheese, under the shadow of the Rock of Cashel, a bold outcrop overlooking the Tipperary plains. The milk comes from their own pedigree herd.

When young, Cashel Blue is firm yet moist, with just a hint of fresh tarragon and white wine. With age, its true character emerges, mellowing to a rounder, more spicy style. The interior softens, then – when the cheese is at the peak of perfection – it gives up the battle of the bulge and collapses, providing a challenge for the retailer but a treat for the connoisseur.

Cashel Blue is available pasteurized, unpasteurized, vegetarian and non-vegetarian. It matures in eight to 14 weeks and has a fat content of 45 per cent.

LEFT: Cashel Blue (left) and Ardrahan (right)

COOLEA
REGION: *West Cork*
TYPE: *Modern, farmhouse, unpasteurized, hard cheese*
SOURCE: *Cow's milk*
DESCRIPTION: *900g/2lb, 5.5kg/12lb and 9kg/20lb cheeses shaped like millstones, with smooth, shiny, orange, natural rind*
CULINARY USES: *Table cheese, snacks, sauces*

Coolea is made by the Willems family, immigrants from Holland. Their Gouda-style cheese is widely considered to be as good as any made on Dutch farms, while having its own unique character. The rich grazing of this isolated part of Cork produces a rich, nutty cheese with a fruity tang on the finish.

Coolea matures in six to 12 months. Occasionally, the family makes a larger cheese that can be matured for up to two years, when its fruity character intensifies, the colour deepens and the small holes gather drops of moisture. The fat content is 45 per cent.

COOLEENEY
REGION: *Tipperary*
TYPE: *Modern, farmhouse, unpasteurized, soft-white cheese*
SOURCE: *Cow's milk*
DESCRIPTION: *200g/7oz or 1.5kg/3¼lb round with soft-white rind*
CULINARY USE: *Table cheese*

Breda Maher makes this Camembert-style cheese by hand. Full-flavoured and grassy, with a distinct aroma of mushrooms when ripe, Cooleeney's rich, semi-liquid interior benefits from the lush pastures for which Tipperary is famous. The cheese ripens in four to eight weeks and has a fat content of 45 per cent.

BELOW: Doolin

ABOVE: *Cooleeney (bottom) and, Croghan (top)*

CROGHAN
REGION: *Wexford*
TYPE: *Modern, farmhouse, unpasteurized, organic, vegetarian, semi-soft cheese*
SOURCE: *Goat's milk*
DESCRIPTION: *1.2kg/2½lb round, shaped like a flying saucer. The smooth, brine-washed, leathery rind is brown-pink to terracotta in colour and has some mould*
CULINARY USE: *Table cheese*

Luc and Anne Van Kampen who make this cheese live in an idyllic part of the world with their small herd of goats. Croghan is loosely based on Gouda. The intensity of flavour is the result of inspired cheesemaking coupled with superb coastal grazing. The flavour suggests grass and hay, while the finish is aromatic without being pungent. Croghan matures in four to 12 weeks. Made only from spring to autumn, it can be difficult to find, but is worth searching for.

DOOLIN
REGION: *Waterford*
TYPE: *Modern, co-operative, vegetarian, hard cheese*
SOURCE: *Cow's milk*
DESCRIPTION: *11kg/24lb wheel with smooth, hard, golden-yellow, waxed rind*
CULINARY USES: *Table cheese, grating, grilling, sauces*

The vintage version of this Gouda-style cheese made a spectacular debut on to the market when it won both the Cheese Lover's Trophy and the Best Irish Cheese at the 1995 British Cheese Awards. Although Doolin is made in a creamery, it is turned by hand and matured slowly to bring out the best from the wonderful, local milk. There are three versions of the cheese. Young Doolin, which is sold after only two months, is pleasant enough, but dull; Mature Doolin has a more distinctive, fruity character; and Vintage Doolin has a deep golden paste, fine grainy texture and layers of flavour – rich, wonderfully buttery and fruity. The tangy finish is long and lingering. Doolin has a fat content of 45 per cent.

GUBBEEN

REGION: *Cork*
TYPE: *Modern, farmhouse, vegetarian, semi-soft cheese*
SOURCE: *Cow's milk (Friesian, Kerry and Brown Swiss)*
DESCRIPTION: *1.5kg/3¼lb round. The terracotta, brine-washed rind has fine, white and pale blue moulds*
CULINARY USE: *Table cheese*

Tom and Gina Fergusson's washed rind cheese has twice won silver medals at the British Cheese Awards. There is a wonderful, earthy sweetness to Gubbeen, as the yeasts and moulds work to produce the rugged rind. The taste of this dense, full-bodied cheese is rich and savoury. The finish is of burnt onions and grilled cheese.

ABOVE: Gubbeen

LAVISTOWN

REGION: *Kilkenny*
TYPE: *Modern, farmhouse, unpasteurized, vegetarian, hard cheese*
SOURCE: *Cow's milk*
DESCRIPTION: *1.4kg/3lb and 3.5kg/8lb cheeses in the shape of millstones. The natural rind is smooth and firm*
CULINARY USE: *Table cheese*

Crumbling and fine, Lavistown resembles a Cheddar but is less compact. Made by Olivia Goodwillie to a Swaledale recipe, it has a sharp acidity and green, leafy taste.

DURRUS

REGION: *West Cork*
TYPE: *Modern, farmhouse, unpasteurized, vegetarian, semi-soft cheese*
SOURCE: *Cow's milk*
DESCRIPTION: *1.4kg/3lb round. The zipper-patterned, washed rind is fawn in colour, with blotches of blue, grey and white moulds*
CULINARY USE: *Table cheese*

The milk for Durrus comes from a neighbouring farm each morning and is processed in a magnificent copper vat in Jeffa Gill's charming dairy. Over the next few weeks the natural moulds and yeasts in the air gradually form a coat, which both protects the cheese and helps in the ripening process.

When young, Durrus is buttery, mild and slightly acidic, mellowing out to a silky-smooth, compact cheese that resembles a French Tomme. There is the smell of the earth on the rind and the medley of flavours includes caramel toffee, tart apples and a hint of smoke, with a nutty creaminess on the finish. The cheese matures in four to eight weeks and has a fat content of 45 per cent.

Durrus has twice won a bronze medal at the British Cheese Awards.

GABRIEL

REGION: *West Cork*
TYPE: *Modern, farmhouse, unpasteurized, hard cheese*
SOURCE: *Cow's milk*
DESCRIPTION: *6.75–27kg/15–60lb wheel with sharp edges. The natural rind is smooth, dark brown or khaki and very hard*
CULINARY USE: *Table cheese*

This wonderful, Gruyère-type cheese is full of flavour and has a strong, fruity zing. Lightly salted in brine, it is cured for many months with neither wax nor plastic to hinder its path to maturity. It seems the climate of this part of West Cork lends itself particularly well to these slow-ripening, hard cheeses. Bill Hogan and Sean Ferry of West Cork Natural Cheese Limited produce two more: Desmond, which is similar to Gabriel but smoother, with a sharp, resonant finish; and Mizen, a huge cheese, often over 45kg/100lb in weight, hard, almost brittle and not unlike the Swiss cheese Sbrinz or Italian Parmesan.

RIGHT: Durrus (top) and Gabriel

MILLEENS
REGION: *West Cork*
TYPE: *Modern, farmhouse, unpasteurized, semi-soft cheese*
SOURCE: *Cow's milk*
DESCRIPTION: *225g/8oz or 1.4kg/3lb rounds, with wrinkled, rather uneven, pinkish-orange, brine-washed rind*
CULINARY USE: *Table cheese*

Veronica and Norman Steele have been making Milleens on the Beara Peninsula for more than 10 years, and it is seldom the same twice, though never disappointing. The aroma is of farmyard, wet rocks and heather, the heather recurring in the flavour of the firm, supple, sweet cheese, which also has hints of cream and butterscotch. At its peak, the paste becomes almost fluid, and the taste is yeasty and savoury, with a strong, herbaceous tang and a suggestion of sea breezes. Milleens has the sweet-sour taste associated with genuine Trappist cheeses. It matures in four to 10 weeks and has a fat content of 45 per cent. It was Supreme Champion at the 1997 British Cheese Awards.

BELOW: Mine-Gabhar (back) and Milleens (front)

MINE-GABHAR
REGION: *Wexford*
TYPE: *Modern, farmhouse, unpasteurized, organic, vegetarian, soft-white cheese*
SOURCE: *Goat's milk*
DESCRIPTION: *225g/8oz round with mould-ripened, dove-grey coat*
CULINARY USE: *Table cheese*

Another award-winning cheese from Luc and Anne Van Kampen, Mine-Gabhar was declared Best Irish Cheese and Best Soft White Rind Cheese at the 1996 Cheese Awards. It matures in three weeks.

ORLA
REGION: *Cork*
TYPE: *Modern, farmhouse, unpasteurized, organic, vegetarian, semi-hard cheese*
SOURCE: *Sheep's milk*
DESCRIPTION: *2kg/4¹/₂lb round with fine, orange, brine-washed crust*
CULINARY USES: *Table cheese, grilling, snacks*

One of the cheeses that sits between semi-soft and hard, depending on the degree of maturity, Orla is supple and decidedly semi-soft when young. After being aged in cellars for up to six months, it more closely resembles Manchego in texture, although it is less oily. The mature cheese is sharp and salty, while retaining the earthy, burnt-sugar flavour so typical of sheep's milk. The texture is firm and breakable, with some holes.

ST KILLIAN
REGION: *Wexford*
TYPE: *Modern, farmhouse, vegetarian, soft-white cheese*
SOURCE: *Cow's milk*
DESCRIPTION: *250g/9oz hexagonal cheese with velvety, smooth, soft, white rind*
CULINARY USE: *Table cheese*

Attractively boxed, this Camembert-style cheese has taken the market by storm. Although the rind can be a little whiffy, the prevailing smell is of mushrooms and cellars, while the soft, nearly melting interior has the rich flavour of warm butter, with a bite that suggests green grass. St Killian is produced by Patrick Berridge.

BLUE RATHGORE
REGION: *Antrim, Northern Ireland*
TYPE: *Modern, creamery, vegetarian, blue cheese*
SOURCE: *Goat's milk*
DESCRIPTION: *2.2kg/5lb wheel. The natural crust is creamy white, fine and wet*
CULINARY USES: *Table cheese, dressings and salads*

Blue goat's milk cheeses are seldom made anywhere in the world. But Britain can boast several: Harbourne Goat, Clawson's Blue Goat, Brendon Blue and, of course, Rathgore, which was created in 1989 for the local and American markets. Problems with supply meant that production almost ceased until 1995, when the producer decided to start again. That same year, Blue Rathgore gained a gold medal in the New and Experimental Class at the British Cheese Awards. The cheese is moist and crumbly, with the smattering of blue giving it a spicy, slightly burnt taste. Through the blue you can still identify the almondy freshness of the goat's milk. Blue Rathgore matures in three to six months.

SCOTTISH CHEESES

Scotland has only a small number of indigenous cheeses. A harsh climate and rugged terrain are not conducive to the development of a cheese industry, although some soft cheeses were made by the crofters (tenant farmers). Caboc, the oldest of these, can be traced back to the fifteenth century. Crowdie, another soft cheese, is thought to have been introduced by the Vikings, although there is no record of it by name until the eighteenth century, possibly because it was usually made for home consumption.

Dunlop, the only indigenous hard cheese, was first made in the time of James II by Barbara Gilmour, the most influential figure in Scottish cheese history. She learnt how to make cheese in Ireland, where she was driven at the time of the religious troubles. On her return to Scotland around 1688, she started making a sweet, milk cheese, which was named after the village in which she lived. The making of Dunlop went on to become a flourishing industry in the eighteenth and nineteenth centuries, then all but died out until Anne Dorward revived the tradition in the mid-1980s.

In the last 15 years there has, however, been a revolution in the Scottish cheese industry. Today there are over 30 different artisan cheeses. Ironically, the very qualities that mitigated against the industry in the past have become its strength. It is the toughness of the climate and terrain and the hardy nature of the milking animal that makes the new Scottish cheeses worthy of mention.

RIGHT: The wash for Bishop Kennedy includes a generous dash of whisky

BISHOP KENNEDY
REGION: *Perthshire*
TYPE: *Modern, creamery, unpasteurized, vegetarian, semi-soft cheese*
SOURCE: *Cow's milk*
DESCRIPTION: *1.4kg/3lb disc with sticky, orange-yellow, brine-washed rind*
CULINARY USE: *Table cheese*

It was not the Vikings, the Romans or the monks who introduced washed-rind cheese to Scotland, but a young French cheesemaker lured to Howgate Cheese in 1992. With his first success, St Andrews, under his belt, he set about creating a washed-rind cheese with a more Scottish attitude. He finally perfected a secret concoction that included a generous dram of whisky. This is rubbed or smeared over the cheese during maturation.

Bishop Kennedy – named after a fifteenth-century bishop of St Andrews – is smooth and velvety, with a spicy finish. The distinctive odour, typical of a washed-rind cheese, has been likened to damp washing or old socks, although more polite people describe it as yeasty. When the cheese is mature, it almost runs and virtually hums with flavour. No doubt it would make an excellent hangover cure. It ripens in eight weeks; the fat content is about 45 per cent.

BONCHESTER
REGION: *Roxburghshire*
TYPE: *Modern, farmhouse, unpasteurized, soft-white cheese*
SOURCE: *Cow's milk (Jersey)*
DESCRIPTION: *275g/10oz round cheese with soft, white crust*
CULINARY USE: *Table cheese*

John and Christian Curtis created this unique, Camembert-style cheese using the milk from their own herd. Theirs is one of the few farms to retain the old practice of resting the herd: the cows are milked from March to December, then dried off until the spring. The Jersey milk gives the cheese its rich, butter-yellow colour and velvety texture. If cut when still "under age", the curd will be slightly chalky. It needs a few weeks to soften to a custard-like consistency, take on a richer colour and acquire a more rounded flavour. There is a hint of mushrooms from the rind and the interior has a fresh, grassy taste.

Bonchester is a past bronze medal winner at the British Cheese Awards and was Champion Cheese at the Royal Highland Show. It ripens in four to eight weeks and has a fat content of 48 per cent.

ABOVE: Bonchester

CABOC

REGION: *Ross and Cromarty*
TYPE: *Traditional, farmhouse, vegetarian, fresh cheese*
SOURCE: *Cow's milk*
DESCRIPTION: *900g/2lb chubby log rolled in oatmeal*
CULINARY USES: *Table cheese; also spread on oatcakes*

Made with cream-enriched milk, Caboc is buttery and wickedly rich. The toasted oats give it a nutty, yeasty flavour. This is one of Scotland's indigenous cheeses, made to an ancient recipe. According to legend it was created by Mariota de Ile, daughter of a fifteenth-century Mac-Donald, Lord of the Isles. When she was 12 years old, Mariota was in danger of being abducted by the Campbells, who planned to marry her to one of their own and seize her lands. Mariota escaped to Ireland, learned how to make cheese and brought the knowledge back to her people. Caboc was popular for many years, but then went into decline. It was revived by Susannah Stone, a descendant of Mariota de Ile, in 1962.

Caboc ripens in five days and has a fat content of 69 per cent.

CAIRNSMORE

REGION: *Dumfries and Galloway*
TYPE: *Modern, farmhouse, unpasteurized, hard cheese*
SOURCE: *Sheep's milk (East Friesland)*
DESCRIPTION: *1.4kg/3lb truckle. The hard, crusty rind has rusty red ferments. Available with natural rind or clothbound*
CULINARY USE: *Table cheese*

A past winner of a bronze medal at the British Cheese Awards, this delicious sheep's milk cheese from Galloway Farmhouse Cheese looks irresistible with its sometimes slightly lopsided shape. The rind develops a series of wonderful, furry moulds as it reaches maturity. The aroma hints at old leather and moss and the texture is firm, rather like Cheddar but more moist. Aromatic and decidedly nutty, with the sweetness of caramel and burnt toffee, Cairnsmore ripens in seven to nine months. The cheese is made only from April to October.

CROWDIE

REGION: *Ross and Cromarty*
TYPE: *Traditional, farmhouse, vegetarian, fresh cheese*
SOURCE: *Cow's milk*
DESCRIPTION: *125g/4¹/₂oz log; also packed in tubs*
CULINARY USES: *Table cheese, baking, snacks and breakfast*

The author's wonderful Scottish granny, one of many pioneers to brave the long sea voyage to New Zealand in the late nineteenth century, used to make her own hand-churned butter by skimming the cream off the milk. The buttermilk went into her exquisite scones and from the skimmed milk she would make Crowdie. The fresh, unpressed curd would be ready to eat the following day.

Crowdie is thought to have been introduced into Scotland by the Vikings in the eighth century. It is called Gruth in Gaelic. Slightly sour-tasting, it has a creamy yet crumbly texture and collapses gently on the palate.

Cheesemaker Susannah Stone recently introduced a blend of Crowdie and double cream called Gruth Dhu (Black Crowdie). This is formed into oval shapes and covered in toasted pinhead oats and crushed peppercorns.

BELOW: Cairnsmore (left) and Caboc

DUNLOP

REGION: *Ayrshire*
TYPE: *Traditional, farmhouse, unpasteurized, vegetarian, hard cheese*
SOURCE: *Cow's milk (Ayrshire)*
DESCRIPTION: *250g/9oz round with pale yellow, natural, rind finely dusted with moulds*
CULINARY USE: *Table cheese*

Anne Dorward started making traditional Dunlop 10 years ago at the farm where it was first established. Firm yet springy, it is very mild and buttery, with the sweetness of fresh milk and a gentle acidity on the finish. It ripens in six months. The producer, Dunlop Dairy, also makes Bonnet and Swinzie.

BELOW: Dunlop

DUNSYRE BLUE

REGION: *Lanarkshire*
TYPE: *Modern, farmhouse, unpasteurized, vegetarian, blue cheese*
SOURCE: *Cow's milk (Ayrshire)*
DESCRIPTION: *1.4–1.8kg/3–4lb cylinder wrapped in foil. The moist, white rind attracts a variety of moulds*
CULINARY USE: *Table cheese*

Dunsyre Blue is wrapped in foil to keep its rind moist. When aged, the smooth, creamy-coloured interior is penetrated by chunky streaks of blue-green mould that impart a spicy flavour to the cheese. The flavour is strongly suggestive of the clover and grasses of the pastures where the cows graze. Dunsyre Blue ripens in six to 12 weeks and has a fat content of 45 per cent. It is made by Humphrey Errington, who also produces Lanark Blue.

GALLOWAY GOAT'S MILK GEMS

REGION: *Dumfries and Galloway*
TYPE: *Modern, farmhouse,
unpasteurized, fresh cheese*
SOURCE: *Goat's milk*
DESCRIPTION: *20g/³/₄oz spheres*
CULINARY USES: *Table cheese, grilling,
spreading, salads*

These tiny, pure white balls of fresh goat's cheese are marinated with fresh herbs and garlic in jars of olive oil. Although garlic is the overriding flavour, you can still identify the freshness of the herbs and the herbaceous, lemony character of the milk.

The same cheese is available as a 450g/1lb round, coated in yellow wax. Very moist and crumbly, it melts in the mouth and has a subtle, goaty aroma and taste, with a slightly smoky finish. The producer, Galloway Farmhouse Cheese, also makes Cairnsmore.

GOWRIE

REGION: *Perthshire*
TYPE: *Modern, farmhouse, hard cheese*
SOURCE: *Cow's milk*
DESCRIPTION: *27kg/60lb cylinder with
natural rind, bound in cloth*
CULINARY USES: *Table cheese, grating,
in sauces*

Wrapped in locally made linen to produce a natural rind, Gowrie is a large and impressive cheese. It is made using traditional Cheddar techniques, but is softer and less dense, more closely resembling Scotland's famous hard cheese, Dunlop. It ripens in seven to 12 months.

ABOVE: *Lairobell*

ISLE OF MULL

REGION: *Isle of Mull*
TYPE: *Traditional, farmhouse,
unpasteurized, hard cheese*
SOURCE: *Cow's milk*
DESCRIPTION: *25kg/55lb cylinder. The
pale yellow rind bears the marks of
the cloth in which it is bound*
CULINARY USES: *Table cheese,
grating, grilling*

The milk from this part of Scotland produces a pale cheese, but its taste does not suffer from a lack of colour. Jeff Reade uses traditional methods but with a local twist: his herd, mainly Friesians with the odd Ayrshire and Jersey, are fed with hops in the winter months. The cheeses, having been bound in cloth, are matured for up to 12 months in the Tobermory Distillery. The cheese is very dense and packs a powerful punch – the classic Cheddar tang being laced with savoury overtones of garlic and onions, and a barely perceptible flavour of parsley and coriander. A headstrong cheese, Isle of Mull is also available in a gift size, with such flavourings as herbs, caraway seeds and peppers.

RIGHT: *Isle of Mull*

LAIROBELL

REGION: *Orkney*
TYPE: *Modern, farmhouse,
unpasteurized, vegetarian,
hard cheese*
SOURCE: *Goat's milk*
DESCRIPTION: *1.8kg/4lb cylinder. The
firm, smooth, natural rind is beige
in colour*
CULINARY USE: *Table cheese*

The cheesemakers are Jock and Hattie Bell, a retired policeman and his wife, who moved from Glasgow to the remote island of Shapinsy in the Orkneys. Lairobell is slightly open in texture and has a dry, crumbly feel. The unspoilt, natural meadows of the island, with their wild flowers and grasses, give the milk a subtle herbaceous flavour with a hint of almonds and a slightly goaty tang.

In the capable hands of an experienced affineur like Iain Mellis, Lairobell can become quite strong and goaty. It ripens in two to eight weeks.

LANARK BLUE

REGION: *Lanarkshire*
TYPE: *Modern, farmhouse,
unpasteurized, vegetarian, blue cheese*
SOURCE: *Sheep's milk*
DESCRIPTION: *1.4–1.8kg/3–4lb cylinder
wrapped in foil. The moist, white
rind has some grey and blue mould*
CULINARY USE: *Table cheese*

Cheesemaker Humphrey Errington, who also makes Dunsyre Blue, was the first person this century to milk sheep commercially in Scotland (they had been replaced by higher-yielding cows). His flock of 400 graze the wild heather pastures some 300 metres above the Clyde Valley. The unique grazing, coupled with Humphrey's skill and enthusiasm, produces an aromatic, slightly sweet yet pungent, Roquefort-style cheese. The superb, green-blue veins spreading through the cheese are the result of a Roquefort mould having been sprinkled into the milk vat before the cheese is curdled. It is then moulded by hand and allowed to mature for three months.

Lanark Blue is a past winner of a silver medal at the British Cheese Awards. It has a fat content of 45 per cent.

LEFT: Loch Arthur Farmhouse is a traditionally made clothbound Cheddar produced using organic milk

LOCH ARTHUR FARMHOUSE

REGION: *Dumfries and Galloway*
TYPE: *Modern, farmhouse, unpasteurized, organic, vegetarian, hard cheese*
SOURCE: *Cow's milk*
DESCRIPTION: *9kg/20lb clothbound cylinder with pale brown-grey, natural rind*
CULINARY USE: *Table cheese*

Made by Loch Arthur Creamery, part of the Loch Arthur Community and Camphill Village Trust, this is a traditionally made, clothbound Cheddar. Firm and quite dry, it melts in the mouth like hard chocolate, revealing a wonderful, nutty character overlaid by fresh, green shoots and a strong, fried-onion tang on the finish. Loch Arthur Farmhouse is less aggressive than mature Cheddars, so the fragrance and subtleties of the organic milk are able to come through.

Loch Arthur Farmhouse ripens in six to nine months and has a fat content of 48 per cent.

The creamery also produces their own Quark and Crannog. A recent addition to the range is Cebuck, a Dales-style cheese, made by putting the fresh curd into a cloth and then hanging it up so that it dries and matures in the shape of a teardrop.

ORKNEY EXTRA MATURE CHEDDAR

REGION: *Orkney*
TYPE: *Traditional, creamery, hard cheese*
SOURCE: *Cow's milk*
DESCRIPTION: *20kg/44lb block cheese, without rind; also made in smaller rounds*
CULINARY USES: *Table cheese, grating, salads, snacks, sauces*

Produced on the island of Orkney, which is renowned for the richness and flavour of its milk, this was declared Best Scottish Cheese at the British Cheese Awards in 1996. An excellent example of a creamery-made cheese, it is strong-bodied and biteable, with the tiny crystals of calcium lactate sometimes found in well-aged, hard cheeses like Parmesan. Orkney Extra Mature is nutty and creamy, with a savoury, burnt-onion taste. It is no surprise that it has achieved around 9 per cent of the UK market, despite the distance it must travel.

Orkney Extra Mature is matured for at least 12 months and has a fat content of 50 per cent.

ABOVE: Orkney Extra Mature Cheddar

SERIOUSLY STRONG CHEDDAR

REGION: *Dumfries and Galloway*
TYPE: *Traditional, creamery, hard cheese*
SOURCE: *Cow's milk*
DESCRIPTION: *20kg/44lb block cheese, without rind*
CULINARY USES: *Table cheese, grilling, grating, sauces*

This blockbuster of a Cheddar is aged from 18 to 24 months and the flavour is strong and savoury, with a mouthwatering tang to balance the creamy richness. The texture is sometimes slightly crunchy, due to the calcium lactate crystals that form in old, hard cheeses. For the Scottish market it is coloured with annatto, while a "white" version is available for those on the English side of the border.

BELOW: St Andrews

ST ANDREWS

REGION: *Perthshire*
TYPE: *Modern, creamery, unpasteurized, semi-soft cheese*
SOURCE: *Cow's milk*
DESCRIPTION: *2.2kg/5lb disc or small square with sticky, deep orange, brine-washed rind*
CULINARY USE: *Table cheese*

This is one of only two Trappist-style, washed-rind cheeses made in Scotland. It has a supple, "holey" texture and a sweet-sour, slightly yeasty taste.

WELSH CHEESES

The most famous Welsh cheese – and the only traditional one still made – is Caerphilly, named after the Welsh mining village where it was first produced in 1831. With its high moisture content and raised salt content, it was the ideal cheese for the miners, replacing the salt lost as they sweated far below the pastures.

The economic advantages of this quick-ripening cheese were quickly recognized by the major Cheddar makers of Somerset. Cheddar, which was made in huge cylinders, took months to mature, occupying valuable space and creating cash-flow problems in the interim. Caerphilly, on the other hand, weighed less and, thanks to its high moisture content, it ripened in a week, but would keep for two to three months. The Somerset cheesemakers could make the small, Welsh cheeses in the summer months when milk was abundant, and still produce their Cheddars.

By the end of the Second World War production had all but ceased in Wales, having been taken up by the large factories in England. Uniformity of feed and pasteurization eroded the subtleties of Caerphilly, and in its block form it became almost indistinguishable from the other "crumblies" – Wensleydale, Lancashire and Cheshire.

Fortunately, with the revival of the old ways by a new generation of cheese-makers, including recent immigrants from Italy and Holland, authentic Welsh farmhouse Caerphilly is back on the shelves. New cheeses, such as Llangloffan and Pant ys Gawn are there too, together with Teifi, a buxom Gouda. Sheep's and goat's milk cheeses are on the increase and the fire is back in the Welsh dragon's tail.

ACORN

REGION: *Cardiganshire*
TYPE: *Modern, farmhouse, unpasteurized, vegetarian, hard cheese*
SOURCE: *Sheep's milk (East Friesland)*
DESCRIPTION: *1.8kg/4lb truckle with golden, crusty, natural rind*
CULINARY USES: *Table cheese, grating*

Acorn is loosely based on an old-style Wensleydale. Firm yet crumbly, it melts in the mouth, releasing the flavours of cream caramel and crushed nuts, with a citrus finish. The cheese ripens in three to six months. It has a fat content of 52 per cent.

In addition to Acorn, cheesemakers Karen and Don Ross produce Skirrid, which is soaked in mead.

CAERPHILLY

REGION: *South and West Wales*
TYPE: *Traditional, farmhouse, unpasteurized, vegetarian, hard cheese*
SOURCE: *Cow's milk*
DESCRIPTION: *900g/2lb and 3.25kg/7lb wheels, with ivory-white rind dusted with fine flour. As the cheeses are aged in a moist cellar, the white and grey moulds become thicker and more leathery*
CULINARY USES: *Table cheese, grilling, grating*

One of the four British cheeses fondly known as "the crumblies", Caerphilly is only lightly pressed and has a higher moisture content than other traditional British cheeses. It was first made in Caerphilly (Castle Town) in about 1831. The brine baths in which the cheese was soaked overnight sealed in the moisture, and the cheese proved popular with Welsh miners who had lost salt during their labours.

One of the best-known producers today is the Duckett family of Walnut Farm in Somerset, who have been making traditional Caerphilly for generations. When young, their Caerphilly has a fresh, citrus taste with a background of crushed bracken and riverside reeds. The texture is moist, friable yet supple, like a school eraser. With maturity, the edges become wonderfully creamy, and the flavour becomes more rounded. Duckett's Caerphilly won a silver medal at the 1996 British Cheese Awards.

Other traditional makers include Caws Cenarth, Glynhynod Farmhouse Cheese, Nantybwla and Abergavenny Fine Foods. Caws Cenarth has converted an old barn into a cheese room with a special viewing gallery for visitors.

While a good factory-made Cheddar can still retain some of the character of a traditionally made cheese, the same cannot be said of Caerphilly. It is worth seeking out the traditionally made cheese, which is not only delectable in its own right, but also makes a marvellous ploughman's lunch or Welsh rarebit.

ABOVE: Caerphilly

CELTIC PROMISE
REGION: *Carmarthenshire*
TYPE: *Modern, farmhouse,
unpasteurized, vegetarian,
semi-soft cheese*
SOURCE: *Cow's milk*
DESCRIPTION: *500g/1¼lb round.
The smooth, brine-washed
rind ranges from orange to
terracotta and has a dusting
of moulds*
CULINARY USE: *Table cheese*

John and Patrice Savage-Ontswedder only recently started making this small, dumpling-shaped, washed-rind cheese under the guidance of the "inventor", James Aldridge. James is one of Britain's most talented cheesemakers, who willingly passes on his legendary knowledge to those willing to work hard and listen attentively.

Once drained, the young, freshly shaped curds are washed, rubbed or smeared with brine to encourage and spread the growth of the orange-pink moulds that contribute to the taste and texture of the final cheese. Supple, smooth, spicy, aromatic and pungent, Celtic Promise is absolutely delicious and is a past winner of a bronze medal at the British Cheese Awards. Available only from some specialist cheese shops, it ripens in about eight weeks.

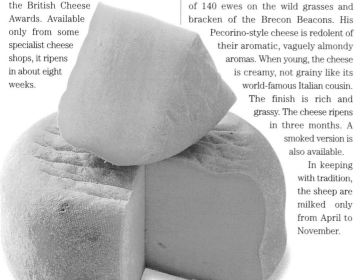

*ABOVE: Llangloffan
Farmhouse*

CWMTAWE PECORINO
REGION: *Swansea*
TYPE: *Modern, farmhouse,
unpasteurized, vegetarian,
hard cheese*
SOURCE: *Sheep's milk*
DESCRIPTION: *1.8kg/4lb tall round. The
hard, ridged rind is brine-washed
and is brownish in colour*
CULINARY USES: *Table cheese, grating*

It is rare to find an Italian cheesemaker outside Italy, but to find one in Wales is unique. Giovanni Irranca farms his flock of 140 ewes on the wild grasses and bracken of the Brecon Beacons. His Pecorino-style cheese is redolent of their aromatic, vaguely almondy aromas. When young, the cheese is creamy, not grainy like its world-famous Italian cousin. The finish is rich and grassy. The cheese ripens in three months. A smoked version is also available.

In keeping with tradition, the sheep are milked only from April to November.

*LEFT: Celtic
Promise*

LLANBOIDY
REGION: *Pembrokeshire*
TYPE: *Modern, farmhouse,
unpasteurized, vegetarian,
hard cheese*
SOURCE: *Cow's milk (Red Poll)*
DESCRIPTION: *4.5kg/10lb wheel. The
crusty, wrinkled, yellow rind has
some mould*
CULINARY USES: *Table cheese,
grilling*

Sue Jones, the cheesemaker, is a past winner of a silver medal at the British Cheese Awards for this Cheddar-like cheese. It is firm yet crumbly and has a dense and creamy consistency. The aroma is of fresh cut hay and meadows and the cheese has a mouthwatering, sharp, green and grassy tang. Llanboidy ripens in two to four months.

LLANGLOFFAN FARMHOUSE
REGION: *Pembrokeshire*
TYPE: *Modern, farmhouse,
unpasteurized, vegetarian,
hard cheese*
SOURCE: *Cow's milk (Brown Swiss
and Jersey)*
DESCRIPTION: *4.5kg/10lb wheel. The
natural rind is quite rough and
pitted. It has a stone-like texture
with some moulds, along with the
imprint of the cloth in which
it is moulded*
CULINARY USE: *Table cheese*

In Castle Morris, near Fishguard, Leon and Joan Downey have been making cheese for 20 years, ever since Leon retired from the Hallé Orchestra. A born entertainer, Leon has created a dairy where he can make cheese for an audience.

Llangloffan Farmhouse is a traditional, hand-made cheese with a rich yet dry, almost crumbly texture that melts in the mouth. Fruity and slightly grassy, it has a hint of fire on the finish. It has twice been declared Best Welsh Cheese at the British Cheese Awards and won the Dougal Campbell Memorial Trophy.

The cheese ripens in two to six months and has a fat content of 45 per cent.

A chive and garlic version of the cheese, coloured with the natural red dye, annatto, is also available.

PANT YS GAWN
REGION: *Monmouthshire*
TYPE: *Modern, farmhouse, vegetarian, fresh cheese*
SOURCE: *Goat's milk*
DESCRIPTION: *100g/3¾oz disc or log*
CULINARY USES: *Table cheese, snacks, grilling, spreading, salads*

This small, delightful, goat's milk cheese has a very clean, fresh, citrus flavour with a tantalizing suggestion of tarragon. The texture resembles that of fromage frais.

The soft, moist curds are carefully drained in tiny moulds and are ready for sale in only a few days, yet with clever packaging the cheeses have a remarkably long shelf life. Pant ys Gawn is now sold quite extensively in supermarkets throughout Britain – its mild, goaty flavour has a wide appeal. Varieties of the cheese include mixed herbs, cracked black peppercorns, and garlic and chives. The producer, Abergavenny Fine Foods Limited, also makes Castle Meadow Caerphilly, Welsh Goat's Log (a log-shaped version of Pant ys Gawn), St David's (a spicy semi-soft cheese), and a number of blended or speciality cheeses.

RIGHT: Pant ys Gawn has a clean, fresh, citrus flavour

PENBRYN
REGION: *Carmarthenshire*
TYPE: *Modern, farmhouse, unpasteurized, organic, vegetarian, hard cheese*
SOURCE: *Cow's milk*
DESCRIPTION: *2.25kg/5lb round. The natural rind has a dusting of blue and white moulds and wild yeasts*
CULINARY USE: *Table cheese*

Penbryn, an organic cheese based on Gouda, is firm yet really creamy, with a host of flavours. Nutty, fruity, sweet and grassy. All these adjectives have been used to describe a cheese that also tastes of melted butter. It ripens in two months.

ABOVE: Pencarreg, a modern Brie-style cheese, is one of a range of organic cheeses made by Welsh Organic Foods

PENCARREG
REGION: *Cardiganshire*
TYPE: *Modern, farmhouse, organic, vegetarian, soft-white cheese*
SOURCE: *Cow's milk (Ayrshire, Shorthorn and Friesian)*
DESCRIPTION: *200g/7oz oval or 1.8kg/4lb round, each with a thick, soft-white penicillium rind*
CULINARY USE: *Table cheese*

Pencarreg is a Brie-style cheese with a texture that feels like solid, whipped cream as it melts in the mouth. The aroma is of mushrooms, while the slightly bitter, green-grassy character is balanced by a buttery sweetness. Pencarreg ripens in two to eight weeks.

The cheese was developed by the late Dougal Campbell, who fell in love with cheese while on holiday in Switzerland. He stayed to learn about cheesemaking, then brought his new-found skills and passion home to create Tyn Grug, a hard, cow's milk cheese.

As more organic milk became available, Dougal embarked on an ambitious project to set up a small creamery, Welsh Organic Foods, and developed a range of organic Welsh cheeses, of which Pencarreg was the first. This was followed by Pencarreg Blue, in which the blue is dotted through the cheese to give a gentle, spicy, blue flavour that becomes more pronounced with age. Pencarreg Blue has a fine, white, Camembert-style crust.

Sadly, Dougal was killed in a tragic farm accident in 1995, but his memory and vision lives on with the cheesemakers at Welsh Organic Foods.

ST DAVID'S

REGION: *Monmouthshire*
TYPE: *Modern, farmhouse, vegetarian, semi-soft cheese*
SOURCE: *Cow's milk*
DESCRIPTION: *2kg/4½lb round. The orange, brine-washed rind is smooth and slightly moist*
CULINARY USE: *Table cheese*

One of only two Welsh washed-rind cheeses, St David's has a pungent, yeasty taste, with an undercurrent of smoked bacon. The texture of this semi-soft, vegetarian cheese is quite supple and squidgy, with tiny holes.

Bryson Craske and his team at Abergavenny Fine Foods also produce Pant ys Gawn and Castle Meadow Caerphilly. The company's speciality cheeses include Tintern and Y Fenni.

TEIFI

REGION: *Carmarthenshire*
TYPE: *Modern, farmhouse, unpasteurized, organic, vegetarian, hard cheese*
SOURCE: *Cow's milk*
DESCRIPTION: *450g/1lb, 900g/2lb and 3.5–4.5kg/8–10lb millstones with smooth, polished, natural rind*
CULINARY USES: *Table cheese, snacks, grating*

Similar to a Gouda in both shape and texture, Teifi has a deep sunshine-yellow interior. Firm, dense and fairly fruity when young, the cheese becomes hard and almost flaky when mature. The flavour intensifies and tingles the taste buds with a suggestion of bitter chocolate and young celery.

Made by John and Patrice Savage-Ontswedder, Teifi ripens in two to nine months. A smoked version of the cheese is also produced, as are versions flavoured with nettles and cumin.

RIGHT:
St David's

TYN GRUG

REGION: *Cardiganshire*
TYPE: *Modern, farmhouse, unpasteurized, organic, vegetarian, hard cheese*
SOURCE: *Cow's milk*
DESCRIPTION: *7.5kg/16½lb and 15kg/33lb clothbound cylinders. The rough, deep golden-yellow rind bears the faint outline of the cloth and has some greyish moulds*
CULINARY USE: *Table cheese*

Loosely based on Cheddar, with a Swiss influence, Tyn Grug is dense, firm and slightly grainy. It has a wonderful complexity of flavours that are gradually released on to the palate. At first there is a hint of young celery leaves, then a rich Gruyère nuttiness and finally a delicious, peppery acidity on the finish. One of the author's favourites, it has won bronze medals at the British Cheese Awards.

Tyn Grug ripens in five months.

BELOW: Tyn Grug (left) and Teifi (right) are both unpasteurized, organic cheeses

SPANISH CHEESES

Wherever you go in Spain, from the vast, barren plains of Extremadura to the majestic beauty of the Sierra Nevada, you will find wonderful cheeses. At the last count, there were more than 600, many owing their idiosyncratic nature to the numerous varieties of indigenous sheep, cows and goats that have developed over the centuries.

In 1988, aware that this marvellous heritage could easily be lost as a new generation of Spaniards turned its back on tradition and moved to the cities, the government initiated an ambitious survey. Its aim was to catalogue every cheese made in Spain. Much of the survey had to be carried out on horseback or on foot, in order to reach artisan cheesemakers in isolated, mountain regions whose cheeses had been made for centuries, but were unknown in the wider world.

Recipes were compared, and eventually 81 distinct varieties of cheese were identified. A national quality-control system, Denominación de Origen (DO) was introduced. This regulates where a specific cheese must be made, which breed of animal must supply the milk, exactly how the cheese must be made and what size it must conform to. It also details any distinguishing characteristics. Similar to the systems that exist in France and Italy, it protects producers and consumers from inferior or foreign copies, as only those cheeses that meet the criteria may carry the official stamp on their rind.

Discovering this astonishing bounty can be a wonderful pilgrimage for the cheese lover. Northern Spain, from Galicia on the Atlantic coast to Catalonia on the Mediterranean, offers the most extensive choice, but the Basque Country, with over 40 different cheeses, should not be neglected. Follow St James' Way, a network of byways that stretches for about 800km/500 miles over Roman causeways, medieval cattle tracks, through ruins and walled cities, and discover delectable cheeses that have been made in virtually the same way for over a thousand years.

The Spanish are warm and welcoming. The food is fascinating and enjoying it amounts to a way of life. Stop in one of the many tapas bars and sample slivers of the local cheese with slices of air-dried Serrano ham, a dish of marinated red peppers and some fresh anchovies. Add a glass of fino sherry – heaven!

BELOW: Mahon

AFUEGA'L PITU
REGION: *Asturias*
TYPE: *Traditional, farmhouse, unpasteurized, fresh cheese*
SOURCE: *Cow's milk*
DESCRIPTION: *500g/1¼lb cone or pumpkin-shape. The rind is buff to deep orange in colour and has a dusting of white mould*
CULINARY USE: *Table cheese*
When the author was first offered a taste of this innocent-looking cheese in a tapas bar, she was unaware of its reputation. Local Asturians hooted with laughter as she took a bite – then reached for a glass of fruity León wine to quench the fire. It was only then that they translated the name: Afuega'l Pitu means "a fire in the gut". Fresh red chilli pepper is added to the cheese and more is rubbed into the rind as the cheese is allowed to mature. The pumpkin or bishop's mitre shape is obtained by straining the cheese in a cloth that is knotted at the top, rather than folded. A plain version of the cheese is also made. Both are well worth trying.

BURGOS
REGION: *Castile-León*
TYPE: *Traditional, farmhouse and creamery, unpasteurized, fresh cheese*
SOURCE: *Cow's and sheep's milk*
DESCRIPTION: *1–2kg/2¼–4½lb wheel with corrugated grooves down the sides and ridged wedges marked on the top and bottom*
CULINARY USES: *Baking; also often eaten for dessert, with sugar and honey*
This fresh cheese takes its name from the Castilian city that used to hold a weekly market. Throughout the winter and spring, farmers from the surrounding areas would gather at the market to sell their sheep's milk cheese. Ready within hours of being made, Burgos, also known as Requeson, is pure white, smooth and slightly rubbery. It tastes of fresh milk, with a hint of acidity and salt. If you can, find a hand-made example. The markings on the cheese come from the moulds into which the fresh curd is pressed.

CABRALES (DO)
REGION: *Asturias*
TYPE: *Traditional, farmhouse,
unpasteurized, blue cheese*
SOURCE: *Cow's, sheep's or goat's milk*
Description: *3kg/6½lb cylinder
with natural rind, wrapped
in either maple leaves
or foil*
CULINARY USES: *Table cheese;
also served for dessert,
with honey*

This, Spain's best-known blue cheese, is made by hand in the north-east corner of the Picos de Europa (Peaks of Europe) where rugged mountain peaks tower above beech, oak and birch forests. The best cheeses are produced in spring and summer, when the shepherds take their animals to the high pastures and the cheese is made from a mixture of cow's, goat's and sheep's milk. In winter, when only cow's milk is available, the cheese lacks the wonderful complexity of the mixed-milk version.

The cheese was traditionally wrapped in maple or plane tree leaves, which covered the coarse, sticky, orange-yellow rind, with its pervasive aroma. Today, foil is used as it holds the cheese together better. The inside can be off-white or yellow, with brown around the edges. It is streaked like a banana cake, with irregular lines and patches of crunchy, grey-green to purple-blue mould. The texture is unusually complex: soft and creamy, yet grainy and almost crumbly. The pungent smell suggests fermenting fruit, moulds and yeast, and the cheese has a spicy, lip-smacking finish.

Cabrales is ripened in natural limestone caverns for two to three months. The rind is penetrated with rods to encourage the blue mould naturally present in the caves (*Penicillium glaucum*) to penetrate the rind. The locals are said to prefer the cheese at six months old, when it is almost totally blue and *con gustano* (with maggots). This the author has not experienced, nor does she intend to!

Similar cheeses include Picos de Europa and Valdeon.

CASTELLANO
REGION: *Castile-León*
TYPE: *Traditional, farmhouse and
creamery, unpasteurized, hard cheese*
SOURCE: *Sheep's milk (Churro
and Castilian)*
DESCRIPTION: *1–3kg/2¼–6½lb round
(half cylinder). The pale fawn,
natural rind is marked with the
zigzag pattern of the draining hoop*
CULINARY USES: *Table cheese: serve with
the classic Spanish quince cheese –
membrilla – whose fruity tang makes
it the perfect companion*

Castile-León is now the largest cheesemaking region in Spain, accounting for 85 per cent of pure sheep's milk cheeses. Like Manchego, Castellano is a hooped cheese, which means that the fresh curds are drained in special plastic hoops, which leave distinctive zigzag marks on the rind. The top and base of the artisan cheeses also carry a motif or design from the carved wooden or plastic bases, which are placed below the cheese as it drains in the hoops. The motif (a flower, geometric pattern or pair of initials) identifies the cheesemaker – or did. Today, as more of the cheeses are made in factories or co-operatives, the size and shape of Castellano is becoming more uniform, confusing shoppers accustomed to recognizing their favourite cheese by the markings on the rind.

Extremes of climate, the distinctive milk of the Churro and Castilian sheep and the origin of the individual cheesemaker's recipe all contribute to the character of the artisan cheese. The pale yellow interior of a good Castellano is firm and dense. Compared to Manchego, it is quite moist, and has a few rice-sized holes. The wonderfully delicate, cream-caramel taste is perfectly offset by the fresh acidity and hint of salt.

CUAJADA
REGION: *Various*
TYPE: *Traditional, farmhouse and
creamery, fresh cheese*
SOURCE: *Sheep's and goat's milk*
DESCRIPTION: *Sold in pots of
various sizes*
CULINARY USES: *Use instead of yogurt;
often served with honey or fruit
for breakfast*

Cuajada originally came from northern Navarre, where the shepherds used the local thistle rather than animal rennet to coagulate the milk. This gave the traditional cheese a unique and more floppy consistency than the modern equivalent, which is made, like junket, by adding rennet to fresh milk and then heating it gently. The mixture is poured into small, earthenware or plastic pots, where it sets lightly.

*LEFT: Cuajada – this
fresh cheese is widely available in Spanish supermarkets*

ABOVE: Garrotxa

GARROTXA

REGION: *Catalonia*
TYPE: *Modern, farmhouse, unpasteurized, hard cheese*
SOURCE: *Goat's milk*
DESCRIPTION: *1kg/2¼lb round with natural rind covered in thick, furry, grey mould*
CULINARY USE: *Table cheese*

Disillusioned with the stress of city life, a steady stream of professionals in many industrialized countries have moved to the country, bringing their entrepreneurial skills to a range of enterprises, including cheesemaking.

Although this cheese is based on an old recipe, it has been developed and marketed using modern methods by several groups of what the Spanish people refer to as "neo-rurals" working together as a co-operative in a village north of Barcelona.

Garrotxa is one of the author's favourites. The pure white milk seems to have absorbed the flavour of fresh walnuts and the scent of mimosa, while retaining the fresh crispness of young grass. The texture is firm yet springy, becoming smooth and velvety as you reach for more.

RIGHT: Idiazabal

IDIAZABAL (DO)

REGION: *Basque and Navarre*
TYPE: *Traditional, farmhouse and co-operative, unpasteurized, hard cheese*
SOURCE: *Sheep's milk (Lacha and Carranzana)*
DESCRIPTION: *1–3kg/2¼–6½lb cylinder. Pale yellow to amber in colour, the natural rind is smooth and hard*
CULINARY USES: *Table cheese, grilling, grating, tapas*

For centuries Idiazabal has been made by shepherds in the high mountain pastures of the Urbia and Aralar mountains. It was traditionally sold at the end of September, when the shepherds and their herds of sheep were forced down from the mountains by the first snows of winter.

The cheese has a compact texture, with a few pinprick holes. It is dry, but not crumbly, and feels pleasantly oily in the mouth. The rind carries the marks of the wooden moulds in which it is drained.

The characteristic, smoky flavour was originally the result of the cheeses having been stored near the shepherds' night fires. There were no chimneys in the simple mountain huts, so the cheeses absorbed the sweet, aromatic smoke.

Artisan cheesemakers continue to make the cheese in the way their fathers and grandfathers did, but Idiazabal is also produced industrially. Producers wishing to carry the DOs stamp of approval must, however, adhere to traditional methods.

MAHON (DO)

REGION: *Minorca*
TYPE: *Traditional, farmhouse and creamery, unpasteurized, hard cheese*
SOURCE: *Cow's milk (Friesian)*
DESCRIPTION: *1–4kg/2¼–9lb square with rounded edges. The hard, orange rind carries the imprint of the cheesecloth and tends to be greasy*
CULINARY USES: *Table cheese, grating (especially over pasta), snacks*

This cheese comes from Minorca, one of the Balearic Islands off the north-east coast of Spain. It was originally made from the local sheep's milk, but during the brief British occupation in the eighteenth century, cattle were shipped in and the local cheesemakers were persuaded to change to cow's milk.

Although the unpasteurized cheese is sold fresh, a few days after being made, it is at its most bold and delicious when age has given it a hard and slightly granular texture, like that of Parmesan. The ivory interior, with its small, irregular holes, contrasts with the bright orange rind whose colour comes not from bacteria, but from being rubbed with butter, paprika and oil. The taste is sharp, with a salty tang due to the proximity of the grazing to the sea. Some of the traditional cheesemakers add a small proportion of sheep's milk to their cheese.

The curd is piled in the centre of a cloth square, alternate corners are knotted and twisted together and the cheese is pressed for a few days. This gives the cheese its characteristic "cushion" shape and the indentation in the centre.

Mahon is sold at various stages of maturity. If fresh, it must be consumed within 10 days. The semi-cured cheese has been matured for at least two months, while the cured cheese has been matured for five months and the aged cheese for 10 months. Pasteurized Mahon is also available. It is usually sold young, when the texture is smooth and supple and the aroma is sweet and fruity.

MANCHEGO (DO)

REGION: *La Mancha*
TYPE: *Traditional, farmhouse and creamery, hard cheese*
SOURCE: *Sheep's milk (La Mancha)*
DESCRIPTION: *2–3.5kg/4½–8lb cylinder with flat surfaces. The natural rind is distinctively patterned*
CULINARY USES: *Table cheese, grating, grilling*

The plains where the legendary Don Quixote tilted at windmills and protected the shepherds from attack by marauding bandits are now irrigated. There are vineyards where once only the hardy La Mancha sheep survived. Much has changed, but the sheep are still there, grazing on the shrubs and grasses of the Dahesa and producing the thick, aromatic milk that gives Manchego its character.

This remarkable cheese has been made in La Mancha since the time of the Romans. However, it is now produced in large, modern co-operatives and the milk is frequently pasteurized, but this has not markedly altered the flavour.

To qualify for the famous Manchego label, the cheese must be firm and dry, yet rich and creamy. Only sheep's milk from La Mancha may be used. The distinctive pattern on the waxed rind – originally the result of encircling the curd with a plaited

BELOW: Manchego, from left, aged for 4 months, 6 months and 10 months

(braided) band of esparto grass – must be visible. (The colour of the wax denotes the age of the cheese.) The interior should be ivory in colour, with small, irregular eyes. The complexity of the flavour will depend on the age of the cheese, but there should be a richness, reminiscent of Brazil nuts and burnt caramel, with a slightly salty finish. The aroma should suggest lanolin and roast lamb.

Manchego is sold at various stages of maturity: at the age of 13 weeks, it is described as *curado* (cured) and when over three months old, it is referred to as *viego* (aged). There is a peppery bite to cheeses that have reached a great age.

MATO

REGION: *Catalonia*
TYPE: *Traditional, farmhouse, fresh cheese*
SOURCE: *Goat's and cow's milk*
DESCRIPTION: *1–2kg/2¼–4½lb bowl-shaped cheese; also sold in pots*
CULINARY USES: *Cooking, as a breakfast cheese, snacks*

This fresh cheese resembles fromage frais. It has a delicate citrus and herb tang. No salt is added before it is potted or drained in basketweave moulds shaped like pudding basins, so it does not keep long. Often made at home, it is used for both savoury and sweet dishes, and is freqently served with honey, aniseed and fruits.

PENAMELLERA

REGION: *Asturias*
TYPE: *Traditional, farmhouse and co-operative, natural-rind cheese*
SOURCE: *Cow's, goat's or sheep's milk*
Description: 500g/1¼lb disc. The thin, wrinkled, yellowish-orange crust has a dusting of fine, white mould
CULINARY USES: *Table cheese, snacks*

Named after the high peak that rises behind the village where the cheese has been made for centuries, Penamellera has a slightly greasy appearance and oddly meaty smell. The interior is more elegant. Supple and dense, with a few small, irregular holes, it has a mellow, vaguely nutty taste. The finish is fresh and lemony.

Similar cheeses include Quesuco, Porua and the locally produced Rozagas. In 1984 concern that the number of local producers was gradually dwindling led some Asturian farmers to form a co-operative to market their unique cheese. Production has increased and Penemellera is now well known throughout northern Spain.

PICOS DE EUROPA (DO)

REGION: *Cantabria*
TYPE: *Traditional, farmhouse and creamery, blue cheese*
SOURCE: *Cow's milk*
DESCRIPTION: *3kg/6½lb cylinder with natural rind wrapped in plane tree leaves*
CULINARY USES: *Table cheese, often eaten with wild honey*

The recipe for this creamy, moist cheese is thought to have been brought to Spain by early French pilgrims as they followed St James' Way to the Atlantic coast.

Picos de Europa is usually made from cow's milk, but farmhouse cheesemakers will add a little goat's or sheep's milk, as available. The cheese has blue-green veins, a pungent aroma, a pleasantly salty bite and a clean, piquant finish. Wrapped in plane leaves, it gives a cheeseboard a rustic yet elegant look. If the rind darkens and becomes sticky, pat it dry and leave it in a cool place to breathe for a few hours.

Also known as Valdeon, Picos de Europa ripens in two to three months and has a fat content of 45 per cent.

QUESO IBERICO (DO)
REGION: *Central Spain*
TYPE: *Modern, creamery, hard cheese*
SOURCE: *Cow's, goat's and sheep's milk*
DESCRIPTION: *3kg/6¹/₂lb wheel. The hard, dry rind bears the marks of the esparto (plaited/braided grass) bands used in the draining process*
CULINARY USES: *Table cheese, grating, grilling, snacks*

The mixture of cow's, goat's and sheep's milk gives this modern, uniquely Spanish cheese a truly three-dimensional character. Regulations require that it contain not less than 25 per cent and not more than 40 per cent of any one type of milk, and the flavour has elements of all three.

The creamy texture melts in the mouth gradually, releasing a rich, full-bodied nuttiness before delivering a fruity tang on the finish. It is made by large consortiums, in much the same way as Manchego. It is sometimes mistaken for Manchego, partly because the cheese looks very similar and also because the words "Manchego Blend" appear on some labels. Queso Iberico ripens in one to six months.

QUESO IBORES
REGION: *Extremadura*
TYPE: *Traditional, farmhouse and co-operative, unpasteurized, hard cheese*
SOURCE: *Goat's milk (Retinta and Verata)*
DESCRIPTION: *3kg/6¹/₂lb round. The smooth, reddish-brown, natural rind is rubbed with oil and paprika*
CULINARY USES: *Table cheese, tapas*

Queso Ibores takes its name from the area in Extremadura – Los Ibores – where it has been made since Roman times. The unusual, deep red of the rind provides a wonderful contrast to the pure white interior. The aroma of the paprika is distinctive and penetrates the cheese as a subtle spicy tang. This is offset by the aromatic and creamy nature of the goat's milk.

QUESO MAJORERO
REGION: *Fuerteventura*
TYPE: *Traditional, farmhouse and co-operative, unpasteurized, hard cheese*
SOURCE: *Goat's milk*
DESCRIPTION: *5–7kg/11–15¹/₄lb cylinder. The pale amber, natural rind has a geometric pattern printed at top and bottom*
CULINARY USES: *Table cheese, grilling*

Also known as Queso Fuerteventura, from the barren yet beautiful island on which it is made, this cheese is one of the author's favourites. Firmly pressed to create the hard texture, its tough rind bears the traditional marks typical of many Spanish cheeses. Although the interior seems dense, it melts in the mouth to leave a trail that suggests wild honey, the scent of wild thyme and almonds. The finish is peppery and rounded, like a fine, red wine. It is excellent with a fino sherry or robust red wine.

Fuerteventura, like all the Canary Islands, is short of water, yet the prickly pear, thistles, cacti and straggly bushes provide the native goat with a veritable feast. The arid conditions mean a reduced milk yield, but the flavour of the milk is intensely aromatic, almost perfumed.

BELOW: Queso Iberico

ABOVE: Queso Majorero

QUESO DE MURCIA
REGION: *Murcia*
TYPE: *Traditional, farmhouse and co-operative, fresh cheese*
SOURCE: *Goat's milk*
DESCRIPTION: *1–2kg/2¹/₄–4¹/₂lb pure white, round cheese with indented ridges from the wooden bases on which it drains*
CULINARY USES: *Table cheese, cooking*

Driving through hot, barren Murcia, one could be forgiven for wondering what the straggly flocks of sheep and goats find to eat in the gravelly soil. Closer inspection reveals tough scrub and intensely scented wild thyme, oregano, rosemary and other hardy plants, each contributing to the flavour of the milk. The low moisture content of the grazing also means that the yield of milk is low, but rich and thick and ideal for cheesemaking.

Queso de Murcia is pure white, with innumerable small holes. The texture is spongy and the cheese is subtly flavoured with rosemary and tarragon, balanced by a refreshing acidity. The fresh cheese has been made in the same way for centuries, but because it has a short shelf life and does not travel well, the local government decided to create a cured or aged local cheese that would keep well and have a wider appeal outside the region and abroad. The result was Queso de Murcia al Vino, a delicious and highly successful cheese, made by washing the cheese in the local red wine. The naturally porous rind takes on a deep burgundy colour and the cheese absorbs the fruity, slightly spicy flavour and aroma of the wine.

QUESO DEL MONTSEC

REGION: *Catalonia*
TYPE: *Modern, farmhouse, unpasteurized, vegetarian, soft-white cheese*
SOURCE: *Goat's milk*
DESCRIPTION: *2kg/4¹/₂lb round with rustic-looking, patchy rind coated with wood ash*
CULINARY USE: *Table cheese*

Like Garrotxa, this was developed by a group of young professionals who were looking for a more meaningful lifestyle for themselves and their families. The press dubbed them "neo-rurals" and did not always take them seriously, but had to reconsider when they successfully made and marketed Montsec.

The cheese has a dense, fairly grainy texture that feels very creamy in the mouth, yet has a definite bite. The distinctive taste of goat's milk is instantly apparent, and the cheese has a strong, herbaceous, spicy finish.

Queso del Montsec requires two to three months to ripen. It is also known as Cendrat.

QUESO DEL TIETAR

REGION: *Avila*
TYPE: *Traditional, farmhouse, unpasteurized, fresh or hard cheese*
SOURCE: *Goat's milk*
DESCRIPTION: *Fresh – in pots; aged – in 2.5kg/5¹/₂lb cylinders. The natural rind on the aged cheese is blue-grey*
CULINARY USES: *Table cheese, cooking (fried with the local pequilla peppers, garlic and plum tomatoes, it makes a perfect partner for pasta)*

Seldom found outside Avila, Queso del Tietar comes in two distinct styles. The fresh cheese is called Cabra del Tietar. Sold when it is only a few days old, the cheese is pure white and rindless, with a lemon-fresh flavour that hints at the aromatic goat's milk. It is often mixed with wild thyme, oregano and rosemary or paprika.

If the cheese is aged for two to three months, the texture hardens. It resembles Sierra de Zuheros and is firm but spongy, with a pronounced, nutty flavour.

RONCAL (DO)

REGION: *Navarra*
TYPE: *Traditional, farmhouse and co-operative, unpasteurized, hard cheese*
SOURCE: *Sheep's milk (Lacha and Aragon)*
DESCRIPTION: *2kg/4¹/₂lb wheel with hard, natural rind covered with a velvety-smooth layer of blue-grey mould*
CULINARY USES: *Table cheese, tapas, grating, grilling*

Roncal was the first Spanish cheese to be awarded the protection of the Denominacion de Origen, but regulation of its production goes back to the thirteenth century, when the local council controlled the movement of the indigenous Lacha and Aragon sheep. In July, the animals were taken to the summer alpine pastures, returning at the end of September. On 13 October they were on the move again, this time to the winter pastures in the south of Navarre, where they remained until 15 May.

This migratory pattern (transhumance) is still practised by a few shepherds, but change of ownership or usage of the land makes it difficult. In 1974 a cheese factory was set up near Pamplona to ensure that this delicious cheese would continue to be produced.

Roncal is aged for at least four months and has a fat content of 45 per cent. The firm, elastic interior is slightly grainy, with small, irregular holes. The flavour owes much to the richness of the milk. Distinctly "sheepy" and quite pungent, it retains a sweet, herbaceous flavour, thanks to the natural pastures of wild grasses, herbs and flowers on which the sheep graze.

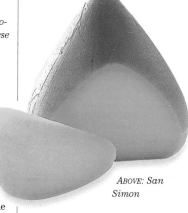

ABOVE: *San Simon*

SAN SIMON

REGION: *Galicia*
TYPE: *Traditional, farmhouse and creamery, semi-soft cheese*
SOURCE: *Cow's milk (Galicia)*
DESCRIPTION: *1–2kg/2¹/₄–4¹/₂lb pear shape with glossy, honey-coloured, natural rind*
CULINARY USE: *Table cheese*

Another quirky Spanish cheese, this has the shape of a bullet or a pear. Enquiries as to the origin of its shape provoke wide grins or unprintable stories, but it has been made for generations on the western tip of Spain, where the lush, green pastures nourish the Galacia cows.

San Simon is lightly pressed, then smoked. It has a supple, open consistency and an attractive, polished rind, which ranges in colour from honey to reddish-brown. The smoke gives the cheese a woody taste to add to the buttery quality and slight acidity from the milk.

ABOVE: *Queso del Montsec – also known as Cendrat*

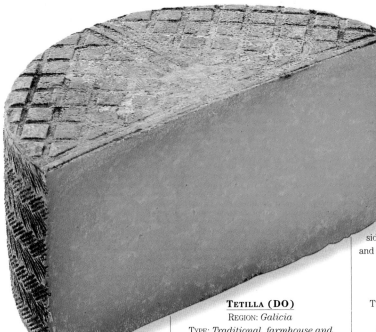

ABOVE: Zamorano

ULLOA
REGION: *Galicia*
TYPE: *Traditional, farmhouse, semi-soft cheese*
SOURCE: *Cow's milk (Galicia and Friesian)*
DESCRIPTION: *1kg/2¹/₄lb round with smooth, waxy, pale yellow, natural rind*
CULINARY USE: *Table cheese*

Ulloa is almost identical to Tetilla, differing only in the shape and the area where it is made. Ulloa is round, with convex sides. It has a fat content of 45 per cent and ripens in about one month.

ZAMORANO (DO)
REGION: *Castile-León*
TYPE: *Traditional, farmhouse and co-operative, hard cheese*
SOURCE: *Sheep's milk (Churro)*
DESCRIPTION: *2 or 3kg/4¹/₂ or 6¹/₂lb drum. The hard, dry, natural rind is covered in a thin, grey mould*
CULINARY USE: *Table cheese*

A hard sheep's milk cheese, Zamorano has something in common with both Castellano and Manchego, but is less grainy. It is matured in conditions of high humidity in order to encourage the growth of the natural, grey mould rind. The flavour has the appealing intensity of burnt caramel and green grass, balanced by the buttery nature of the milk.

Until late this century, Zamoran shepherds and their families were itinerant cheesemakers, trekking from farm to farm with their rennet, hoops, hand-carved wooden boards and curdling vats. The cheeses they made were often matured in the deep, humid, underground "caves" of neighbouring vineyards, which imparted a musty yet fruity character to the cheese and encouraged the growth of a thick, grey mould rind. This practice is frowned upon by modern winemakers.

Zamorano ripens in three to nine months and has a fat content of about 50 per cent.

SIERRA DE ZUHEROS
REGION: *Andalusia*
TYPE: *Traditional, farmhouse and creamery, hard cheese*
SOURCE: *Goat's milk (Murcia)*
DESCRIPTION: *1kg/2¹/₄lb cylinder with smooth, pale yellow, hard rind*
CULINARY USES: *Table cheese, tapas*

Sierra de Zuheros is made from the milk of the Murcia goat on small farms and co-operatives near the old town of Trujillo. Like many Spanish cheeses, it was traditionally moulded in hoops made of plaited (braided) esparto grass. Today, these are slowly being replaced by plastic moulds, which have the distinctive pattern imprinted on the inside. They look rather incongruous hanging up against ancient stone walls.

The cheese is dry, fine and almost crumbly. It has a discernible but not pervasive goaty character, with hints of sweet smoke, wild thyme and lemon zest. The rind of Sierra de Zuheros is sometimes rubbed with paprika and oil, which gives the cheese a spicy finish.

TETILLA (DO)
REGION: *Galicia*
TYPE: *Traditional, farmhouse and creamery, semi-soft cheese*
SOURCE: *Cow's milk*
DESCRIPTION: *750g–1.5kg/1³/₄–3¹/₄lb pear-shaped cheese with pale yellow, ridged rind*
CULINARY USE: *Table cheese*

Tetilla looks like a large, finely ridged fig or breast – hence the name. Made from cow's milk, it has a mellow, fresh, lemony taste with a hint of green grass. The consistency is supple, with a creamy feel on the palate. It ripens in two to three weeks.

TRONCHON
REGION: *Aragon*
TYPE: *Traditional, farmhouse and creamery, semi-soft cheese*
SOURCE: *Sheep's, cow's or goat's milk*
DESCRIPTION: *600g–1.5kg/1¹/₃–3¹/₄lb flattened globe with deep crater. The natural rind is smooth, glossy and the colour of butter*
CULINARY USES: *Table cheese, grilling, snacks*

In terms of texture, Tronchon resembles a young Caerphilly. The taste is aromatic, with a background of white wine acidity. The origin of the shape is obscure, but it is replicated today with special moulds.

PORTUGUESE CHEESES

Unlike Spain, Portugal avoided invasion by the Goths, Vandals and Moors, thanks largely to the Atlantic ocean on one side and the high mountains of the east. This led to the development of a proud, independent race, who to this day value and preserve the old ways.

With a long expanse of coastline, it was inevitable that the Portuguese would become great sailors. In the fifteenth and sixteenth centuries they led the search for new trade routes. The Azores, off the coast of Portugal, were the last port of call for the great explorers on their long journey to the New World. In the fifteenth century, a small settlement was established on the islands. The climate was more temperate than that of the mainland, and a herd of cows was soon established to provide hard, long-lasting cheese, similar to Cheddar, for the seafarers and the islanders. The cheese is known as Queijo da Ilha (island cheese).

The climate on mainland Portugal does not lend itself to cheesemaking and dairy products play a very minor role in the national cuisine. Those cheeses that are made, however, are outstanding: ancient cheeses produced on small farms or dairies in the isolated valleys and mountainsides, where agile, tenacious goats thrive on a diet of wild herbs, scrub, gorse blossoms and brambles. Their milk is thick, luscious and aromatic, and makes superb cheese. The milk from the woolly sheep of the magnificent Serra da Estrela in the centre of Portugal is equally rich and fragrant and shepherds have for centuries used it to make Queijos de Serra. Several similar cheeses, including Queijo Serpa, are made in other areas.

As in other parts of Europe, milk was a precious commodity, and the whey was made into a ricotta-type cheese called Requeijao. Wrapped in fig or cabbage leaves and sold fresh in local markets and small village shops, it is equally useful in desserts or savoury dishes.

During the 1960s and 70s, Portugal underwent rapid social and economic change. The tourist industry boomed and there was a vast migration of people from rural areas to the new coastal developments. This stimulated a need for a more sophisticated dairy industry and large factories were built to bottle fresh milk and produce yogurt and copies of foreign cheeses, such as Camembert, chèvre and Edam.

In the last decade, however, the Portuguese have seen the Spanish revive and revitalize their cheese industry, and have started a drive to do something similar in their own country. 10 Portuguese cheeses recently qualified for Protected Designation of Origin (PDO) and Protected Geographical Indication (PGI) status in Europe (a scheme to recognize and preserve indigenous cheeses, introduced by the European Community and based on the French AOC system). Some, like Queijo Evora, are small discs made with goat's milk; others are made from cow's milk, like Queijo de São Jorge; while others, such as Serra da Estrela, are made with sheep's milk or a blend, like Queijo Rabacal, a fresh cheese.

There is no doubt that, in the next few years, these wonderful Portuguese cheeses will become more readily available outside their country of origin.

SÃO JORGE/ILHA DE SÃO JORGE
REGION: *Azores*
TYPE: *Traditional, farmhouse, unpasteurized, hard cheese*
SOURCE: *Cow's milk*
DESCRIPTION: *8–12kg/18–26lb cylinder. The hard, natural rind is yellowish-brown and slightly mottled*
CULINARY USES: *Table cheese, grating, sauces*

São Jorge is a small island in the Azores. The high plateaux and craters, reminders of the island's violent volcanic past, give way to lush pastures, vibrant local flora and fertile soil.

A Flemish settlement was established on the nearby island of Faial in the fifteenth century. Isolation from the mainland made it necessary for the islanders to become self-sufficient. Cows were brought over and traditional cheesemaking was established both here and on neighbouring islands.

The Azores were the last stop for explorers *en route* to the New World, so the cheeses were much sought after. Like Gouda or Edam, São Jorge improves with age and keeps well, so it continues to prove popular with seafarers like the trans-atlantic yachtsmen who call at the Azores today for provisions. Over the centuries the recipe has been adapted to the local climate and conditions: the result is a unique cheese with the look of Gouda but the savoury tang of Cheddar.

SERRA DA ESTRELA
REGION: *Beira*
TYPE: *Traditional, farmhouse, washed-rind cheese*
SOURCE: *Sheep's milk*
DESCRIPTION: *900g/2lb flat round. The fine, leathery, washed rind is orange-brown and slightly sticky. When aged, it becomes smooth and firm*
CULINARY USE: *Table cheese*

Described as the king of Portuguese cheese, Serra da Estrela has been made for centuries by shepherds in the mountains of Serra da Estrela in the Beira region. Most is still made by small cheesemakers, who used the flowers or leaves of a wild thistle to coagulate the sheep's milk. This gives the cheese a subtle but distinct character, and is a contributing factor in the final texture. The curds are broken by hand rather than cut, and matured in caves for one to four months.

The cheese is so soft and voluptuous that it is almost spreadable. It has a rich, perfumed intensity as a result of the superb grazing, and the sweet, slightly burnt toffee character of the sheep's milk comes through on the finish, which is certainly discernible, but not as strong as you might expect.

When the cheese is allowed to age, the rind toughens and the interior becomes denser and more supple. It can then be sliced with ease.

SWISS CHEESES

Switzerland is a tiny country, whose success is largely due to the commitment of the Swiss to quality, hard work and co-operation. Other nations look with envy at their strong economy, efficiently run cities and excellent road system.

Originally known as Helvetia, Switzerland was home to a Celtic tribe, which in 58BC invaded the southern part of Gaul until the Romans forced them back. From the Romans they learnt the art of cheesemaking.

In the fifth century, Helvetia was invaded by tribes from northern Germany, who ruled the area until three of the cantons (provinces) joined forces in 1291 and defeated their foreign rulers. Eventually other cantons joined the battle and in the fifteenth century independence was won and the foundations for the Swiss Federation were laid.

Today Switzerland is a confederation consisting of 22 cantons, each with its own parliament, courts of law and education system. The people are very much involved in governing their own regions. This ability to work together is seen all over Switzerland, but nowhere is it more effective than in the dairy industry, where most of the cheese is made in mountain chalets or in small co-operatives owned by farmers or cheesemakers.

The primary objective of the Swiss agricultural policy is to uphold this system to ensure that

the large number of meadows and pastures are maintained and the beauty of the countryside remains unchanged. This is essential in a country where tourism is a major source of revenue. With only 25 per cent of the land suitable for grazing, many of the cows, even in summer, are fed indoors so that the grass is not trampled down. Except in the relatively inaccessible mountain pastures, you will seldom see cows grazing in Switzerland; instead farmers cut and gather the fresh grass in a system known as zero grazing.

Early in its history, cheese was used as currency in Switzerland. Much of what was made was taken over the Alps to be exchanged with the Romans for rice, spices and wine.

Cheese is still a vital part of the Swiss economy, and the Swiss guard its quality fiercely. All hard cheeses have to be purchased by the Swiss Cheese Union. The price of the cheese is laid down by the government, as is the price of the milk. Although Swiss cheeses can be extremely expensive, their quality is guaranteed. None of the foreign copies can compare with the originals, which include some of the best-loved cheeses in the world.

BELOW: Tilsiter

ABOVE: Appenzeller

APPENZELLER
REGION: *Appenzell and St Gallen*
TYPE: *Traditional, farmhouse and creamery, unpasteurized, hard cheese*
SOURCE: *Cow's milk*
DESCRIPTION: *5–6.75kg/11–15lb convex wheel. The hard, brushed rind is pale yellow to burnt orange*
CULINARY USES: *Table cheese, melting, grilling*

One of Switzerland's oldest cheeses, Appenzeller dates back to the time of Charlemagne. As the name suggests, it originated in the Appenzell region, but today it is also made in the canton of St Gallen. Its quality and character are protected by rules similar to those operated by the AOC system in France, and it is at its best when made in mountain chalets from the milk of the summer pastures.

The dry, flat, pale yellow to orange rind derives its colour from being washed in a secret concoction of spices, white wine and salt. The aroma hints at spicy, fermenting fruit. If the cheese has been wrapped in plastic, it may sweat and develop a less than appealing, farmyard whiff. The cheese is firm and dense, yet retains a certain suppleness. A few peanut-sized holes are scattered throughout the yellow interior. At first, the taste is buttery, with fruity overtones. As it matures, the flavour becomes fuller and is reminiscent of hot toast and yeast extract. Appenzeller ripens in three to four months, with a fat content of 45 per cent.

BELOW:
Emmental

EMMENTAL
REGION: *Central cantons*
TYPE: *Traditional, farmhouse,*
unpasteurized, hard cheese
SOURCE: *Cow's milk*
DESCRIPTION: *60–130kg/132–286lb*
wheel with convex rim and slightly
concave sides. The thin, hard, natural
rind is a beige-yellow and is covered
by paper identifying the producer
CULINARY USES: *Table cheese,*
grilling, fondue

The history of Emmental can be traced back to 1293, but it was first mentioned by name in 1542, when it was given to the people of Langehthal whose lives had been devastated by fire. It takes its name from the valley of the upper Emme River, but is now made throughout Switzerland, wherever there are high pastures.

Although Emmental resembles Gruyère, the aroma is sweeter, with hushed tones of fresh-cut hay. Squeeze the rind to savour the wine-like aroma. Smoother and more elastic than Gruyère, Emmental has holes the size of hazelnuts or even walnuts. The promise of the aroma is fulfilled in the flavour, which is very fruity, with a mouth-tingling acidity.

FRIBOURGEOIS
REGION: *Fribourg*
TYPE: *Traditional, farmhouse,*
hard cheese
SOURCE: *Cow's milk*
DESCRIPTION: *8kg/18lb wheel. The dry,*
pale beige, natural rind is covered
with a fine, orange,
plastic coat
CULINARY USES: *Table cheese,*
fondues, grilling

Like most traditional Swiss cheeses, Fribourgeois can trace its family history back through the centuries to a significant event. According to local documents, it was served to the wife of Duke Sigismund of Austria in 1448. Firm but breakable, it has a very full-bodied, slightly cloying feel, a delicious, meaty quality and a lingering savoury tang. A traditional, hard, mountain cheese, it resembles a small Gruyère, with a spicy rather than nutty taste that intensifies when the cheese is grilled or melted. It is sometimes referred to as Fribourgeois Vacherin, but should not be confused with the better-known Vacherin Mont d'Or, which is much softer.

Fribourgeois is matured for at least three months.

FROMAGE À RACLETTE
REGION: *Various*
TYPE: *Traditional, farmhouse,*
hard cheese
SOURCE: *Cow's milk*
DESCRIPTION: *8–11kg/18–24lb*
cylindrical wheel. The smooth,
natural rind varies in colour from
pale yellow to orange-brown and can
be dry or slightly sticky and rough
CULINARY USES: *Table cheese, grilling*

Until the nineteenth century, this wonderful melting cheese was known as Valais. It acquired its modern name from the French verb *racler*, meaning "to scrape". The cheese was traditionally cut in half and placed with the cut surface facing the fire. As the cheese started to bubble, it would be scraped on to boiled potatoes to make a delectable treat.

Raclette is very supple. The pale golden interior has a sweet, earthy taste and a pleasant, citrus tang that deepens to a savoury bite. When heated, the cheese bubbles, melts and intensifies in flavour. Also known as Bagnes or Conches, Fromage à Raclette (or simply Raclette) is available in both raw and pasteurized versions, and can be purchased ready-sliced for easy grilling. Some Raclette are made with peppercorns providing a hot, peppery finish to the cheese. It ripens in three to four months and has a fat content of 45 per cent.

ABOVE: Fromage à Raclette – this cheese melts extremely well

Gruyère
REGION: *Gruyère*
TYPE: *Traditional, co-operative and creamery, unpasteurized, hard cheese*
SOURCE: *Cow's milk*
DESCRIPTION: *20–45kg/44–99lb wheel. The natural, rusty brown rind is hard, dry and pitted with tiny holes*
CULINARY USES: *Table cheese, grilling, fondue*

Gruyère is part of the canton of Fribourg and Gruyère cheese has been made here for centuries. In 1115 a quantity of Gruyère was recorded as the tithe paid by local farmers to the monks of Rougement Abbey. Each of the enormous cheeses is made by a group of farmers or by a co-operative, since it takes 400 litres/88 gallons of milk to produce a single 35kg/80lb wheel.

The cheese is a darker yellow than Emmental and has a hint of brown in the colouring. The texture is dense and compact, yet flexible. It is this density that makes it stronger and less stringy than Emmental when heated, so it is better for gratins, grilling and in soups.

When Gruyère is first cut, the aroma suggests a million meadow flowers trapped in rich, creamy milk. Slightly grainy, the cheese has a wonderful complexity of flavours – at first fruity, then revealing more earthy, nutty characteristics that linger on the palate.

Royalp-Tilsiter
REGION: *St Gallen*
TYPE: *Traditional, unpasteurized, hard cheese made in small creameries*
SOURCE: *Cow's milk*
DESCRIPTION: *4kg/9lb wheel with smooth, polished, yellow, natural rind*
CULINARY USES: *Table cheese, melting, grilling, breakfast*

Compared with Switzerland's ancient cheeses, this is a relative newcomer, having been introduced in the latter half of the nineteenth century by a Swiss cheesemaker who had learnt to make Tilsiter while in eastern Prussia after the Franco-Prussian war. The rich, creamy milk of the alpine pastures produced a cheese with a robust smooth texture and small, distinct holes, unlike the original Tilsiter, which had irregular cracks running through it.

Royalp-Tilsiter is smaller than other Swiss cheeses and has a fat content of 45 per cent. It is lightly pressed and ripened for at least two months, but is better after six months. To distinguish it from the other Tilsiter cheese, it is known as Royalp abroad.

BELOW: Royalp-Tilsiter

ABOVE: Gruyère

Saanen
REGION: *Fribourg*
TYPE: *Traditional, farmhouse, hard cheese*
SOURCE: *Cow's milk*
DESCRIPTION: *20–40kg/44–88lb wheel. The natural, very tough rind is brushed and oiled*
CULINARY USE: *Cooking cheese*

Saanen is a very hard, brittle cheese, with a deep yellow interior that is intensely fruity. It resembles Parmesan or Sbrinz and is a good grating cheese that will keep almost indefinitely. Saanen was traditionally reserved for special occasions, when pieces of the cheese would be shaved off and served with a glass of fruity, local wine.

Sapsago
REGION: *Glarus*
TYPE: *Traditional, farmhouse and creamery, hard cheese*
SOURCE: *Cow's milk*
DESCRIPTION: *150g/5oz truncated cone. Pale green and rindless. Sold in foil*
CULINARY USES: *Grating, as a condiment*

Sapsago owes its unusual, pale lime green colour to the addition of fenugreek. Very hard and gritty, it melts like Parmesan when heated. It is astringent, salty, sour – and mouthwatering. The aroma suggests warm cows and farmyards, with exotic, spicy overtones. Not a cheese to be taken lightly. Also known as Schabziger.

SBRINZ
REGION: *Various*
TYPE: *Traditional, farmhouse, hard cheese*
SOURCE: *Cow's milk*
DESCRIPTION: *Flat, cylindrical wheel, 60cm/24in in diameter*
CULINARY USES: *Table cheese, grating*

Sbrinz is thought to be the cheese Pliny the Elder referred to as *Caseus Helveticus* in his writings in the first century AD. The method of production is similar to that for Parmesan and the cheeses share similar traits. Sbrinz has the same fresh, pineapple taste and aroma. It has a lovely fruitiness, against a background of ground nuts, and a deliciously spicy finish. Not as potent as Parmesan, it makes a good and generally significantly cheaper alternative.

Sbrinz is matured for two to three years and has a fat content of 45 per cent.

TÊTE-DE-MOINE
REGION: *Bern*
TYPE: *Traditional, farmhouse and creamery, hard cheese*
SOURCE: *Cow's milk*
DESCRIPTION:
600g–2kg/1¹/₂–4¹/₂lb drum. The hard, ochre to terracotta rind tends to be smelly and sticky
CULINARY USES: *Table cheese, also shaved over salads as a garnish*

It is often thought that the name of this cheese – which translates as "head of the

ABOVE: Tête-de-Moine

monk" – derives from its shape, but there is a rather more prosaic explanation. The cheese was originally called Bellelay, after a monastery in the Jura Mountains. Following the French Revolution it was renamed Tête-de-Moine, after the monks who made it.

Tête-de-Moine has a strong, earthy flavour, like burnt toast with yeast extract. It is usually served in thick strips or ruffles, made by passing it through a special machine called a girolle. The ruffles are used to garnish salads, platters of cooked meats and other dishes.

Tête-de-Moine ripens in three months and has a fat content of 45 per cent.

VACHERIN MONT D'OR
REGION: *Vaud*
TYPE: *Traditional, farmhouse and co-operative, washed-rind cheese*
SOURCE: *Cow's milk*
DESCRIPTION: *500g/1¹/₄lb or 3kg/6¹/₂lb round cheese. The supple, undulating, brownish-pink rind has a dusting of white mould. The cheese is girdled with a band of spruce bark and sold in a pine box*
CULINARY USE: *Table cheese*

During summer, the milk produced by the cows in the upper and lower reaches of the Jura Mountains is used to make Gruyère. When winter sets in, the animals are confined to their warm, cosy barns and fed on hay, and the richer, thicker milk is pasteurized and used to make Vacherin Mont d'Or. The same cheese, produced on the other side of the mountains in France, is simply called Mont d'Or and is made with raw milk.

When ripe, Vacherin Mont d'Or is so smooth and runny it can be eaten with a spoon. The aroma of resin from the bark girdle is absorbed by the cheese, and the taste is reminiscent of the flowers and herbs of the mountain pastures. The cheese ripens in four to six weeks.

If you can afford it, buy a whole Vacherin Mont d'Or. Enjoy the cheese with a bottle of full-bodied, fruity white wine or a smooth Pinot Noir.

ABOVE: Sbrinz can only be made in Switzerland

THE CHEESES OF HOLLAND

More than half the land in Holland is below sea level, and the sea is held back only by the intricate system of dykes and canals that was begun by the Romans. The superb grazing on this reclaimed land, known as the Polders, is the foundation on which the cheeses of Holland were built. Surprisingly, unlike other major cheese-producing countries of Europe, which produce a vast range of different cheeses, Holland concentrates on only two – Edam and Gouda – on which all the other Dutch cheeses are based.

Edam and Gouda played a major role in the economy of Holland in the Middle Ages, when their smooth texture and long-lasting qualities made them highly desirable. In 1621, the founding of the Dutch East India Company gave Holland a powerful trading base, as it held the monopoly on the spices from Indonesia. Cloves, aniseed, cumin and caraway were much sought after, and were soon incorporated into cheeses. Kruidkaas, which includes either caraway or cumin, is still made today, as is Nagelkaas (with cloves) and Leidsekaas (with cumin or aniseed).

By about the middle of the seventeenth century, Edam and Gouda were being exported to virtually every country in Europe. In France in the time of Louis XIV, the passion for Dutch cheese was so great that when the Treasury banned its importation on grounds of cost, the French started developing their own (the forerunner of Mimolette Française).

Artists of the day included cheeses in many masterpieces and it is rumoured that in 1841 the Uruguayan fleet, under American command, defeated the British by substituting Dutch Edams for cannonballs when their supply ran out.

With nearly a third of Holland dedicated to dairy farming, cheese plays a significant role in the economy and over 75 per cent of the annual production is exported. Most cheese is made in highly mechanized factories, a necessary development that has sadly led to a decline in the number of artisan cheesemakers. The few that remain largely make farmhouse Goudas, while some sheep's milk cheeses are produced on the island of Texel and in the province of Friesland, which gave the Friesian cow its name.

Copies of Gouda and Edam are now made all over the world, both in factories and by artisan cheesemakers, often Dutch emigrants seeking a better quality of life and a less regimented environment. To identify authentic Dutch cheeses – and ensure that their quality is maintained – production is governed by strict rules. Each cheese must carry a label that includes detailed information on origin, producer and fat content.

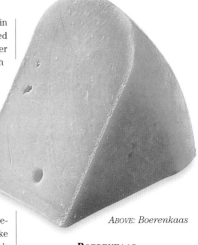

ABOVE: Boerenkaas

BOERENKAAS
REGION: *Various*
TYPE: *Traditional, farmhouse, unpasteurized, semi-hard cheese*
SOURCE: *Cow's milk*
DESCRIPTION: *8–40kg/18–88lb wheel with convex rim and glossy, brushed, natural rind*
CULINARY USES: *Table cheese, often sliced for breakfast; also melted in sandwiches*

Though most of Holland's cheese manufacture is highly mechanized, some farmhouse Gouda is still made by artisan cheesemakers using raw milk. This cheese gets its name – Boerenkaas – from the Dutch words for farmer (*boer*) and cheese (*kaas*). It is quite difficult to obtain in Holland today, due to the decline in the numbers of artisan cheesemakers, which in turn is linked to the scarcity and cost of agricultural land.

Boerenkaas is, however, made in the traditional way. The only modern touch is the porous plastic coating, which is "painted" on to the newly formed cheese to protect it during the months of slow ageing. When young, it is nutty and rich, with a dense, creamy texture and a fragrance reminiscent of meadow pastures and fresh hay. With age, its flavour intensifies, becoming strong and fruity. Tiny calcium crystals, like those in Parmesan, develop in well-aged cheeses.

ABOVE: Maasdam – one of the newer cheeses

BELOW: Gouda (left), and Edam (right), the majority of which is exported, because the Dutch prefer the stronger flavour of Gouda

FRIESEKAAS
REGION: *Various*
TYPE: *Traditional, creamery, semi-hard cheese*
SOURCE: *Cow's milk*
DESCRIPTION: *Large round, at least 10kg/22lb in weight, with waxed, natural rind*
CULINARY USES: *Table cheese, snacks, breakfast, grilling*

A spiced Dutch cheese, this is similar to Leyden, but is flavoured with a combination of cumin and cloves. It ripens in three to 12 months and has a fat content of 40 per cent.

GOUDA
REGION: *Various*
TYPE: *Traditional, creamery, hard cheese*
SOURCE: *Cow's milk*
DESCRIPTION: *5–10kg/11–22lb round with very smooth, yellow, waxed rind. Mature cheeses are hard and slightly granular, with a black wax coating*
CULINARY USES: *Table cheese, snacks, breakfast, grilling*

Gouda accounts for more than 60 per cent of the cheese produced in Holland. An ancient cheese, its history dates from the sixth century, when it was made on small farms around the village of Gouda. It has been exported since the thirteenth century and is now enjoyed worldwide.

Other European countries, notably Sweden, have adopted the Dutch style of cheesemaking, and produce cheeses that are similar to Gouda. Since the last century, Dutch immigrants in America and Australia have been making farmhouse versions by meticulously adhering to the old methods, although regulations prevent many of them from using raw milk.

When only a few months old, Gouda is firm, smooth and supple, with a scattering of small holes. The flavour is sweet and fruity. As time passes, the taste intensifies and becomes more complex. Mature Gouda (18 months plus) is coated in black wax, which provides a stark contrast to the deep yellow interior. At this age, the texture of the cheese is granular, and it can be grated. Gouda has a fat content of 40–45 per cent.

DUTCH MIMOLETTE/ COMMISSIEKAAS
REGION: *Various*
TYPE: *Traditional, farmhouse and creamery, hard cheese*
SOURCE: *Cow's milk*
DESCRIPTION: *3–4.5kg/6–9lb ball. The natural, pitted rind ranges from light brown to deep orange*
CULINARY USES: *Grating, in sauces and pastries, snacks*

Seldom seen outside northern Europe, this magnificent, fruity cheese looks like a giant orange with rough, pitted skin. Known as Commissiekaas in Holland and Dutch Mimolette everywhere else, the cheese is actually a matured Edam coloured with carrot juice.

At around five months Dutch Mimolette is firm, compact and slightly oily, with a fruity aroma and nutty flavour. The best is yet to come, however. When aged, the colour darkens to a deep orange, the texture becomes rock hard, granular and brittle and the flavour is pronounced. It is fruity, with a hint of orange zest (real or imagined). The nutty flavour intensifies to reach a mouth-watering crescendo.

This cheese ripens in six to 12 months and has a fat content of 45 per cent.

EDAM
REGION: *Various*
TYPE: *Traditional, creamery, semi-soft or hard cheese*
SOURCE: *Cow's milk*
DESCRIPTION: *1.5kg/3¼lb ball with barely perceptible rind covered in distinctive, red wax*
CULINARY USES: *Table cheese, popular for breakfast and in sandwiches, also grilled*

Named after the small port of Edam, just north of Amsterdam, this is a pressed, semi-soft or hard cheese in the shape of a ball. The red wax coat, first used in the fourteenth century, makes it a distinctive sight in delicatessens and supermarkets the world over. Most Edam is still produced from skimmed or semi-skimmed milk and has a fat content of between 30 and 40 per cent. Authentic Edam is mostly sold young, when the texture is still supple and elastic, and the flavour is mild, sweet and nutty. Imitations can be bland and rubbery.

A black wax coat indicates an Edam has been aged for at least 17 weeks. Some of the cheese is aged for up to 10 months, when it becomes strong, nutty and excellent for cooking.

LEYDEN/LEIDSEKAAS
REGION: *Leiden*
TYPE: *Traditional, farmhouse, hard cheese*
SOURCE: *Cow's milk*
DESCRIPTION: *3–10kg/6½–22lb boulder-shaped cheese with brushed, natural rind which is either rubbed with annatto or "painted" with red plastic*
CULINARY USES: *Table cheese, grilling*

Made on farms around Leiden, the famous university city, this cheese is similar in texture to Gouda, but because it is made with semi-skimmed milk it feels slightly drier. The curd is coloured with annatto and mixed with cumin seeds before being pressed and washed in brine. The cumin provides an aromatic flavour that contrasts well with the creamy, nutty character of the cheese.

A genuine Leyden will be identified as such by having the imprint of the city's emblem, the famous crossed keys, on the rind. To further distinguish the cheese, the rind is rubbed with annatto until it acquires a shiny reddish-orange colour.

The traditional custom of treading the spices into the curd has, needless to say, been replaced by machine.

Leyden is also called Komijnekaas.

ABOVE: Leyden

BELOW: Leerdammer is one of the best-known brand names for Maasdam

LEERDAMMER
REGION: *Zuid-Holland*
Modern, creamery, semi-hard cheese
SOURCE: *Cow's milk*
DESCRIPTION: *6–12kg/13–26lb boulder-shaped cheese. The smooth, natural rind is polished and may be waxed*
CULINARY USES: *Table cheese, grilling*

Most of the large cheesemaking factories in Holland have begun to produce their own branded versions of Maasdam. Leerdammer is one of the better-known, along with Ronduer, Goyweter and Fricotal.

MAASDAM
REGION: *Various*
TYPE: *Modern, creamery, semi-hard cheese*
SOURCE: *Cow's milk*
DESCRIPTION: *6–12kg/13–26lb boulder-shaped cheese. The smooth, natural rind is polished and may be waxed*
CULINARY USES: *Table cheese, grilling*

Created in the early 1990s as an alternative to the more expensive Swiss cheese Emmental, Maasdam has attracted a large following. The market continues to increase, and it is already being copied in other countries.

Although there are similarities with Emmental, it is higher in moisture and therefore more supple. It ripens faster than other Dutch cheeses, being ready in four to 12 weeks. The flavour is sweet and buttery, with a fruity background, making it ideal for serving as a snack or breakfast cheese. It can also be grilled.

GERMAN CHEESES

The Germanic tribes, originally from Scandinavia and the Baltic, gradually expanded east of the Rhine and by 200BC were beginning to invade the Roman Empire. It was not, however, until the arrival of the Franks and the rule of Charlemagne that the cheeses of Germany began to emerge. Charlemagne's love of food is legendary, a fact that helped to shape German cuisine, which has a reputation for being both hearty and substantial.

Germany's dairy industry is huge, now rated fourth or fifth in the world, yet surprisingly its cheeses are far less well known beyond its borders than are its sausages, beers and breads. One of the main reasons for this is that many of the cheeses are either processed varieties, or copies of other European cheeses.

Quark is the notable exception. Now found all over Europe, it is a fresh curd cheese with a sharp, yogurt-like taste. Thought to have originated in the Iron Age, it led to the development of other types of *Sauermilchkäse* (sour milk cheese), which are often very pungent.

Limburger, adopted by the Germans from Belgium, is a Trappist-style cheese, as is Münster. Both have a strong, robust flavour that appeals to the German love of rich, spicy food.

As in Switzerland, the quality of German cheeses is very strictly controlled. Labelling must be precise, which is helpful for the informed local consumer, but not necessarily for the visitor.

ALLGÄUER EMMENTALER

REGION: *Bavaria*
TYPE: *Traditional, creamery and co-operative, hard cheese*
SOURCE: *Cow's milk*
DESCRIPTION: *40–90kg/88–198lb wheel with smooth, waxed, natural rind*
CULINARY USES: *Grilling, melting, snacks, breakfast*

The mountain pastures of Allgäu in southern Bavaria resemble those of their Swiss neighbours, and the cattle are similar, so it is not altogether surprising that the Bavarians produce a cheese that has much in common with that made on the other side of the mountains. Allgäuer Emmentaler is a sweet, fruity cheese, with holes the size of walnuts. It is less expensive than the Swiss original.

Since the end of the last century, when the makers of Allgäuer Emmentaler adopted the same stringent standards of quality maintained by the Swiss, it has been hard to tell the two cheeses apart, although lovers of Swiss Emmental would claim that their cheese has the edge in terms of flavour.

Determined to maintain their unique identity, the Swiss ensure that the rinds on their exported cheeses are completely covered with the words "Switzerland" and "Emmental", leaving the consumer in no doubt about where the cheese is made.

BAVARIAN BERGKÄSE

REGION: *Bavaria*
TYPE: *Traditional, farmhouse and creamery, unpasteurized, hard cheese*
SOURCE: *Cow's milk*
DESCRIPTION: *20–50kg/44–110lb wheel with natural rind, similar to but darker than Emmental*
CULINARY USES: *Table cheese, grilling, melting*

Bergkäse simply means "mountain cheese" and is a smaller version of the popular Allgäuer Emmentaler. Firm but supple, and almost chewy, Bergkäse is a superb melting cheese. More aromatic than Emmental but still fruity, Bergkäse is made only in the summer months from the milk of cows grazing the mountain pastures, which explains why it is also known as Alpenkäse.

Control is less strict than for the Allgäuer Emmentaler and quality can vary from maker to maker, but it is nonetheless a good buy.

Bergkäse ripens in three to nine months and has a fat content of 45 per cent.

BRUDER BASIL

REGION: *Bavaria*
TYPE: *Modern, creamery, semi-soft cheese*
SOURCE: *Cow's milk*
DESCRIPTION: *1kg/2¼lb flattened brick with convex sides. The natural rind is dark mahogany in colour and is waxed*
CULINARY USES: *Grilling; also used in snacks and sandwiches, often served with beer*

This is a traditionally made version of the Bavarian smoked cheese (Rauchkäse) found almost everywhere. The smooth, firm, yellow cheese has small holes. The taste is creamy and pleasantly smoky, but can be rather "plastic".

Bruder Basil ripens in one month and has a fat content of about 45 per cent. A version flavoured with chopped ham is also available.

RIGHT: Bruder Basil

ABOVE: Cambozola, which as the name implies, is based on Camembert and Gorgonzola, appeals to those who find other blue cheeses too ferocious. Bavarian Blue and Blue Brie are similar cheeses

BUTTERKÄSE

REGION: *Various*
TYPE: *Traditional, creamery, semi-soft cheese*
SOURCE: *Cow's milk*
DESCRIPTION: *1–4kg/2 1/4–9lb rectangular loaf or wheel with golden to red, natural rind*
CULINARY USES: *Snacks, breakfast*

Made in both Germany and Austria, this cheese lives up to its name and has a buttery taste and colour. Very supple, but odourless and rather bland, it needs pickles and beer to give it life.

Also called Damenkäse (ladies' cheese), Butterkäse ripens in one month and has a fat content of 50 per cent.

CAMBOZOLA

REGION: *Various*
TYPE: *Modern, creamery, blue cheese*
SOURCE: *Cow's milk*
DESCRIPTION: *2kg/4 1/2lb flat round with penicillium rind*
CULINARY USES: *Table cheese, snacks*

Cambozola is a modern success story. Since its creation in the 1970s, others have tried to copy it, but few have achieved the consistency of quality and texture, which are responsible for Cambozola's success. The smooth, rich texture is achieved by adding cream to the milk, and the taste is mildly spicy and slightly sweet-sour.

LIMBURGER

REGION: *Various*
TYPE: *Traditional, creamery, washed-rind cheese*
SOURCE: *Cow's milk*
DESCRIPTION: *200–675g/7oz–1 1/2lb brick. The smooth, sticky, washed rind is reddish-brown, with corrugated ridges*
CULINARY USES: *Table cheese, grilling, melting over potatoes*

The aroma is unmistakable – powerful, outspoken and impossible to ignore. The yellow interior hints at sweetness, but the overwhelming taste is spicy and aromatic, almost meaty. Despite its robust nature, Limburger has its limits and passes these if it is allowed to become runny, with a slimy rind. It is best when the texture is firm, yet yielding.

Limburger undoubtedly originated with the cheese-loving Trappist monks in Belgium, but was hijacked by German cheesemakers in the nineteenth century. It is now so popular that most Germans and even some Belgians believe it to be a German cheese.

The cheese ripens in six to 12 weeks and has a fat content that fluctuates between 20 and 50 per cent. A milder version is popular in the United States, having been introduced by German immigrants.

LEFT: Limburger has an unmistakable odour

AUSTRIAN CHEESES

BERGKÄSE

REGION: *Voralberg Massif*
TYPE: *Traditional, creamery, unpasteurized, hard cheese*
SOURCE: *Cow's milk*
DESCRIPTION: *6–30kg/13–65lb wheel with smooth, dark yellow, natural rind*
CULINARY USES: *Table cheese, melting, grilling, fondue*

Closely resembling the Bavarian Bergkäse, this has a creamy, fudge-like flavour with a hint of hazelnuts. The holes in the paste are smaller than those in the German cheese and the cheese is matured for six months or longer.

KUGELKÄSE

REGION: *Danube*
TYPE: *Traditional, creamery, fresh cheese*
SOURCE: *Cow's milk*
DESCRIPTION: *Speckled, white balls in various sizes*
CULINARY USES: *Added to local dishes; also served solo, with beer*

This is a simple local speciality. Once the fresh curd has formed – and while it is still warm – pepper, caraway seeds and paprika are added so that the curd becomes infused with their aroma and character. The cheese is then rolled into balls, which are salted and dried for weeks or even months.

MONDSEER

REGION: *Salzburg*
TYPE: *Traditional, creamery, semi-soft cheese*
SOURCE: *Cow's milk*
DESCRIPTION: *500g–1kg/1¼–2¼lb round. The soft, washed rind is deep orange, dusted with powdery, white mould*
CULINARY USES: *Grilling, snacks*

Firm yet moist, Mondseer is open-textured with a few irregular eyes. It has a slightly spicy aroma and a sweet-sour taste. Although it is related to other washed-rind cheeses, it tends to be milder and less pungent.

Mondseer ripens in about two to three months and has a fat content of 45 per cent.

MÜNSTER

REGION: *Schwarzwald*
TYPE: *Traditional, creamery, washed-rind cheese*
SOURCE: *Cow's milk*
DESCRIPTION: *125–500g/4½oz–1¼lb round cheese with sticky, orange, washed skin*
CULINARY USE: *Table cheese*

Münster is a smooth, fairly soft, yellow cheese with a thin, orange skin and a mildly piquant flavour that can become quite pungent with regular washings. In the Middle Ages the cheese was made by the monks at Munster Abbey in modern-day Alsace. When Alsace became part of Germany, the name of the cheese gained an umlaut, and it became Münster, after the Westphalian town. Ownership of Alsace switched from Germany to France several times after that, but the cheese continued to be made on both sides of the border. Today, it is also produced in the USA, where it is known as Muenster.

QUARK

REGION: *Various*
TYPE: *Traditional, creamery, vegetarian, fresh cheese*
SOURCE: *Cow's milk*
DESCRIPTION: *Moist, white cheese sold in pots*
CULINARY USES: *Cooking, spreading, in dips and cheesecakes, with fruit for breakfast*

Quark simply means "curd" in German, and the cheese is said to date from the Iron Age, when nomadic tribes discovered the means of fermenting milk without the use of rennet.

Quark can be made from whole, skimmed or semi-skimmed milk or even buttermilk. Soft and moist, like a cross between yogurt and fromage frais, it should taste lemon-fresh. Some versions have skimmed milk powder added and can be rather gritty. Quark ripens within a few days.

RIGHT: Quark

ROMADUR/ROMADURKÄSE

REGION: *Various*
TYPE: *Traditional, creamery, washed-rind cheese*
SOURCE: *Cow's milk*
DESCRIPTION: *200–500g/7oz–1¼lb rectangular loaf with yellowish-orange, washed rind*
CULINARY USE: *Table cheese*

Similar to Limburger, but milder and smaller, Romadur has a sweet-sour flavour with a hint of smoke. It can be made with whole or semi-skimmed milk and has a fat content between 20 and 60 per cent.

TILSIT

REGION: *Various*
TYPE: *Traditional, co-operative or creamery, semi-hard cheese*
SOURCE: *Cow's milk*
DESCRIPTION: *4.5kg/10lb wheel. The thin, dry, yellow-beige crust has some moulds*
CULINARY USES: *Table cheese, grilling, snacks*

The original Tilsit was apparently discovered accidentally by Dutch cheese-makers living in Tilsit, which was then in East Prussia. At the time, they were trying to make their beloved Gouda, but various factors combined to create a cheese that was markedly different, especially in relation to the rind.

The cheese is washed and brushed regularly for the first two months so that the crusty rind forms. This protects the smooth, supple interior, with its tiny, irregular holes, from drying out. The aroma is mildly pungent, while the taste is buttery and fruity, with a spicy tinge.

BELGIAN CHEESES

Belgium's cheeses are virtually unknown outside her borders, being overshadowed by those of her famous neighbour, France, yet the country produces over 250 varieties of cheese.

There is evidence that the Belgae, a Celtic people, had some knowledge of basic cheesemaking, and although the Romans introduced more sophisticated techniques, it was the Franks who were to have the most influence on cheesemaking in Belgium. Between AD771 and 800, their king, Charlemagne, developed an extensive empire, and encouraged the building of over 50 abbeys. The monks not only set about spreading the word of God, but also worked with the people to improve their herds and their cheesemaking skills.

The records kept by Charlemagne provide us with an insight into his world. At Aachen, his seat of power, cellars were dug to store and ripen his cheeses. As Charlemagne's empire faded, the country split into independent duchies and trade brought wealth and prosperity. Despite being governed in turn by the Austrians, Spanish and Dutch, Belgium emerged in 1831 as an independent kingdom, with its own culture and cuisine.

Respect for the past, and a determination not to allow the older varieties of cheese to become extinct, led several

LEFT: *Herve is Belgium's most famous cheese*

cheesemakers in 1960 to embark on a campaign to rediscover old recipes. Their research, in monasteries, farms and libraries, has revitalized the industry, creating a new identity for Belgian cheese, based on its rich and varied history.

Regrettably, the majority of cheeses produced in Belgium today are factory-made copies of traditional Belgian and other European cheeses, but those described here can be found and savoured in the many elegant restaurants and cafés for which Belgium is famous.

BEAUVOORDE

REGION: *Various*
TYPE: *Traditional, creamery, semi-hard cheese*
SOURCE: *Cow's milk*
DESCRIPTION: *3kg/6¹/₂lb or 6kg/13lb hexagonal cheese with grey, natural rind*
CULINARY USES: *Table cheese, also used in snacks and sandwiches*
Beauvoorde cheese was created in the early 1900s by Arthur Djes, innkeeper of Beauvoorde village. His family continued to make the cheese until the Second World War forced them to abandon production. Recently revived, it is now made in creameries. Firm yet supple and open-textured, Beauvoorde has a mild flavour and a spicy aroma.

BRUSSELSE KAAS/FROMAGE DE BRUXELLES

REGION: *Brabant*
TYPE: *Traditional, creamery, washed-rind cheese*
SOURCE: *Cow's milk*
DESCRIPTION: *150g/5oz flattened rounds, sold in tubs*
CULINARY USES: *Spreading, snacks*
Made with skimmed milk, Brusselse Kaas is smooth, sharp and citric, with a bite that is surprisingly strong and salty. This is the result of the cheese having been regularly washed and dried over a period of at least three months. It is shaped into rough rounds and packed in tubs.

HERVE

REGION: *Liège*
TYPE: *Traditional, farmhouse and creamery, washed-rind cheese*
SOURCE: *Cow's milk*
DESCRIPTION: *200g/7oz brick with glossy, orange-brown rind*
CULINARY USES: *Table cheese, snacks*
Belgium's most famous cheese, Herve, has an autumn-coloured crust that is pungent and yeasty. Beneath it, the supple, tender interior ranges from sweet to powerful and spicy, depending on how long the cheese has been ripening. Small quantities of unpasteurized cheese are still made, and there is a double-cream version.

BELOW: *Beauvoorde*

MAREDSOUS
REGION: *Various*
TYPE: *Traditional, farmhouse and creamery, washed-rind cheese*
SOURCE: *Cow's milk*
DESCRIPTION: *1kg/2¼lb or 2.5kg/5½lb loaf-shaped cheese. The firm, orange, washed rind sometimes has a fine dusting of white mould*
CULINARY USES: *Table cheese, grilling*

This is another of Belgium's Trappist-style cheeses and is made by the monks at Maredsous Abbey. It is lightly pressed, then washed in brine to create the firm, orange crust and pungent aroma. The supple, smooth interior is pale yellow with a slightly smoky tinge. Not as aggressive as Herve, it has perhaps more in common with France's Saint-Paulin.

PASSENDALE
REGION: *Flanders*
TYPE: *Modern, creamery, semi-soft cheese*
SOURCE: *Cow's milk*
DESCRIPTION: *3kg/6½lb round, shaped like a country loaf and with a dusting of fine, white mould that resembles flour*
CULINARY USES: *Table cheese, grilling, snacks, breakfast*

With its warm, brown crust lightly dusted with white mould, this looks like a loaf of country bread. A modern cheese, based on an old monastic recipe, it is firm, with small holes. The flavour is mild and creamy. The cheese takes its name from the Flemish village of Passchendaele, where thousands of British soldiers lost their lives in the First World War.

PLATEAU DE HERVE
REGION: *Herve*
TYPE: *Traditional, creamery, washed-rind cheese*
SOURCE: *Cow's milk*
DESCRIPTION: *1.5kg/3¼lb dome with sticky, orange, washed rind wrapped in foil*
CULINARY USES: *Table cheese, snacks*

This lightly pressed cheese has a pale yellow interior with a creamy consistency. Washed regularly in brine, it has the flavour without the pervasive aroma of Herve. It ripens in two to three months.

POSTEL
REGION: *Various*
TYPE: *Traditional, farmhouse, washed-rind cheese*
SOURCE: *Cow's milk*
DESCRIPTION: *4kg/9lb rectangular cheese with orange, washed rind*
CULINARY USE: *Table cheese*

The monks at the Abbey of Postel resumed making this classic Trappist cheese in the 1960s, using the milk from their herd of 160 cows. Volume is small, but those who have discovered this cheese willingly travel to the abbey to buy it.

PRINC'JEAN
REGION: *Various*
TYPE: *Modern, creamery, fresh cheese*
SOURCE: *Cow's milk*
DESCRIPTION: *150g/5oz rindless round*
CULINARY USE: *Table cheese*

This triple cream cheese has a wonderfully rich texture. There is a peppercorn version as well as a softer type, which has a white rind and creamy flavour. The cheese is packed into small, wooden crates for sale.

LEFT: *Maredsous*

REMEDOU
REGION: *Liège*
TYPE: *Traditional, farmhouse and creamery, washed-rind cheese*
SOURCE: *Cow's milk*
DESCRIPTION: *200–675g/7oz–1½lb square with shiny, moist, red-brown, washed rind*
CULINARY USE: *Table cheese*

Also known as Piquant, which is something of an understatement, this is a larger and particularly aggressive version of Herve. Its size means that it takes longer to ripen, which gives the surface bacteria time to exude the powerful aroma for which the cheese is famous. It is known locally as "stinking cheese" and is best eaten in the open air with a glass of robust, red wine or local beer.

The name of the cheese is said to come from *remoud*, which was an old Walloon word for the rich milk produced towards the end of a cow's lactation period.

ABOVE: *Rubens*

RUBENS
REGION: *Lo*
TYPE: *Traditional, farmhouse and creamery, semi-soft cheese*
SOURCE: *Cow's milk*
DESCRIPTION: *3kg/6½lb oval with firm, smooth, red-brown, washed rind*
CULINARY USE: *Table cheese*

A chubby, wholesome-looking cheese with a rich, smooth, subtle taste, Rubens is covered with a smooth, reddish-brown, protective coat. One of many old Belgian cheeses revived in the 1960s, it carries a label bearing a portrait of the Flemish painter after whom it is named.

DANISH CHEESES

Denmark's maritime climate and flat meadowlands make it an ideal environment for the comfort-loving cow that becomes a familiar sight as you travel through the picturesque countryside.

Thanks to its geographical position and its Viking past, Denmark has always been a trading nation. The cheese industry was originally based upon varieties made in neighbouring Germany and Holland – cheeses like Gouda, valued for the way it withstood the rigours of sea travel, and Limburger. There are few original Danish cheeses: most are highly efficient copies, many of which now carry Danish names as a result of the Stresa Convention of 1951.

The classic example of Danish cheese is Samso, which was developed in the nineteenth century along the lines of a Swiss-style cheese. Outside Denmark, its best-known cheese is, however, Danish Blue (Danablu), which is based on the French blues.

Danish Feta, a popular cheese that is even exported to the Middle East, was recently at the centre of a controversy over the name. A fierce battle is now brewing between Greece and the European Parliament as to whether Greece should be allowed sole rights to use the name feta for its own cheese.

Over 60 per cent of all cheese made in Denmark is exported, and its Ministry of Agriculture is fiercely protective of the industry. It demands very high standards and has banned the production of raw milk cheeses. Although the cow is by far the most important dairy animal, some goat's milk cheese is made, but mainly for home consumption.

BLA CASTELLO/BLUE CASTELLO
REGION: *Various*
TYPE: *Modern, creamery, blue cheese*
SOURCE: *Cow's milk*
DESCRIPTION: *150g/5oz and 1kg/2¼lb half-moon-shaped cheese. The moist, natural rind may develop some grey, brown or white moulds*
CULINARY USE: *Table cheese*

Developed in the 1960s to meet the growing demand for mild, creamy blues, Bla Castello has a Brie-like texture, with the the blue in fairly thick, horizontal lines. Enriched with cream, it has a fat content of 70 per cent. The aroma is of mushrooms and the taste is mildly spicy. A popular cheese, but one which some regard as rather bland.

DANABLU/DANISH BLUE
REGION: *Various*
TYPE: *Modern, creamery, blue cheese*
Source: *Cow's milk*
DESCRIPTION: *3kg/6½lb drum or block. The sticky, yellow, natural rind has some brownish-grey or blue moulds*
CULINARY USES: *Table cheese, snacks, also crumbled in salads*

This cheese was invented in the early twentieth century by Marius Boel as an alternative to Roquefort, although the two cheeses are very different. It is now known throughout the western world and sales show no signs of abating. The name Danablu is protected by the Stresa Convention; Danish Blue, however, is not.

The appeal of the cheese lies in its sharp, almost metallic taste, salty bite and creamy feel in the mouth. The interior is very white and makes an attractive contrast to the blue-black mould, which is rather gritty and salty (additional salt is added to some exported cheeses).

Danablu ripens in two to three months and has a fat content of 50–60 per cent. It is also known as Marmora.

LEFT: Danish Blue (top) and Mycella

RIGHT: *Kefalotiri is made from sheep's milk*

KASERI

REGION: *Various*

TYPE: *Traditional, farmhouse and co-operative, unpasteurized, stretched curd cheese*

SOURCE: *Sheep's and goat's milk*

DESCRIPTION: *1–9kg/2¼–20lb wheel. There is no rind, but the white crust is smooth, creamy and springy*

CULINARY USES: *Table cheese, melting, grilling, baking (in pastries)*

Kaseri must be at least 80 per cent sheep's milk, with the remainder goat's milk. It is a young version of Kefalotiri, which has been immersed in hot brine to create the characteristic, rubbery, stringy texture. As such it resembles the Italian Provolone Dolce, but has a much stronger flavour. Quite salty and pungent, with a dry feel in the mouth, it has an underlying sweetness due to the sheep's milk. Kaseri is used in Greece in place of mozzarella and appears in numerous local dishes.

KEFALOTIRI/KEFALOTYRI

REGION: *Various*

TYPE: *Traditional, farmhouse and co-operative, unpasteurized, hard cheese*

SOURCE: *Sheep's milk*

DESCRIPTION: *6–8kg/13–18lb drum with thin, hard, natural rind ranging in colour from white to rich yellow*

CULINARY USES: *Breakfast cheese, grating, baking, snacks*

Kefalotiri was already well known and respected by the time of the Byzantine era. It is said to take its name from *kefalo*, a Greek hat. Historically, it was the first cheese to be made at the start of the new season. As soon as the young lambs were weaned, the sheep's milk was used to make this popular cheese. The colour varies from white to yellow, depending on the mix of milk and the grazing, and the firm, dry cheese has numerous irregular holes. The flavour is pleasantly fresh, with a distinct taste of sheep's milk and a slightly sharp finish, not unlike a very fruity, herbaceous olive oil.

Kefalotiri is described as a "male" or "first" cheese to indicate that it is made with full-cream milk; the more delicate whey cheeses (like Manouri, Myzithra or Anthotiro) are called "female" or "second" cheeses. The cheese ripens in two or three months and has a fat content of 40–55 per cent.

MANOURI

REGION: *Crete and Macedonia*

TYPE: *Traditional, farmhouse, unpasteurized, whey cheese*

SOURCE: *Sheep's or goat's milk*

DESCRIPTION: *Made in various sizes, in shapes ranging from large, tapered logs to truncated cones, this smooth, white cheese has no rind*

CULINARY USES: *Mainly used in pastries such as spanakopita or drizzled with honey and served for breakfast as a low-fat alternative to Greek yogurt*

An ancient cheese, made from the whey from feta or Kefalotiri, Manouri is creamy and white, with the texture of a light cheesecake. It melts in the mouth and has a fresh, milky, slightly citrus flavour. Firmer than Myzithra, it is also known as Manoypi.

MYZITHRA/MITZITHRA

REGION: *Various*

TYPE: *Traditional, farmhouse and co-operative, unpasteurized, whey cheese*

SOURCE: *Sheep's milk*

DESCRIPTION: *Rindless rounds of various sizes, showing the imprint of the cloth in which they were drained.*

CULINARY USES: *Baked in light pastries or with vegetables. Also eaten fresh*

Myzithra is a mild, refreshing cheese with a fine, crumbly texture. It was originally made with the whey from Kefalotiri or feta, to which some milk or cream was added. It can be eaten after a few days or ripened for several months. Where milk is abundant, Myzithra may be preserved in salt and dried as a firm, grating cheese. A sour form is sold as Xinomyzithira.

XYNOTYRO

REGION: *Various*

TYPE: *Traditional, farmhouse, unpasteurized, whey cheese*

SOURCE: *Sheep's and goat's milk cheese*

DESCRIPTION: *Made in various shapes and sizes and marked by the reed baskets in which they are drained, these cheeses do not have any rind*

CULINARY USES: *Baking, salads*

The name means "sour cheese", which is a rather inadequate description for a hard, flaky cheese that melts in the mouth to leave a distinct, sweet-sour sensation on the palate. The flavour of Xynotyro is a combination of sweet, burnt caramel, lanolin (typical of sheep's milk cheeses) and the sour taste of the whey. It ripens in a few days and has a fat content of 20 per cent.

LEFT: *Kaseri has a similar texture to Italian Provolone Dolce*

TURKISH CHEESES

The forefathers of the modern Turks migrated from Central Asia and arrived in Anatolia in the tenth century. Like many nomadic tribes, they travelled with the sheep on which they depended for their survival, and which provided them with wool for their clothing and rugs, meat and – most important – fresh milk for both their yogurt (*sivi tas*) and cheese (*peynir*).

In parts of Turkey, shepherds still wander the hills with their flocks and cheeses are still made from recipes handed down over many years from one generation to the next. Milking is done in ancient, stone enclosures, and cheeses can still be seen hanging over open fires, or draining in bags made from goat skins slung under the branches of trees.

In local markets, you may encounter the soft, white, sheep's milk feta (Beyaz Peynir) alongside Gravyer Peynir (Turkish Gruyère) and rustic cheeses, but the majority of cheese is now made in factories, from cow's, goat's or sheep's milk.

Other cheeses you may come across as you travel through this fascinating country include Taze Kaser (fresh cheese), which, despite its name, is a hard cheese, mainly used as a filling for the delicious Turkish-style toasted sandwiches. Another favourite is Eski Kaser (old cheese), which is rather like a Pecorino, though less salty. Firm, dry and white, it becomes softer and a turns a deep yellow with age. Eski Kaser is often served with honey for breakfast. Alternatively, it can be cut into blocks and preserved in brine.

Made from sheep's milk, Kasar Peynir is a hard, tangy cheese that is pale lemon in colour; Los Peynir is a light, creamy whey cheese, which resembles yogurt; Tulum is a cheese that is made and stored in the stomach or skin of a goat; Mihalic Peynir is a rich, unsalted sheep's milk cheese and Dil Peynir is a mild, stretched-curd cheese.

LEFT: Beyaz Peynir

One of the simplest cheeses, Koy Peynir, is made in village homes throughout Anatolia. Milk is warmed to blood heat, salt and rennet are stirred in, and the mixture is then pulled off the heat, covered and left overnight. Next morning, the coagulated milk is tipped into a cloth-lined sieve and left for six hours to drain. The cheese that remains in the sieve should be soft and creamy. It is either eaten as it is or used in cooking.

BEYAZ PEYNIR
REGION: *Various*
TYPE: *Traditional, farmhouse and co-operative, unpasteurized, vegetarian, fresh cheese*
SOURCE: *Sheep's milk*
DESCRIPTION: *Pure white and rindless, the cheese has a grainy appearance. It is usually sold in blocks or slices*
CULINARY USES: *Fresh in salads, cooked in pastries and many local dishes*
The most popular Turkish cheese, Beyaz Peynir is made in factories and co-operatives and by shepherds. Vegetable rennet is used to clot the milk. The curds are pressed for a few hours, then roughly chopped and strained, sometimes in attractive wooden or woven moulds. After draining, the cheese is cut into slices before being salted and covered with brine. Beyaz Peynir is usually stored in brine for more than six months. It resembles feta and has a fat content of about 45 per cent. It is usually soaked in cold water or milk before use, to remove the excess salt.

MIHALIC PEYNIR
REGION: *Bursa*
TYPE: *Traditional, farmhouse, unpasteurized, vegetarian, hard cheese*
SOURCE: *Sheep's milk*
DESCRIPTION: *Made in various sizes and shapes – often as balls or slices – the cheese is smooth and white with no rind*
CULINARY USES: *Fresh in salads, also used in baked dishes*
The fresh curd is divided into small portions, which are placed in hot water, which is then stirred. The curds are left in the water to harden and acquire a firm, slightly elastic texture, then they are tied in a cloth, which is twisted to force out the whey. Finally, the curds are rolled into small balls, or shaped and sliced, then salted and dried. Mihalic Peynir is stored in brine to preserve and protect the cheese until it is needed. It often goes by the name of the village where it is made.

THE CHEESES OF CYPRUS

Traces of civilization dating back to the fifteenth century BC have been discovered in Cyprus. The modern city of Larnaca was once the centre of the Phoenician civilization and the island was for centuries an important trading post for the Aegean sea and the eastern Mediterranean. The discovery of rich copper deposits in the third century BC brought considerable wealth to the country and attracted often uninvited attention from a succession of invaders, including the Romans, the Byzantines and the Ottoman Turks.

Through all the centuries of conflict, the shepherds in the rugged interior continued to herd their goats and sheep, making cheese in the same way as their fathers and forefathers had before them. Feta, Kaskavali, which is similar to the Bulgarian Katschkawalj or the Italian Caciocavallo, and Halloumi are the most common varieties. Despite the on-going battle between the Greek and Turkish communities, Cyprus is an increasingly popular holiday destination.

HALLOUMI
REGION: *Various*
TYPE: *Traditional, farmhouse and creamery, stretched curd cheese*
SOURCE: *Sheep's, cow's or goat's milk*
DESCRIPTION: *Small, rectangular block or loaf shapes in various different sizes. The cheese is shiny, white and smooth, without rind*
Culinary uses: *Frying, grilling, barbecuing*

Originally a sheep's or goat's milk cheese, Halloumi is now more often produced from cow's milk. The curd is heated in hot water, then kneaded. Chopped mint is usually added and the elastic, squeaky curd is rolled out like pastry and cut into small blocks. These are stored in light brine until needed.

Halloumi has a fibrous, rubbery texture and its otherwise bland, milky taste is heightened by the herby flavour of the chopped fresh mint and the salt from the brine. Denser than mozzarella, it is fundamentally a cooking cheese, whose true character is only revealed when it is heated. Halloumi is one of the few cheeses that will hold its shape when it is fried or grilled. If thin slices of the cheese are placed in a hot, non-stick pan, the outside will rapidly become crisp and slightly charred, while the centre melts deliciously, rather like mozzarella.

In recent years Halloumi has become more popular, particularly amongst the young chefs of Australia, New Zealand and the West Coast of America. To respond to their demands, this traditional Cypriot cheese has begun to be made by cheesemakers in Australia where it is called Halloumy, and by Pelusso Cheese in California who call their version Haloumi.

Halloumi is also made in Romania and the Lebanon.

LEFT: Halloumi is a cooking cheese similar to mozzarella

EASTERN EUROPEAN CHEESES

Eastern Europe has been in turmoil since AD552, when the original settlers, the Slavs, were forced from what is now the Ukraine, by the tribesman of the Russian Steppes. The Slavs crossed into Romania and Bulgaria during the sixth century BC taking with them their knowledge of farming and how to preserve milk in the form of yogurt and Sirene (a cheese similar to feta). Later, Roman occupation lead to the introduction of the style of cheese preferred by the Roman forces, although the only obvious survivors today are Katschkawalj and Halloumi.

Hungary, too, has few indigenous cheeses, although Turkish invaders introduced Brynza, a soft feta-like sheep's milk cheese. In Poland in the tenth century BC Polish cheesemakers began producing and exporting copies of European cheeses. Tylzscki, based on Tilsit, is one of the few that is still made.

By the end of the Second World War artisan cheesemaking had all but died out and throughout Eastern Europe, huge factories were constructed to produce bland, industrial copies of European cheeses like Gouda, Cheddar, Camembert. Emmental, Tilsit and Limburger. However, in the late 1980s small cheese production began to flourish and artisan cheeses began to be made again.

ABERTAM
COUNTRY: *Czech Republic*
TYPE: *Traditional, farmhouse and co-operative, hard cheese*
SOURCE: *Sheep's milk*
DESCRIPTION: *500g/1¼lb irregular ball with thin, yellow to orange, natural rind*
CULINARY USES: *Table cheese, melting, grilling*

Abertam is made in Karlovy-Vary (formerly Carlsbad), the famous spa town. The natural pastures of this mountainous part of Bohemia provide the native sheep with a rich diet that is revealed in the robust flavour of the hard, pressed cheese. Abertam ripens in two months and has a fat content of 45 per cent.

BALATON
COUNTRY: *Hungary*
TYPE: *Traditional, farmhouse and creamery, hard cheese*
SOURCE: *Cow's milk*
DESCRIPTION: *9–12kg/20–26lb loaf shape with thin, greasy, natural rind*
CULINARY USES: *Table cheese, grilling*

Named after the beautiful Lake Balaton, this Hungarian cheese has a firm, compact texture with a scattering of small holes. The flavour is mild, with a pleasant acidity.

BRINZA/BURDUF BRINZA
COUNTRY: *Romania*
TYPE: *Traditional, farmhouse and co-operative, fresh cheese*
SOURCE: *Sheep's milk*
DESCRIPTION: *White, slightly grainy cheese made in blocks*
CULINARY USES: *Cooking cheese*

Brinza is the local name for cheese in the Carpathian region. Its origins go back to Roman times and beyond, and similar cheeses have been made for centuries. It is mild, moist, creamy and crumbly. Usually eaten within a day or two of being made, it has a delicate, sweet, aromatic character. Some of it is also preserved in salt for use during winter, when it more closely resembles feta.

BRYNDZA
COUNTRY: *Slovakia*
TYPE: *Traditional, farmhouse and co-operative, fresh cheese*
SOURCE: *Sheep's milk*
DESCRIPTION: *Stark, white cheeses in various shapes and sizes, without rind*
CULINARY USES: *Spread on rye bread, used in salads, baking*

Made throughout Eastern Europe, particularly in the Carpathian Mountains, this is a subtly flavoured sheep's milk cheese, which is cut into cubes and stored in brine. Crumbly and moist, it resembles feta, but is not as salty.

Bryndza can also be made with cow's or goat's milk, either of which will result in a different consistency. The cheese can range from soft and spreadable to firm and crumbly. As the shepherds and their flocks are often some distance from the co-operatives, they turn their milk into simple curds, press these into cloth sacks and leave them to drain. They are then taken to the dairies, where the curds are broken up, salted, milled and remoulded into blocks. Bryndza is also sold in wooden barrels, packed with yet more salt.

Bryndza is matured for four weeks or more. It has a fat content of around 45 per cent. Similar cheeses include the Romanian Brinza, Hungarian Brynza, Sirene from Bulgaria and Greek feta.

LEFT: Hermélin, made in the Czech Republic, is a soft-white Camembert-style cheese – just one of the many copies of the better-known European cheeses produced in Eastern Europe

EASTERN EUROPEAN CHEESES 127

HALLOUMI
COUNTRY: *Romania*
TYPE: *Traditional, farmhouse and creamery, stretched-curd cheese*
SOURCE: *Cow's milk*
DESCRIPTION: *300–675g/11oz–1¹/₂lb plaited cheese with smooth, shiny, pale yellow, natural rind*
CULINARY USES: *Frying, grilling, melting*

Like many Eastern European cheeses, Halloumi's origins are blurred by the migratory nature of the ancient peoples who once roamed this area. It seems likely that the Romans learned the stretched-curd technique from the Indo-Europeans who, before the Iron Age, spread over Europe from the Russian steppes. Their language and influence can be traced through Persia, Greece, Eastern Europe, the Middle East and down through Turkestan and northern India.

Halloumi is supple and stringy, becoming harder the longer it remains in the brine in which it is traditionally cured. It is also made in Cyprus and Lebanon.

KATSCHKAWALJ
COUNTRY: *Bulgaria*
TYPE: *Traditional, farmhouse and creamery, stretched-curd cheese*
SOURCE: *Sheep's milk*
DESCRIPTION: *6–9kg/13–20lb irregular round, with thin, pale yellow to yellowish-brown, natural rind*
CULINARY USES: *Table cheese, snacks, also fried or baked in local dishes*

Katschkawalj is a *pasta filata* (stretched-curd) cheese made from sheep's milk and found right across Eastern Europe and into Central Asia. It is thought to have originated before the days of the Roman Empire, and may have been the progenitor of the Italian Caciocavallo. Like all *pasta filata* cheeses, it is made by kneading and stretching the fresh curd before it is salted and aged. It keeps well and is valued for its versatility in cooking. Originally made principally by shepherds for their own consumption, it is now largely produced in factories.

Although the best Katschkawalj is made from sheep's milk, mixed milk and pure cow's milk versions are on the increase. The texture of the sheep's milk cheese is firm but flexible and crumbly. Underneath the pale yellow rind (which deepens in colour as the cheese matures), the cheese is salty, sharp and slightly bitter. The flavour has a hint of caramelized onion. Both eaten as a table cheese, and used extensively in cooking, Katschkawalj is sometimes referred to as the "Cheddar of the Balkans". It matures in two months and has a fat content of 45 per cent.

LAJTA
COUNTRY: *Hungary*
TYPE: *Traditional, farmhouse and co-operative, unpasteurized, semi-soft cheese*
SOURCE: *Cow's milk*
DESCRIPTION: *1kg/2¹/₄lb rectangular cheese with moist, deep orange, washed rind*
CULINARY USE: *Table cheese*

This was undoubtedly introduced to Hungary by some order of intrepid monks, determined to convert the local populace, but missing the cheeses of Western Europe. The slightly sticky, washed rind covers a supple interior containing numerous small, irregular holes created as a result of the starter culture used and the ensuing vigorous fermentation process. Lajta has the robust aroma and taste characteristic of washed-rind cheeses. It ripens in four to six weeks and has a fat content of 50 per cent.

LIPTAUER
COUNTRY: *Hungary*
TYPE: *Traditional, farmhouse and co-operative, unpasteurized, fresh cheese*
SOURCE: *Sheep's or cow's milk*
DESCRIPTION: *Spiced, white cheese sold in pots*
CULINARY USE: *Forms the basis of numerous local dishes*

The Hungarians developed Liptauer from a simple, white, sheep's milk cheese called Liptoi, which was made by shepherds in their mountain huts. The curd was hung in cloth sacks for up to a week before being taken to a small dairy, where it was mixed with paprika and salt.

Each family has its own recipe for what has become known as Liptauer cheese.

Onions, caraway seeds, capers, anchovies or other ingredients whose proportions are often secret are added to the curd, together with varying amounts of paprika. Hungarians have a great love of spicy food, so Liptauer can be exceedingly hot, even vicious. It has a fat content of around 50 per cent.

LIPTOI
COUNTRY: *Hungary*
TYPE: *Traditional, farmhouse and co-operative, unpasteurized, fresh cheese*
SOURCE: *Sheep's milk*
DESCRIPTION: *White, mousse-like cheese sold in pots*
CULINARY USES: *Snacks, hors d'oeuvres, salads*

For centuries, this simple cheese has been made by shepherds in the Tatra mountains. Fine and mousse-like, with the subtle, sweet taste of sheep's milk and rosemary, it is mixed with various spices and herbs. There are as many recipes for this cheese as there are makers, as the recipes are handed down from one generation to the next.

Liptoi is the basis for Liptauer, the best-known cheese of Eastern Europe, which combines paprika, caraway, onions and capers in a heady, sometimes wickedly hot spread. This is most often served as a dip, with celery – and copious amounts of the local beer.

MANUR/MANDUR
COUNTRY: *Serbia*
TYPE: *Traditional, farmhouse and creamery, unpasteurized, hard cheese*
SOURCE: *Sheep's or cow's milk*
DESCRIPTION: *2–3kg/4¹/₂–6¹/₂lb sphere with thin, white or straw-coloured, natural rind*
CULINARY USES: *Grating – as a condiment or in soup*

This unusual cheese is unique to Serbia. The fresh milk (cow's or sheep's, depending on the season) is gradually heated until it boils. It is then cooled to hand-hot and a mixture of buttermilk, fresh whey and rennet is added. Once set, the curd is drained in a cloth before being salted, shaped and dried. It ripens in a few days and has a fat content of 40 per cent.

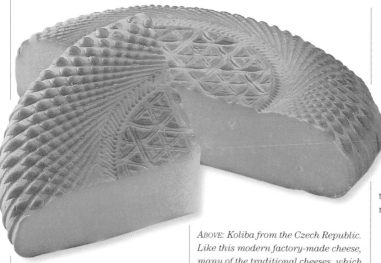

ABOVE: *Koliba from the Czech Republic.
Like this modern factory-made cheese,
many of the traditional cheeses, which
were made in what was once known as
Czechoslovakia, had intricate designs
carved into the moulds by the cheesemaker – giving each a unique pattern*

OSCHTJEPKA
COUNTRY: *Slovakia*
TYPE: *Traditional, farmhouse,
unpasteurized, semi-
hard cheese*
SOURCE: *Cow's and sheep's milk*
Description: *500g/1¼lb round
cheese with natural rind
marked with slight indentations
from the cloth used for draining
and drying*
CULINARY USES: *Table cheese,
grilling, melting*

Supple and elastic, Oschtjepka is similar
to Bulgarian Katshkawalj. It has been
made for centuries in the magnificent
Carpathian Mountains, a mecca for sheep,
with its fresh mountain streams and natural pastures.

Most of the cheese is still made by the
shepherds themselves. The soured milk is
pressed into balls, each the size of a small
melon, and hung to dry from the ceilings
of their mountain chalets. The sweet,
aromatic smoke from the shepherds' fires
gradually dries the cheese and adds to its
flavour. Similar cheeses, which are also
produced in Eastern Europe, include
Parenica, which is made in Slovakia, and
the Polish cheese, Oszczpek.

Oschtjepka ripens in about two to three
months and has a fat content of around
45 per cent.

OSZCZPEK
COUNTRY: *Poland*
TYPE: *Traditional, farmhouse and
co-operative, unpasteurized,
semi-hard cheese*
SOURCE: *Cow's and sheep's milk*
DESCRIPTION: *Made in various
sizes and shapes (usually oval),
with smooth, polished, pale
lemon, natural rind which can be
chocolate brown if the cheese is
heavily smoked*
CULINARY USES: *Table cheese,
grilling, melting*

Oszczpek is one of the few remaining traditional cheeses to be found in Poland.
Most of the other cheeses on sale there
are factory-made imitations of the more
popular European cheeses.Made in the
Tatra Mountains, Oszczpek belongs to the
same family as the Slovakian Oschtjepka.

The curd is kneaded, then pressed into
hand-carved, wooden moulds. Once
drained, the young cheeses are traditionally stored in the eaves of the house,
where they gradually absorb the smoke
from the fire.

Oszczpek ripens in one to four weeks
and has a fat content of 45 per cent.

PODHALANSKI
COUNTRY: *Poland*
TYPE: *Traditional, farmhouse and
creamery, unpasteurized,
semi-hard cheese*
SOURCE: *Cow's and sheep's milk*
DESCRIPTION: *500g/1¼lb brick or loaf
shape with hard, pale yellow,
natural rind that darkens to
burnt orange if smoked*
CULINARY USES: *Table cheese, grilling*

Firm, but supple, Podhalanski has tiny
holes throughout the pale yellow interior. Some cheeses are lightly smoked in
the style of earlier times. Podhalanski
ripens in two months.

SIRAZ
COUNTRY: *Serbia*
TYPE: *Traditional, farmhouse,
unpasteurized, semi-hard cheese*
SOURCE: *Cow's milk*
DESCRIPTION: *200–400g/7–14oz flat
disc. The rough, yellow, natural rind
has some yeasts*
CULINARY USES: *Table cheese, baking;
often crumbled into local dishes*

To make this unusual Serbian cheese, the
young curd is pressed into flat discs, about
15cm/6in in diameter. The cheese is then
left in the sun to dry, often on a balcony
wall, until the fat begins to ooze. The surface is rubbed and salted several times
over the next few days until a crust forms,
when the cheeses are stored in wooden
containers of brine. The cheese ripens in
a few weeks. It has a mellow, slightly sour,
salty tang and a compact body.

SIRENE
COUNTRY: *Bulgaria*
TYPE: *Traditional, farmhouse and
creamery, unpasteurized, fresh cheese*
SOURCE: *Sheep's and cow's milk*
DESCRIPTION: *White, slightly grainy
cheese without rind, sold in blocks*
CULINARY USES: *Salads, spreads, baking;
also as a table cheese, with fresh herbs*

The most popular and most widely produced Bulgarian cheese. Moist, crumbly,
fresh and lemony, it is stored in barrels or
tins of brine. Sirene is richer and creamier
than many similar cheeses, and has a fat
content of 45–50 per cent.

THE CHEESES OF INDIA AND THE MIDDLE EAST

The culture and climate of India, and of many of her neighbours, have inadvertently conspired against the development of a dairy industry. The combination of high temperatures and humidity causes rapid growth of moulds, cracking of the cheese surface, excessive drying out and rapid putrefaction. Installation of equipment to alter the environment is expensive and inappropriate where the volume of available milk is low and the potential producers and customers widespread and isolated.

Such indigenous cheeses as do exist are generally very simple, and are dried over fires, often fuelled by cattle dung rather than wood, which is scarce, particularly in the Himalayas. Karut is a very dry, hard, skimmed-milk cheese made in Afghanistan and north-west India, while Krutt is made by the nomadic tribes in the middle Asiatic steppes, using skimmed milk from cows, goats, sheep or camels. The milk is coagulated by natural souring, and the curd is hung up in sacks to drain.

Elsewhere, milk is normally coagulated using rennet obtained from a young milk-fed calf, but this is not possible in India, where the cow is a sacred animal. Non-animal rennet can be used, but seldom is. Instead, the practice is to make simple, quick-ripening cheeses, which are coagulated by the action of the acid in milk, and not by bacteria or moulds.

In the mid-1990s, milk consumption in India has more than doubled; it is said to be the fastest-growing market in the world. Production of some of the popular cheeses of European origin is developing. Herds of cows and water buffalos are increasing, but the milk yield is still insufficient to meet the demand and it is necessary to import milk products.

Paneer, a simple cheese made in the home and eaten within a few days of being made, is very popular. It is used in various traditional Indian dishes, including meat and vegetable curries and spicy vegetable dishes.

To make your own paneer, bring 2 litres/3½ pints fresh whole milk to the boil. Stir in 30ml/2 tbsp vinegar or lemon juice and set aside. When the milk has curdled, pour it into a clean, scalded muslin cloth set in a strainer. Rinse with fresh water and drain well, then bring up the sides of the cloth to enclose the curd and shape it into a ball. Place under a heavy saucepan or similar weight and press for 10–15 minutes. This makes about 225g/8oz paneer.

BELOW: Paneer is one of the few cheeses that can easily be made at home

THE MIDDLE EAST

Centuries ago in Iran, simple dried cheeses were produced, then, when milk was abundant, the people made a softer sheep's milk cheese, similar to feta, which was preserved in brine to last through the leaner months. The nomadic bedouins, too, made a soft cheese that was either eaten fresh or preserved in salt.

Nowadays, the most common cheese found in the region are small balls of fresh curd, sometimes rolled in herbs or spices, and served at breakfast time. They are called Lebneh in the Lebanon and Israel, Lebney in Syria, Gibne in the Arabic countries and Labaneh in Jordan. A similar cheese, Serat, made in the high mountains of Iran and Afghanistan, is smoked and dipped in beeswax to help preserve it.

Although most exported Halloumi comes from Cyprus, this cheese was originally made by the Bedouin tribes from sheep's milk. It is still made today, popular because of its ability to hold its shape even when grilled on a skewer.

Kashakawan, found in the Lebanon and Syria, is similar to both Bulgarian Katshkawalj and Turkish Kasar Peynir. The name means "cheese on horseback", and is thought to originate from when the cheeses were tied in pairs and slung acrss a pole like saddle bags to dry. A kosher version of the cheese is made in Israel, where they also make the smaller, Smoked Basna.

Most other cheeses from Israel are copies of popular European cheeses. One of the most common, Bulgarian cheese, is actually feta, but is so-called because the best feta was considered to come from Bulgaria where the cheese is softer and less salty than the Greek varieties. Other cheeses include Bin-Gedi, a Camembert-type cheese; Galil, a sheep's milk cheese modelled on Roquefort; Golan, a hard Provolone-style cheese; Tal Ha'emek, a hard cheese with holes like Emmental; and Gilead, which is similar to mozzarella.

THE CHEESES OF THE USA

All too often, the prevailing attitude to cheese in the USA appears to be that it is something you have to cook, grate or melt for it to be useful. There is also a widely held belief that cheese is too fattening and too high in salt to indulge in more than occasionally. Unfortunately, the supermarket shelves reflect public opinion. They are laden with ready-to-go shredded or sliced Jack, Cheddar, Swiss or processed cheese, kept "fresh" with preservatives. Sanitized, sterilized and standardized – who can blame Americans for thinking cheese is just a commodity that you have to do something with?

How did this happen in a country where, by 1890, nearly a third of the population were European-born immigrants? Ironically, it was the enormous influx of immigrants that helped to create the situation. Mass production was seen as the only way to feed the soaring population. There was no time to invent new cheeses, and distribution of small-volume farmstead cheeses was impossible in such a huge country, so milk was processed, mainly into Cheddar, and "big" was the byword. By 1900, a thousand cheese factories had grown up along the East coast alone.

The first all-American cheese was Brick, set apart from European cheeses as much by name as by the process by which it was made. In 1877, John Jossi, a Wisconsin cheesemaker of Swiss

RIGHT: New York State Cheddar

extraction, discovered that if he squeezed fresh curd between two bricks, the result was a brick-shaped cheese similar to the popular German Limburger, but firmer and more rubbery. His cheese was ideal for cutting, and had a mild aroma and taste. Today, Brick is vacuum-packed in slices, strings or blocks and is sold right across the USA.

Next (in 1882) came Colby, named after a town in Wisconsin. Similar to Cheddar, but softer and more elastic, it also matured more quickly and could be eaten within weeks rather than months. Sweet and bland, Colby was soon accepted as an all-purpose, family cheese. It remains a favourite.

The origin of Monterey Jack, although attributed to the Scot, David Jacks, can actually be traced back to the Spanish Franciscan monks who came north during the early days of the missions, when California was still part of Mexico. Finding themselves with surplus milk, they set about making *queso blanco*, a delicate, creamy cheese that originated in Spain and which had spread to South America.

David Jacks' contribution was to recognize its potential. He set up factories, and by the mid 1880s was producing his own cheese. To distinguish it from others on the market, it was known as Jack's cheese and ultimately Jack. To differentiate this cheese from the firmer, industrially produced Jack, it is usually referred to as Monterey, Sonoma or California Jack.

Like many great cheeses, Dry Jack was created by accident rather than design. In 1915 another San Franciscan found himself with a surplus of young Jack

BELOW: Dry Jack

cheese. Needing the shelf space for other cheeses, he stored the Jack cheese on the floor, hand-salting each one in the hope that it would survive. Weeks later, he found that the Jack cheese had become fruity, rich and hard, not unlike Parmesan. Dry Jack proved instantly popular and has been a favourite ever since.

By 1930 most of the familiar European cheeses were being produced. However, the paranoia over raw milk in the 1950s closed down all but the most intrepid cheesemakers. The few remaining artisans relied on the loyalty of the local community to survive, while those in more isolated areas found success through mail-order sales.

The influence of the Vietnam War, coupled with the growth of the hippie movement, were just two of the catalysts that spawned a new generation of farmstead cheesemakers who had decided to embrace a different way of life.

By the late 1970s, production had moved into the hands of large companies. Small co-operatives disappeared as cheese became another commodity to be distributed as cheaply and efficiently as possible to the increasing number of supermarkets.

A new era of American cooking was emerging, with young chefs turning their backs on the imported cheeses in favour of seeking out regional produce. Mediterranean-style menus called for fresh mozzarella, ricotta and goat's milk cheeses. Delis and fancy food shops were on the increase and the wonderful farmers' markets, with their emphasis on quality rather than quantity, provided a showcase from California to New York for the American farmstead cheeses.

Many of the new generation of cheese-makers turned to goats or sheep. They were easier to handle, required less investment and there was a better return on their milk. The strict laws enforcing pasteurization had been relaxed, and raw cheese could be sold so long as it was matured for more than 60 days.

The consumers' attitude has also changed. When people buy farmstead cheeses, they feel they are supporting the old ways and encouraging those who practise sustainable farming methods. Today there are more than 80 producers of American farm-stead cheeses. Seek them out, give them support and enjoy them.

ABOVE:
Monterey Jack

In addition to the smaller cheese-makers, the USA has large manufacturers producing different types of cheese, which are often versions of European varieties. In this section of the book, you will find entries for individual cheeses, as well as listings for companies whose entire range sets a standard that makes them worth looking out for.

BEL GIOIOSO CHEESES
REGION: *Wisconsin*
TYPE: *Various unpasteurized, Italian cheeses*
SOURCE: *Cow's milk*
DESCRIPTION: *Various sizes and shapes, including bell, wheel, pear and wedge*
CULINARY USES: *Various*
Bel Gioioso is the name given to a range of Italian cheeses that have their origins

in the Auricchio Cheese Company, which was founded near Naples in 1877. The company flourished, ultimately becoming the world's largest producer of aged Provolone. In 1979, they set up a factory in Wisconsin, using Italian equipment and cheesemakers.

Today, Bel Gioioso Cheeses produces Fontina, Parmesan, Romano, Asiago and Gorgonzola as well as mascarpone and fresh mozzarella, plus the Provolone with which they began. Adherence to tradi-tional Italian cheesemaking methods has given Bel Gioioso cheeses authenticity. However, the differences in climate and grazing, together with the need to meet the demands of the local market, has sub-tly altered the flavour and texture of the vari-ous cheeses. Fortunately, their fundamental char-acter has not been lost.

BERGÈRE BLEUE
REGION: *New York State*
TYPE: *Modern, farmhouse, organic, blue cheese*
SOURCE: *Sheep's milk*
DESCRIPTION: *Cylindrical cheese, 16cm/6¹⁄₂in in diameter and 10cm/4in tall. The sticky, moist, natural rind has occasional blotches of natural yeasts and moulds*
CULINARY USES: *Table cheese, omelettes and salads*
Bergère Bleue is a Roquefort-style cheese with a rich aroma of lanolin and yeast. It melts in the mouth like butter, releasing the flavour of burnt caramel. The blue-green streaks of *Penicillium roquefortii* give a spicy piquancy to the pale lemon-coloured cheese, which is moist and slightly crumbly. The more mature cheese is spreadable.

The cheesemaker is Jane North, who learnt her craft in the French and Spanish Pyrenees. When she returned to the USA, she and her husband Karl built their farm at Freetown. Eight years later, in 1988, they established Northland Sheep Dairy and started cheesemaking. In addition to Bergère Bleue, the dairy also produces Tomme Bergère and Folie Bergère.

BRIER RUN CHEESES
REGION: *West Virginia*
TYPE: *Traditional, farmhouse, organic, fresh and aged cheeses*
SOURCE: *Goat's milk (Nubian, Alpine and Saanen)*
DESCRIPTION: *Various sizes and shapes, ranging from 115g/4oz to 1kg/2¹⁄₄lb in weight*
CULINARY USES: *Table cheeses, also used in salads and for grilling*
Goats are hardy creatures, producing their best milk when conditions are tough and varied. The narrow valley, scrub-covered grey crags and herbaceous pastures of the Appalachian foothills provide Greg and Verena Sava's goats with the perfect envi-ronment. Their natural existence also means that they breed at their own whim, not man's, so there are times when milk is in short supply and the cheese can be difficult to find. Greg and Verena handle the flavoursome milk with care, hand-ladling the curd to give a creamier, fuller flavour. Their goat's milk cheeses are among America's finest.

BULK FARM CHEESES
REGION: *California*
TYPE: *Various traditional, farmhouse, European-style cheeses*
SOURCE: *Cow's milk*
DESCRIPTION: *Various*
CULINARY USES: *Table cheese, grating, grilling*
Dutch cheesemakers are among the finest exports from Europe, adapting the traditional recipes of their native cheeses to their new pastures and climates. The Bulk family have been cheesemakers for generations, and Walter and Lenneke are doing a fine job of upholding the family tradition at their farm in California.

Those who have sampled the cheeses sold at their small retail store tend to come back, impressed by the quality. To ensure their Gouda has the authentic taste and texture, they import the traditional starter culture and rennet from Holland. This affects every stage of the cheesemaking process and has a direct bearing on the rich, nutty flavour of Gouda. Bulk Farm also produces its own Leyden, Edam and Quark.

CAPRIOLE BANON
REGION: *Indiana*
TYPE: *Traditional, farmhouse,*
fresh cheese
SOURCE: *Goat's milk (Alpine)*
DESCRIPTION: *180g/6¼oz disc wrapped*
in marinated chestnut leaves
CULINARY USE: *Table cheese*

Judy Schad's cheeses are exceptional in quality and character. Not only do the shapes and names reflect her wicked sense of humour – Wabash Cannonballs and Fromage à Trois are just two of the cheeses from her list – but her concentration on ageing the cheeses to the point of perfection demonstrates her belief that the American palate loves to experience new flavours.

Her Capriole Banon looks like an exquisitely wrapped gift, with its covering of interwoven chestnut leaves that have been marinated in brandy and white wine. Their aroma permeates the soft, creamy curd to devastating effect – a sensational blend of flavours.

Judy's company, Capriole Inc., also makes Mont St Francis, Old Kentucky Tomme and Festiva, which is a wonderful combination of a Jack-style goat's milk cheese with pine nuts, basil and flavoursome sun-dried tomatoes.

CHÈVRE DE PROVENCE
REGION: *Alabama*
TYPE: *Modern, farmhouse, organic,*
fresh cheese
SOURCE: *Goat's milk (mixed breeds)*
DESCRIPTION: *Various shapes and sizes,*
without rind
CULINARY USES: *Table cheese, grilling*
or baking, spreading, salads

Like great pastry chefs, some cheesemakers seem to possess an almost arcane touch. The judges at the 1994 and 1995 American Cheese Society conference certainly recognized Liz Parnell's talents, awarding both her Chèvre de Provence and her fromage frais first place.

Liz's chèvre has been described as an American treasure. The subtle flavour of the tiny discs of fresh, lemony, goat's milk cheese is enhanced by the mixture of olive oil and fresh herbs in which it is packed.

COACH FARM CHEESES
REGION: *New York State*
TYPE: *Modern, farmhouse, fresh and*
soft-white cheeses
SOURCE: *Goat's milk (French Alpine)*
DESCRIPTION: *Various shapes and sizes,*
textures and tastes
CULINARY USES: *Table cheeses, grilling,*
baking as filling for pastries, sauces
and salads

From fresh, mild and lemony to creamy, aromatic and mushroomy, Coach Farm Cheeses are of a consistently high quality. They set the standard by which many small farms match themselves, and it is not surprising that nowadays they are among the most widely distributed cheeses in America.

Miles, Lilian and Susan Cahn are perfectionists, taking as much trouble with the varied diet of their 800 goats as they do in finding a wrapping that will protect the cheese while allowing it to breathe.

Their fresh cheeses are ready to eat within days. The aged varieties grow a soft-white penicillium mould and are best eaten when still firm and flaky. Mild, but not bland, they dissolve like ice cream. Both types are available in a variety of flavours. One of their best-known cheeses is Pyramid, in which the young curd is flavoured with aromatic and spicy green peppercorns.

COTTAGE CHEESE
REGION: *Various*
TYPE: *Modern, creamery, fresh cheese*
SOURCE: *Cow's milk*
DESCRIPTION: *Creamy, lumpy cheese*
sold in pots
CULINARY USES: *Table cheese, snacks,*
salads, baking

Americans have come to think of cottage cheese as their own invention, but it originated with the rural labourers of Europe, who had been making it for centuries before it crossed the Atlantic.

Cottage cheese is an acid curd cheese, relying on the natural tendency of warm milk to curdle, rather than requiring the addition of rennet. Once the soft, floppy curd has formed, it is cut into pea-sized cubes and heated gently in the whey until it reaches the desired texture and body. The whey is then drained off and the lumpy curd is rinsed in cold water to remove the excess whey and lactose. What remains is cottage cheese. Salt and a little milk or cream are routinely added, and many varieties are flavoured to lift what is essentially a bland and often rather boring flavour.

Cottage cheese accounts for nearly 25 per cent of all cheese consumed by weight-conscious Americans. It is produced in factories across the country, each fighting for their share of the market. The cheese ripens in one or two days and has a fat content of five to 15 per cent.

ABOVE: A young Capriole
Banon

BELOW: Cream cheese

COUGAR GOLD

REGION: *Washington State*
TYPE: *Modern, creamery,
semi-soft cheese*
SOURCE: *Cow's milk*
DESCRIPTION: *1kg/2¼lb round
cheese without rind, packed
in a can*
CULINARY USES: *Table cheese, snacks*

Established in 1948 by Washington State University to encourage the growth and quality of cheesemaking in the state, Cougar Gold remains popular – partly, no doubt, due to the novelty of buying a cheese that is packed in a can.

Cougar Gold is creamy, smooth and rich, with a mellow cheese-and-onion-sauce aroma and taste. An enthusiast once sent the author two cans, one 12 months old and the other two years old, in order to prove that cheese in a can could be good and could be aged. The author was suitably impressed but not necessarily converted.

CREAM CHEESE

REGION: *Various*
TYPE: *Modern, creamery, fresh cheese*
SOURCE: *Cow's milk*
DESCRIPTION: *White, rindless cheese
sold in pots*
CULINARY USES: *Spreads, baking,
dips, cheesecakes*

Like cottage cheese, this is an acid curd cheese, but requires a starter culture to curdle the milk, which it does by turning the milk sugar (lactose) into lactic acid. Low-fat varieties may require the addition of a little rennet to help the milk to coagulate. The freshly formed, soft curd is poured into close-weave linen cloth (or a sack of woven plastic), the ends are knotted together and the bundle is left to drain. After two to three hours, the curd on the sides of the cloth is scraped into the centre, the cloth is re-tied and the bundle is placed on a draining tray under a weight and pressed for two to three hours. At this stage, salt is added. Theoretically, the cream cheese could now be packed into tubs for immediate use, but it is more often heated and extruded before being poured into moulds for sale.

Cream cheese is generally mild and velvety, with a fresh, lemony zing balanced by the buttery richness of the cream. Low-fat versions may contain whey powder, which gives them a slightly grainy feel. Cream cheese made at home must be eaten within a few days, but the commercially produced product can have a shelf life of up to 60 days depending on the method used to make and preserve it. Stabilizers are seldom used, but some manufacturers use a gum of sorts to hold the cheese together and improve its keeping qualities.

CROWLEY

REGION: *Vermont*
TYPE: *Traditional, farmhouse,
semi-hard cheese*
SOURCE: *Cow's milk*
DESCRIPTION: *Cylindrical
or oblong cheeses in
various sizes. The natural
rind carries the imprint
of the cheesecloth
and has some
natural mould*
CULINARY USES: *Table cheese,
grating, grilling*

This farmhouse cheese is made by washing the freshly cut curd with cool spring water. This removes much of the acidic whey, creating a cheese that is similar to but sweeter than Cheddar. The curd is then salted, loosely packed to allow the small holes to develop, then placed in wooden presses and hand-cranked for just long enough to ensure it develops a firm, yet moist texture. When aged for between three and six months, the cheese is magnificent; at around six months, while retaining some sweetness, it has the pungent, cheese-and-onion tang of mature Cheddar; at over 12 months and labelled "extra sharp" it is Crowley's best-seller.

The story of the cheese starts in the family kitchen, where Winfield and Nellie Crowley made cheese for friends and family. In 1882 they built their creamery. Demand soon grew for their cheese, which was made from a combination of recipes, modified over the years to suit the preferences of individual family members.

Although officially designated as a Colby cheese, Crowley was actually made decades before Colby cheese existed. Nor is it a Cheddar, as the cheesemaking process is different.

In 1967 the factory was in serious danger of closing. Randolph Smith, who had come to Vermont to retire, heard the rumours, stepped in and saved Crowley from extinction. His sons continue to produce this simple, farmhouse cheese by hand in the original wooden barn, often watched by the many thousands of visitors who come every summer to view the cheesemaking.

CYPRESS GROVE CHEVRE

REGION: *California*
TYPE: *Modern and traditional, farmhouse, vegetarian, fresh and aged cheeses*
SOURCE: *Goat's milk (Alpine)*
DESCRIPTION: *Various shapes and sizes*
CULINARY USES: *Table cheese, salads and sauces, grilling and baking*

Consistent quality and distinctive packaging have spelt success for cheesemaker Mary Keehn and her daughter Malorie. Their fresh cheeses are made in the traditional, French, farmhouse style. Light and mousse-like, they have a pleasant acidity and herbaceous finish. When aged, the cheeses develop a white penicillium mould that forms a shell. The herbaceous character becomes more pronounced and the mushroom aroma of the rind penetrates the cheese. Although harder than the young cheeses, the aged cheeses melt in the mouth. Their other cheeses include Chèvre Log, Pee Wee Pyramid, Goat's Milk Cheddar, Tomme and feta.

ABOVE: *Dry Jack*

CANADIAN CHEESES

Canada's early settlers, from Britain and France, were mainly trappers, traders and foresters with little interest in either cheesemaking or farmsteading, so it is not surprising that cheesemaking was slow to develop in this beautiful, but often inhospitable land. When cattle were introduced, it was for meat, not milk. Cheese was hardly a consideration, since game and meat were plentiful sources of protein. Only in winter, when snow and isolation prevented fresh supplies from reaching large farms, were some rudimentary cheeses made.

It was the arrival of French Trappist monks that really began Canada's cheesemaking tradition. Their first monastery was in Quebec, and by 1881 they were producing a semi-soft, washed-rind cheese, Oka, which has been made commercially since 1960. The Benedictine monks at the abbey of Saint Benoit du Lac in Quebec created Canada's first blue cheese, Ermite (Hermit) in 1943. It, too, is still being made.

British immigrants gradually established dairy herds. They set up co-operatives to process the milk into Cheddar, as they have done in Australia, America and New Zealand.

Canadian Cheddar made its presence known in a big way when a 10-ton Cheddar was made in Ontario for the 1893 World Exhibition in Chicago. The cheese finally ended up in a London restaurant. As a marketing exercise, it was extremely successful, and Canadian Cheddar was placed firmly on the map – and in the minds of the British. It continues to sell well in supermarkets across Britain, industrially made but often aged to a mouth-puckering degree of acidity, a taste staunch supporters insist is the mark of the perfect Cheddar. Epicures who prize the firm, rich nuttiness of traditional British Cheddar, with its final savoury bite, might disagree, however.

Cheddar continues to dominate the Canadian cheese market, although the growth of tourism and the skiing industry has brought about a dramatic increase in sales of Canadian Raclette and Oka. So far, the revival of artisan cheesemaking, which has had such a beneficial affect in America and Great Britain, has scarcely begun in Canada, but cannot be too far away, as a few small cheesemakers scattered across the provinces are already finding a market for their hand-made cheeses.

LEFT: *Canadian Cheddar*

DRY JACK

REGION: *California*
TYPE: *Traditional, farmhouse, unpasteurized, vegetarian, hard cheese*
SOURCE: *Cow's milk*
DESCRIPTION: *4kg/9lb square with rounded edges. The natural rind is hand-rubbed with oil, cocoa and pepper*
CULINARY USES: *Table cheese, grating, salads*

Like many great cheeses, Dry Jack was created by accident rather than design. In 1915 a San Francisco wholesaler found himself with an over-abundance of young Jack cheese. To clear shelf space for new arrivals, he reluctantly stacked the Jack on the floor, hand-salting each one in the hope that it would survive.

Weeks later, he found that the cheeses were fruity, rich and hard, not unlike the Pecorino and Parmesan he had run out of at the time. Necessity being the mother of invention, he coated each cheese with oil, pepper and cocoa, to imitate the lamp black being used on imported Italian cheeses at that time, and offered "Dry Jack" to his customers. A star was born.

Today the cheese, made by the Vella Cheese Company, is among the finest in the world. The rind looks like chocolate icing. Underneath, the deep yellow cheese is hard and when cut, the cheese shatters rather than breaks, releasing layer upon layer of flavour: sweet and fruity; sharp and mouth-watering, rich and full-bodied like a fine wine.

FRESH JACK
REGION: *California*
TYPE: *Traditional, farmhouse and creamery, semi-soft cheese*
SOURCE: *Cow's milk*
DESCRIPTION: *Rounds in various sizes. The straw-coloured, natural rind is fine and springy*
CULINARY USES: *Table cheese, snacks, melting, salads*

Another cheese from the famous Vella Cheese Company, Fresh Jack resembles Edam in texture, but is creamier and more springy. It has a distinctive taste: aromatic, with a hint of green-grass bitterness. Factory-made Jack tends to be bland, mild and milky, with a rubbery feel compared to this excellent cheese.

GRAFTON VILLAGE CHEDDAR
REGION: *Vermont*
TYPE: *Traditional, farmhouse, unpasteurized, hard cheese*
SOURCE: *Cow's milk*
DESCRIPTION: *Blocks of various sizes, without rind*
CULINARY USES: *Table cheese, grating, melting, grilling, in sauces*

By keeping to small-batch production and traditional methods, Grafton continues to produce excellent white (uncoloured) Cheddars, with the depth of flavour and character possible only with raw milk and long ageing.

The Grafton Village Cheese Company was established in 1890 in the village of Grafton, now meticulously restored. It draws its milk from local dairy farms, where cattle graze the rich grasslands of the southern Vermont mountains. The result is milk that is high in butterfat, with a consistent quality and texture, qualities that are essential for the production of cheeses that will develop real character and depth as they mature.

Grafton Village Cheddar ripens in six to 24 months and has a fat content of 50 per cent. The company makes several flavoured Cheddars (with sage, garlic or dill), plus a version that is smoked over corn cobs.

HOLLOW ROAD CHEESES
REGION: *New York State*
TYPE: *Traditional, farmhouse, organic, fresh and aged cheeses*
SOURCE: *Sheep's milk (also mixed Sheep's and cow's milk)*
DESCRIPTION: *Various shapes and sizes*
CULINARY USES: *Table cheeses, snacks, salads*

Joan Snyder and Ken Kleinpeter produce a range of excellent cheeses, each of which offers a wonderful insight into the character of sheep's milk, with its burnt-caramel sweetness and rich, nutty finish.

Joan and Ken adhere strictly to the principles of organic farming, aiming to produce "healthy food from well cared for and humanely raised animals". In addition to producing fresh sheep's milk cheese logs, ricotta, feta and Camembert, they make their own yogurt, using a mixture of sheep's and cow's milk when sheep's milk is in short supply.

HUBBARDSTON BLUE COW
REGION: *Massachusetts*
TYPE: *Modern, farmhouse, fresh cheese*
SOURCE: *Cow's milk*
DESCRIPTION: *Small round with natural rind covered in blue-grey mould*
CULINARY USE: *Table cheese*

Not a conventional blue, this is so called because of the soft, fuzzy rind of blue-grey mould that helps to speed up the ripening process, softening the cheese close to the rind to the point where it almost runs. The flavour is gentle and aromatic, with a hint of almonds.

Hubbardston Blue Cow is made by Westfield Farm, who also make some goat's milk cheeses.

IDAHO GOATSTER
REGION: *Idaho*
TYPE: *Modern, farmhouse, hard cheese*
SOURCE: *Goat's milk (Saanen)*
DESCRIPTION: *2kg/4$\frac{1}{2}$lb wheel with natural, waxed rind*
CULINARY USES: *Table cheese, grating, grilling*

Exchanging their potters' wheels and artists brushes for milking machines and curd cutters seems to have been a natural progression for Charles (Chuck) and Karen Evans, who have turned cheese-making into almost an art form. Their Idaho Goatster looks very attractive, with its annatto-rubbed and waxed rind. The hard, almost dry texture of the cheese is similar to that of an Italian Pecorino, while the flavour of the goat's milk gives it a nutty, almond-like quality.

Chuck and Karen also make Bleu Age, a surface-ripened cheese with the blue mould on the outside. Here it differs from traditional blue cheeses, which blue from the inside out. Bleu Age is creamy and quite sharp, with a spicy quality not unlike Stilton's. At the American Cheese Society's 1990 conference it was judged Best of Show and also took a gold award.

Cranberry Torta consists of alternate layers of plain chèvre and chèvre mixed with cranberries and lemon zest, liberally sprinkled with walnuts. The company also makes Idaho Goatster with Porcini.

ABOVE: Grafton Village Cheddar – an excellent uncoloured Cheddar made in Vermont using raw milk. It is aged for up to a year

LAURA CHENEL'S CHÈVRE

REGION: *California*

TYPE: *Various fresh and aged, traditional, farmhouse cheeses*

SOURCE: *Goat's milk*

DESCRIPTION: *Various sizes and shapes*

CULINARY USES: *Table cheese, salads*

Laura Chenel is to chèvre what Pavarotti is to opera. She has brought these simple yet complex cheeses to the attention of the people of America, and in doing so she has destroyed the myth that goat's cheese is harsh and only for sophisticated palates. Her cheeses are hand-made and matured to the point where the subtlety of the milk is at its most revealing. Inspired by the French artisan cheesemakers she worked with in 1979, Laura adheres to the ancient traditions while allowing the vagaries of the Sonoma climate, the soil and her goats to influence each cheese.

She makes a range of shapes and sizes, from the tiny Cabecou in oil to the aged Tomme. All are highly sought after, not only by the thousands of visitors to the wine-growing region of Mendocino, but also by chefs and restaurateurs. When Alice Waters of the famous Chez Panisse restaurant put the cheeses on her menu and cheeseboard, it was like receiving the royal seal of approval.

MAYTAG BLUE

REGION: *Iowa*

DESCRIPTION: *Traditional, farmhouse, unpasteurized, vegetarian, blue cheese*

SOURCE: *Cow's milk*

DESCRIPTION: *2kg/4¹/₂lb cylinder. The ivory-coloured, natural rind has some grey, blue and white moulds*

CULINARY USES: *Table cheese, blue cheese dressing, dips, salads*

Since 1941 the name Maytag has become synonymous in America with the unlikely combination of washing machines and blue cheese. The link began in the 1920s when the sons of the founder of Maytag Appliances decided to demonstrate their own entrepreneurial skills and started the family farm. They gradually built up a pedigree herd of black and white Holstein/Friesian cows. Selling milk proved to be high in effort and low in profit, so they turned to cheesemaking. Since 1941 they

have not looked back, thanks largely to their recognizing the potential of the mail-order business: today, close to 50 per cent of their cheese is sold that way.

You might expect that a cheese that is as well known as Maytag Blue would be produced in huge volumes, but the makers have kept production small to ensure that they retain the quality only achievable when the cheese is made by hand. Maytag Blue has a dense, crumbly texture. Like Roquefort, it melts in the mouth, revealing a very spicy flavour from the fine streaks of blue-grey mould that are scattered throughout the creamy, moist cheese. The finish is hot, with a delicious bite that tempts you to try another piece.

Part of Maytag Blue's success is due to the company's "caves" or cellars, built into the side of a hill. Here the natural moulds and yeasts reside. The temperature and humidity are controlled by nature rather than pure technology, and the cheeses are permitted to ripen slowly over six months. This ensures a creamy texture and a depth of flavour comparable to that achieved by some of the famous European blues.

In addition to Maytag Blue, Maytag Dairy Farms also make White Cheddar and Edam.

MOSSHOLDER CHEESE

REGION: *Wisconsin*

TYPE: *Modern, farmhouse, semi-soft cheese*

SOURCE: *Cow's milk*

DESCRIPTION: *Supple cheese with tiny holes*

CULINARY USES: *Table cheese, melting, grilling*

Like Crowley, Mossholder was invented on the kitchen stove. Grandfather Mossholder's ambition to make a cheese with a bit of punch became something of an obsession, but his patience paid off when he invented Mossholder, which was loosely based on the Trappist cheeses of Europe. Aromatic, pungent and meaty, the supple cheese is full of tiny holes that positively ooze flavour – it is almost as good to breathe in as eat. It is regarded by cheese-lovers as one of the great American farmhouse cheeses.

ABOVE: *One of Sally Jackson's sheep's milk cheeses*

MOZZARELLA

REGION: *Texas*
TYPE: *Traditional, creamery, vegetarian, stretched-curd cheese*
SOURCE: *Cow's and goat's milk*
DESCRIPTION: *Small, irregularly shaped balls in various sizes*
CULINARY USES: *Salads, baking, pizzas and pastries*

Paula Lambert started the Mozzarella Company when she returned to America after living in Italy and really missed the cheeses she left behind. Undaunted, she set out to make her own. That was in 1982. Today she produces over 20 different cheeses. In addition to Italian specialities, she makes classic French and Mexican-style, soft and semi-soft cheeses. At the annual conferences of the American Cheese Society in 1992, 1994 and 1995, her Scamorza was voted number one in its category.

Paula's mozzarella di bufala was virtually indistinguishable from the classic Italian cheese, but the supply of buffalo's milk dried up and another source has not yet been found. Fortunately, both the cow's milk mozzarella and Capriella (made from a mixture of cow's and goat's milk) are equally delicious.

MUENSTER

REGION: *Wisconsin*
TYPE: *Traditional, creamery, washed-rind cheese*
SOURCE: *Cow's milk*
DESCRIPTION: *Loaf-shaped cheese without rind, coloured with paprika*
CULINARY USES: *Table cheese, grilling*

If you are expecting something which runs across your cheese-board, trailing a strong, pungent aroma and meaty, nutty flavour – in other words, a typical French Munster – you are likely to find disappointment at the end of your knife. American Muenster is closer to the Dutch or German copies, which are decidedly less formidable than the French. It has a supple, springy texture and sweet-sour, savoury tang, but is still a weak copy, best used for cooking as it melts superbly.

PEEKSKILL PYRAMID

REGION: *New York State*
TYPE: *Modern, farmhouse, fresh cheese*
SOURCE: *Cow's milk*
DESCRIPTION: *Pyramid-shaped cheese without rind*
CULINARY USES: *Table cheese, snacks*

Peekskill Pyramid has a rich, wickedly buttery taste and a texture like creamy caramel. Whipped into a pyramid shape, it looks as impressive as it tastes, and has a delicious roundness on the finish.

The cheesemaker is Jonathan White. Like so many newcomers to the world of artisan cheeses, he came not from a rural background but was a disillusioned computer engineer with a fascination for making his own cheese. In 1994, Charles Palmer, the New York restaurateur, suggested he turn his hobby to real purpose. Together they set up Egg Farm Dairy, which neither sells eggs nor is a farm. If the name of the dairy is quirky, so is the setting, next door to a hair salon in a row of small shops. Step inside, however, and you will discover a real haven for cheese and cheese-lovers.

In addition to Peekskill Pyramid, Jonathan makes Muscoot, Amawalk, Hudson and Wild-ripened Cheddar. Muscoot has a rich, creamy feel and a sweet, buttery taste that becomes more complex as it melts in your mouth, while Amawalk is an aged cheese, with a more distinctive, nutty style.

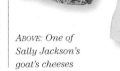

ABOVE: One of Sally Jackson's goat's cheeses

PLYMOUTH CHEESE

REGION: *Vermont*
TYPE: *Traditional, creamery, unpasteurised, hard cheese*
SOURCE: *Cow's milk*
DESCRIPTION: *Granular cheese with smooth, golden-yellow, natural rind, sold in various sizes and flavours*
CULINARY USES: *Table cheese, melting, baking*

The supple, granular texture of this traditional New England cheese is achieved by washing the newly formed curds, then kneading them by hand. The elastic curd is then salted, pressed and matured for several months. It is at its best after six months, when maturity has allowed the distinct fruity tang to come through.

The Plymouth Cheese Company is a family business, dating back to 1890. It was founded by John Coolidge, father of President Calvin Coolidge, in the small, village of Plymouth, now lovingly restored. During the recession it was forced to close, but young John, the President's son, reopened the factory in 1960, using the original recipe to make the cheese. Today it is as successful as a tourist attraction as it is for its cheese, which is sold mainly through the shop and by mail order.

SALLY JACKSON CHEESES

REGION: *Washington State*
TYPE: *Modern, farmhouse, unpasteurised, aged cheeses*
SOURCE: *Goat's and sheep's milk*
DESCRIPTION: *Various shapes and sizes*
CULINARY USES: *Table cheeses, cooking*

Sheep's milk cheeses seem to be emerging as the new stars of the cheese world, and Sally Jackson makes some of the best. Her mild, nutty, sheep's milk cheese wrapped in brandy-soaked chestnut leaves has a wonderful texture – it glides like silk across the palate, and the chestnut leaf wrap gives a vegetal, earthy, vaguely alcoholic subtlety to the final flavour.

RIGHT: The rind of Sonoma Dry Jack has a coating of cocoa

SEA STARS GOAT CHEESES
REGION: *California*
TYPE: *Modern, farmhouse, fresh cheeses*
SOURCE: *Goat's milk (Alpine)*
DESCRIPTION: *Small rounds and logs, garnished with edible flowers*
CULINARY USE: *Table cheese*

Cheesemaker Nancy Gaffney fell in love with goats 20 years ago, when she met and cared for Fanny – a capricious, beguiling and extremely fertile Alpine goat.

Nancy's small, beautifully presented cheeses are gentle, moist and lemon-fresh. Soft and spreadable, with just a hint of goat, they are exquisitely garnished with nasturtiums, marigolds and other edible flowers. The range includes two chèvre tortas, one with layers of sun-dried tomatoes and basil and the other with layers of pistachio and dried apricots. Nancy's cheeses have won her first place at the American Cheese Society's conferences, and are now to be found in all the best places up and down America's West Coast.

BELOW: Sonoma Jack flavoured with hot peppers

SHELBURNE CHEDDAR
REGION: *Vermont*
TYPE: *Traditional, farmhouse, unpasteurized, vegetarian, hard cheese*
SOURCE: *Cow's milk (Brown Swiss)*
DESCRIPTION: *Block cheese without rind*
CULINARY USES: *Table cheese, also widely used in cooking*

Mariano Gonzales uses the traditional cheddaring process to make this prize-winning cheese for Shelburne Farms. The cheese has a firm, biteable texture, and the milk yielded by Brown Swiss cows gives the flavour a rich complexity. Shelburne Cheddar is matured for 18–24 months and has a fat content of 51 per cent. At the annual conference of the American Cheese Society in 1990, it was declared Best of Show. Four years later, it won the Best Farmhouse Cheese category.

SONOMA JACK
REGION: *California*
TYPE: *Traditional, farmhouse, semi-soft cheese*
SOURCE: *Cow's milk*
DESCRIPTION: *Block cheese in various sizes without rind*
CULINARY USES: *Table cheese, grilling*

This mild, white cheese has won the hearts of Americans since it was introduced by David Jacks in the late nineteenth century. Supple and moist, it was probably modelled on the Scottish cheese, Dunlop. The sweet and creamy taste is balanced by a citrus bite. Now made in a wide range of flavours, including hot pepper, it has become a cheese for all seasons and occasions.

In 1931, Celso Viviani and Tom Vella started the Sonoma Cheese Factory to make Jack, which was already popular in northern California. When the partnership dissolved, Tom formed the equally well-regarded Vella Cheese Company down the road. A new generation of Vivianis continues to maintain the traditional cheesemaking methods, despite the strong pressure of demand for this popular cheese. They also produce Teleme, Cheddar, Havarti, Dry Jack (the rind of which is coated with cocoa) and their own ricotta.

ABOVE: Shelburne Cheddar – a prize-winning cheese made in the traditional way

TELEME

REGION: *California*
TYPE: *Traditional, farmhouse, vegetarian, semi-soft cheese*
SOURCE: *Cow's milk*
DESCRIPTION: *5kg/11lb square, 30cm/12in across. The pale pinkish-orange rind is dusted with rice flour*
CULINARY USES: *Table cheese, baking, salads*

The Peluso family have been making Teleme for three generations. Delicious when young, it really comes into its own when ripened. The pale pinkish rind, mottled with moulds and yeasts, literally bursts at the seams, and the aroma is utterly compelling. The taste conjures up conflicting images – meadow flowers, wild game and sour cream – and the cheese has a yeasty finish.

Teleme was introduced to America by Greek immigrants over a century ago. It is based on Touloumotyri or Touloumi, a goat's milk cheese similar to feta but not as salty. The immigrants did not have access to goat's milk, so used cow's milk instead. Italian cheesemakers found the cheese to their liking, made a few adjustments, and Teleme was born.

Peluso Cheese is one of only two companies currently making Teleme. They also produce Monterey Jack, Dry Jack, Halloumi and Raw Milk Cheddar.

BELOW: Teleme develops a wonderful aroma when it is left to ripen

TILLAMOOK CHEDDAR

REGION: *Oregon*
TYPE: *Traditional, creamery, vegetarian, hard cheese*
SOURCE: *Cow's milk (90 per cent Holstein; 10 per cent Jersey)*
DESCRIPTION: *White and annatto-coloured block cheeses*
CULINARY USES: *Table cheese, grating, grilling, baking, sauces*

Tillamook Cheddar is made using milk that has been heat-treated rather than pasteurized, a process that allows some of the bacteria essential for producing top quality Cheddar to be retained. To comply with American health regulations, the Cheddar must be over 60 days old before being sold, although most is aged for longer, to allow the cheese to reach the level when it can be labelled "sharp" or "extra sharp".

The white, uncoloured Cheddar is made with animal rennet, as it was found that aged cheeses made using non-animal rennet failed to achieve the desired quality and taste. Its mouth-watering, fruity tang is hard to resist.

Tillamook County Creamery Association, a co-operative of 160 dairymen, also produce Monterey Jack, Jalapeno, Colby and Smoked Cheddar. The plant handles a third of all the milk produced in Oregon. To do this, it runs 24 hours a day, 365 days a year. To maintain its enviable reputation as producer of one of America's finest Cheddars, every batch of milk is tested, and farmers are paid according to the quality and butterfat content of their milk.

TOSCANA

REGION: *California*
TYPE: *Modern, farmhouse, vegetarian, hard cheese*
SOURCE: *Sheep's milk*
DESCRIPTION: *900g/2lb round with convex sides. The hard, yellowish-grey, waxy, natural rind has a criss-cross pattern on top and bottom*
CULINARY USES: *Table cheese, grating*

Like many of America's modern cheese-makers, Cindy Calahan and her son Liam arrived at that position by accident, rather than design. When they left the city, they planned to produce superb, farm-raised lamb for the chefs of California. They were successful, but the excess milk after lambing proved too much of a temptation for Cindy, who could not resist making it into cheese. After some coaching in Tuscany they returned to the wild pastures of Bellwether Farms and now produce a magnificent American-style Pecorino.

The texture is hard and flaky, with small eyes irregularly scattered throughout the cheese. At first, Toscana feels dry in the mouth, but it dissolves to reveal a symphony of flavours and aromas, reminiscent of a warm summer's day in the mountains. Floral, aromatic, nutty and earthy, with the underlying sweetness of caramelized onions, Toscana is a wonderful cheese with a character all its own.

VERMONT CHEDDAR

REGION: *Vermont*
TYPE: *Traditional, creamery, hard cheese*
Source: *Cow's milk (Friesian and Jersey)*
DESCRIPTION: *Cylinders and truckles in various sizes, with waxed rind*
CULINARY USES: *Table cheese, grating, cooking*

Despite the time, money and space it takes to make a good Cheddar, the Cabot Farmers Co-operative Creamery has never faltered. Founded in 1919, the creamery is now owned by over 500 farmers, and produces both hard and soft cheeses. Once tasted, the rich, robust flavour, smooth texture and mouth-watering, tart finish of the Extra Sharp or Private Stock Cheddars are unforgettable.

VERMONT SHEPHERD
REGION: *Vermont*
TYPE: *Modern, farmhouse, unpasteurized, hard cheese*
SOURCE: *Sheep's milk*
DESCRIPTION: *4.5kg/10lb wheel with convex sides. The natural rind is hard and rustic-looking*
CULINARY USES: *Table cheese, grating*

When David Major took over the family sheep farm in 1983, he realized they would have to diversify to survive. Since 1989, David and his wife Cynthia have been making Vermont Shepherd cheese.

It is a modern, artisan cheese based on traditional cheesemaking methods. Each cheese is turned and scrubbed every day during the three-month ageing process to ensure that the good moulds survive and the bad die young.

Firm and dense, rather than hard, Vermont Shepherd is deliciously nutty. The sweetness of cream caramel that is so typical of sheep's milk cheese is balanced by a green-grass tang, reminiscent of meadow flowers and lanolin.

WIENINGER'S GOAT CHEESE
REGION: *New York State*
TYPE: *Modern, farmhouse, unpasteurized, hard cheese*
SOURCE: *Goat's milk*
DESCRIPTION: *6kg/13lb Gouda-style wheel with smooth, pale lemon, polished, natural rind*
CULINARY USES: *Table cheese, grating over pasta, in salads and sauces*

Sally and Ted Weininger base their cheese on Dutch Gouda, but have adapted the recipe to create a cheese that belongs in a class of its own. Using minimal salt, they still achieve a real depth of flavour.

A well-rounded, buxom, pale yellow wheel, Wieninger's Goat Cheese is sold young (at four to eight months) or aged (eight to 13 months). When young, the texture is firm and dense, yet still creamy, and the cheese has a sweet, fruity, herbaceous flavour. With age, the texture becomes more like that of Pecorino. The cheese is best eaten in chunks so that the coarse, grainy texture can be enjoyed and the layers of complex flavours can be fully appreciated.

THE CHEESES OF CENTRAL AND SOUTHERN AMERICA

The Altiplano or High Andes, the backbone and natural border dividing Chile from Argentina and running north through Bolivia and into Peru, is the home of the indigenous llama, alpaca and vicuna. The native Indians domesticated these fascinating creatures, relying on them not only as beasts of burden but also as a source of meat, milk, wool and hides. Cheese, however, was unknown until the Spanish and Portuguese missionaries arrived in the sixteenth and seventeenth centuries.

Even then, there was no instant conversion to cheesemaking. The High Andes were a hostile territory to all but the native beasts, and the lowlands were too humid for cows or goats. Only in the cooler areas in between did cows thrive.

As cheesemaking became established, it was the mild, fresh *queso blanco* that proved most popular, partly because it suited the diet of the people and partly because the cooler temperatures made it less important to mature the cheese. In Peru, where a few hardy goats survive the rigorous climate, the locals suspended sacks or skins containing the curd over slow-burning wood fires to speed up the draining process. More recently, in Chile, there has been a move to imitate the sheep's milk cheese of the Pyrenees.

Argentina is famous the world over for the quality of its beef, but was never a great cheese producer. The greatest influence on the cheese industry, such as it is, was the immigration of large numbers of Italians in the middle of the nineteenth century. Unable to survive without their cheese – and too far away to rely totally on imports – they started making a Parmesan equivalent, Treboligiano, together with a mozzarella-type cheese called Moliterno.

In Brazil, too, cattle are regarded principally as a source of meat. The humid conditions make cheesemaking extremely difficult, so cheese has never really caught the imagination – or the palates – of the people. Most of the cheese that is consumed is imported, but some local cheese is made in the Minas Gerais region, north of Rio de Janeiro. Minas Frescal (fresh cheese) and Minas Prensado (a stretched curd cheese) are no doubt based on recipes introduced by the early missionaries.

YERBA SANTA SHEPHERD'S CHEESE
REGION: *California*
TYPE: *Modern, farmhouse, unpasteurized, hard cheese*
SOURCE: *Goat's milk (Alpine)*
DESCRIPTION: *1.6kg/3¹/₂lb oval. The thick, beige to yellow, natural rind is hard and slightly oily*
CULINARY USES: *Table cheese, cooking*

Easily as good as any of the hard, artisan, goat's milk cheeses of Spain, Yerba Santa Shepherd's Cheese is very hard, dry and flaky, with small holes. The intensity and diversity of flavour is magnificent: at first the cheese has an almost minty freshness that tingles on the palate, then its more powerful, aromatic character, suggesting toffee, herbs and almonds, kicks in.

A consistent winner in the hard aged section at the annual conference of the American Cheese Society, Yerba Santa Shepherds Cheese is made by Chris and Jan Twohy at their farm near Clear Lake. They take pride in the quality of their milk and use no pesticides, artificial feed supplements or stabilizers.

BELOW: Yerba Santa Shepherd's Cheese

MEXICAN CHEESES

Although Mexican civilization dates back to at least 2000BC, it wasn't until the Spanish conquest of 1521 that cheeses were first introduced to Mexico. The Spanish brought with them chickens, pigs, cattle, goats and a few sheep. They established huge estates for themselves. Trade with the Old World created considerable wealth, not only from precious metals, but also from the export of the hitherto unknown tomatoes, peppers, chillies, potatoes and cocoa beans. The intrepid monks who travelled with the conquerors introduced cheesemaking. Pecorino, Manchego, fresh cheeses and hard cow's milk cheeses were welcome reminders of home.

Maize (corn), the main crop of Mexico, played an integral part in the national cuisine, especially in the form of tortillas. In addition, the ubiquitous beans ensured the diet was rich in fibre. These staples, plus tomatoes, chillies and peppers, along with cheese, have created some of Mexico's most famous dishes.

Queso blanco – a crumbly, soft, white cheese – is famously used in enchiladas, when it is mixed with raw onion and wrapped in a hot tortilla, which is then covered with a tomato and chilli sauce. Queso anejo, a clothbound goat's or cow's milk cheese, is crumbled into numerous dishes, while the stretched-curd cheese Asadero is popular as a melting cheese.

In the last 20 years, travel and the influence of a growing multinational community have created new markets for cheese in Mexico. Local producers now make versions of Gruyère, Camembert and Port Salut. Cream cheese is also produced, often with a flavouring of jalapeños or other chillies.

ASADERO
REGION: *Various*
TYPE: *Traditional, creamery, stretched curd cheese*
SOURCE: *Cow's milk*
DESCRIPTION: *Various shapes, ranging in weight from 225g–5kg/8oz–11lb. The rind is smooth and polished*
CULINARY USES: *Grilling or baking*
The name of this cheese means "fit for roasting". It melts superbly and is used in numerous dishes. Originally from Oaxaca – and sometimes referred to as queso Oaxaca – it is similar to Provolone. The curd is stretched, then shaped into balls, loaves or plaits (braids). White and supple, it ranges from bland to buttery and sweet.

QUESO ANEJO
REGION: *Various*
TYPE: *Traditional, farmhouse and creamery, hard cheese*
SOURCE: *Cow's and goat's milk*
DESCRIPTION: *5–10kg/11–22lb rounds or blocks, without rind*
CULINARY USES: *Grilling or baking*
Queso anejo (aged cheese) was originally made with goat's milk, but today cow's milk is often used. Crumbly and salty, it resembles feta when fresh. When dried, it acquires a texture not unlike that of Parmesan.

ABOVE: Queso anejo

QUESO BLANCO
REGION: *Various*
TYPE: *Traditional, creamery, fresh cheese*
SOURCE: *Cow's milk*
DESCRIPTION: *Various shapes and sizes, often in block form*
CULINARY USES: *Grilling, pan-frying, baking, salads*
The name simply means "white cheese". Queso blanco is made in most Latin American countries, and resembles a cross between mozzarella and salty cottage cheese. Traditionally, it is produced from skimmed milk or whey, coagulated with lemon juice, although recently some creameries have begun making it with full-cream milk coagulated with rennet. The curd is scalded and pressed to create an elastic texture which holds its shape when heated. Like Halloumi, it can be sliced and fried. The flavour is mild, creamy and lemon-fresh.

QUESO FRESCO
REGION: *Various*
TYPE: *Traditional, farmhouse and creamery, fresh cheese*
SOURCE: *Cow's or goat's milk*
DESCRIPTION: *Various sizes and shapes, often round*
CULINARY USES: *Grilling and baking, also used fresh in salads*
Based on the Spanish cheese Burgos, queso fresco (fresh cheese) is normally eaten within a few days of making. Soft and breakable, rather than crumbly, it has a grainy feel and very mild, fresh acidity. It holds its shape when heated.

LEFT: Asadero, which is also known as queso Oaxaca

AUSTRALIAN CHEESES

Australia's often inhospitable climate, extraordinary marsupials and abundant wildlife did not exactly inspire the nomadic Aborigines to set up homesteads, domesticate their animals and start cheesemaking, unlike their counterparts in the Northern Hemisphere. Instead, cheesemaking had to wait until the first European settlers arrived in the late 1700s, bringing with them cows, goats and sheep.

At first, cheese was made in kitchens on the isolated farms with tree stumps and boulders as presses, but gradually, as herds grew, the dairy farmers formed co-operatives.

Until the late 1960s, however, butter and Cheddar or variations on those themes were virtually the only dairy products being made, for it was largely the British and Irish who colonized Australia, and much of their production was exported back to the "home country".

The cheese revolution was fired by immigrants from Italy, Greece, Yugoslavia, Holland and Germany, who arrived in droves after the Second World War. Cheese was an integral part of their culture, and before long European cheesemakers were setting up factories. Most notable of these was Czech-born Milan Vyhnalek, who established Lactos in 1955 to make Brie, Camembert, Gouda

ABOVE: Gabriella Kervella, one of Australia's new breed of artisan cheesemakers with her herd of goats

and Edam. Kraft followed suit, developing a Pecorino-style cow's milk cheese and a Parmesan.

In the 1980s, when soft, smelly, flavoursome cheeses were first airfreighted in by Bill Studd, rather than being shipped, the large dairy companies and wholesalers watched in disbelief as chefs responded with almost indecent haste, snapping up the new arrivals as fast as they became available, despite the high prices and the availability of indigenous (if bland) copies.

It took about another 10 years before the number of modern, Australian, farmhouse cheeses could be

BELOW: Surprise Bay Cheddar

counted on more than one hand, but things were changing. A new breed of Australian cheesemaker was emerging.

Despite the revolution, farmhouse production remains small and industrial Cheddar dominates the market. However, as with wines, the best cheeses are made by individuals striving to perfect their craft. Unlike Europe, where land is scarce and cattle must often live in barns, having their fodder delivered on the back of a tractor, the majority of Australian cows graze on natural pastures – clean, pure and healthy. Regrettably, regulations in Australia ban the production of unpasteurized cheese, a ban shared by New Zealand and South Africa, so much of the character and flavour of the milk is lost.

Unlike their European counterparts, Australian cheeses tend to be made by one cheesemaker in an area, rather than several. This section therefore lists the makers to look out for, and highlights one or two examples of their cheeses. Also included is the occasional exception from a large creamery that has proved to be particularly good.

Other names to look out for are Elgaar Farm Cheddar from Tasmania, which also makes the herb- and spice-flavoured Meadow cheeses, and Faudel Farm in South Gippsland, whose goats yield fine fromage frais and curd cheese.

GIPPSLAND BLUE

REGION: *Victoria*

TYPE: *Modern, farmhouse, blue cheese*

SOURCE: *Cow's milk (Friesian)*

DESCRIPTION: *5kg/11lb round with natural, orange crust covered with a dusting of white and blue-grey moulds*

CULINARY USES: *Table cheese, grilling, salads*

Gippsland Blue is produced by the Tarago River Cheese Company, a joint venture begun in 1982 by Laurie Jensen, Richard Thomas and Robert Johnson, cheese lovers with a pioneering spirit that led them to make one of Australia's finest and best-known blue cheeses. Using milk from their own herd (and occasionally making their own starter cultures), they have adapted methods learnt in Europe to their own climatic and grazing conditions.

Gippsland Blue was probably the first genuine farmhouse cheese to be made in Australia. It resembles traditional Dolcelatte: sharp, yet sweet and buttery, with a spicy, lingering, blue-cheese tang.

ABOVE: Meredith Blue (left), Bass Straight Blue (right) and Gippsland Blue (front)

The chunky veins of blue mould spread unevenly through the dense, rich cheese, which ripens in eight to 10 weeks.

Learning from the marketplace and continuing to build on their own experience, the cheesemakers have created a variety of other blues as well as softer Camembert and Brie-style cheeses, using Jersey milk to obtain a deeper yellow colour and a more velvety, smooth texture. Committed to both good quality and consistency while acknowledging the seasonal nature of milk, they have successfully introduced numerous other cheeses, the more eclectic being Tarago Lavender, whose unusual additive has inspired local chefs to create some interesting dishes.

Shadows of Blue is milder than Gippsland Blue, with a Brie-like texture and taste, whereas Blue Orchid has a somewhat more vicious, intense nature

and should not be treated lightly. Thanks to the richness of the Jersey milk, Gippsland Brie is in the Double Brie category, with a buttery texture softened by the white moulds, which also help create the mild, milky flavour with its mushroomy overtones.

GRABETTO

REGION: *Victoria*

TYPE: *Modern, farmhouse, cheese (fresh and aged)*

SOURCE: *Goat's milk*

DESCRIPTION: *25g/1oz thimble-like cheese. The fine, crusty, natural rind has touches of white and grey*

CULINARY USE: *Table cheese*

When young, Grabetto has a taste not unlike crushed Brazil nut ice cream with a tingle of lemon sorbet. With age, the cheese becomes very hard and flaky in texture. It develops a sharp, mouthwatering flavour with more than just a hint of the goat's milk. Grabetto is produced by Yarra Valley Cheese. It ripens in three to six weeks.

ABOVE: *Two of the many different Kervella goat's cheeses – Affine (back) and Chèvre Frais log (front)*

HEIDI GRUYÈRE

REGION: *Tasmania*
TYPE: *Traditional, farmhouse, vegetarian, hard cheese*
SOURCE: *Cow's milk (Friesian)*
DESCRIPTION: *20–35kg/44–80lb wheel. The classic, crusty, Beaufort-type, natural rind looks almost polished*
CULINARY USES: *Table cheese, grilling, fondue*

Experienced in the traditional cheese-making techniques of his native country, Switzerland, Frank Marchand was brought out to Tasmania by Lactos in the 1970s. Like so many others, he fell in love with his adopted country. In 1985, with a small herd of 100 Friesians, he started Heidi Farm in order to make the cheeses of his childhood: Tilsit, Gruyère and Raclette.

Frank is fascinated by cheese and loves develop new varieties. Heidi Gruyère has a firm yet supple texture, similar to French Beaufort, with tiny, crunchy crystals and a profusion of flavours. The sweet, fruity taste initially suggests pineapple, then becomes nutty. The more mature the cheese, the better it tastes.

JINDI BRIE

REGION: *Victoria*
TYPE: *Modern, farmhouse, soft-white cheese*
SOURCE: *Cow's milk (Shorthorn/Jersey)*
DESCRIPTION: *2.75kg/6lb round with smooth, velvety, white penicillium rind*
CULINARY USES: *Table cheese, also used in salads*

George Ronalds has been farming in Gippsland since the early 1980s. He saw the opportunities for European-style cheeses in Australia and he and his team have concentrated on Camembert- and Brie-style cheeses.

Jindi Brie is semi-stabilized to give it a longer shelf life. The texture is rich and buttery and has slightly sweet tones. The flavour of the cheese resembles young mushrooms in melted butter. It ripens in four to five weeks.

Other cheeses made by George Ronalds include Jindi Camembert and a triple cream cheese.

LEFT: *Heidi Gruyère*

KANGAROO ISLAND BRIE

REGION: *Adelaide*
TYPE: *Traditional, farmhouse, soft-white cheese*
SOURCE: *Cow's milk*
DESCRIPTION: *20cm/8in wheel with a smooth, velvety, white penicillium rind*
CULINARY USE: *Table cheese*

Mos and Liz Howard have been making cheese at the family farm on Kangaroo Island for the past five years, using only milk from their own cows. Each cheese is made by hand, the curd being gently ladled into the moulds or hoops.

The young curd is drained and turned; after about 12 hours it will reduce to about half the original volume. Some four to six weeks later, each batch is tasted, tested and checked, then labelled and sent to the mainland.

Kangaroo Island Brie is smooth and voluptuous, with the sweet, creamy taste of fine mushroom soup. It melts like butter in the mouth, with just a hint of lush, green grass and a whisper of sea breezes. As the cheese is made all year round, and the curd is not stabilized, it is subject to subtle seasonal changes – the mark of a true hand-made cheese.

Like all cheeses, Kangaroo Island Brie is at its best when eaten at room temperature. It has a fat content of 55 per cent.

KERVELLA AFFINE

REGION: *Western Australia*
TYPE: *Modern, farmhouse, organic, soft-white cheese*
SOURCE: *Goat's milk*
DESCRIPTION: *100g/3¾oz round or log with soft, fine, white rind*
CULINARY USE: *Table cheese*

Named for the cheesemaker, Gabrielle Kervella of Fromage Fermier, this goat's milk cheese can be eaten at two weeks, when it has a mild, sweet taste. More often, though, it is allowed to mature to eight weeks, when the soft curd becomes hard and flaky and the aromatic character of the goat's milk intensifies. The distinct, lingering taste of this more mature cheese suggests crushed, salty macadamia nuts.

KERVELLA CHÈVRE FRAIS

REGION: *Western Australia*
TYPE: *Modern, farmhouse, organic, fresh cheese*
SOURCE: *Goat's milk*
DESCRIPTION: *Round or log-shaped cheese, made in various sizes*
CULINARY USES: *Table cheese, grilling, spreading, soufflés*

Gabrielle Kervella has become synonymous with Australian cheese, yet she only started making her traditional French-style goat's cheese in Gidgegannup around the mid-1980s. In the years that followed, she worked alongside French artisan cheesemakers, returning to Australia to adapt the recipes to prevailing conditions that were very different from those she encountered in Europe. Heat, dust and significant seasonal variations in the pastures were just some of the difficulties she had to contend with, but she has produced a range of delicious cheeses.

Kervella Chèvre Frais is a classic, French-style, fresh chèvre. It ripens in a few days, has no rind and has a light mousse-like texture. Smooth and lemon-fresh, it melts in the mouth with a hint of almonds and just a suggestion of goat's milk. The finish is slightly sweet. It is sometimes dusted with ash or herbs.

KING ISLAND CAPE WICKHAM BRIE

REGION: *Tasmania*
TYPE: *Modern, creamery, soft-white cheese*
SOURCE: *Cow's milk*
DESCRIPTION: *1kg/2¼lb wheel with thick, velvety, soft rind*
CULINARY USE: *Table cheese*

Small and exposed, King Island guards the western entrance to Bass Strait, which separates Tasmania from the Australian mainland. The winds that buffet the island are legendary, and flotsam and jetsam from wrecked ships have often fetched up on these shores.

Straw from shipwrecked sailors' mattresses is thought to have been responsible for the unusual and varied grasses on which the King Island cattle graze all year round, contributing to the unique character of the island cheeses.

Founded in 1902, King Island Dairy became a co-operative in 1939, but it was not until 1988 that the company started producing the cheeses that have made it a household name – rich, sweet-tasting cream cheeses, spicy, aromatic blue cheeses, the famous Cape Wickham Brie

BELOW: Cape Wickham Brie (front) and Jindi Brie (back)

and the rich, full-flavoured, hand-made Surprise Bay Cheddar.

King Island Cape Wickham Brie is a stabilized cheese, with cream added. It ripens in 20–45 days and is covered in a soft-white rind with a mushroomy aroma and taste. The creamy yellow interior melts like butter in the mouth and the flavour hints of sea breezes and sweet pastures.

KING RIVER GOLD

REGION: *Victoria*
TYPE: *Modern, farmhouse, semi-soft cheese*
SOURCE: *Cow's milk (Jersey/Friesian)*
DESCRIPTION: *600g/1¼lb round. The washed, natural rind is pinkish-orange, with a dusting of grey mould*
CULINARY USES: *Table cheese; also good if the rind is removed and the cheese sliced and melted over vegetables*

David and Anne Brown have come a long way since they stumbled across an old butter factory in Milawa, 200km/125 miles north of Melbourne. With the help of Richard Thomas for the first two years, they developed the Gorgonzola-style Milawa Blue. As David's expertise increased, they gradually widened their repertoire, and today they produce a wide range of excellent cheeses, including several made from Sheep's and goat's milk.

A pilgrimage by one of their cheese-makers to France to work alongside the artisan makers of Reblochon, Chevrotin des Aravis, Cabicou and Beaufort has obviously influenced the quality and flavour of cheeses like Oxley Traditional Blue, Milawa White (a fresh, acid cheese) and their two washed-rind cheeses, King River Gold and Milawa Gold.

The rind of King River Gold is washed and rubbed to encourage the pinkish-orange bacteria to spread over the cheese, sealing in the flavour and creating a smooth, dense, voluptuous interior with random small holes. The flavour hints at warm cow's milk and the cheese has a slightly sharp, green-grass finish. Milawa Gold is a stronger, more piquant version of the same cheese. Inspired by the Trappist-style cheeses of Europe, it has a distinctive, red-gold rind and a supple, smooth texture.

MEREDITH BLUE
REGION: *Victoria*
TYPE: *Modern, farmhouse, blue, cheese*
SOURCE: *Cow's milk*
DESCRIPTION: *1.5–2kg/3–4½lb round. The crusty, natural rind is orange, covered with grey, white and blue moulds*
CULINARY USE: *Table cheese*

Now in her fifth year at Meredith Dairy, Julie Cameron, the cheesemaker, is producing a number of different types of cheeses using sheep's milk, including a version of the fresh French cheese, fromage blanc. She also makes a delicious, sweet, caramel-tasting yogurt that has just a hint of fresh rosemary and eucalyptus flavours. More recently, she has been experimenting with goat's milk and makes a lovely, fresh chèvre and a goat's milk fromage frais.

Although described as Roquefort-style, Meredith Blue is a mild and creamy blue cheese with its own unique character. The sweetness of the sheep's milk comes through the distinct and spicy, but not overly strong finish.

Meredith Blue ripens in two months and, because it is made using sheep's milk, is a seasonal cheese.

The dairy also produces Woodburne, which is a small moulded, white, sheep's milk cheese.

MILAWA BLUE
REGION: *Victoria*
TYPE: *Modern, farmhouse, blue cheese*
SOURCE: *Cow's milk*
DESCRIPTION: *6kg/13lb squat cylinder. The rugged, wrinkled, natural rind is grey or pink, with various shadings of mould*
CULINARY USE: *Table cheese*

Made by David and Anne Brown of the Milawa Cheese Company. The streaks of blue invade a rich, buttery interior that melts in the mouth. Milawa Blue has a lovely, vegetal taste, with undertones of bitter chocolate. Matured for eight to 12 weeks, it ranges from the sublime to the slightly disappointing.

POLKOLBIN
REGION: *New South Wales*
TYPE: *Modern, farmhouse, semi-soft cheese*
SOURCE: *Cow's milk*
DESCRIPTION: *250g/9oz square. The fine, slightly wrinkled, orange rind tends to be sticky*
CULINARY USES: *Table cheese; grilling*

At the Hunter Valley Cheese Company, set up in 1995 by David Brown of Milawa, cheesemaker Peter Curtis produces the popular Polkolbin. Similar to the French cheese Pont l'Evêque, it has the aroma of damp washing or a farmyard. Sharp and spicy, it has a lingering, piquant, almost meaty taste.

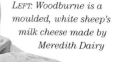
LEFT: *Woodburne is a moulded, white sheep's milk cheese made by Meredith Dairy*

PURRUMBETE MOZZARELLA
REGION: *Victoria*
TYPE: *Traditional, farmhouse, stretched-curd cheese*
SOURCE: *Water buffalo's milk*
DESCRIPTION: *200g/7oz ball*
CULINARY USES: *Melting, grilling, in salads*

The water buffalo grazing at the edge of beautiful Purrumbete Lake look as though they have been there for ever, yet it took a man with determination and a dream to make it happen. Roger Haldane's fascination with the animal kingdom began when he introduced alpacas into Australia, but it was the magnificent water buffalos of southern Italy that really captured his imagination and drove him through red tape to import 55 of the animals in 1996.

Roger's imposing blue-stone homestead overlooks the meadows running down to the lake. The milking parlour has been upgraded to house the buffalo (which demand more tranquil surroundings and more privacy than their bovine cousins) and, with the help of confirmed cheese addict Nick Haddow, Roger has developed Australia's first buffalo's milk mozzarella.

Purrumbete Mozzarella has the authentic perfume and nutty taste of Italian mozzarella and is a tribute to the months Nick spent in Italy learning the process from artisan producers. The porcelain-white colour is equally accurate, but most importantly, the texture – springy, stringy and wet – is entirely right.

The company also produces Dancing Brolgo, a washed-curd cheese named after a native bird famous for its weird dance.

ABOVE: *Purrumbete Mozzarella – Australia's first true buffalo's milk cheese*

PYENGANA CHEDDAR

REGION: *Tasmania*
TYPE: *Modern, farmhouse, hard cheese*
Source: *Cow's milk*
DESCRIPTION: *8kg/18lb and 18kg/40lb truckles. The natural rind has the imprint of the cloth, with some moulding*
CULINARY USES: *Table cheese, grilling, grating*

Firm, but neither as hard nor as smooth as traditional Cheddar, this cheese has a slightly granular feel to it. After about 12 months, the natural bacteria in the milk produce a rich, nutty cheese with a real depth of flavour. The cheesemaker is John Healey, who took over the old Pyengana cheese factory in the mid 1990s. He uses pasteurized milk from his own farm and continues to follow the old Pyengana methods, which are often labour-intensive but produce wonderful results.

RACLETTE

REGION: *Tasmania*
TYPE: *Traditional, farmhouse, vegetarian, semi-soft cheese*
SOURCE: *Cow's milk (Friesian)*
DESCRIPTION: *5kg/11lb flat wheel. The brown, leathery rind is drier than that of traditional Raclette and can be somewhat sticky*
CULINARY USES: *Table cheese; also marvellous if sliced and grilled*

Frank Marchand's Raclette comes close to the original French cheese, and is elastic and supple, yet dense. Small holes, spread through the paste, give it a slightly open texture. There is a hint of sweetness, but the overriding taste is savoury, meaty and yeasty. Made by Heidi Farm, the cheese is produced only in spring and summer, and it matures in two months.

ROMNEY MATURE

REGION: *Victoria*
TYPE: *Traditional and modern, farmhouse, semi-soft cheese*
SOURCE: *Sheep's milk (Romney)*
DESCRIPTION: *1.5kg/3¼lb cylinder with natural rind imprinted with the marks of the cheesecloth, and some light grey mould*
CULINARY USES: *Table cheese; also used for cooking*

Robert Manifold's family have been in this area for so long that you expect to find mountains or rivers bearing the names of his ancestors. He bases his cheesemaking at the Mount Emu Creek Dairy in Camperdown and uses the milk from two or three local farms. Romney (named for the breed of sheep) is a washed-curd cheese and comes in two different forms. For the waxed version, the young curd is shaped and drained in a mould, then waxed while still moist. As a result, the finished cheese is fresh, moist and springy, with tiny holes and a mild, sweet flavour.

For Romney Mature, the curd is bound in cloth and allowed to mature for up to six months. The sweet, caramel taste of the sheep's milk intensifies and the cheese develops a more nutty flavour and a hard, flaky texture.

Mount Emu Creek Dairy also makes Romney Fresca, as well as its own feta.

BELOW: Pyengana Cheddar is not as hard as some traditional Cheddars

ABOVE: Romney Mature

ST CLAIRE

REGION: *Tasmania*
TYPE: *Traditional, creamery, hard cheese*
SOURCE: *Cow's milk*
DESCRIPTION: *9kg/20lb wheel with fine, leathery, waxed, yellow rind*
CULINARY USES: *Table cheese, grating, grilling*

Made in the style of a traditional Gruyère, the deep yellow St Claire is smooth and firm (and a little too rubbery for the author's taste). Sweeter and milder than traditional Gruyère, it has a fairly mellow, fruity finish.

It is made by one of Australia's oldest manufacturers of Continental-style cheeses, Lactos, which was founded by Milan Vyhnalek in 1955. Bongrain, the huge French cheese company, soon realized its potential and bought Lactos in 1981. Now highly successful, with plants in several locations, Lactos makes a range of cheeses and consistently wins prizes around the world for their quality. Although best known for its Brie- and Camembert-style cheeses, it also makes Edam, Gouda, Neufchâtel and several blues in addition to cream and processed cheeses. St Claire is its only Gruyère-style cheese.

TASMANIA HIGHLAND CHÈVRE LOG
REGION: *Tasmania*
TYPE: *Modern, farmhouse, fresh cheese*
SOURCE: *Goat's milk
(Toggenberg/Saanen)*
DESCRIPTION: *150g/5oz log*
CULINARY USES: *Table cheese, grilling*

John Bignell's chèvre is fresh and lemony, with a moist, cheesecake texture. It has a distinct, but not overpowering, goat taste, redolent of thyme and white wine. Both plain and ash-covered versions are available. They mature in one to three weeks and have a fat content of 35 per cent.

John and Jill Bignell also make sheep's milk cheeses, both fresh and aged. Their semi-hard Sheep's cheese has a natural rind, a spongy, Havarti texture and a sweet, fruity finish. The author has yet to track this cheese down, but had it described to her by Bill Studd, joint owner of the Richmond Hill Cafe and Larder in Melbourne, who stocks a marvellous selection of Australian artisan cheeses.

The Bignells' newest venture, is a wickedly rich, triple cream cheese based on the French Brillat-Savarin.

TIMBOON BRIE
REGION: *Victoria*
TYPE: *Traditional and modern, soft
white, organic cheese*
SOURCE: *Cow's milk*
DESCRIPTION: *1kg/2¼lb round with
soft-white, velvety penicillium crust*
CULINARY USE: *Table cheese*

Herman Schultz and his family must have felt like pioneers when they started making cheese in 1984. Today there are more than 30 farmhouse dairies in Australia, but Herman is still an innovator. His cheeses are made using only bio-dynamic milk (a type of organic milk).

Timboon Brie ripens in 45–60 days. It is not stabilized, and therefore has a more tempestuous nature and a greater depth of flavour than many cheeses of the same type. Because the milk is pasteurized, the rind does not develop the wild yeasts and pigments that would give Timboon the authenticity of a traditional Brie, but it comes closer than most.

Other Timboon Farmhouse Cheeses include Buetten and Fleurie.

ABOVE: Washed Rind (back) and Timboon Brie (front)

TOMME DE CHÈVRE
REGION: *New South Wales*
TYPE: *Modern, farmhouse,
semi-soft cheese*
SOURCE: *Goat's milk*
DESCRIPTION: *1kg/2¼lb cylinder with
orange, natural rind patched with
blue and white moulds*
CULINARY USES: *Table cheese, grilling,
baking, salads*

Hunter Valley Cheese Company's Tomme is smooth and dense, with a slightly salty tang and the subtle background flavour of tarragon and white wine that is characteristic of goat's milk cheese. It is slightly firmer than an unpasteurized French Tomme, and does not have quite the same depth of flavour.

Cheesemaker Peter Curtis also produces Chèvre Brie, which is based on an old French recipe for Brie de Melun. The fresh curd is dusted with vine ash and salt.

WASHED RIND
REGION: *Victoria*
TYPE: *Modern, farmhouse,
semi-soft cheese*
SOURCE: *Cow's milk (Red Shorthorn)*
DESCRIPTION: *3kg/6½lb flat wheel. The
sticky, orange, washed rind is dusted
with blue, grey and white moulds*
CULINARY USE: *Table cheese*

Fred Leppin entered the world of cheesemaking in the late 1980s. His English and French-style cheeses are not mere copies of the originals. Instead, he creates new world versions. His semi-soft, washed-rind cheese, while made in the Trappist style, has different qualities from the original. The cheese has a meaty, pungent aroma with a soft, springy texture, and the flavour seems to have absorbed the warm, minty aroma of the eucalyptus trees.

Fred Leppin's washed rind cheeses – Whitelaw, Bass River Red, Wine Washed Rind, Cronwell, Ranceby, Loch and Kardella – have been greeted with great enthusiasm in Australia.

WOODSIDE CABECOU

REGION: *Adelaide*
TYPE: *Traditional, farmhouse, fresh and aged cheeses*
SOURCE: *Goat's milk*
DESCRIPTION: *30g/1¼oz disc. The thin, natural crust is yellowish and wrinkled. It may develop rogue moulds, but these can easily be brushed off*
CULINARY USE: *Table cheese*

Paula Jenkins has a passion and an innate talent for cheesemaking. Much of her knowledge was acquired through working alongside artisan cheesemakers in France and Britain, and she is skilled at adapting their recipes and methods for the Australian climatic conditions and milk.

Along with chef Simon Burr, Paula has been running Woodside Cheese Wrights for just over two years. The cheesery is located in the old Farmers' Union factory at Heritage Park in Woodside, where Paula makes a variety of cheeses from both goat's and cow's milk.

Woodside Cabecou is ivory-white, soft and mousse-like when young, with a fresh acidity. After a few days, it develops a fine surface skin which blossoms into a delicate, white

mould. This helps to ripen the fresh curd. With age, the cheese hardens, the herbaceous, mushroomy flavour and aroma become more obvious and some furry, grey mould may appear.

The fresh chèvre curd makes an excellent alternative to cream cheese, adding an extra dimension to salads, grilled vegetable dishes and snacks.

Edith takes its name from an artisan cheesemaker with whom Paula worked in Burgundy. A soft cheese with a luxurious texture, it is encouraged to grow its velvet coat before being rolled in vine ash and aged for a few weeks. The texture is the result of the laborious task of hand-ladling the curd into the moulds. This, together with the lingering goaty flavour, is ensuring its success.

The company also produce Capricorn and Charleston, a cloth-matured Cheddar.

LEFT: Yarra Valley Feta

SOUTH AFRICAN CHEESES

Most cheeses sold in South Africa today are factory-made copies of Gouda and Cheddar, which is not surprising, given that the majority of European immigrants who first settled in this country came from Holland and Great Britain. Small amounts of feta, Edam and Brie are produced locally, and it is possible to obtain industrial imports of European cheeses, but cheeses that are uniquely South African are difficult to come by.

Cheesemakers like Christine Briscoe are doing their best to change the situation, however. Christine farms Ayrshires in Natal, some 3,000 miles from her main market, Cape Town. This does not prevent her from ensuring her cheeses are delivered in peak condition to the wine farms where they sell extremely well. She simply air freights them in from Durban. Her range, sold under the name Galtee Mare, consists mainly of English-style territorials like Sage Derby, Leicester and Cheddar, and she even makes two blues. All her cheeses are hand-made.

The Harris family also farm in Natal, but their herd consists of Jerseys, not Ayrshires. They make small volumes of several cheeses under the name Bellavigne. These include Saint-Paulin, Tilsit and a soft, creamy, sweet cheese that looks like Edam.

Fairview Estate, a wine farm near Paarl, in the Cape Province, has been producing a soft, Brie-style blue since the early 1980s. It can be found in supermarkets and speciality shops.

The booming tourist industry will undoubtedly lead to a demand for more locally produced cheeses, as has happened elsewhere in the world. When it does, South African cheesemakers – as determined and dedicated as any of their international colleagues – will come into their own.

YARRA VALLEY PYRAMID

REGION: *Victoria*
TYPE: *Modern, farmhouse, fresh cheese*
SOURCE: *Goat's milk*
DESCRIPTION: *Small pyramid, plain or ash-covered*
CULINARY USES: *Table cheese, grilling*

Firm, yet light in texture, Yarra Valley Pyramid resembles Sainte-Maure. Creamy, lemon-fresh and slightly salty, it melts in the mouth like ice cream. If left to age, the cheese becomes firmer and may develop some mould.

The cheese is produced by Richard Thomas, a man who is in danger of becoming a living legend in the Australian cheese world. His name first appeared when, in partnership with David Brown, he started the Milawa Cheese Company. Next, he helped to set up Meredith Dairy. Yarra Valley is his first venture with goat's milk cheese, but looks like becoming another Australian success story.

They also make Yarra Valley Feta. This cheese is sold packed into small cans. The little balls of refreshingly salty, moist cheese are immersed in olive oil and fresh herbs to give extra flavour to the cheese.

THE CHEESES OF NEW ZEALAND

It is thought that the Maoris, travelling in canoes from Polynesia, were the first to settle New Zealand, around the first century AD. Some historians say that the red-headed Morioris arrived first, but were wiped out by the Maoris. In any event, the early settlers found no indigenous mammals to provide milk or meat, and their diet consisted mainly of ferns, roots, birds, fish and shellfish.

The absence of indigenous mammals meant that when the first British settlers arrived in the late eighteenth century, they had to bring their cattle with them. To provide grazing for their Friesian, Jersey and Guernsey cows, they hacked and burned vast areas of primeval forest. The sheep were chosen for their meat and wool rather than for milking, and the few goats that survived the treacherous sea voyages were mainly for domestic use.

Co-operative dairies, owned by the farmers, were established throughout New Zealand to process milk from the many small and isolated farms. From the late 1840s Cheddar became a major export to

BELOW: A cheesemaker at Kapiti turning Aorangi cheeses to ensure the white mould coats the entire cheese

the home country. Blue cheese was also being made in small quantities by the middle of the nineteenthth century.

During the Second World War, Cheddar from New Zealand was welcomed in a Britain enduring rationing. Customer loyalty and consistency of quality have kept it on British tables, although the volume has been cut back considerably since Britain's entry into the Common Market.

New Zealand has been forced to look elsewhere for trading partners, and today large volumes of cheese and other dairy products are exported to North America, the Middle East, Russia and Japan.

Over the past 30 years or so, the small co-operatives have merged, and New Zealand now has some of the largest and most efficient milk-processing factories in the world. However, much of the cheese is being made to meet the requirements of large overseas customers. Consistency is important and regional characteristics are quashed so that a buyer can purchase cheese with an identical profile – good news for buyers looking for uniformity, but disappointing for those seeking subtle nuances of flavour.

In a country the size of Britain, but with a population of just over 3.5 million,

it is a challenge for the large co-operatives to produce a variety of cheeses and yet remain profitable. Blue cheese was introduced commercially in the 1950s by the New Zealand Rennet Company, now Ferndale Dairies, who are the country's largest producer of speciality cheeses, especially blue cheeses.

The redoubtable Ross McCallum saw the potential for more specialized cheeses, and started his own company – Kapiti Cheese – in 1985. His aim was to produce New Zealand cheeses rather than European imitations, and he set about developing a range of cheeses with Maori names. Equally important, he created an image that would encourage New Zealanders to buy the local cheese by choice and not just because there was nothing else. His strategy has worked, and Kapiti Cheese now produces over 50 different cheeses.

Several resourceful Dutch cheesemakers emigrated to New Zealand in the 1980s. Combining traditional methods with modern practices, they recreated the traditional cheeses of their homeland – Gouda, Leiden, Edam and Maasdam, many of which are delicious when aged.

Change was afoot. Large factories started to mass-produce Camembert and Brie, and a few took courage and introduced New Zealanders to chèvre, but it was not until Kapiti's small, feta-like, sheep's milk cheese, *hipi iti* (which means "little sheep" in Maori) hit the market in 1990 that New Zealand could boast a commercially produced sheep's milk cheese. Considering that at the time there were over 40 million sheep in New Zealand, this seems quite extraordinary.

Today there are around 14 factories and 19 independent or artisan cheesemakers, producing over 200 different cheeses. Many are uniquely New Zealand discoveries, bearing local names and exhibiting distinct characteristics and considerable charm. Because it would be impossible to list them all, they have been selected on the basis of their success at the New Zealand Cheese Awards.

AIREDALE

REGION: *Oamaru*

TYPE: *Modern, farmhouse, vegetarian, semi-hard cheese*

SOURCE: *Cow's milk*

DESCRIPTION: *2kg/4¹/₂lb straight-sided round. The thin, natural crust has a coating of red cheese "paint"*

CULINARY USES: *Table cheese, grating, grilling*

Made by Bob Berry for Whitestone Cheese, Airedale is compact, rather than elastic. Its texture is on the borderline between semi-soft and hard. Special red cheese "paint" conceals its deep sun-yellow centre and encourages the cheese to develop a real depth of flavour. Fruity when young, it becomes full-bodied, with an onion aroma and memorable savoury aftertaste.

BARRY'S BAY CHEDDAR

REGION: *Banks Peninsula*

TYPE: *Traditional, creamery, hard cheese*

SOURCE: *Cow's milk*

DESCRIPTION: *35kg/80lb cylinder, waxed and clothbound*

CULINARY USES: *Table cheese, grating, grilling*

Cheesemaking was first introduced to the Banks Peninsula around 1844 by English and Scottish settlers. By the late 1890s there were at least nine factories, producing butter, Cheddar and other cheeses; today Barry's Bay is the only one left. Here cheesemaker Don Walker and his team successfully combine modern technology and traditional cheesemaking methods to produce a range of European cheeses, which consistently win medals at the New Zealand Cheese Awards. Their rinded Cheddar is the only traditional, cloth-bound Cheddar in New Zealand. It is made in large cylinders, which are first waxed and then left to mature for six to 36 months. This results in a firmer texture than that of Cheddars that are made in blocks and matured in plastic. At around 18 months, the flavour intensifies and the cheese seems to develop a mind and style of its own. Barry's Bay Cheddar is a past gold medal winner at the New Zealand Cheese Awards.

BLEU DE MONTAGNE

REGION: *Various*

TYPE: *Modern, creamery, blue cheese*

SOURCE: *Cow's milk*

DESCRIPTION: *200g/7oz and 1.8kg/4lb tall cylinders. The fine, straw-coloured rind has a dusting of white, pale blue and sometimes red moulds*

CULINARY USE: *Table cheese*

Made by Ferndale Dairies, Bleu de Montagne is smooth and quite creamy, with a spicy, blue tang that becomes more pronounced with age. A few weeks after the cheese is made, the natural crust is rubbed with salt, then pierced with stainless-steel rods. This allows the blue mould already present in the cheese to breathe in the oxygen and weave the threads and patches of blue-grey mould through the open-textured, creamy interior. Bleu de Montagne ripens in 60 days. It won a gold medal at the 1997 New Zealand Cheese Awards.

BRICK

REGION: *Wellington*

TYPE: *Modern, small, creamery, semi-soft, vegetarian cheese*

SOURCE: *Cow's milk*

DESCRIPTION: *2kg/4¹/₂lb brick with sticky, burnt-orange, washed rind*

CULINARY USE: *Table cheese*

Brick was first made in America in the early nineteenth century, based upon the traditional, monastery-style cheeses of Europe. Kapiti Cheese began experimenting with Brick in the 1990s. Having tried it in America, they tested it in New Zealand by entering it for the 1994 Cheese Awards. It won a gold medal that year and the Cheese Lover's Cheese Award in 1995.

The rind has a marvellous, pungent aroma with overtones of yeast and roast lamb. The pale yellow interior is velvety-smooth and dense – typical of a washed-rind cheese. It has a sweet and savoury taste, with a spicy tang.

The sticky orange rind has,

however, not responded well to being entombed in plastic film – a prerequisite in New Zealand supermarkets. This factor, combined with the pungent aroma, has caused retailers some concern. Sadly, Kapiti have either withdraw it or sold a younger, less exciting version. Fortunately the young chefs of New Zealand love Brick and it continues to find its way on to numerous cheeseboards. Hopefully, it is the first of many washed rind cheeses to be made in New Zealand.

BRIE

REGION: *Various*

TYPE: *Modern, creamery, soft-white cheese*

SOURCE: *Cow's milk*

DESCRIPTION: *Various sizes and shapes, with thick, white penicillium rind*

CULINARY USE: *Table cheese*

Numerous Brie- and Camembert-style cheeses are made in New Zealand. The quality is uniform and consistent. Because most of these soft-white cheeses are stabilized, there is little variation in taste. Stabilization means that once the curd has broken down and the cheese has a dense but creamy consistency, it will remain in that state rather than continuing to ripen.

It is becoming more usual for the locally produced cheeses to be given Maori names. Kapiti's Aorangi, for instance, is a Brie-style cheese whose Maori name means "white cloud".

BELOW: Brick

CHEDDAR

REGION: *Various*
TYPE: *Traditional, creamery,*
hard cheese
SOURCE: *Cow's milk*
DESCRIPTION: *Sizes vary, but they are*
typically block-shaped
and free of rind
CULINARY USES: *Table cheese, grating, in*
salads and sauces, baking

Block Cheddars are never as hard as those matured in cloth, but when aged for 18 months or more, they develop a firm, bite-able texture and a delicious cheese-and-onion tang that intensifies when the cheese is cooked. The natural carotene in the grass gives New Zealand Cheddar extra depth of colour and strict controls imposed by the dairy boards ensure that Cheddars of the same age will have a virtually identical profile, no matter where in New Zealand they are produced.

It is this predictable uniformity, regardless of season or place of origin, that has made New Zealand Cheddar the popular choice of buyers the world over. However, because the grazing and climate are so diverse, there is a move by smaller producers to produce Cheddar-style cheeses that celebrate these differences.

A recent development (presumably a marketing initiative) has seen the word Cheddar disappearing from the labelling on some pre-packed cheeses, leaving only the strength of flavour to identify the cheese. Degrees of strength are as follows: Mild, Medium, Mature, Tasty, Extra Mature and Vintage.

There are so many New Zealand Cheddars it would be impossible to name them all or say which were the best. However, in recent years Duke of Marlborough, Marlborough Tasty Cheddar and Tararua BONZ Cheddar and have each been declared to be Champion Cheddar at the New Zealand Cheese Awards. One of the "Best Cheddars up to 12 months" is Anchor Mild Cheddar, which is made by Anchor Products.

COLBY

REGION: *Various*
TYPE: *Traditional, creamery,*
semi-soft cheese
SOURCE: *Cow's milk*
DESCRIPTION: *Sizes vary, but they are*
generally block-shaped and free
of rind
CULINARY USES: *Table cheese, grating,*
grilling, snacks and salads

Colby was named after the town in Wisconsin, USA, where it was first made. It came to New Zealand in 1882 and is still one of the most popular cheeses.

It is a washed-curd cheese, which means that the curds are thoroughly rinsed in fresh water to remove all excess whey and any stray lactose. This prevents the acidity in the curd from rising, so the cheese remains soft and springy, with a sweet and mild flavour.

Colby has a higher moisture content than Cheddar and feels more elastic. It is also sweet, rather than savoury, thus lacking the depth of flavour acquired by a good Cheddar. For this reason, it is seldom cooked; if it is used in recipes, it is for reasons of texture rather than flavour.

Colby ripens in four months.

EVANSDALE FARMHOUSE BRIE

REGION: *South Island*
TYPE: *Modern, farmhouse, vegetarian,*
soft-white cheese
SOURCE: *Cow's milk*
DESCRIPTION: *Thick rounds in various*
sizes, with soft, fine, white rind
CULINARY USE: *Table cheese*

Colin Dennison seems to make the impossible look easy. A school teacher, he makes cheese in his "spare time", helped by members of his family. Self-taught, he has

BELOW: New Zealand
Cheddar

a zealous desire for perfection and a strong dose of the New Zealand attitude that if you need something doing you do it yourself.

He had not planned to become a cheesemaker, but when Daffodil, their house cow, produced more milk than the family could consume, Colin entered the challenging cheese world. His first attempt, Monterey Jack, was not a great success, but Colin persevered. The result was Evansdale Farmhouse Brie, still his most popular cheese.

Deeper in hieght than traditional Brie, Evansdale Farmhouse has a soft-white rind and a smooth, creamy texture that melts in the mouth, gradually releasing its flavour of mushrooms, melted butter and green grass. The cheese ripens in six weeks. Seldom found outside Dunedin, it is available by mail order from Colin at Evansdale Cheese, who also make Caerphilly, Komene Kaas, Sage Derby, Wensleydale, ricotta and feta.

FOUR HERB GOUDA

REGION: *Christchurch*
TYPE: *Traditional, farmhouse,*
organic, vegetarian, hard cheese
SOURCE: *Cow's milk*
DESCRIPTION: *5kg/11lb boulder-shaped*
cheese with waxed, natural rind
CULINARY USES: *Table cheese*

Rients Rympa grew up in Holland, close to a cheese factory. When he and his wife Karen decided to emigrate to New Zealand, they first spent a year studying and learning about cheese in Holland. Nearly 15 years later, they have a thriving business and the Karikaas brand is familiar throughout South Island.

Their Four Herb Gouda is made from organic milk from a nearby farm's herd of Friesian/Holstein cows, the same breed that is used in Holland to make the traditional cheese. The creamy, rich and nutty taste of the cheese marries well with the flavour of the fresh, finely cut herbs that are distributed through it. Four Herb Gouda is matured for three to six months.

They also produce Leyden, Maasdam, plain Gouda and Kwark (Quark).

HIPI ITI

REGION: *Wellington*
TYPE: *Modern, creamery, vegetarian, fresh cheese*
SOURCE: *Sheep's milk*
DESCRIPTION: *90g/3¹/₂oz cylinder*
CULINARY USES: *Table cheese, grilling, baking, salads*

In a country where sheep vastly outnumber people, it is perhaps surprising that New Zealand had to wait until 1990 for its first sheep's milk cheese to appear. Using the milk from an experimental herd, Kapiti created a fresh cheese similar to feta. It is called Hipi Iti, from the Maori meaning "little sheep", and is packed with herbs in jars of oil.

Fresh and lemony, with the characteristic sweet, caramel taste of sheep's milk, Hipi Iti is crumbly like feta but is only slightly salty. It gradually absorbs the subtle taste of the herbs in the oil in which it is stored.

Hipi Iti ripens in two months and has a fat content of 52 per cent. It won silver medals at the New Zealand Cheese Awards of 1996 and 1997.

JUBILEE BLUE

REGION: *Various*
TYPE: *Modern, creamery, blue cheese*
SOURCE: *Cow's milk*
DESCRIPTION: *250g/9oz log with smooth, velvety-soft-white rind*
CULINARY USES: *Table cheese, salads*

The first New Zealand blue cheese, Blue Vein, was launched in 1951 by the NZ Rennet Company. Jubilee Blue was created to celebrate Blue Vein's 40th anniversary and the 75th anniversary of the founding of the company. Smooth, creamy and Brie-like, it has small blotches of blue mould scattered throughout the white paste. There is a delicate aroma of mushrooms, and the taste suggests melted butter with rather spicy, slightly bitter overtones, reminiscent of rocket (arugula) or radiccio. Jubilee Blue ripens in 40 days.

RIGHT: Hipi Iti (front) and Aorangi, a Brie-type cheese (back), are just two of the many excellent cheeses made by Kapiti Cheese in Wellington on the North Island

KIKORANGI

REGION: *Wellington*
TYPE: *Modern, creamery, vegetarian, blue cheese*
SOURCE: *Cow's milk*
DESCRIPTION: *2kg/4¹/₂lb cylinder. The slightly moist, natural rind is cream in colour, with grey and blue moulds*
CULINARY USE: *Table cheese*

Another fine cheese from Kapiti, Kikorangi is superbly creamy, almost buttery, with a slightly gritty texture. The distinct, blue veins give the cheese a very strong, piquant, blue taste. Vibrant rather than vicious, it makes the tastebuds hum.

MAHOE AGED GOUDA

REGION: *Kerikeri*
TYPE: *Traditional, farmhouse, vegetarian, speciality cheese*
SOURCE: *Cow's milk*
DESCRIPTION: *6kg/13lb millstone. The smooth, pale yellow, natural rind is coated in yellow wax*
CULINARY USES: *Table cheese, grilling, grating*

Mahoe Cheese began as an experiment in the kitchen. When Anne and Bob Roastrevear decided to make cheese, they originally made varieties from their native Holland – Edam and Gouda – but demand and the desire for experimentaition led to the production of other cheeses, including feta, ricotta and Mahoe Aged Gouda.

Mahoe Aged Gouda is a very firm, smooth cheese with a slightly pliable texture that is almost chewy. It has a fruity, fresh tang and is rich and buttery in the mouth. The finish suggests caramel. The cheese is matured for 15 months and is a consistent medal winner at the New Zealand Cheese Awards.

MERCER GOUDA

REGION: *Hamilton*
TYPE: *Traditional, farmhouse, hard cheese*
SOURCE: *Cow's milk*
DESCRIPTION: *10–12kg/22–26lb boulder-shape. The smooth, pale yellow, natural rind is waxed*
CULINARY USES: *Table cheese (enjoyed for breakfast), grilling, snacks*

Like many artisan cheesemakers, Albert Alfernick believes that the best cheeses are made with unpasteurized milk, which gives them a deeper, more complex flavour. Regulations in New Zealand do not permit either the production or the importation of cheeses made with raw milk, but this does not stop Albert from producing a range of wonderful cheeses.

Enter Albert and Enika's tiny shop in Mercer, just off the main Auckland to Hamilton road, and you will be faced with shelves groaning with golden orbs of cheese, just begging to be tasted: Goudas of all ages, some with cumin, cracked pepper, garlic or herbs; delicious aged Edam; and sweet, fruity Maasdam.

MEYER VINTAGE GOUDA

REGION: *Hamilton*
TYPE: *Traditional, farmhouse, semi-hard cheese*
SOURCE: *Cow's milk*
DESCRIPTION: *10–12kg/22–26lb boulder-shape with smooth, mellow yellow, waxed rind*
CULINARY USE: *Table cheese*

Declared Supreme Champion at the New Zealand Cheese Awards of 1994, Meyer Vintage Gouda is firm, smooth, dense and creamy. The peach-coloured interior won the hearts and palates of the judges with its aroma of almonds and rich, nutty flavour. Phrases like "sweet and fruity"; "hard, granular and crunchy" and "wonderful depth of character" were bandied about. The pronounced tang and lingering, fruity finish were also lovingly described.

It is therefore not surprising that demand has grown steadily for Ben and Fieke Meyer's Vintage Gouda, which takes about 12 months to develop its full potential. The price reflects the time and labour involved in its production, but it is definitely value for money.

Ben and Fieke emigrated to New Zealand in 1994 and set up a small dairy near Hamilton. They brought with them a passion for cheese and a belief in the traditional methods of their native Holland. What they had not encountered before, however, was the way the composition of milk could alter with the seasons when animals had natural grazing. Their first cheese, made with rich, spring milk, was "very hard indeed", according to Fieke. With the help of Albert Alfernik, another Dutch cheesemaker, they tried again and this time met with success.

Their shelves are now filled with wonderful, round, yellow cheeses – over 3,000 at the last count – each one turned and brushed by hand as they slowly reach maturity. The Meyers produce Gouda at various stages of maturity, some plain, others flavoured with cumin, cloves or pepper.

LEFT: Sainte Maure

PORT NICHOLSON

REGION: *Wellington*
TYPE: *Modern, creamery, vegetarian, semi-soft cheese*
SOURCE: *Cow's milk*
DESCRIPTION: *1.8kg/4lb round with smooth, bright orange, washed rind*
CULINARY USES: *Table cheese, grilling, melting*

Port Nicholson has the characteristic, sweet-sour, slightly smoked aroma and taste of the Trappist-style cheese Port-Salut, upon which it is based, but is more supple and open textured. The producers, Kapiti, named the cheese after the magnificent harbour of New Zealand's capital city, Wellington.

BELOW: Port Nicholson

SAINTE-MAURE

REGION: *Wellington*
TYPE: *Modern, creamery, vegetarian, soft-white cheese*
SOURCE: *Goat's milk*
DESCRIPTION: *200g/7oz log with thick, white penicillium rind*
CULINARY USES: *Table cheese, grilling, salads*

Ross McCallum and his wife Glenys founded Kapiti Cheese in 1985 and rapidly made their mark on the gourmet world with an impressive range of quality speciality cheeses. Their meteoric rise is due to the passion Ross has for cheese, his vision and uncompromising attitude to quality and his desire to create cheeses with a unique New Zealand identity. Using names inspired by the Maori language, traditional cheesemaking methods and elegant and informative packaging, he set out to conquer the local market.

In the early 1990s, Kapiti began working alongside young chefs excited at the possibilities of their wonderful range of cheeses. Sainte-Maure, was Supreme Champion at the 1997 New Zealand Cheese Awards. It is firm yet velvety-smooth and melts in the mouth to release a medley of flavours – aromatic, distinctly nutty and deliciously sweet.

SARATOGA

REGION: *Masterton*
TYPE: *Modern, farmhouse, vegetarian, fresh cheese*
SOURCE: *Goat's milk*
DESCRIPTION: *100–150g/3³/₄–5oz rounds, waxed in various colours*
CULINARY USES: *Table cheese, grilling, salads and pastries*

Dee Lever is a woman of extraordinary courage. Before a serious car accident left her severely disabled, she had never made cheese. A few years ago her tiny, fresh, goat's milk cheese, Saratoga, won two of the top New Zealand Cheese Awards. Not only was it declared Best Fresh Cheese, but it also scooped the Cheese Lover's Cheese Award.

Saratoga has a moist, almost mousse-like texture. Lemon-fresh, it has just a hint of almonds, tarragon and white wine, characteristics of good goat's milk. Each cheese is carefully dipped in wax to protect it and prevent it from drying out.

Production at Saratoga Dairy Goats is small, but the cheeses improve from year to year. The latest additions – Piccolo, Encore, Sonata, Minuet and Opus – have a delicate, aromatic flavour, achieved not merely through careful handling of the curd, but also through good feeding and care of the goats and a commitment to consistent quality. Piccolo was declared Best New and Experimental Cheese at the 1997 New Zealand Cheese Awards.

WAIMATA FARMHOUSE BLUE

REGION: *Gisbourne*
TYPE: *Modern, farmhouse, vegetarian, blue cheese*
SOURCE: *Cow's milk*
DESCRIPTION: *2.5kg/5¹/₂lb cylinder with sticky, natural rind blotched with some grey and blue mould*
CULINARY USES: *Table cheese, salads and sauces*

Unanimously chosen Best Blue at the 1997 New Zealand Cheese Awards, where it was also declared to be Best Vegetarian Cheese, Waimata Farmhouse Blue is creamy without being rich, spicy without being vicious: in short, it is everything a blue should be.

Cheesemaker Carol Thorpe is a relative newcomer to the New Zealand cheese scene. She and her husband Rick first became interested in cheesemaking when they visited Wales in the late 1970s to further their knowledge and experience of self-sufficiency, but it was only in 1992, when the kiwifruit industry looked rather gloomy, that Carol examined the prospect of making cheese on a commercial basis.

By late 1994, Carol felt that her cheeses were ready for the market. Making blue and white moulded cheeses at the same location proved a challenge, but less than a year later, her success at the New Zealand Cheese Awards proved she was a master of the moulds.

Her company, Waimata Cheese, now makes various Brie-style blues, plus both a traditional Camembert and a version made with double cream. Also on the list are Port Gisborne, Vine Ash and feta.

WHITESTONE FARMHOUSE

REGION: *Oamaru*
TYPE: *Modern, farmhouse, vegetarian, soft-white cheese*
SOURCE: *Cow's milk*
DESCRIPTION: *800g/1³/₄lb or 1.5kg/3¹/₄lb cylinder with a fine powdering of penicillium mould*
CULINARY USE: *Table cheese*

This is one of a handful of cheeses that are uniquely New Zealand. Produced from Friesian cows grazing the North Otago limestone country, it is made in an open vat. Covered in a fine, penicillium rind, it has the fragrance of grass and an elasticity, rather like a young Caerphilly. The curd remains moist and crumbly in the centre, becoming softer towards the rind, and there is a slight fruity tang, reminiscent of feijoa (pineapple guava), on the finish.

Unlike many New Zealand cheeses, which are stabilized to improve their shelf life, Whitestone Farmhouse is allowed to continue to ripen, developing more character as it does so. At the 1995 New Zealand Cheese Awards, it was declared Best Original New Zealand Cheese.

Whitestone Cheeses, owned by Bob Berry also produces Airedale, Mt Dasher, Monte Cristo and Windsor Blue.

THE NEW ZEALAND CHEESE AWARDS

In 1993 the New Zealand Cheese Awards were created. The aim was to raise the profile of New Zealand cheese both nationally and internationally and to provide a recognized symbol of excellence for those judged to be of a high standard. The judges, working in pairs, are assigned to a class of 15–20 cheeses. One judge will be an industry expert, the other a well-respected chef or food writer. Between them they must agree a final score based on texture, taste and general appearance.

Unlike most competitions, there are no guaranteed first, second or third prizes awarded. Only those reaching a high level of quality and flavour will receive a gold, silver or bronze medal. Some classes may have several gold, silver and bronze medal winners. Others may have none.

After the initial judging, the gold medal winners from the 10 main categories are grouped together, and one cheese is chosen as the "Best of Each" category: Best Blue cheese, Best Cheddar cheese and so on. From these the Supreme Champion for that year is selected – an accolade that is guaranteed to bring huge increases in sales and popularity.

The medals are printed on the wrappers or labels of the winning cheeses, making it easy for the consumer to identify the very best of New Zealand cheese.

ABOVE: *The New Zealand Cheese Awards "symbol of excellence", which medal winners are allowed to print on their cheese labels or wrappers*

SHOPPING FOR CHEESE

For most of us, finding a good cheese means first finding a good cheese shop. The best shops are those that buy in immature cheeses and nurture them until they are ready to reveal their true character and subtlties of flavour. Regrettably, most shops simply order cheese and sell them with little thought as to their ripeness.

Try to buy cheese as near to the time you want to eat it as possible. If there is a particular cheese that you want, order it well in advance to give the cheesemonger time to find it and ripen it, or ask his or her advice about what will be at its best on the day that you need it. Maturing cheese is a time-consuming labour of love, so do not expect to pay the same for a cheese from an affineur as you would from a supermarket. Shop where you are allowed to taste before you buy, and where the assistant can suggest a choice of cheeses that provides a balance of mild and strong, hard and soft, with differing flavours, types of milk, shapes and characters.

If the cheese is strangled in plastic film it will become sweaty and develop bitter flavours. A good cheese shop will use plastic film sparingly on the cut-surfaces, so that the cheese can breathe. They will know the name of the cheese, the name of the farm or creamery where it is made, and perhaps even how it was made.

In recent years, mail order has become a popular way for small producers and retailers to reach a wider audience. It is an extremely effective way of obtaining hard-to-find cheeses, and, in general, if the cheeses are well packed and sent overnight, they seem to suffer no ill-effects. Some companies will send the cheese by refriger-ated transport, but this adds to the cost.

The following cheese shops are worth visiting.

AUSTRALIA
Ambrosia
Shop 44
Adelaide Central Market
Adelaide SA 5000
Tel (08) 8212 5810

Botega Ritolo
43 The Parade West
Kent Town SA 5067
Tel: (08) 8362 0455

Diamaru Food Hall
  Delicatessen
211 Latrobe Street
Melbourne VIC 3000
Tel: (03) 9660 6569

Simon Johnson, Purveyor of
  Quality Foods
181 Harris Street
Pyrmont, Sydney NSW 2009
Tel: (02) 9552 2522
and 12–14 Saint David Street
Fitzroy VIC 3065
Tel: (03) 9486 9456

David Jones Food Hall
Cnr. Market and Castlereagh
  Streets
Sydney NSW 2000
Tel: (02) 9266 6065

Myer Food Hall – Perth City
Forest Chase
200 Murray Street
Perth WA 6000
Tel: (09) 221 3444

Richmond Hill Cafe and Larder
48–50 Bridge Road
Richmond, Melbourne VIC
Tel: (03) 9421 2808

BELGIUM
La Baratte
rue de Tervaete, 55
1040 Etterbeek, Brussels

CANADA
Denninger's
284 King Street East
Hamilton, Ontario
Tel: 905 528 8468

ENGLAND
Blue Bird
350 Kings Road
Chelsea, London SW3 5UU
Tel: 0171 559 1173

Cambridge Cheese Company
4 All Saints Passage
Cambridge
Cambridgeshire CB2 3LS
Tel: 01223 328 672

Fortnum and Mason
181 Piccadilly
London W1A 1ER
Tel: 0171 734 8040

La Fromagerie (below)
30 Highbury Park
London N5 2AA
Tel: 0171 359 7440

Gastromania
The Market Place
Cirencester
Gloucestershire GL7 2PE
Tel: 01285 644 611

Harvey Nichols
109 Knightsbridge
London SW1X 7JR
Tel: 0171 235 5000

Jeroboams
96 Holland Park Avenue
London W11 3RB
Tel: 0171 727 9359

Neals Yard Dairy
17 Shorts Gardens

London WC2H 9AT
Tel: 0171 379 7646

Paxton and Whitfield
93 Jermyn Street
London SW1Y 6JE
Tel: 0171 930 0259
and 13 Wood Street
Stratford-upon-Avon
Warwickshire CV37 6JF
Tel: 01789 41544
and 1 John Street
Bath, Avon BA1 2JL
Tel: 01225 466 403

Ticklemore Cheese Shop
1 Ticklemore Street
Totnes, Devon TQ9 5EJ
Tel: 01803 865 926

Vivian's
2 Worple Way
Richmond
Surrey TW10 6DF
Tel: 0181 940 3600

Wensleydale Creamery
Gayles Lane
Hawes
North Yorkshire DL8 3RN
Tel: 01969 667 664

FRANCE
Roland Barthelmy
92 rue Grande
77300 Fontainebleu

Barthelmy
51 rue de Grenelle
Paris

Bon Marche – La Grande
Epicure de Paris
38 rue Sevres
75006 Paris

M. Daniel Boujon
7 rue Saint-Sebastien
74200 Thonon-les-Bains

Marie Cantin
12 rue du Champ de Mars
75006 Paris

La Ferme Savoyarde
22 rue Meynadier
06400 Cannes

Fromagerie Maréchal
Halle de Lyon
112 cours Lafayette
69300 Lyon

La Fromagerie de Phillippe
Olivier, Artisan-Affineur et
Marchand de Fromages
43–45 rue Thiers
62200 Boulogne-sur-Mer

Galleries Lafayette (Lafayette
Gourmet)
48 boulevard Haussmann
Paris

M. Jacques Ponnelle
12 rue St Vincent
71100 Chalon/Saone

M. Quatrehomme
Quatrehomme
62 rue Sevres
75006 Paris

IRELAND
Cavistons
59 Glasthule Road
Sandycove, Dun Laoghaire
Co Dublin
Tel: 003531 280 9120

SCOTLAND
I.J. Mellis Cheesemonger
492 Great Western Road
Glasgow G12 8EW
Tel: 0141 339 8998
and 30A Victoria Street
Edinburgh EH1 2JW
Tel: 0131 226 6215
and 205 Bruntsfield Place
Edinburgh EH10 4DH
Tel: 0131 447 8889

Valvona and Crolla
19 Elm Row
Edinburgh EH7 4AA
Tel: 0131 556 6066

NEW ZEALAND
Kapiti Cheeses
Lindale
Main Road North
Paraparaumu 6450
New Zealand
Tel: (04) 297 0450

SWITZERLAND
J.P. and J.A. Dufaux
4 rue Centrale
110 Morges
Canton de Vaud-Suisse

UNITED STATES OF AMERICA
Balducci's
424 6th Avenue (9th Street)
New York NY 10011

Campanile
524 South La Brea Avenue
Los Angeles
California CA 90036
Tel: 213 938 1447

Dean and Deluca
560 Broadway (Prince Street)
New York NY 10012

EAT
1064 Madison Avenue
New York NY 10028

Grace's Marketplace
3rd Avenue and 71st Street
New York NY 10021
Sutton Place Gourmet
6903 Rockledge Drive
Suite 900 Bethesda
Maryland 20817
Tel: 301 564 3100

Wholefoods
4663 Mt Sinai Road
Durham
North Carolina 27706
Tel: 919 419 7354

Zabar's
2245 Broadway (80th Street)
New York NY 10024

Zingerman's Delicatessen
422 Detroit Street
Michigan M1 48104
Tel: 313 683 3354

WALES
Llangloffan Farm Shop
Castle Morris
Haverford West
Pembrokeshire SA62 5ET
Tel: 01348 891 241

BIBLIOGRAPHY

Androuet, Pierre, *Guide du Fromage* (Aidan Ellis, 1973)
Basan, Ghillie, *Classic Turkish Cookery* (Tauris Parke, 1997)
Bilson, Tony, *Cheeses – The Australian Kitchen (Buying, Preparing and Cooking)* (Barbara Beckett, 1995)
Boxer, Arabella, *Mediterranean Cookbook* (Penguin, 1983)
Burton, David, *The New Zealand Cheese Book – Cooking and Serving Dairy Produce* (Reed Methuen, 1988)
Carr, Sandy, *The Mitchell Beazley Pocket Guide to Cheese* (Mitchell Beazley, 1986)
Cheke, Val, *The Story of Cheese-Making in Britain* (Routledge & Kegan Paul, 1959)
Chenel, Laura and Siegfried, Linda, *American Country Cheese* (Aris, 1989)
Corato, Ricardo di, *Italian Cheeses – A Pocket Guide* (Idealibri, 1985)
Del Conte, Anna, *Secrets from an Italian Kitchen* (Corgi, 1993)
Halliday, James, *Australian Wine Guide* (Angus and Robertson, 1990)
Hickman, Trevor, *The History of Stilton Cheese* (Alan Sutton, 1995)
Jenkins, Steven, *Cheese Primer* (Workman, 1996)
Jones, Evans, *The Book of Cheese* (Macmillan, 1981)
Lambert, Gilles and Roche,

Narcisse, *La Cuisine au Fromage* (Stock, 1971)
Montagné, Prospe, *Larousse Gastronomique* (Crown, 1965)
Nichols, Lourdes, *Mexican Cookery* (Fontana, 1986)
Rance, Patrick (foreword), *Cheeses of the World* (Little, Brown, 1993)
Rance, Patrick, *The French Cheese Book* (Macmillan, 1989)
Rance, Patrick, *The Great British Cheese Book* (Macmillan, 1982)
Rewi, Adrienne and Nicholas, Juliet, *Fine Cheese – Gourmet Cheesemaking in New Zealand* (Hazard, 1995)
Robuchon, Joel, *French Cheese* (Dorling Kindersley, 1996)

Scott, R., *Cheesemaking Practice* (2nd edn, Elsevier Applied Science, 1986)
Simon, André, *Cheeses of the World* (Faber and Faber, 1961)
Smith, John, *Cheesemaking in Scotland – A History* (Scottish Dairy Association, 1995)
Stubbs, William, *Guide to the Cheese of France* (Apple Press, 1984)
UNALAT (ed), *DOC Cheese of Italy – A Great Heritage* (Angeli, Franco, 1992)
United States Department of Agriculture, *Cheeses of the World* (Dover, 1969)
Whittle Fiona (ed), *Australian Farmhouse and Speciality Cheese Book* (Publicity, 1992)

INDEX

NOTES

NOTES

NOTES

NOTES

NOTES

NOTES

NOTES